Moravian Missionaries in Western Trans-Himalaya

(Lahul, Ladakh and Kinnaur)

Moravian Missionaries in Western Trans-Himalaya

(Lahul, Ladakh and Kinnaur)

Tobdan & C. Dorje

2008

Kaveri Books

New Delhi-110002

ISBN-10 : 81-7479-084-5

ISBN-13 : 978-81-7479-084-2

First Published in 2008

Published by
Kaveri Books
4697/5-21 A, Ansari Road
New Delhi-110002 (India)
Ph.: 011-23288140, 23245799
E-mail : kaveribooks@vsnl.com

Laser Composed in Baskerville BE Regular Font by
Vaishnav Graphics & Systems, New Delhi-110 055

PRINTED IN INDIA

Preface

Arrival of the Moravian Missionaries in this part of Western Trans-Himalaya marks an important moment in the history of the region. They were responsible for introduction of western system of education and health and other services, benefiting a large number of people. They also brought the ancient tribal society into brief contact with the western culture and manners. Their intensive scholarly activities like the studies conducted on a variety of subjects including folk art, local dialects and languages, customs, art and archaeology, literature, etc. of the region during the period of their stay extending to nearly a century resulted in accumulation of a good quantity of important literatures and other materials.

The grand tradition of Francke is being carried out by the qualified and trained western scholars in Ladakh and Zanskar. However, in respect of Lahul, the time of Moravians was its golden age, in this respect.

The present work is intended to be in continuation of and carry forward our previous attempt entitled "Historical Documents from Western Trans-Himalaya-Lahul, Zanskar and Ladakh (1996), besides treating some new related topics.

Facsimile of some works concerning Trans-Himalayan region, printed through lithographic process and published at Kyelang by the Moravians, are reproduced as appendix so that the the curious readers and serious scholars in the field will have the glimpse of the earnest efforts made by them in the remote and inaccessible Himalayan region. Some of the original texts have appeared in Roman transcription in the work referred to above with their English rendering. Texts forming introductory sentences of each item in German have been reproduced here as far as they are legible, together with the English translation or a brief description.

The present treatise draws heavily from the works and accounts of the predecessors and other learned scholars which we acknowledge with due regard and are thankful to them. It is hoped that this work will be of interest to the general readers as well as the serious scholars, as our former work had acceptance among them. The authors are thankful to Shrimati Meenakshi Sharma for preparation of Index of this monograph and Shri Rakesh Goel of M/s Kaveri Books for accepting and taking the publication in a record time.

C. Dorje
Archaeological Survey of India,
Janpath, New Delhi-110001

Tobdan
Miyan Behad,
Kullu-175101 (H.P.)

Contents

Contents

1.
Introduction of Christianity in Western Trans-Himalaya

In the history of expeditions of the missionaries into Central Asia it is said that the earliest mission of the Catholic Church was dispatched from Europe to meet Changez Khan, after he conquered Central Asia in 1206. The aim of the mission was to win his subjects into the Christian faith. The missionaries received favourable response from the Emperor, encouraging them for requesting for reinforcement batches. Reference is made of the Franciscan Friars, "who distinguished themselves in giving new life to those ancient records, and among them special mention must be made of John of *Plano Carpini* (1246), *William Roebroek* (1254) and *Odorico de Pordenone* (1316-1328)." Wessels has been successful in tracing their travelogues which he found praiseworthy. "Their writings are only surpassed by the engrossing narrative of the famous Venetian Marco Polo," says Wessels (Wessels, 1992: 4). All the travellers to the region speak of the great number of Christians in those remote regions, but they were mostly Nestorians. There were repeated encounters between them and the Franciscans, when the latter were called to Cathay by Kublai Khan towards the close of the thirteenth century. In the course of the following years the Catholics increased in such numbers that Pose Clement V thought it necessary to send them bishops, and in 1307, John Monte Corvino was appointed Archbishop of Cambaluc in Cathay (Wessels, 1992: 5).

These explorers to Central Asia were all destined to head towards Cathay located on the outskirts of north-west China. It was like the legendary holy land Shambhala existing in Tibetan sacred mythology. "By all of them the country they described was called Cathay" (Wessels 1992: 5). The capital of Cathay is called Cambaluc, a corrupt form of the Mongolian term *Khan-balig* which means 'Khan's Town'. Ekai Kawaguchi, a Japanese explorer, discovered a reference in Tibet referring to one of these

Christian missionaries sent to Central Asia who perhaps made an excursion to Tibet where he contacted the residents there.

Thereafter followed Bento de Goes, a great explorer. He has left an engrossing account of his long and gruelling journey. Bento de Goes was born in 1562 on the island of San Miguel. His education was thorough. Leaving to India, he met the Great Mughal Akbar. Entering the life of a soldier he begged for admittance into the Society of Jesus. His request was granted and he entered the novitiate of Goa in February 1584. He was a man of talent. Goes started his journey leading to Central Asia, rather Cathay, leaving Agra on October 29, 1602 and reached at Lahore on December 8. Nearly in the same period the great Siddha lama sTag-tshang Ras-pa, (AD 1574-1651), from Tibet, contemporary of King Senge Namgyal of Ladak, visited these areas of Jalandhar and Uddyan. Their further journey from Lahore began on 24 February, 1603. It was a great train of 500 animals with the traders, which later on was enhanced by adding 400 soldiers as protectors against the bands of marauders attracted by the merchandise. Finally the whole party entered Yarkand, the then capital of the kingdom of Kashgar. It was probably November 1603. The explorer stayed about a year in Yarkand, but the stay was not comfortable, being always under threat of life from the fanatic Mohammedans. Under great difficulty he moved towards Cathay. Thus he reached Central Asia, facing many obstacles and ultimately died in April 11, 1607.

Later on in the early twentieth century the missionary work in Central Asia is found in the charge of an organization named Central Asian Mission. Nicholas Roerich, a renowned international figure, while on his way to Turkistan, met some members of this organization across the Karakoram pass. He has made some observations on their physical and mental health. One can easily imagine the harsh environmental conditions under which they were desired to work.

On 23rd September, 1925, when Nicholas Roerich and his party camped in village Panimikh across Karakorum, they were told that two *Sahibs* from Yarkand were campping in the same village. "We had hardly had time to unfold our tents when they approached us; they were two Swedish missionaries, one of them the ailing Germanson. They return to Stockholm. Germanson tells of the difficult places on the road. About Chinese Turkestan he speaks without special enthusiasm" (Nicholas Roerich, 1929: 131).

At another place the author puts down the facts in the manner: "To our camp came riding a missionary from Yarkand. On yaks, he had just crossed Khardong Pass, losing all sense of days and dates. His watch had stopped. He repeated constantly: 'It is a staggeringly hard journey.' He told us that the worst spots were Khardong and Sasser Pass, while Karakorum, though higher was easier. He praised highly the people of Turkestan. He informed us that the Amban is already awaiting us and considers us his guests" (Nicholas Roerich, 1929: 113).

At Leh, Roerich, understandably was meted out with altogether a different kind of experience by the Moravians, about whom otherwise we observe every traveller leaving a note of appreciation for their cordial behaviour and selfless services. The experience he had on 18th September, 1925, is related, in the words: "At last one can finally leave all of Kashmir's falseness and dirt. One can forget half-ruined Srinagar. One can forget the attack made on our caravan by armed bandits. The Moravian mission in Leh has some strange restrictions and informs us of its consent to rent us one of its houses on condition that I sign an agreement to do no 'Religious, semi-religious, etc. propaganda.' No one could explain just what meaning the mysterious semi and etc had? We were able to get along without the headquarters of the mission - in the Palace of the Ladaki King. Only in the mountains does one feel safe. Only in the desert passes ignorance does not reach one" (Roerich,1929:125).

Speculations were made proclaiming spread of Christianity into Tibet sometime very early in its history stating that "The Tibetan Buddhists have a religious service in which they use bread and cider. It is said that this religious service came from China through the Nestorian Christians, for there is a tradition that St. Thomas introduced Christianity into China" (Biscoe, 1922: 213).

In the same manner, D'Adranda, when speaking of Tsaparang, Guge, in Western Tibet, in 1623-24, feigned that there are many symbols of Christianity in this place. Wessels rejects D'Adranda's statement outrightly in the words, "They were only based on a superficial and outward similarity of some Buddhist ceremonies to those of the Catholic Church" (Wessels, 1992: 47).

Francke too discovered D'Adranda's expressions unfounded. He has stated that, "I have not yet been able to make out what he means by this, whether he mistook Buddhist symbols (for instance svastikas) for Christian symbols, or whether there were actually crosses of a Christian type among the rock carvings of this place, like the Maltese crosses of Drangtse of the Pangkong lake" . He also attempted to verify the facts but found nothing to support the statements of D'Adranda. While on scientific tour of the border areas of Tibet in 1909, he sent Lobzang, a competent person, to Guge. He could not bring anything which could prove the assertions of D'Adranda. "I had hoped that Lobzang would find it possible to clear up this question, but I was disappointed. Lobzang said that he had seen many rock sculptures (without inscriptions) at Tsaparang, but nothing to suggest the former presence of Christians in this place" (Francke, 1926-I: 28).

The earliest occasion of Tibet's actual contact with Christianity is connected with a possible excursion made by Odorico de Pordenone, one of the missionaries sent to Central Asia (1316-1328) during the course of his expedition. Ekai Kawaguchi, an erudite scholar and explorer from Japan, while in Tibet, found the event dated 1328 preserved in the Tibetan literature. But at the time they did not think of starting any exertion there. Kawaguchi writes, "The first authentic story of the arrival of a foreigner in Tibet is recorded in the year 1328, when a priest of Pordenove, named Friar Odoric, entered Tibet as a propagandist of the Roman Catholic Church. His attempt failed, chiefly because the Tibetans of the time had nothing in particular to learn from Odoric, for Tibet possessed many priests of its own who were able to perform many things differing little from those recorded of Jesus Christ in their miraculous character. Indeed Odoric himself seems to have profitted by what he saw in Tibet instead of imparting anything new to the natives. He took notes of many wonderful things performed by Tibetan priests and took them home, but he burnt most of those notes for fear that their publication might compromise the interests of his own religion. So only a fragment of the account of his travel was preserved" (Ekai Kawaguchi, 1995: 400).

The real efforts towards this object in Tibet began after a long interval from the above event. In fact, this too was initiated in Western Tibet, rather than in Central Tibet. The regions of Western Tibet and Central Tibet are, in reality, two distinct geographical entities, physically separated by the vast cold steppe. Western Tibet, the ancient Zhang Zhung, comprised a vast region of small states consisting of Guge, Spiti, Kinnaur, Lahul, Ladak, and extending to Gilgit, Baltistan, Turkistan, etc. These states were located quite close to each other and were separated only by some minor natural barrier, which could be crossed without much difficulty. But the tract between Central and Western Tibet, which was conquered by Central Tibet in the seventh century A.D., was very wide. The land was uninhabited except by the mobile shepherds (*Dokpa*) who rear cattle and sheep. The land is extremely cold and infested with robbers (*Jagpas*). It took one and half month's journey to reach Lhasa from Tsaparang through a dangerous and inhospitable track. One had to carry the baggage and ration, and were under constant threat of the lurking *Jagpas.* This route was taken up in the event of urgent necessity such as war time, or by the traders in large caravans and rarely by the pilgrims. Ordinary travellers generally avoided the route. The would-be lama-students from mNgaris of Ladak, Lahul, the Punjab and then through Uttar Pradesh and Nepal entered the territory of Tibet from southern direction. This was convenient and less risky route, although circuitous and long. Some of the students, in later times when the railway lines were laid, were lucky enough to take advantage of and enjoy the railway ride for the first time in their life. They feel pride in sharing such experiences.

Wessels traces detailed history of the various attempts of the missionaries sent to Central Asia and Tibet, viz Central and Western Tibet, in his work (1924) and in his 'Introduction' to the work on the same subject in Fillipo De Fillipi (1932 ed.).

The missionaries were ordinarily doing not only religious propaganda but some of them are also known for their scientific and scholarly work. They studied the geography and culture of the people inhabiting those areas of the high Himalayas. Wessels writes in appreciation of the pioneer works executed by the missionaries, "Yet there were men among them who, though but pioneers, not scientific explorers, may lay claim to undeniable merits in the vast field of the history of discovery. Such a one is the Portuguese Jesuit Antonio de Andrade, who nearly 300 years ago was the first European to claim those stupendous mountain walls, to discover one of the principal sources of the sacred Ganges, and starting from Hindostan, to penetrate into the unknown regions of Tibet" (Wessels,1992: 43).

The Christian mission launched from Europe began their work in Western Tibet in 1624, with the expedition led by Father Antonio de Adranda. Adranda was born at Oleiros, in Portuguese, in 1580, and entered the Society of Jesus on December 15, 1596. Four years later he was sent to India, where he completed his studies. Adranda's journey to Tibet started from Agra on March 30, 1624. He together with Brother Manuel Marques left Agra to follow the Moghul Emperor (Jahangir) on his journey to Kashmir. On arriving at Delhi he left with a group of Hindu pilgrims to the

Himalayas. He took the shortest route through Srinagar, Badrinath (Garhwal) and Mana pass, the region which at the time of Alberuni in the 10th-11th century A.D. and till late after the Independence of the country, was known as 'Bhot'. In Tibet, he settled at Tsaparang, the capital of Guge. "Thus in the beginning of August 1624 the first European entered the 'citadel real', the Tibetan town of Chaparangue." The missionary had an interview with the king in 1625 to whom he explained the reason of his coming and obtained the king's favour in preaching his faith. "At first the king, unable to believe that a man, not a trader, could undertake such a journey, was somewhat displeased, but after the first interview, in which the missionary explained the reason of his coming, both he and the queen showed themselves quite pleased. A religious conviction prompting such deeds of daring did not fail to impress him, and when a few weeks later Andrade insisted on being allowed to leave, as otherwise the pass would be closed, he could only obtain permission on condition of his returning the following year".

At the beginning of November 1624 he was back at Agra and on the 8th he narrated the account of the first journey to the land of the living Buddha. Keeping his determination unfaded, not only did Andrade himself return to Tsaparang the following year, but with him and after him several missionaries laboured in the basin of the upper Sutlej. He was given three men. But before their arrival at Agra, Andrade, probably unwilling to risk missing the season, had started his next journey to Tibet on June 17, 1625, accompanied by Father Ganzales D' Sousa and his companion in former perils, Brother Manuel Marques.

In this new territory then, where no neglected Christians were found, though many religious ceremonies of the people bore some outward resemblance to those of the Catholic Church, they started the work they had come to do. The king kept his promise, gave some gifts including gold to the missionaries, and himself urged in April 1626 the building of a church and of a house for the missionaries. An excellent site was secured in the town near the king's palace. On Easterday, April 12, 1626, was laid the foundation-stone of the first Christian church in Tibet. On August 15 of the same year, came the new arrivals from India. The mission kept gaining strength. A second station was opened in Rudok and received a fresh arrival of an assistant in 1627. Efforts were carried on with the new men, but the achievement appears to have been quite unsatisfactory. "In ten years' time the Fathers have not administered a hundred baptisms, and even of these converts the greater part had been amongst the retainers either of the mission or of the king." Andrade, instead of engaging him in abating the problems in Tibet, was recalled on a new assignment in India. "Though the exact date is not known, it is certain that before 1630 he was recalled from Tibet to take upon him the honourable task of governing the whole mission-province of Goa. Thus the Tsaparang mission in losing its energetic and enterprising head sustained a loss that could not be compensated for by the solicitude and care of a distant Superior. His antagonists seized the opportunity and within a short time after his departure, in the same year 1630, a revolution broke out which put an end to the reign of the friendly king," (Wessels, 1992: 75). 'Shortly after the departure of the missionary some powerful military commanders probably lamas rose in open revolt, called in aid the king of Ladak and offered him the crown. With their help the latter laid siege to Tsaparang'. Following the revolt, the king was overthrown and the reign of the kingdom was taken over by Ladakh. Andrade's record of the incident occurring in Guge during this period amounts to add an important chapter to the history of Ladak, details of which otherwise would have been lost in oblivion. Adranda writes that for a long time there had been a violent quarrel between Guge and Ladak. Eighteen years before the king of Guge had a son, the heir to the throne born to him, but at his birth the queen had lost her reason, "so that she is still ailing. When after two years all efforts to cure her proved useless, the king resolved to contract a fresh marriage although the Tibetan religion permits no bigamy. The new bride was a sister of the king of Ladakh and Mariul. The marriage contract was made by proxy, but when the new queen, on her way to her husband, was at two day's distance from Tsaparang, he suddenly forbade her to proceed and ordered her to go back to Ladakh." Ladakh immediately began war, which with occasional intervals continued for eighteen years impoverishing the country by rendering impossible the working of fields and or mines. Another cause of conflict was the great discontent among the numerous lamas at the conduct of the king. The latter had proceeded somewhat hastily in introducing the new religion and some of the measures adopted against the lamas were decidedly imprudent. Thus in 1626 the king had taken away from his brother, the Chief lama, all his revenues.

The king and his family were kidnapped and carried off to Leh. The whole country was conquered and the Christians, numbering about 400, were singled out for retribution, many were reduced to slavery and had to share king's exile. "The new governor appointed by the king of Ladakh, who had returned to Leh taking with him the late king, and leaving a garrison in the town, was very hostile to the mission", (Wessels 1924: 75, 101). Adranda died in 1634, but the mission continued somehow for some more times even though under very unfavourable circumstances.

Father de Azevedo, who spent nearly the whole of his life in India, came to Tsaparang with the object of removing the difficulties arising as a result of the turmoil. Born at Lisbon in 1578 he left his native country when still a boy and joined the Society of Jesus at Goa at the age of nineteen. On completing his studies he was stationed at different places. In 1627 he went to the Mogor mission and was already fifty-two when he received his commission for Tsaparang. Azevedo left Agra on June 28, 1631. He took the same route as taken by Andrade. On August 25 he joined his brethren at Tsaparang. Father Azevedo learned that the Commander of Leh was hostile against Christians although the king of Guge was inclined to allow him to preach among his people. The forlorn state in which he found the much-tried Christian community at Tsaparang soon convinced Azevedo that ordinary measures would not suffice and he resolved to take a bold step. It was impossible to do anything here, for the new governor, appointed by the king of Ladakh. Therefore Azevedo came to Leh to meet the king. The journey from Tsaparang to Leh undertaken in September, took him 21 days. Azevedo met the king, Singe Namgyal, at Leh in 1631 and obtained a kind of *firman,* "authorizing us to continue to work as we had done during the reign of the late king, not only in the kingdom of Coge, but also in Ridocho and even in his own capital." Thereafter in the same year passing through Lahul and Kullu, Azevedo proceeded to the plains of the Panjab, and finally to Agra. The missionaries in Western Tibet were ultimately banished and they arrived in Agra in December, 1635.

While at Tsaparang, Father Adranda had gathered information about U-Tsang, Central Tibet, situated at one and a half months' journey east of Tsaparang. On his suggestion, three Fathers; Estevao Cacella and Joao Cabral, together with an Italian lay-brother, Bartolomeo Fonteboa, were sent from Bengal on 30th April, 1626. The mission, however, could not move beyond Shigatse and it was ended there like that of Guge.

Wessels muses on the subject: "Thus both attempts at spreading the Gospel in Western and Central Tibet had miscarried. Brother Marques remained in bonds at Tsaparang and at far-away Shigatse there was no one to take up Cacella's work and pray over his lonely grave." The missionaries had, however, not given in their endurance. "Though nothing was done in the ensuing years the missionaries in India never forgot those earlier attempts. As a kind of advanced post they continued and developed mission work at Srinagar among the Garhwal Mountains; they never quite relinquished all hope of going back some time in the future, but they had to wait for the man of push and position required to take the matter up." Thereafter a number of attempts were made to revive the toil in Tibet, but due to many difficulties, like the health of the volunteers, it could not commence.

Appointment of Father Ippolito Desideri in November 1713, in charge of the 'Tibet Mission' gave a starting point to a new movement. He, with Father Emanuel Freyre, who had passed some twenty years in India, proceeded with the objectives. Their first target was Kashmir, whence they were to traverse Little Tibet or Baltistan, and thus to penetrate into Great Tibet or Ladak, where they hoped to make a successful start in the missionary work.

When they reached Leh, on 26th June, 1715, they struck upon a second thought. Freyre, Desideri's companion, decided to proceed to the Third Tibet, U-Tsang, instead of staying at Ladakh. Desideri was at first confounded but ultimately decided to take up the plan put forth by Freyre. After staying for two months in Ladakh, they moved towards Lhasa and on 18th March, 1716, they were able to set foot within the holy city of Lhasa.

Freyre, resting for a few weeks returned to Hindustan on 16th April. Desideri stayed back at Lhasa, the only European staying there. His labours in Tibet extended over a period of five years. At his first audience with the king (?), on 1st May, 1716, he obtained permission to preach and also to buy a house at Lhasa, a mark of special favour, since foreigners could only rent houses. With undivided zeal he now addressed himself to the study of the language. Desideri's dedication and hard labour he put may be gauged from his own statement, "From that day to the last which I passed in the kingdom, I studied from morning till night." Nor without success, for by the end of December of the same year he had finished an expose of the Christian religion, which was presented to the king at an audience on 6th January, 1717. He then joined the University of Sera, at two miles from Lhasa. His plan was to write in the Tibetan language a refutation of the errors of Buddhism, their doctrine and a defence of the Catholic religion. But he had hardly set to work when he was interrupted by a violent catastrophe. The Tartars invaded the country. Lhasa was taken over and sacked. On 3rd December, 1717, the king and his ministers were murdered. Not thinking himself safe at Sera, Desideri retired to the province of Takpo Khier at eight days' journey from the capital, where he found time and opportunity to finish his book. His retirement lasted till April, 1721, with the exception of a few months at Lhasa. In one of his visits to the capital he gave his book to read to his former teacher of Tibetan, one of the cleverest among the lamas. It consisted of three volumes containing many points causing rise to a great debate. He also translated the *Lam rim chenmo* into Italian, before he left Lhasa, in 1721. As Desideri left Tibet, the missionary labours of the Society of Jesus in Tibet came to an end once more.

In the middle of the nineteenth century a group of dedicated volunteers connected with a Christian missionary organization, known as Moravian Mission, was sent out on a mission from Europe. They entered India and established their working stations in the Western Trans-Himalayan regions in Lahul, Kinnaur and Ladak: the areas which lay along the border with Tibet. They were, in fact, originally on way towards the Central Asian states to work among the Mongolian Buddhist tribes, but were stopped by the Russian authorities before they could enter the countries of their destination. They then turned back and without changing their destination chose to take more circuitous route. They came to India and selected places on the borders with Tibet, for their operations, having population similar in ethnicity, language, culture, etc. to those of the countries where they proposed to visit. Here they intended to familiarise themselves with the culture, environment and other essential aspects, till they got opportunity to actually move towards their destination. It was thus a chance instance that they chose this area for their activities, even though these were the toughest areas for them to live. The incident was analogous to the journey of the team of Moorcroft and Trebeck who happened to pass through this route of Beas valley, Lahul and Ladak. Otherwise their original plan was to go to Tibet across Niti Pass through Garhwal.

The missionaries worked here for about a century, until they had to ultimately discard their plan. They worked encompassing a variety of activities of development, viz. health, education, agriculture, industry, language, history, archaeology, and the like. Much more than this, they put the movement of Tibetan studies on much stronger footing, the foundation of which had been laid down already shortly before this by a great scholar like Csoma de Koros. Incidentally, Csoma also was exerting in the same geographical areas of Zanskar and Kinnaur, as the Moravians were operating in. The Mission had posted some highly talented individuals who took up the task very seriously and shortly put themselves on the world map. A few of them earned place among the leading international scholars in the field of Tibetology, like Jaeschke: *The Tibetan-English Dictionary;* Francke: *Antiquities of Indian Tibet;* Ribbach: *Dokpa Namgyal,* etc. There were also some excellent women who educated the neglected women and children with great love and care, as we learn from the descriptions of the various visitors. But we know none of them individually for they are all garbed in one small word 'Mrs', as is the European system of naming the worthy wives.

The *Gazetteer of the Kangra District, Lahul,* 1917, traces the origin and history of the Moravian Mission in the following words: "The Central Asian stations are at Leh and Khalatse in Ladak, at Poo in Bashahar and at Kyelang in Lahul. These fields were opened after attempts to settle in Tibet had been frustrated by the Russian and Chinese Governments...... The Unitas Fratrum, known as the Moravian Church, is remarkable for its Missionary endeavour. It began life in 1457 A.D. and passed through a period of persecution in Bohemia before it migrated to Saxony. It is a small church, but the congregations of the Mission fields number three times as those at home, and every member takes some part in Mission work. The fields are in remote places, including Labrador, Central America, South Africa and Central Asia, with a leper asylum at Jerusalem. The tenets of the Church are Evangelistic Protestant, the orders are Episcopal, the Government is by representative Synods and elected Boards. There are three Provinces in (i) Great Britain and Ireland, (ii) The United States of America, with Canada, and (iii) Germany, with several continental countries. The general Synod meeting every ten years controls the policy and funds of the Church as a whole, and appoints a Board to control the Missions, which is composed of an elected Bishop from each Province and a Finance Member. Each Province has its own legislative Synod and Executive. There is no Bishop in the Central Asian Mission field, which is financed from England. The Secretary of the Mission Board in Saxony is an Englishman and the Pastors in Central Asia are now either English, naturalized British or Swiss. They are paid very small salaries and credit all revenue (e.g. from trade or farming) to the funds of the Mission and at Kyelang, they live cut off for many months together from the outside world" (Gazetteer, 1917, part III, Lahul: 205-206).

Markham goes in more detail in searching their past history, their real objectives and efforts: "For upwards of a century the attention of the Moravian missionaries has been turned towards the Kalmuk and Mongol tribes, and in 1765 a Moravian settlement was formed near Czarizin on the Volga, affording opportunities of communicating with the nomad tribes of the steppes. In the beginning of the present century some slight progress was made among the Kirghis tribes, but the mission terminated in 1821, owing to the interference of the Russian government. Having been refused permission to pass through Russian territory, two Moravian missionaries set out in 1853 with the intention of penetrating into Mongolia by way of India. They were stopped on the borders by the Chinese officials and then received orders from Herrnhuth to settle down where they best could among the Tibetans. A place called Kaelang, in British Lahaul, was selected, and a few years afterwards the mission was placed on a more regular footing, under Brothers Jaeschke, Rechler and Heyde. In 1873, the staff consisted of Brothers Heyde and Redslob, with their wives and twenty converts. The mission house is 10,000 feet above the sea, and has fields and carefully tended gardens and orchards attached to."

"Brother H.A. Jaeschke, after eleven years' residence in Lahaul, returned to Germany in the end of 1868. He is the highest authority in Europe on the modern Tibetan language and its dialects, and is the author of more than one valuable work on the subject. The Moravian Brethren will continue to occupy their present important station in North-Western India, as a basis of operations, until they are permitted to cross the Chinese frontier into Tibet. Their knowledge of the Tibetan language, and their intercourse with the Lamas, will be one influential means of preparing the way for future unrestricted intercourse between India and Tibet" (Markham, 1876: Introduction, cvii-cviii).

When the Moravians arrived in the Western Himalayas, the economy of the people was dependent, besides agriculture, on petty seasonal trading and animal husbandry. The residents were not familiar with such modern institutions as school, dispensary and printing press, which the Moravians founded.

As they were pursuing their own objectives, further benefits were expected to accrue them from their works. "From Western Tibet it is also probable that much will be done to restore the old friendly intercourse between India and the Central region. Something indeed has already been effected, on the one hand, by the Moravian missionaries in Lahul, headed by Mr. Jaschke and Mr. Heyde, who have learned the Tibetan language, and will be able to convey intelligence of the policy of the British government, through the heads of Buddhist monasteries in Ladak; on the other hand by the explorers, who are instructed and sent forth on long journeys of discovery from the headquarters of the Great Trigonometrical Survey of India" (Markham, *ibid*).

There were many Christian Religious Agencies working during the British period at various places in the areas now falling in the present state of Himachal Pradesh.

Sabathu Mission: The Ludhiana Mission of the American Presbyterian Church had a branch at Sabathu since 1837. Sabathu or Subathu is presently located in district Solan. It was, however, chiefly intended as a sanatorium for old Missionaries and invalids in the Mission. Strength of the native population, depended almost entirely upon the military force present at the station, which was constantly fluctuating; and there had been long intervals during which missionary operations had to be suspended. A leper asylum was attached to the Mission. There were originally two Mission schools for boys and girls respectively. But the attendance fell off so that the schools had been abandoned, and then the Mission school-house was used for a small private school, which had no connection with the Mission.

Simla Baptist Mission: Information about the early activities of the missionaries in Shimla, obtained from the Rev. Gulzar Shah, have been described in the Gazetteers "This may be called an indigenous Mission originated by the Rev. Gulzar Shah in the year 1865. He was then the pastor of the Baptist Church in South Colinga Street, Calcutta. His employment as a clerk in the Public Works Department of the Government of India brought him up to Simla for the first time that year. The Mission has since been carried on by him on his own responsibility with the help obtained, as regards work, from a few of his Bengali brethren, and, as regards money, chiefly from officials of the Government of India, from the Simla Union Church, and from the Baptist Missionary Society. The Mission did not belong to any Church or Society till the year 1880. That year Mr. Shah, fearing further complications that might arise after his death made over the Mission property to the Baptist Missionary Society, in consideration of their being the largest subscribers to the Mission for some years past, and especially of the help they gave in the building of the new chapel. Since the year 1881 the Mission has been still more closely connected with the Baptist Missionary Society.

'In May 1865 Mr. Shah commenced Sabbath services for native Christians of all denominations, there being no such services held in any other place in Simla at the time. He preached to the Hindus and Muhammadans that came up from the plains, also to the hill people in their villages, and received much encouragement in his work. In 1866 two male and one female teacher were appointed, but there were no direct conversions, and no additions to the Church. From that year the staff increased steadily. In 1882 the staff constitued as follows: one Missionary, one Assistant Missionary, six Voluntary helpers, one Evangelist, three teachers, one Bible-woman and two Colporteurs.

'In 1868 the first chapel was built and two new converts were obtained, and since that year additions have been named to the Church by conversions from among the Hindu, Muhammadan and Sikh population. The total converts baptized in connection with the Mission since its commencement till the year 1883 have been 134. A new chapel on the cart road was opened in June1879. The number of the congregation was increased with the increasing number of native Christians who have come up to Simla year after year as employees of the Secretariat and other government offices. Separate services are held for Bengali and Hindustani congregations.

'The converts who have been baptized, do not, as a rule, reside at or near the Mission premises, but go back to their work in the distant villages. Many are in isolated positions where they cannot meet for Christian worship, but those who are at a convenient distance from the chapel or branch station usually assemble for public worship. The branch stations are at Jatogh, Kalka and Gandauli. The number of converts is increasing year by year, and the converts of one year are generally the fruits of the labours of the converts of the preceding year."

Francke visited the office of a missionary organization located at Kotgarh in 1909 and remarks, "We left Simla on the 14th June and reached Kotgarh on the 16th at noon. At Kotgarh I enjoyed the hospitality of the C.M.S. missionary, the Rev. Mr. Beutal, who is an authority on the language, customs and geography of his district" (Francke, 1926-I: 2).

Baptist Mission Schools: The leading schools situated in Shimla today like B.C.S., Tara Hall, Saint Edward, all are managed by Christian Organisations. History of founding of these reputed schools and their initial forms which were contrary to what they appear at present, again gathered by Gulzar Shah, is recorded in the Gazetteers "A school was opened in 1866 for the benefit of the hill children; and, although there is a Government School in Simla, the Mission School supplied a real necessity. Many a poor man's son who could not go to the Government School there received a sound primary education in the vernacular, and as much English as now enables him to earn him his living as Compositors in the Government Press or Record Daftari in other offices. We have sent forth from our school about 40 boys, many of whom are now grown up young men and heads of families; some have embraced the Christian faith, and others are still non-Christians.

'We are unable to keep our boys for an extended course' as soon as they learn enough to carry some sort of work either as Compositors, Daftaris or shop keepers, our pupils leave us; but we do not regret this, as we intended our school to be a good primary school. The main object of our school is to teach our boys to read the Bible in their own vernacular, and this we are able to accomplish in the course of two years' tuition; but in conjunction with the Bible we teach our boys reading, writing and arithmetic, and also a little geography and general history in the vernacular, and just as much English as helps them to manage the kinds of work above specified.

'The classes or castes from which our pupils are principally drawn are Brahman, Kanet, Rajput, Koli and Gurkha and other Hindu castes, also a few Muhammadans; but we do not exclude the lowest castes, even sweepers' children being welcomed. We have a Boarding School for hill boys of distant villages and for orphans; and in order to show the parents that we have no desire to break their caste, we always keep a Brahmin cook to dress the boarders' food, and all our arrangements are open to the parents' inspection. No complaints have ever been made on this score, but of course the numbers of our boarders fluctuate, the highest number accommodated having been 18 in 1879. Our school is situated on the east of our chapel, on the cart road. The school has been managed under the superintendence of the Rev. Gulzar Shah by a staff of the three to four teachers, some of these teachers being old pupils of the school. Average number of scholars, 50 males, 6 females" (*Gazetteer of the Simla District, 1888-1889, 1890:* 42).

At present the Christian Associations are managing hospitals, besides schools, at many places in Himachal Pradesh. The Christian population according to the Census of 1881 in district Kangra which included the present districts of Kullu, Lahul-Spiti and Hamirpur, is given as under:

Area	Persons	Males	Females
	a) Christians		
District Kangra	327	180	147
Kangra	244	–	–
Nurpur	8	–	–
Hamirpur	1	–	–
Kullu Sub Div.	74	–	–
Villages	177	–	–

Area	Persons	Males	Females
	b) European & Eurasian Christians		
District Kangra	210	116	94
Kangra	192	–	–
Nurpur	3	–	–
Hamirpur	14	–	–
Kullu sub Div.	1	–	–

(Kangra Distt Gazetteer, 1883-84, Statistical Tables, Table no. vii, p.vi.).

Christian in Kullu: Moravian missionaries were staying at Kyelang since 1854. The figure for Lahul might have been included under that of Kullu Sub Division, as Lahul then formed part of Kullu. There were 117 Christians in Kullu, in around 1915. They included the English officers, fruit planters and their families, and some natives settled at Ani, near Dalash in Outer Saraj. The Gazetteer informs that 'there is no ecclesiastical administration in Kulu or Saraj, but missionaries from the Canadian Mission in Kangra occasionally visit Kulu. There is a Salvation Army Mission and Settlement at Ani. The Native Christians there were settled by Dr. Carleton of the American Presbyterian Mission whose property was taken over by the Salvation Army seven years ago in about 1910. A fruit farm, weaving school, and two educational schools are managed, one school being at Dehuri' (Gazetteer 1917: 73).

Presently there are number of organizations working here, some in the shape of NGO. The preachers hail ordinarily from Kerala, Tamilnadu, Manipur, etc. There is a church in Kullu which was constructed in 1985. There was land already there where there were graves and the building was constructed on this site. It is managed by the Indian Evangelical Mission (IEM) which has churches, besides in Kullu, at Manali, Shamshi and Ani. Another organization is based at Mohal, about six kilometers from Kullu towards Mandi. They too are planning to build a Church. These organizations are cut off from the old traditions and also appear possessing no such interest. All old literature including the knowledge about their existence are lost. There was a gramophone record in Kulluvi language. There are still four graves with writings thereon but no effort has been made to read them. Presently one booklet has been brought in the Inner Saraji Language of Kullu entitled *'Markuse Likhidi Shobhli Galla'*, 2004, Silchar, Assam, pp.112.

Chamba Mission: Christian missionaries arrived in Chamba quite early as the Gazetteers of the district says, "In 1863 a Christian Mission was founded in the Chamba town by a minister of the Church of Scotland. The mission continued and flourished noticeably for some years and, to this day, which according to the old gazetteer, was gifted to the mission by the Raja Ram Singh, the then ruler of the Chamba state. The mission is no longer as flourishing, and in its present state it commands a total Christian population of one hundred and five, and is locally run by a padre" (*Chamba District Gazetteer,* 1963: 172-173). "By 1906, the town had an Anglo-vernacular middle school maintained by the Church of Scotland Mission, in addition to a high school, run by the State, which was what the above mentioned primary school had blossomed into several years earlier" (*ibid:* 397). The Church also maintained a dispensary in Chamba in which 6080 new patients were treated in 1906. J. Hutchison, a missionary stationed here, was a scholar of great repute and has made valuable contributions in the study of the history and many other aspects of Chamba.

2.
Moravian Missionaries in Lahul

Rev. A.W. Heyde and Rev. E. Pagell arrived in Lahul in 1854. They selected village Kardang in Punan, on the left bank of river Bhaga and settled there. Soon, after a couple of months they shifted to Kyelang on the other side of the river. Kyelang falls on the right side of river Bhaga and pleasantly faces the rising sun. As compared to Kardang, Kyelang is located slightly at lower height and is comparatively more populous. It is broader, flatter and less sloppy. They immediately began constructing their own house which was completed within two years, by 1856.

When Andrew Wilson visited Kyelang in 1873, the staff at the station consisted of Brothers Heyde and Redslob with their wives and nearly twenty baptised converts including the children of the native Christians (Andrew Wilson, 1876: 265).

The Kangra District Gazetteer of 1897, for its note on the activities of Moravian Mission, which it calls Protestant Mission, in Lahul obtained details from one of its own active members, Rev A.W. Heyde, whose narrative is reproduced here: "The Mission belongs to the Church of the Moravians or United Brethren (Unitas Fratrun). It was established in the year 1854. From the beginning, its object was to reach the Mongol tribes of Central Asia who profess Buddhism. The first two missionaries appointed in 1852 were to have gone by European Russia and Siberia into Central Asia, but after repeated applications had been made, the Russian government refused to let them pass through their territories. After that the route by China would have been taken, but China being then still obstructive to missionary enterprise, this way had also to be abandoned and a third to be chosen, viz. that via Ladak. From Ladak the missionaries were to penetrate to the Mongolian tribes of the Khalmaks who inhabit the northern parts of Eastern Turkistan. In Ladak the first station was to have been established it being hoped that from thence it would be possible to advance gradually. This, however, proved impracticable, as the Kashmir government refused to give the necessary permission for the desired station. Thus it came to pass that Lahul was fixed upon as a suitable place for a first settlement, because the province was situated close to Ladak, and because its inhabitants belong at least partly to the Mongolian race and profess Buddhism. From Lahul the mission hopes still to advance into Ladak as soon as permission can be obtained to do so, thereby pursuing its original object. The name of the station in Lahul is Kyelang, and often spelt Kailing or Keylang which is wrong. The Mission being still a small one, at present only two missionaries carry on its work. Two more missionaries have lately been appointed, who will increase its present staff soon. The mission Department of the Moravian Church organization is the directing board of this as well as all other Moravian missions" (*Gazetteer, 1897 Part III, Lahul:* 21, 22). The narrative explains the circumstances in which the Moravians were constrained to settle in Lahul.

In 1857 Heinrich August Jaeschke joined the mission as Superintendent, the position which he held for eleven years from 1857 to 1868. The particular job, assigned to him, was to translate the Bible into Tibetan, which he accomplished with the assistance of the speakers in Kyelang and Ladak, and pilgrims from all over Tibet who crossed through Lahul. Jaeschke translated and published sections of hymns of the New Testament, besides generating a number of other important works.

Rechler succeeded Jaeschke in 1868. In his account of the mission in 1874 he reported that all Christians in Kyelang were Ladakpas, i.e. they were from Ladak (Stutchbury, 1991: 39). This position remained unchanged perhaps till the winding up of the office. It seems that the people of Lahul, including the Lamas, were prepared to participate in the church services and hymn singing, but were quite resistant to conversion.

The mission had to face a sort of minor setback, sometime after establishment of the office, due to an inauspicious incident which occurred in the area. Elizabeth Stutchbury gathers that within the first fifteen or so years of the mission, one Ladakpa lama who was residing at Jhabjhes Gonpa in Kardang, lost his life under, what the Moravians felt were, in very suspicious circumstances. This Lama apparently had become very interested in the translated Christian scriptures, and is said to have fallen to his death from the top of a house in Kardang village whilst engaged in a drinking session. This incident may be indicative of Lahuli antagonism towards converts, although it may also have been an accident (Stutchbury, 1991: 39-40).

Stutchbury, however, informs that there was no memory of this event among the Kardangpa at the time of her field work. "Given that I had trouble establishing dates and events early this century, I have no reason to suspect suppression of information. Very little mention was made about the presence of the Moravians in Lahul during my field work" (Stutchbury, 1991: 39-40). Hooper, perhaps, is referring to this incident as a suspected case of poisoning, which according to him took place in 1854, and the victim was lama Tashi (Hooper, 1963: 141). On comparison of the date of occurrence of the incident from the two sources, it is at variance widely. It is impossible to say which date is correct.The year 1854 is the year of opening of the mission office.

Walter Asboe joined at Kyelang in 1927 and in 1936 he moved to Leh, then finally left India in 1947. He occupied himself mainly in the study of the agricultural practices and some social customs of the districts. He wrote several brief and interesting monographs on various subjects like disposal of the dead, agricultural practices, scapegoat, pottery, etc. in Lahul and Ladak which were published in *'Man'* between 1932 and 1946. While in Kyelang, Asboe encouraged the locals to make and install the 'combustion' stove with chimney. The introduction of the chimney greatly improved the smoky interiors of the houses. These small metal stoves called *lcags-thab* or *tandoor,* which are these days used in all Lahuli houses, and in Kullu and many parts of Himachal Pradesh as well, have made a considerable improvement to the cleanliness of the interior of the houses, and also have improved the fuel economy.

Heyde was a keen gardener and it is said, he cultivated potato from the original eight that the missionaries had brought with them. He is attributed for introduction of many innovative things into Lahul. The potato soon became popular in local gardens, being well suited to the altitude and climate. Lettuce, spinach, and turnip were also introduced, becoming popular in the local diet. The Lombardy poplar was also introduced, as well as the willow tree, which now grows in considerable numbers along the irrigation channels near the villages. Thus although the missionaries met with little success in spreading the teachings of the doctrine and in recruiting converts, their agricultural activities met with convincing acceptance.

In an official record the information has been preserved in the words, 'the mission introduced potatoes, oats and *rye* on their farm: the *rye* is cultivated by the people chiefly for sake of the straw, but oats have disappeared: potatoes have become widespread. The Lombardy poplar was also brought in by the Moravians and is doing very well" (*Gazetteer 1917, Part III, Lahul:* 207-208).

The Gazetteer does not fail to bring out the important activities of the mission on record, in each of its new edition. 'The Lahul Mission congregation consists of 21 adults and 27 children: there are 15 accredited communicants. The mission has a bungalow, school and dispensary at Kyelang and a branch school at Chot in Pattan. The work done by the Moravians is very valuable: they have assisted investigation into folklore, language, customs and religion: they have introduced the Christian religion and made some converts: their example and assistance on all necessary occasions has been most beneficial to the people at large. Their efforts at education have not prospered as they would have done but for the passive or active opposition of the local lamas, and much difficulty is experienced in obtaining students in the summer and even in the winter. This is not because the schools are Christian: the efforts of Government have also been unsuccessful, though at present there is some demand for a good primary school. The lamas impart a certain kind of education in their monasteries which they think is sufficient and it certainly has elevated the Lahulas above the people of Kulu in point of intelligence and literacy, but the lamas' education is not good enough for modern times and this is apparently being realized by the leading men in Lahul now. The schools at Kyelang and Chot educate chiefly Christians: the Kyelang school was established in 1861 after overcoming much opposition and in 1862 branch schools were opened under lamas in seven villages, but were closed owing to the unreliability of the lamas. In the last winter, for which figures are available, Kyelang school was attended by 17 boys and 2 girls. Knitting classes are held for women and girls in the winter with satisfactory results, and there is much promise in this branch of the work. In Manchat (Pattan) there were schools opened at Gushal and Shansha, but they were soon closed. The Chot school had 16 boys and 4 girls in the winter of 1914-1915" (*Gazetteer 1917, Part III Lahul:* 206-207).

It is stated that it was difficult to encourage the girls to attend school, though the wives of the pastors had greater success with their knitting classes. "The knitting of the colourful jaquared socks worn by the Lahulis these days was learnt from the wives of the three missionaries who joined their husbands to be in 1859". The Moravians are also credited with the introduction of glass window panes. In some cases double glazing is employed for extra insulation.

The position of the schools and the pupils attending the schools has been reported in the earlier Gazetteer in the manner, "Schools are in at both stations, at Pu for boys as well as for girls, while at Kyelang at present only one for girls is attached to the mission, about thirty girls receive instructions in reading, writing, arithmetic, religious instructions, singing, sowing, and knitting stocking, etc. Pupils of Christian parents attend the whole year, non-Christian only during the winter months; the latter being employed by their parents otherwise during summer. Several schools for boys were formerly connected with the mission in different villages of Lahul, the aim of all being to impart a good primary education suiting a rural population, among which the mission chiefly works. After a course of five years or less, the boys were dismissed to their homes, others taking their place. However, circumstances arose which made it desirable to amalgamate these schools into one government school at Kyelang, and thus it came about that the mission at least for the present, has no boys' school. The number of pupils at Kyelang is at present about thirty girls, at Pu about ten girls and from ten to fifteen boys".

The Moravians opened a lithographic press in Kyelang in 1859 and they first published Dr Barth's Bible Stories in Tibetan. Thereafter they carried on a number of other kinds of jobs on the machine. The archaic machine, as some scholars say, enhanced the literary activities of the Moravians greatly, as we learn from the official reports. 'As to literary works the mission has published ten school books, including a geographical work with maps and compendiums of general and sacred history, one small and two large dictionaries in Tibetan language (Tibetan-English and Tibetan-German). The New Testament has been translated and printed, while portions of old Testament are also ready for the press etc." (*Gazetteer, 1897, Part III Lahul:* 22-23).

The machine remained most active during the time of Jaeschke's stay, but after that it appears to have been left idle most of the time as a later document relates, "The printing press at Kyelang has not been used of late except for a reprint of some Tibetan school books in 1904 and Tibetan Census Forms in 1910. It had, however, done much valuable work. Among other publications the following have been listed by the present Pastor Kunick: Gospels, Epistles, Hymn book, Pentateuch, Books of Samuel, Literature of Christian Evidence, tracts, school books, Tibetan Primer and Reader, Geographical Reader, Arithmetic, Tibetan letter-writer, Instructor in English for Tibetans, Instructor in English, Tibetan, and Urdu in one book,

Tibetan Dictionary and Grammar, repeated issues of Census forms in Tibetan for use in Lahul and Spiti: the gospel of St. Mark in Bunan, Tinan and Manchat dialects, a Gospel Harmony of the life of Christ in colloquial Ladaki, a compilation of folklore in the three Lahul dialects, and a second collection of Tibetan Historical Inscriptions on rock and stone from Western Tibet" (*Gazetteer 1917, Part III, Lahul:* 207-208).

The Mission had also a dispensary and its performance is explained in the words, 'The daily attendance at the dispensary is about 10, but it has fallen off since the people have been asked to contribute an anna or two for the medicines. The pastor in charge is not medically trained but has been through a short course in medicine". The Mission was also assigned some other small items of works, but quite important, by the Government as it is reported that, 'The mission keeps statistics of rain and snowfall at Kyelang for the Meteorological Department."

Pastor Schnabel and his wife were at Kyelang for about ten years, and were repatriated to Germany in the autumn of 1915 (*Gazetteer, 1917:* 206).

Peter was at the mission in Leh and Kyelang between 1930-40, and was interned at the outbreak of World War II at the Yule Camp in Kangra. He also worked at Poo. He is said to have been the most troubled man, among all the missionaries. He is stated to have been the last person to leave from Kyelang office.

Theos Bernard, a member of the Kyelang mission, is reported to have been murdered, in 1945. Office of the mission in Lahul is said to have been closed thereafter.

Heinrich August Jaeschke (1817-1883), the linguist, was born in Herrnhut, Saxony, Germany in 1817. He was educated and taught at the Paedagogium at Niesky. At Kyelang he had been commissioned to devote himself to the task of translating the Bible into Tibetan. He was about forty years of age, when he came to Kyelang. Markham comments on his merits saying that it 'would hardly have seemed fitted to commence living at altitudes between ten and eleven thousand feet above sea level; but in other respects he was well equipped. He was already fluent in seven languages, and had some knowledge of several others, including Sanskrit, Persian and Arabic'. After joining at Kyelang he went to Ladakh and stayed there for a while to learn the initial lessons in Tibetan language. Jaeschke's achievements are further summarized by Markham, 'Brother H.A. Jaeschke, after eleven years' residence in Lahul, returned to Germany in the end of 1868. He is the highest authority in Europe on the modern Tibetan language and its dialects, and is the author of more than one valuable work on the subject. He wrote 'A Short Practical Grammar of the Tibetan Language, with Reference to the spoken Dialects' (Kyelang, 1865), a Romanized Tibetan and English Dictionary (Kyelang, 1866), and a Tibetan and German Dictionary, just completed. These works are all auto-lithographed. In 1866, he submitted to the Berling Academy a treatise on the phonetic laws of the Tibetan Language. Since 1873 he has been engaged, for the India Office, on a comprehensive modern Tibetan and English Dictionary, which is now nearly ready for the press' (Markham, 1876: cvii-cviii). He also translated the New Testament into classical Tibetan.

The Gazetteer in the section on Lahul writes reaffirming the above facts, ".... and thither came in 1854 Pastors Heyde, Pagell and Jaeschke. Pastor Pagell was transferred to Poo shortly afterwards and after a few years, Pastor Yaschke, who was a good linguist, went to Saxony to continue his labours. Pastor Francke was stationed chiefly in Leh. Pastor Heyde remained at Kyelang for half a century continuously and only returned to Germany to spend his last two years."

Jaeschke concluded his work quickly and in addition prepared many treatises, textbooks for children as well as for adults and a book on Tibetan grammar. All these were first lithographed and then printed on a small hand machine at Kyelang. The first portion of the scripture *'A Harmony of the Gospels'* was printed in this manner in 1860. Jaeschke was responsible for translation of whole of the New Testament, except a portion. The complete Tibetan Bible, however, could be published only in 1948, with further contributions from Francke and Gergan. Jaeschke brought out a newspaper. However the most important work for which he is known the world over, are the *Tibetan-German Dictionary* and the *Tibetan-English Dictionary.* The dictionary is considered to have been prepared on the original linguistic efforts of Csoma de Koros (1784-1842). The English translation of the *Tibetan-German Dictionary* was published at the expense of the Government of India in 1881.

Mr. Bruce visited Kyelang along with his family in around 1912 and stayed there for about a fortnight. Mrs Bruce met Mrs and Mr Heyde and Schnabel who were there at the time of her visit. The author takes note of the mission house: "It was situated in the centre of the fields, the farmlands owned by the Mission. Just below the cottage was principal farm house, tenanted by Christian Lahoulis. The farmer's wife was Ladakhi by birth, and both she and her husband were very nice people" (Bruce, 1914: 138). She further says that there was no church in Kyelang.

Bruce expresses deep sympathy for the missionaries whom he saw living under extremely harsh climatic conditions of Kyelang. He feels that they had adapted themselves very well to the environment and also had introduced some novel devices in alleviating the severity of the weather as would be most useful in such a desolate place. After obtaining thorough knowledge of the district the author writes, "Moravian Mission have acquired a considerable amount of land, which he and his converts farm. The real difficulties arise when harvest-time comes around, as there is a great demand for labour, and Kyelang does not produce much. Also the cold very quickly arrives, necessitating the rapid garnering of the crops, and grass must be cut for hay, and stored as quickly as possible to avoid loss.

'The Mission has a large farming business, as besides growing all his own grain, potatoes, etc, Mr. Schnabel has large flocks of sheep. As far as it is possible to influence such superstitious folk as the Lahoulis he has improved their methods of agriculture, and to a certain extent made them rely more on common sense than on auspicious omens and favourable days, for beginning either to sow or reap. He and his wife, in fact, live a most practical life among the people, and one of the happiest signs is to see how well his people turn out. Especially there is no attempt made to take them out of their surroundings, or to give them modern English Christian names or clothes when they are baptized.

'The farm was conducted very much as a small European farm might be, and the bailiff and his wife ran everything in much the same way - far better really - and helped to keep the farm accounts," (Bruce, 1914: 149-150).

Bruce further informs that there were 30-40 Christians in Kyelang. "...but these numbers do not represent the enormous amount of good Mr. and Mrs Schnabel have done in a great many really practical ways. For instance, Mrs. Schnabel has taught a great number of Lahouli women and girls to make excellent socks and stockings, jerseys and comforters. In fact a new industry has been established. The knitting is chiefly done during the winter, when there is so little for the people to do and the country is for the greater part of the time under snow. During these months, also schools are in full swing, both Mr and Mrs Schnabel teaching. Besides these many activities, Mr Schnabel is the only person with any medical knowledge in the whole of Lahoul, and is being continually applied to in every kind of illness or accident, for all of which he does his best. Some of the problems he has to tackle are rather startling. While we were at Kyelang some half a dozen men in the Manchat, who were laying a wooden pipe to carry water across the face of a cliff, owing either to stones coming from above or from the face giving way, were precipitated down the cliff, and all more or less broken up. Mr. Schnabel flew off to attend them although the place where the accident had happened was over twenty miles away. This is only one of many proofs of the confidence the people have in him, and that irrespective of the actual making of converts the civilizing influence of the Mission must be great. Even the mere example of doing so much for people without asking anything in return is in itself worth untold gold. 'I made considerable purchases of thick socks and stockings. Very thick and warm they are too, and just the thing for hill-work in cold weather" (Bruce, 1914: 150-151).

The author visualizes the extremely difficult plight of the missionaries in the winter in Lahul, "We were sad when the time actually came for leaving our little cottage and our many Kyelang friends, and it was especially sad to realize that in a very few weeks the kind Schnabel would be cut off from India and would, in all probability, not see another European face for eight months to come; and what is worse, would have no post for quite five of these months. This isolation they endure year after year - a terrible trial and strain, involving, as it does, the impossibility of getting any news of their children in Europe. Mr. and Mrs. Heyde, their predecessors lived, I believe, for fifty years in Kyelang, an extraordinary record. They were both, as also is Mr. Schnabel, notable Tibetan scholars" (Bruce, 1914: 152).

The missionaries also assisted the residents of Spiti whenever they were called upon and was found convenient. The Gazetteer found that, "There are no medical arrangements for Spiti, but Moravian Missionaries from Poo in Bashahr generally pay a visit to the lower part of the valley in the summer and treat any ailments they find, the Kyelang Missionary doing the same for the upper valley" (Gazetteer, 1917: 308).

Biscoe gives account of a memorable incident in which a missionary, probably it was A.H. Francke (Appendix IV), was caught unexpectedly in a tumultuous in the fearful environment that a traveller usually encounters in these regions. In such a moment all have but one to look, to whose refuge he is necessitated to go. Basically all the religions grow from the same root stock writes Biscoe and illustrates the statement from a story, very near to reality, as may be read from his interesting description: "The following story was told me by one of the Moravian missionaries. He was on his way from Leh, which is the capital of Ladakh, to India on important business - viz. to meet his bride at Bombay - and was obliged to travel in the early spring, which is a most dangerous time for crossing the passes. He was nearing the

Zoji La Pass when he was overtaken by a blizzard, and soon he found that he had lost his way as the fresh snow had covered the tracks of the mail runners. It was of course, bitterly cold, and he could see no distance ahead on account of the blinding snow, driven against him by the strong cutting wind. After a vain hunt to find tracks, he was forced to give up the search, and as night was fast approaching he saw no possibility of surviving the night except through Divine help, so he prayed earnestly that his life might be spared. 'He had only just finished praying when he saw a figure which he thought must be a belated mail runner, so with thankfulness and joy he followed this figure, when suddenly it disappeared. He went to the place where he last saw the figure, and there he found a hole in the snow, into which he descended, and found himself in one of the stone shelters built for the safety of the mail runners. But what was his astonishment to find the shelter empty. No one was there! He then realized that his prayer had been answered in a most unexpected manner, and that his life had been spared for future service" (Biscoe, 1922: 199-200).

The missionaries in these difficult areas had to face not only the ruthless environment of the high mountain climatic conditions, but were also pressurized by the unfavourable international political conditions. Thus the mission at Kyelang had a short break as a result of the First World War as the missionary personnel had to be repatriated to their home country.

Yet another traveller and keen observer to Kyelang had a memorable encounter with the missionaries which he has recorded and reads as follows, "No survey of Lahul, however cursory, would be complete without some mention of the Moravian mission at Kyelang. This station was opened in 1854 under Pastors Heyde, Pagel and Jaeschke, and in their and other hands flourished and did good work until 1915, when the mission was closed in consequence of the repatriation of the missionaries as alien subjects. At the time of my visits to Lahul there was only one Ladakhi paster in charge of the mission and the Christian Church in Lahul is perhaps to be regarded as moribund. But in its day the mission had a great and living influence; the actual number of converts was small, but influence of the pastors was good, and they helped people with education and medical aid and by the introduction of potatoes, rye and lombardy poplars. The pastors did good work with their studies of the folk-lore and language of the region, but the greatest work of the Moravian mission was probably done through its printing press. On the press at Kyelang were printed many valuable books in Tibetan and other local dialects dealing with the Christian religion and with the study of the dialects" (Whistler, 1924: 47-48).

In around 1960's there lived a lady at Kyelang, named *achi Leo* (Sister Leu), who was a Christian and her house was named 'Leu Kothi', i.e. the house of Leo. Her offspring have now reverted to Buddhism. Another person was named Yakhob (Yakub) whose house had no name.

Francke has added a small but valuable chapter on the ancient history of Lahul at the end in one of his works entitled 'History of Western Tibet'. He has indicated at one place that more detailed account on the history of Lahul has been given in an article which was likely to be published in the journal 'Indian Antiquary' which, however, failed to come to light. Francke appears to have gathered a good amount of material on the history of Lahul, as he had done for other areas. 'With Pastor Francke, who was also repatriated, has gone an invaluable history of Lahul and much information regarding folklore, which is perhaps lost for good', remarks the Gazetteer.

Ribacch served in Lahul from 1892 to 1896. Thereafter he left for Ladak to work there. John Bray introduces the life of Ribacch: "Samuel Ribbach was a German missionary of the Moravian Church who spent more than twenty years in the Indo-Tibetan borderlands. He first came to India in 1892 to the Moravian mission station at Kyelang, Lahul. There he served under Wilhelm Heyde who had already spent nearly half a century in Lahul. Heyde was an accomplished Tibetan scholar; he was later to work in Darjeeling on a revised version of the Tibetan New Testament (the original translation having been the work of another Moravian scholar, H.A. Jaeschke) and he acted as co-editor of a Tibetan dictionary produced by the Bengali scholar, Sarat Chandra Das. In Heyde Ribbach therefore had a masterly Tibetan teacher. Having served his apprenticeship in Lahul, Ribbach moved in 1896 to Leh" (Ribbach, 1986: Introduction, iv).

Jaeschke's Linguistic Works: Jaeschke moved very fast in learning and mastering the Tibetan language. He accomplished the assigned task of translating the holy scriptures into Tibetan and in addition to this, he wrote a number of text-books and other useful treatises, thereby applying his knowledge to practical test. Carrying on his interest in creating literature for future pupils of Tibetan, Jaeschke prepared two dictionaries, Tibetan-German and Tibetan-English, besides a grammar. Caption of the English version of the work reads: 'A Tibetan-English Dictionary, with special reference to the Prevailing Dialects, to which is added An English-Tibetan Vocabulary.' The work thus displays a special feature of collection of words from the local dialects, as is spoken in the areas of Lahul, Spiti, Ladak and by those coming from Tibet on pilgrimage and passing through these areas.

This was the first attempt of its kind in the history of these areas. He stayed in Lahul for a short period of eleven years and gave the highest output to the scholarly world. The printing machine was installed at Kyelang during his time which remained in use till he was there.

Western scholars often seem to miss the point of wide distinction existing between the cultures and languages of those of the Central and Western Tibet. Central Tibet with Lhasa as its centre of origin of its culture and language, is evolutionary and constantly developing, and the west follows it in many cases, specially in the matter of religious literature. As Jaeschke tells himself, there are numerous dialects in the West. These spoken western languages constitute a number of historical layers such as the kirata (Mon), the ancient Tibetan (specimen found in the Tun-Huang literature); and is being influenced constantly by the Tibetan classical literature, modern Tibetan language from the north-east and the Indo-Aryan languages from the southern direction. Its peculiar geographical location is responsible for this kind of complexity. Its hard living conditions tend to pull it backwards in time, thus having tendency of retaining its ancient character. Even the violent turmoils of long past history had little effect in changing its cultural identity unrecognizably. Thus it carries the burden of the tribal past, habited in small pockets. On the other hand, it being situated on the border of two great international divergent cultures, it is subjected to pulls and pushes from either side from time to time. Moreover in the time of Jaeschke, Central Tibet was yet to be explored fully. Viewed in this context, Jaeschke's work could not but naturally be less popular among the ordinary readers and students, in comparison to similar contemporary works which were based on the classical literature. Yet Jaeschke's work is of rare kind, of high academic value and permanent nature which will always be counted among the most respected works. It is impossible if such kind of work will be undertaken ever again of this stature.

In the area of Tibetan language, after Csoma, perhaps Jaeschke was the next highest European authority. Indeed both the scholars learned the language and began their studies in Tibetan from the same area of Western Trans-Himalayas. However, the objectives of studies, environment, limitations, facilities available for the studies and the precedents for reference and guidance, etc. were different for both the scholars.

Jaeschke was responsible for the translation of the whole of the New Testament, with the exception of Hebrew's Revelation. Jaeschke familiarizes us in detail about his plan, objectives and methods adopted in the preparation of the work in the Preface of his dictionary. This was a moment of historical importance for many, especially for the area where he worked. The learned author reviews whole of the existing lexicographical literature on Tibetan in European languages and traces its origin and development in the Introductory part of his present work. Readers must be interested to learn more from the author in his own words. "This work represents a new and thoroughly revised edition of a Tibetan-German Dictionary, which appeared in lithographed form between the years 1871 and 1876. During a residence, which commenced in1857 and extended over a number of years, on the borders of Tibet and among Tibetan tribes, I and my colleagues gathered the materials for this Dictionary. 'We had to take primarily into account the needs of missionaries entering upon new regions, and then of those who might hereafter follow into the same field of enterprise. The chief motive of all our exertions lay always in the desire to facilitate and to hasten the spread of the Christian religion and of Christian civilization, among the millions of Buddhists, who inhabit Central Asia, and who speak and read in Tibetan idioms. 'A yet more definite object influenced my own personal linguistic researches, in as much as I had undertaken to make preparations for the translation of Holy Scriptures into the Tibetan speech. I approached and carried forward this task by way of a careful examination of the full sense and exact range of words in their ordinary and common usage. For it seemed to me that, if Buddhist readers were to be brought into contact with Biblical and Christian ideas, the introduction to so foreign and strange a train of thought, and one making the largest demands upon the character the imagination, had best be made through the medium of a phraseology and diction as simple, as clear, and as popular as possible. My instrument must be, as in the case of every successful translator of the Bible, so to say, not a technical, but the vulgar tongue.

'Thus, in contrast to the business of the European philologist, engaged in the same domain, who quite rightly occupies himself with the analysis and commentary of a literary language, the vocabulary and terminology of which he finds mainly deposited in the speculative writings of the Buddhist philosophers, it became my duty to embrace every opportunity, with which my presence on the spot favoured me, to trace the living powers of words and of expressions through their consecutive historical applications, till I reached their last signification in their modern equivalents, as these are embodied in the provincial dialects of the native tribes of our own time. 'These circumstances, it is hoped, will excuse, and explain the system of my work. A consistent attempt is here made for the first time to give a rational account of the development of the values and meanings of words in this language; to distinguish precisely the various transitions in period of literature and varieties of dialect; and to make sure of each step by the help of accurate and copious illustrations and examples. I have done my utmost to arrive at certainty where, heretofore, much was mere guess-work, and cherish the hope that, from this point of view, my contribution will be welcomed by the comparative philologist, and will be serviceable to the general cause of learning, as well as a useful volume within that narrower circle, whose requirements I was specially bound not to overlook, of persons whose main purpose is to be taught how to write and speak the modern Tibetan tongue. 'The language of the people has as many dialects, as the country has provinces. Indeed, as in most geographically similar districts, well nigh every separate mountain valley has its own singularities as to modes of utterance and favourite collocations of words. Especially is it interesting to note, in respect to pronunciation, how the old consonants, which would seem to have been generally sounded and spoken twelve centuries ago, when the Tibetan written character came into existence, and which at any rate, are marked by the primitive system of writing, remain still extant; every one of them can still be disinterred, somewhere or other, from some local peculiarity of language, and thus even the very diversity of modern practice can be made to bear testimony to the standards imposed by what was termed above the Classical Period.

'I have already adverted to the circumstances which, especially in the case of the student, who has for immediate object to learn how to read and write the Tibetan language, render existing dictionaries almost if not quite useless. They give but scanty information concerning modes of construction, variations and limits of actual application, shades of meaning, etc. In my own case, I was forced from the beginning to compile my own German-Tibetan dictionary, and found myself for all practical purposes thrown back upon my own resources. But the cause of truth appears to require a further word or two in regard to the Lexicon by Professor I.J. Schmidt of St. Petersburg, the relation of that work to its predecessors having been left by its author in some obscurity.

'The first Tibetan dictionary, intended for European students, was published at Serampore, as long ago as 1826. It contains the collections, amassed in view of a dictionary and grammar, by a Roman Catholic missionary, who was stationed in eastern Tibetan or close to the frontier in

Bhotan. There was nothing to assist him, except the scanty contributions, given by Georgi, in his Alphabetum Tibetanum. He had to cope with an entirely unworked language. He evidently took the one way possible of making acquaintance with it, sufficient to enable him to understand, to speak, to read and write. Each word or sentence was jotted down, as soon as it was heard, or was committed to writing, at the request of learner, by some native expert. After a while, the attempt could be made to a master book. In the instance of our missionary, Padma Sambhava's book of legends appears to have been selected, a work which represents rather a low level of literature, yet just on that account, perhaps, as a specimen of popular and current literature, not unsuitable to start from. Then, step by step, as best he could, our missionary had to possess himself of some abstract views, which would serve as a preliminary basis for a grammar. And had it been granted to this first occupant of the field to reduce his materials to an ordered system and to prepare them himself for publication, it is possible that in Europe the knowledge of the Tibetan language might have reached, some fifty years earlier, the stage at which it has now arrived. The very name of that Roman Catholic missionary, however, has been lost. The papers which left behind him, unsorted and unsifted, came into the hands of Major Latter, an English officer, and were passed on by him to Mr. Schroter, a missionary in Bengal. English was substituted for the Italian of the manuscript, and the East India Company made a grant which defrayed the cost of the Tibetan types and the further expenses of printing. But there was no Tibetan scholar to correct the proofs. The author himself would doubtless, on reconsideration, have detected and dismissed much erroneous or unnecessary matter. As it was, many additional mistakes crept in during the passage through the press. Thus the work, though it has a richer vocabulary than can be found in the later dictionaries, cannot on any questionable point be accepted as an authority and has only value for those who are already competent, for themselves, to weigh and decide upon the statements and interpretations it advances. I have not been able to extract from it much that was serviceable to me. Nevertheless, any one who knows by experience what time and toil such a work must have cost, though its design remained unfulfilled and its object unaccomplished will not easily be able to repress his indignation at the tone, in which this book in the preface to his Grammar is recklessly and absolutely condemned by Professor Schmidt.

'High praise, however, is awarded by the Professor to a second work, the Tibetan English Dictionary by Csoma-de Koros, which appeared in 1834.

This work deserves all eulogy; but the Professor's manner, which imitates that of a master commending a pupil, is, though on other grounds, as unwarranted and as so offensive in this as in the former case. The work of Csoma de Koros is that of an original investigator and the fruit of almost unparalleled determination and patience. The compiler, in order to dedicate himself to the study of Tibetan literature, lived like a monk for years among the inmates of a Tibetan monastery. It is to be regretted that, with the knowledge he certainly must have possessed of the later language and literature, he should have restricted the scope of his labours to the earlier period of literature, and when in his Grammar conversational phrases are quoted as examples, they are almost without exception in the dialects of the Kangyur, and of little practical value.

'This Tibetan English dictionary by Csoma has been adapted for a German public by Professor I.J. Schmidt of St. Petersburg. The translation from English into German is good; in the general alphabetical arrangement improvements have been introduced, and such as are in conformity with the spirit of the language; moreover, three Mongolian dictionaries have been consulted, and from these a certain number of words have been supplemented. But it cannot be said that even on the work of revision Professor Schmidt has bestowed much pains. For example, Csoma's rough grouping of words under the principal headings is left unaltered, though here especially a reduction to alphabetical order was obviously required. Mistakes and superfluities, very pardonable in the case of a first issue of an original publication, are repeated in this translation, and these cannot be so readily overlooked and condoned, when they are made at second hand, and are sanctioned and subscribed to by one, who has assumed so severe a critical and editorial attitude.

'My own dictionary, in the main, pursues the object and accepts the plan of the work, which was published by Mr Schroter. As I said at the beginning, I have not restricted myself to the Classical Period, but I have endeavoured to deal with the Tibetan language as a whole, though I do not pretend to have performed this task exhaustively. My dictionary derives its matter and its principles, so far as possible, equally from the literature and from the speech of the people. Each word has been made the object of observation in its relation to the context as it occurs in books, and in its value and place among others when it is used in common conversation, and then the attempt has been made to define its range and to fix its meaning.

'All the words, cited by Csoma and Schmidt, even such as I myself had never seen or heard, I have embodied in this work, stating, in each case, the source from whence I drew them". Thus he sums up the whole situation existing in his time.

In 1865 the staff were Heyde, Rechler and Jaeschke. Jaeschke died on 24 th September, 1883, in Berlin.

William Heyde left Europe in 1853 and was among the first two missionaries to arrive in Lahul in 1854 who opened mission office here. In 1856 he completed construction of the mission house at Kyelang. William Heyde became a known expert in Tibetan. His contributions in the field of literature, language, besides the community development, are commendable. He in 1868 wrote a section on the history of the Moravian mission in Lahul and their activities which was included in the Gazetteer of the Kangra District, Lahul. He alongwith Graham Sandburg were appointed by the Government of Bengal to revise the Tibetan English Dictionary of Sarat Chander Dass. The scholars worked together for two years from 1899 to 1902 till the completion of the work. In this way he made an important contribution in the development of the lexicographical works of Tibetan into English. He left Darjeeling for Europe in 1903. Heyde remained in Lahul for the longest period, for 50 years. The Gazetteer records his contributions in the words, "Pastor Heyde remained at Kyelang for half a century, continuously, and only returned to Germany to spend the last two years of his life. His record is one of absolute devotion to the work of the Mission: he and his wife have left lasting effects of their life and labours among the people of Lahul as have a succession of other Missionaries" (*Gazetteer, 1917, Part III, Lahul:* 206).

In 1863 Mr. P. Egerton, of the Civil Services, made a tour through Spiti, and Mr. A.W. Heyde accompanied him. Heyde was first scholar to bring the Pu-nan language of Lahul to writing, in 1869 AD. He used Tibetan characters for writing the language. He also made first attempt at writing a Punan grammar. "But Mr. Heyde and his wife (for as a bride Mrs. Heyde arrived in Kyelang, and did not leave it again until she left it for good, forty-three years later) became great scholars also. They revised the New Testament translation, putting it into colloquial Tibetan, more easily taught to and understood by, the humble converts of the peasant class", says Mrs. Bruce (Bruce, 1914: 275). While Heyde remained in India for fifty years, from 1854 to 1903, Mrs Heyde was here for 43 years, roughly from 1860 to 1903.

Kyelang: Some Data

1. William Heyde Joined in 1854 and remained here upto 1899, and then went to Darjeeling from where he was repatriated to Herrnhut, Europe, in 1903 where he died after two years.

2. Pagell was at Kyelang from 1854 upto 1865. Thereafter in 1865, he, alongwith his wife opened the Poo office in Bashahar.
3. Jaeschke joined at Kyelang in 1857 and remained for 11 years. He left for Europe in 1868.
4. In 1873 Heyde and Redslob families were there at Kyelang.
5. Ribbach was here from 1892 to 1896.
6. Francke was in Kyelang from 1906 to 1908, for two years.
7. Asboe was in Kyelang from 1927 to 1936, then he went to Ladakh and left India in 1947.
8. In 1910 there were the families of Heyde and Schnabel. Schnabel and wife remained for 10 years from 1906 to 1915 when they were repatriated to Germany.
9. G. Hettash died in 1908.
10. Peter was at Ladak and Kyelang, and also in Kinnaur between 1930 and 1940, and is stated to have been at Kyelang till the closing of the station.
11. Bruce, while writing in 1914, gives the figure of the Christians in Lahul at thirty (Bruce, 1914: 150). He also notes that there was no church at Kyelang.

Achievements of the Missionaries - An Assessment

Moravians remained in the Himalayan territories for nearly a century and then left for their country. They worked and contributed extensively towards improvement of living conditions of the residents, even though their own stay was not always at ease. They were far away from their home and society, and were living in an alien country. The environment was harsh and unfamiliar, and the people, among whom they were working, were strangers.

The Moravians established their office first in Lahul among all their stations in the Himalayas and it is here that they initiated all their vital and key projects. They installed the basic infrastructures at Kyelang. The personnel of the mission mostly came first to Kyelang. After receiving the initial familiarization course and basic induction, they moved to the other stations of the organization where they were required to work. The fathers who opened office in Khalatse or Leh and Poo had come from Kyelang.

In Lahul, they had opened seven branch schools, besides the one at Kyelang, thus laying down the foundations of modern education so far back. But some of them had to be closed because of the non-availability of suitable teacher-lamas. They established a printing press here which catered to the needs of all their other stations. A newspaper was published from there. School text books on different subjects, in different languages; text books for the training of the personnel of the organization; research papers and many other works were printed here. Jaeschke's grammar and his world famous dictionaries were first printed here. All the endeavours in the linguistics and other studies, and translation of the holy texts were done and printed here. At the same time they were working for the benefit of the residents, through schools and hospitals and crafts classes.

Mission's work of real significance, from the view point of Lahul is the scholarly works done by the missionary scholars in the fields of its history, religion, language, culture, etc. They also collected from the area numerous documents and materials of historical importance and preserved them, which otherwise would have been lost irretrievably. They studied the various dialects of the region and put them to writing for the first time. They also sent materials for the Linguistic Survey of India.

Dr Francke, although stayed only for two years (1906-8) in Lahul, has published at least three collections of inscriptions and other materials of historical importance from Kyelang. More valuable documents have been included in his 'Antiquities of Indian Tibet, Part II'. He has contributed numerous articles on the history and languages of Lahul in several reputed professional international journals.

The missionaries also introduced such new devices into Lahul as the smokeless iron-hearth which is very simple and adapted to the local conditions, is fuel saving and an efficient energy generating device; ventilation of windows by using glass panes; growing of various exotic vegetables; plantation of Lombardy poplar; and imparted training in knitting of socks and pullovers, etc. Even after doing so much, there is nothing to commemorate their presence, if ever they lived here. They had created some motifs, in an attempt to keep the memory alive, but the fast moving and changing world has not spared them unassaulted.

a. **Iron-hearth (lchags-thab):** Iron-hearth, called *lchags-thab* in sTod, has without doubt come from Europe, which was introduced by the missionaries. It is slightly modified in Lahul.

b. **Poplar:** As regards the plantation of Lombardy poplar tree, it may be said that there grow at least two varieties of it in Lahul which in the dialect of sTod are named: Ma-kal and Kyu-lad. Moorcroft and Trebeck mention sight of poplar plantions, when they visited Lahul in 1820.

c. **Willow (Cang-ma):** Of the three varieties of cang-ma found in the area, one called *tsel-cang* (in sTod) grows wild in small bushes, similar to that of bamboo or reed, in shape. Its supple and strong straight branches are useful for weaving basket (*tse-po*) for carrying in it loads on the back. The second variety, *srwang-cang* (in sTod), is similar to cang-ma, in size and shape. It is used for the same purpose as *cang-ma*, but it is planted not like the ordinary *cang-ma*, but by simple method like other plants. It is easily distinguishable from the other one, from its leaves which is covered on its upper side with thin and white woolly substance. People have very low preference for it and its plant is seen only occasionally. Willow (*cang-ma*) is grown along the water channel (*yu-ra*), vacant lands near the cultivated fields and in the open wastelands. Each household is able to identify the trees in the common large groves owned by it. It would not be an exaggeration if we call it 'green gold' of Lahul. It is one of the major items of assets of a household: more the number of trees one owns, richer it is. Willow plantation is a bit a complex operation. Importance of willow may be known from the fact that in the winter, not a single blade of green grass is visible on the ground. No crop and grass grows in the winter. At this time its' soft twigs and the green bark of the branches are used as fodder for all kinds of domestic animals: the large flocks of sheep, goat and cattle that each house owns, on an average between fifty and hundred a house. Animals relish it highly and is equally nourishing. The residual wood is utilized as fuel, and also in the construction of houses for spreading on the beams of flat roofs, upon which are laid straw and again over it a thick layer of earth.

A remarkable fact about the culture of willow is that the distinctive method of raising and growing it is an enviable achievement in the biological engineering which cannot be said to have evolved in the period of a few years, not even within the period of a hundred years; rather it must be a result of several hundred years. The residents learned the technique through the long period by experimenting and adapting against the numerous tough environmental conditions existing in the territory. The plant is grown in the shortest possible period where otherwise the pace of growth of plants is extremely slow; and also harvest bumper yield, again in the least possible period. This method of planting surpasses several technical obstacles. The trees are usually planted on the slopes of the land that cannot be dug up for cultivation. Plantation of willow trees is one of the yearly routine for every household of average wealth. The plantation may be entirely new, or may be done to replace the unsuccessful young plantations done one or two years back, the ones dried out due to old age, those buried under the weight of snow from the snow-slip or avalanche in the winter, etc. The tree itself is never cut, unless it falls down itself, for its stem is of no use other than for fuel. Willow is propagated by planting in bunches of 3 or 4 freshly cut poles, depending upon the thickness of each one, known as *pung-shen* (in sTod, for a single pole or the bunch), around 5 to 6 inches thick and about six-seven feet in height, in a pit around two feet or slightly more deep. They are tied together before planting and the whole plant is wrapped with rags after planting in order to protect it from the bites of the cattle. Although the poles are quite thick, the bark covering it is yet green and juicy, and is a great attraction for the animals. Regular periodical irrigation is necessary, after about each fortnight, for its roots are short and the main body of the plant is voluminous, besides the poor character of the soil. All the new sprouts are allowed to grow at the top of the plant, those growing on the middle of the stems have to be removed, some preventive work is done by the wrappings also. As the tree grows, the poles merge to form a single stem. The plant sheds lush bunch of shoots in the first year and the yield of branches is ready for harvesting after three - four years. Branches sprout from all around the head of each pole. Further each year it is cut at a little higher level so that the tree assumes shape of a mushroom with cap reversed. Each of the freshly cut stump becomes root for the next year. After a few years, some of the stronger branches can be left out to grow thicker which can be cut after some more years for further propagation.

As against this method, if the plants were grown by small cuttings, or saplings, in the normal way like apple or poplar, it would be extremely difficult to keep the plant surviving. Further it may take very long time to reach the crop yielding stage. Yield cannot be obtained as high as it is obtained by this top-cutting method.

This method of plantation has a number of advantages. The thick strong bunch of stems resists the thrust of the snow-slip in the winter, and even though planted without fencing, animals cannot harm. The growth period between the seedling and crop-cutting is greatly reduced, and also the period of each crop season. Above all the shape of the tree makes it safe from the weight of snow received each winter and the yield is definitely much more than that obtained in the normal method. Thus it is a great achievement in the advanced scientific method of management of willow plantation.

Moorcroft and Trebeck, two European explorers, passed through Lahul in 1820 A.D., 34 years prior to the Moravians settled in Lahul. Among many observations they have made, they remarked on the situation of plantation of willow in Lahul. Everything they describe is the same as we see being done today. Typically they saw that the tree is planted for the 'large head of croppings', just as is done now a days, and saw a tree of sixteen feet in girth.

The two learned travellers observed a grove of willow plants at Beeling, where they pitched their tents, about one kilometer before reaching Kyelang from the direction of Tandi, where such thick groves exist even today. "Beling, where we halted, afforded ground for cultivation, and for a grove of willows: one of these near my tent was sixteen feet in circumference. This tree is planted for the large head of croppings which it affords, and which are made up into faggots, and piled round the roofs of the houses as fire wood for the winter. Several of the trees were hollow; for when it is discovered that decay has affected the wood, the interior is scooped out till little but the bark is left. In this state it not only throws out its branches at top, but I noticed in some of them branches descending from the head inside the tree, and taking root in the earth at its base. The people are careful to keep up these plantations" (Moorcroft and Trebeck, 1971-I: 202-203). It is stated in the narrative that the trees are hollowed from inside. This is a natural process observed in the willow tree. Even in the smallest branch of the tree a pore runs in the centre, from its base to the tip, which is filled up with a soft pulp of brown colour, initially being colourless, but browning as it grows older and eventually may get rotten. Thus the tree becomes hollow from inside as its age advances, although the tree keeps on increasing its outer girth. Another important observation has been made here. The branches were hooked towards inside the hollow stem for further propagation. This is not done these days.

Today, although new plantations are being made continuously every year, the survival of the old plants, and that too, so large as seen in the days of the two travellers, is difficult to find. They are now impaired constantly by the passersby, due to manifold increase in the mobile population, and the number is reduced constantly, among many other reasons, by felling for the land required for consruction of road and buildings.

d. **Potato:** Potato of Lahul has peculiar characteristics. Boiled potato is crisp and even if eaten in greater quantity, it does not taste bitter and repulsive. Any kind of seed imported from outside acquires this character after a few years. Therefore potato forms an important part of diet of a Lahula family. The midday food, *za-ra,* essentially consists of boiled potato which may be eaten with a vegetable, commonly wild, and or curd or buttermilk with *tsampa*. Potato is used regularly in *thugpa* (*adu-thugpa,* potato-gruel), in the supper, and for curry. Potato is a universal item of food and is used abundantly.

The Gazetteer of the district notes on the annual routine of the residents of the district, in the manner, "The Lahula does not stay at home except to cultivate his crops and a large proportion of the population is absent whatever time of the year is considered. Hundreds of men go in July to Western Tibet where they pay cash for wool and pashm and dispatch it to Lahul on their own sheep, and the latter are then sent back to Tibet for the winter grazing. Others traffic at the Patseo fair which goes on for a month in August and buy salt, wool and *pashm* and take it to Kulu. Many Lahulas, however, take their sheep to the lower Hill States for the winter. Others work in forests, in Kishtwar, Chamba and Kulu, either as sub-contractors or as coolies. The number of Lahulas who go further afield in India for trade is unknown, but is believed to be increasing" (Gazetteer 1917, Part III, Lahul: 208). It is the compulsion of the habitat. Under these circumstances it is to be wondered that the Lahula remained ignorant, till only a hundred and fifty years back, of the utilities of potato.

e. **Socks:** The missionaries are attributed the introduction of socks. We see socks in Lahul known as 'Lahuli socks' with typically patterned design, which is very popular outside the district. The portion of the socks forming the part of the legs is simple. Designs are knitted with the threads of different colours, usually there is a set of seven colours, on the upper part of the socks forming the portion of foot, which is visible through the net-like upper portion of straw-shoes (*pu-la*), again an object, typical to Lahul.

Many of these designs on the socks may be named in the sTodpa dialect in this manner. The whole system of designs or patterns put on a sock is called *Tshom.* Some of the important *tshom* (designs) may be named as: *nyug-rum* (swastika), *rgya-nag lcags-ri* (Chinese border), *bum-tsang* (auspicious pot), *bum-tsang phyed* (half bum-*tsang*), *Kaljor men-tog* (White Kaljor flower), *Kardang skyod-skyog* (zig-zig, like the path to Kardang), *skyang-gug, par-par-tsi, lab-ri, ka-li cung-ngun, ka-li ched-mo,* etc. While the normal woollen thread is called *sne-ma,* the coloured threads for designs is called *bab-sa'i.* We cannot find the nomenclatures in any other place, because woollen socks are not made so elaborately anywhere other than in Lahul. All the above tasks are attributed to the Moravians having had done in all the three regions of Lahul, Ladak and Bashahar.

The result of a hundred years' labour of total force directed towards the propagation of Christianity is well known to everyone. Instances of such lessons are found filled to the brim in the experiments in the implementation of the rural development projects.

f. **Education:** Efforts of the missionaries in the field of education may be appreciated for opening seven or eight schools in those early times. The people, however, failed to take advantage of the opportunity made available to them. Grievance of some scholars regarding the failure to attract the girls to school is genuine. The straight jacket socio-economic set up of the small society leaves no freedom for the girls to part from their family. Even at the time of marriage the rules are curved and efforts are made to prevent the marriage at the outset from being solemnised, understandably in order to retain the girl at home, even though it is a duty, strictly customary, assigned to the close relatives of the girl, like her maternal uncle. Her individuality is suppressed in order to maintain the socio-economic system. Women are the pillars of home-economy, while the men are on the hunt for paltry gain to the distant lands of the lower hills or Jangthang in the north. Girls were not sent to school in sTod valley, even by the sixtys and seventys of nineteenth century.

Although there came out several scholars from among the educated native converts from Ladak and Kinnaur, there was none to have taken lead among the Christian converts in Lahul, even though the Missionaries had created the best facilities at Kyelang and had stayed substantially for longer period.

g. **Publications:** Besides the publications by the eminent scholars like Jaeschke and Francke, as mentioned above, some holy verses were translated by A.W. Heyde in Punan dialect. In 1908 A.H. Francke completed a version of St. Mark, struck of forty copies of it and circulated among the people and latter lithographed it in 1911. The Manchad version of translation done by Dr. Francke and Lama Zodpa was printed in 1914 by lithography. The two also prepared Tinan version and published it in 1915.

The Sufferings

Among the missionaries who came here and were living far away from their home, separated from their relatives and children, not all were fortunate enough to be able to return to their homeland. Some others returned at the advanced age, only to spend the last few years at home. A few families lost the lives of their children. "Mr. and Mrs. Schnabel had a charge of this centre for some eight years, and one of their little ones was buried in the mission house garden at Poo," (Bruce, 1914: 277). 'The most dedicated brethren gave also of themselves' - 'many old and young lie buried below my house in a clump of willows', says Lady Bruce while giving description of the depressing site, at Kyelang. The author further writes: "The pathos of these isolated lives struck me very forcibly as I walked from the willow shaded path leading from the house to the God's acre below. For enclosed within stone walls and entered by a gate from the lower garden was the little cemetery, full of graves. Under the protecting branches of willows and poplars rested the bodies of two children of this family, as well as those of several other small boys and girls. There are memorial tablets to some adults, too, but the greater proportion are to young children."

Mr. and Mrs. Pagell started the centre at Poo in 1865. Mrs. Pagell came as a young bride and spent the rest of her life in these domains. Mrs. Bruce narrates the stirring story of their end in a foreign land where there was none of their relatives around, none to share their sufferings and to console them, or to shed even a single drop of tear for the loss of their lives. It is a rare example of agony and tragedy having scarcely any comparison. Thus she writes, "For eighteen years they worked there often terribly depressed, but persevering in the face of all difficulties and they had many converts. At last they both fell ill. At all events they became convinced that they could not recover, for they had their coffins and shrouds prepared. It was in the winter, when they were cut off from all communications with the outer world, and could get no help.

'Fortunately, the poor wife only survived her husband three days. He died on January, 4. Then poor brave Mrs. Pagell, feeling her own end was near, laid herself in her coffin. She died on January, 7. They were buried by their converts, and the headman of the village at once sealed up their effects and when in answer to the said news and appeal from the Tibetan Christians the following May, a member of the mission was able to push through to Poo. He found all in perfect order. It is difficult to imagine anything braver or more pathetic" (Bruce, 1914: 276-277).

The Final Withdrawal

Moravians had not come here to stay for ever. They closed their office firstly in Bashahar in 1912, thereafter in Lahul in 1940 or 1945, and lastly in Ladak, after a few years of the Independence of the country. The details of the Moravians' departure from Lahul and India are confused in the political events of the years of turmoil of World War II and India's Independence, says Stutchbury. In fact, there appear a number of external compulsions which forced them eventually to stop their activities in India. The objectives of the Mission for working in India is explained by one of its eminent members, H.A. Jaeschke, in the words, "The chief motive of all our exertions lay always in the desire to facilitate and to hasten the spread of the Christian religion and of Christian civilization, among the millions of Buddhists, who inhabit Central Asia, and who speak and read in Tibetan idioms," (Jaeschke, 1958: Preface, iii). Achievements of the Moravians on this account may be assessed from the observations made by numerous visitors to the area from time to time recorded in their works. The office initially started at Kyelang by Mr. A.W. Heyde and Mr. Pagell was run from the beginning on practical as well as on spiritual lines. The missionaries were initially successful in their main objective, in gaining the followers. There were about twenty converts at Kyelang when Andrew Wilson visited Lahul in 1873. The number of the faithful stood at twenty nine including the children in 1897. The number does not appear to have exceeded much beyond this figure, at any time thereafter. Till some years back, the number had reduced to only one family throughout Lahul. Eventually this too reverted to Buddhism.

One of the impediments coming in the way of their earnest effort may be read in the works of Sir James Layall, an administrator: "The very tolerance of the Boti race in religious matters will, I think, be one obstacle to their conversion. In the Sunday services of the mission house I saw an old and learned lama, who lives there to assist Mr. Jaescke in his Tibetan studies, join in the hymns and responses with great zeal and fervour. I do not think that either he or his friends was anything inconsistent in his so doing, though he had not the least intention of becoming a convert to Christianity. All worship is good, seemed to be his motto" (*Kangra District Gazetteer, 1897*)." This observation was made in 1868, only after 14 years of their stay in Lahul. Mr. Heyde who, commenting on the character of the Lahulas, as he had observed and experienced himself, predicted the same year that, "With regard to sobriety, veracity, fidelity to the marriage tie, and in other ways, the morals, both of the Buddhists and half Buddhists of Lahul, are deplorably loose, but nevertheless they stick to their different religions with a tenacity that gives till now little hope for the spread of Christianity among them" (*District Gazetteer, Kangra, Lahul, 1917:* 200).

The same observation is seen reverberating in the writings of a later visitor, Pran Chopra, a journalist, "The influence of Tibetan Lamaism and the strong institutions of community life which it has created must be held responsible at least in part for the failure of the Moravian mission to find many converts in these valleys." He visited the areas after the Chinese Agression of 1962. The Moravians were to some extent successful in Kinnaur and Ladak. As such this could have been one of the reasons for their abandoning the mission.

Another cause prompting the Moravians to abandon the mission could have been the unfriendly international relationship between England and Germany. The missionaries were repatriated to their homeland during the First World War and there was only one native person to look after the office at Kyelang. During the second World War too some missionaries from Kyelang were confined to jails.

Their plan of advancement towards Central Asia looked uncertain as the international political atmosphere was becoming more and more hardened and unfavourable. Therefore the prospects of their further movement appeared impossible. There was no solution but to stop the mission. Withdrawal from Bashahar in 1912 was their first step in this direction. Various authors have made their own presumptions regarding the closure of the mission office in Lahul. Khosla assumes that it was closed in 1945 when Dr. Bernardo, a prominent member of the mission, was murdered, somewhere beyond Ladakh (Khosla, 1956: 205). According to Randhawa they left Lahul in around 1940 or 1942 because of their differences with the local Thakurs. These causes indeed were minor. Even if these causes were true in respect of Lahul, the same cannot be said about Kinnaur where the office had been sold and closed in 1912 or Ladak. The answer may be sought in the wider perspective.

When the Moravians left Kyelang, they sold their house to the Thakurs of Khangsar, who then rented it out to the Government. Since there was no modern and good house compared to this, it was used as Deputy Commissioner's residence for some years. A resident remarks, "Five rooms, a lift, and a beautiful verandah, all in excellent wood. It was the residence of the Moravian missionaries who were in Lahul from 1854 to 1940."

The Moravians, however, did not confront always failure. Their greatest gift to the scholarly world is their contributions in the study of Tibetan language and preparation of the Dictionary and grammar for the benefit of the interested future scholars. Their contributions in the study of the history and languages of various small states in the region is highly valuable. For the social and economic development of the people they opened schools and hospitals, and introduced exotic implements and techniques in the field of agriculture. Even though few people know that the Moravians had ever lived in Lahul, their gift to the region is unforgettable.

3.
Moravian Missionaries in Kinnaur

In the state of Bashahar, the first office of the Moravian Mission was opened at Poo in Kinnaur, in 1865. The Kangra District Gazetteer of 1897 records the foundation of the first office in Kinnaur in the words: "A second station of the Moravian mission in these parts was founded in 1865 among the Buddhists of Upper Kanawar in the protected Hill State of Basahir (Shimla district). The name of this station is Pu situated on the immediate frontier of Tibet proper, having been established with a view to extend its labours into that country" (*Gazetteer 1897, Part III Lahul:* 22).

Mrs. and Mr. E. Pagell opened the Poo office who had been, before this, at Kyelang in Lahul. They worked here for 18 years till both of them died in 1883. "Thereafter father Screne (?) took over the charge of the Station" (Rahul, 1956: 271).

In around 1870, Andrew Wilson visited Poo and met Mrs. and Mr. Pagell. They had got a house constructed for themselves. Besides, "there was a small chapel in his compound, in which service was conducted on Sundays for the benefit of the few Christians", writes Wilson. He further notes, "Besides himself and his wife, two or three men with their families, constituted entire Christian Community, and of these one was the hereditary executioner of Kunawar, the office having been abolished during the life time of his father, while of another, a true Tibetan who acted as a house servant. Mr. Pagell said that he was a Schandel', or scandal, to the Christian name, from his habits of begging and borrowing money right and left" (Wilson, 1875: 152).

Rahul Sankritayayan was highly appreciative of the services rendered and the works done by these selflessly dedicated missionaries. He visited Kinnaur twice; the second time in 1948. Mahapandita Rahul was very well informed of all the developments going on in whole of the Himalayan region, for he had been roaming continuously in the reigon and the Central Asian countries for long time. He maintained deep knowledge about all these areas. In his valuable work concerning the area, 'Kinner Desh' (1956), he has given account of his excursions to Kinnaur and Bashahar state, and its history. About the missionaries at Poo in Kinnaur, he wrote in 1948, "The Dak Bunglow of Poo was constructed in 1913. Before this, about 35-37 years back, Redslob couple had come and both of them died here, where many other missionaries too are burried. The Church has now disappeared. The inscribed stones are lying neglected in the compound of the Lambardar. The Mission remained functional here upto 1913. Till then there was a school and a post office. Padre Marx was a skilled carpenter. He taught the craft of carpentry to many people and artisans here. The missionaries also taught and imparted training in knitting sweater and socks. They planted apple and peach trees in Chiné" (Rahul 1956: 129).

In 1897 (some authorities say in 1900) a new and the second station, after Poo, was opened in Kinnaur at Chiné (Kalpa) or Pangi where Mrs. Bruske and Mr. J.T. Bruske assumed charge of the station. Before this they had worked at Chhota Nagpur for fourteen years and in 1894 had joined the Moravian Mission at Leh. The Chiné office was closed in 1912. Perhaps Marx also worked here, as Rahul Sankritayayan mentioned that he was responsible for the construction of the bungalow at Chiné. Bruske purchased land from a zamindar with the assistance of Raja Shamsher Singh of Bashahar. He constructed a Bungalow there on the road-side, and a school and remained here for thirteen years. Bruske's experience of working on the language at Chhota Nagpur and then working in similar capacity in Kinnaur helped to reveal the connection between the two languages. Thus, it revealed the secret of an ancient connection between the *Kiratas* of the Himalayas and the pre-Aryan inhabitants of the northern plains of India, the Austrics. This was a highly valued contribution on the history of the ancient Himalayan tribes. Hooper maintains, "After fourteen years with the Gossner Mission in Chhota Nagpur they had joined the Moravians at Leh in 1894, and in 1900 were in charge of a newly opened station of Moravians at Chini on the River Sutluj, about fourteen days March from Simla. They reduced the language to writing, and in spite of Mr. Bruske's ill health succeeded in translating St. Mark. The work at Chini was subsequently taken over by the Salvation Army, and in 1918 a translation of St. John was issued in the Tankri script prepared by F. Mortimer" (Hooper, 1963: 146).

About Chiné, Rahul Sankritayayan maintains that "This building of *Dak Bunglow* (presently Government Rest House) was constructed by Bruske with his money and labour. In 1900 they constructed a beautiful *dak bunglow* besides the other houses. A school was opened for boys (1899-1907). He propagated the art of handicrafts among the people. Then after serving here for 13 years, he died and his wife too left for the heaven. Thereafter the station was taken over by Peter. In 1912 the Mission office was sold to the Salvation Army. Bruske imported from Holland plants of apple and peach. He had planted a lot of flowers here and most of them were perennial including a rose plant" (Rahul 1956: 51-54). The rose plant was in full bloom during Rahul's stay here for three months in 1948.

In 1909 Francke visited Chiné, on his way for archaeological tour of the Tibetan border where he met Mr. Bruske and his wife. While they were staying and serving there, they had gained wide and thorough knowledge of the culture and history of the area. Francke admired them highly for the kind of knowledge they had gained about the region, which he found very useful in his own research work. At Poo Mrs. and Mr. R. Schnabel were on the post. After him Peter was here whom Rahul had met in Ladak in 1933.

The Mission at Chiné remained active upto 1912 and in the same year it was sold to Salvation Army, another missionary group, for rupees 9000. Salvation Army also worked diligently and was very helpful to the people. They opened a hospital where an Anglo-Indian couple Dr. Samuel and his wife worked for a year. They opened a school for training the women in spinning and knitting of wool. The group continued for some years but it could not stay long for it was dependent on state funding for its source of income. The First World War caused financial stress on the government and that dried up the source of funds for the Salvation Army. At last in 1919 it sold all its assets including the buildings etc. to the government at a cost of rupees five thousand and then left the area. Two most memorable members belonging to the latter organization were M/s Walker and Mortimer. However, their contribution and including that of their organization is considered insignificant in comparison to that of Bruske and the Moravian Church.

The Gazetteer reports that there were schools both at Poo and Chiné. At Poo both boys and girls attended the school. They were taught reading, writing, arithmetic, religious instructions, singing, sewing, knitting stockings, growing fruits, etc. The number of students one time at Poo counted ten girls and from ten to fifteen boys.

"The number of native Christians at both stations together is at present 35 including children of which number three adults and three children at

Pu" (*Kangra District Gazetteer, Lahul, 1899, 1994:* 21- 22). Here the Gazetteer refers as first station to Kyelang and the number of converts also included from the same station.

G.M. Young, in 1912, appreciated the Moravian Missionaries working in Kinnaur in the words: "The Moravian Mission contains several Tibetanists, worthy successors of Francke, who could do so, and would moreover, be welcomed by the Tibetans, as they are highly qualified in medicine, on this last account a Moravian Missionary at Poo has been more than once invited by the Tibetans of Guge, to enter their district" (Young, 1982: 273).

It is widely alleged that the Moravian Missionaries introduced handloom from Europe and they introduced the growing of grapes, apple etc. into Kinnaur. There is no denying the fact that they brought fruit plants from Holland and taught handloom, knitting, carpentry, and introduced some improved European implements and techniques in their use. But these arts, artifacts and activities were not unknown in Kinnaur. High quality of such products from Kinnaur was popularly known outside the district. The facts may be learned from the official records and the descriptions left by the European visitors who came to Kinnaur earlier than the establishment of the Mission in 1865.

Official report of an officer from the Administrative department of the British government recorded before 1824, highlights the matter in the following words, "In Kanawar the people chiefly subsist by trade, and live upon flocks. The grape, apple and turnip are extensively and most successfully cultivated, and form a chief source of food during the winter months. Blankets for the chief export to the Chinese territory, raisins, *neozas* (nuts), tobacco, rice, horse-shoes, saddles, stirrups, etc. are sent to tartary" (Murray 1824: 282).

Report of Mr. Lockwood Kipling, Principal of the Lahore School of Art, another official of the British Government wrote for the old edition of the Simla District Gazetteer, earlier to that of 1908, in the words, "In the Bashahr state good blankets and woollen clothes are made. Some of the gudmas are soft and thick and woven in the brown and grey strips. Pretty patterns of parti-caloured yarn are knitted in socks and mittens. Blanket weaving of a coarse kind is a domestic occupation" (Gazetteer, 1908: 17). Thus we observe that all these occupations were practiced in Kinnaur before the coming of the Moravians and constituted a substantial part of their occupation. The Moravians certainly brought about improvement in the already existing status.

Garret, who visited Kinnaur in 1842, has made an impressive remark on the grape vine cultivation as, "For four days I traversed a charming country of secluded valleys where one felt shut off from the world and where I travelled under shady avenues of vines (nowhere else in India have I seen grapes). ...The picturesque villages were hidden among the vines or under the oak trees hoary with age" (Garret, 1971: 116).

Missionaries contributed remarkably in the areas of education, craft, health, agriculture, horticulture, linguistics and archaeology. Mr. Bruske, despite his continuous ill health, studied Kinnauri language painstakingly and succeeded in completing the translation of St. Mark's Gospel in 1908 (Hooper, 1963: 146). The translation was a joint effort of Mrs and Mr J.T. Bruske and was published by the Bible Society at Lahore, the cost being met by the Church of England Congregation at Shimla as their centenary offering. In 1918, a translation of St. John was prepared by F. Mortimer of the Salvation Army who had taken over the charge of the mission at Chine´ from the Moravians. The work was written in Tankri script. In the field of study of linguistics they prepared and supplied material for the Linguistic Survey of India and brought the basic characteristics of the Kinnauri language before the scholarly world.

The Moravian missionaries had brought up in their schools a number of boys and girls. From among them Mr Tharchin (Thar-phyin) grew up to be an outstanding scholar. He belonged to Poo and was imparted good education by his masters. He ultimately shifted to Kalimpong in West Bengal and settled there. He started there a printing press in Bhoti. He brought out a newspaper in Bhoti language and published a number of books in the same language, including a dictionary. He was greatly helpful to the European scholars in making understand ancient and difficult texts and books in Tibetan.

Lobzang, another product of the Moravians, was also educated and trained at Poo. He accompanied Francke in his archaeological tour and was found to be of great help to the archaeologist. While Francke himself was not permitted to go to Tholing and Tsaparang, beyond Shipki in Tibet, he sent Lobzang there who was able to gather valuable information from there on the two towns and was also successful in searching an important historical document with the rdZong-dpon (Castleward) of Tsaparang (Francke, 1926-I: 27). It was a copy of the agreement between the Raja of Bashahar and Tibetan government dating 17th century AD. Another version of the same Document has been treated by Tucci and Petech.

On August 28, 1907, Sven Hedin visited Poo and spent two days in the Mission hospital. Messers Marx and Schnabel, and their families were at Poo at this occasion. The Moravian Missionaries remained in the area for about half a century till 1912, the beginning of the First World War. Peter was holding the office during the last years of the station.

4.
Moravian Missionaries in Ladakh

Jesus Christ if ever set his holy feet among the virgin rocky lands in the Himalayas - is a question of solemn investigation. It seems that this is also one of the serious issues for investigation included in the agenda for explorative journey of the internationally renowned figure, Nicholas Roerich. His first encounter with the question begins in Ladakh. 'Regarding the legends of Jesus - first there was a complete denial. To our amazement denial first comes from the circle of missionaries. Then slowly, little by little, creep in fragmentary, reticent details, difficult to obtain. Finally it appears that the old people in Ladakh have heard and know about the legends.

'Such legends about Jesus and the Book of Shambhala, lie in the 'darkest' place. And the figure of the lama - the compiler of the book of Shambhala - stands like an idol in some sort of fantastic headgear. And how many other relics have perished in dusty corners? For the Tantrik-lamas have no interest in them. It was necessary to see this other side of Buddhism" (Nicholas Roerich, 1929: 114).

Ladakh's actual contact with Christianity began in 1631. If the missionaries visiting Central Asia in the 14th century had not strayed away, by chance, into the kingdom of Ladak, it was Azevedo the first Christian and European to visit Leh in 1631. He even obtained an order from the King Singe Namgyal, the most powerful king known in the history of Ladakh, to open missionary office at Leh. But Azevedo did nothing, nor was there sent anybody instead.

Second such instance happened about a century later when two missionaries, Desideri and Freyre visited Leh, the capital of Ladakh in June, 1715 with the avowed motive of spreading Christianity in Tibet. They, however, changed their mind abruptly and after staying there for nearly two months proceeded to Lhasa, Central Tibet.

The Moravians established office in Leh first in 1885 when Redslob and Dr Marx advanced from Lahul. In due course of time Leh office assumed much greater importance, overwhelming that of Kyelang.

Beginning of operation of the Mission in Ladakh virtually had begun when Jaeschke came to Leh from Kyelang in 1857 for studying Tibetan language. According to local information, it is said that Sonam Tobgey of sTog was his first teacher. Later on Sonam Tobgey and his son Jorldan were converted to Christianity.

J.S.M. Hooper, a chronicler of the movement of Bible translation into Indian languages in India deems Jaeschke's arrival in Kyelang, an important event, saying, "Joining his colleagues at Kyelang, he was delighted to make the acquaintance of educated lamas who helped in his Tibetan studies." Then he reports about Jaeschke's visit to Leh saying that, "Soon after arriving in Ladakh, he lived for three months with a family at the village of sTok near Leh." This was a short trip for getting the initial lessons in Tibetan (Ladakhi) language and also had acquaintance of the wider geographical and cultural expanse of the place of his work. He, however, throughout his stay here, lived and worked at Kyelang.

Francke reached Leh in 1896 and stayed here for three years. He then went to Khalatse (mKhar-la-tse) where he stayed from 1899 to1906. Among his many activities he copied the story of the Gesar of Ling from Meme Dondub Tashi of rGya.tsho and Meme Yeshe Rigzin of Sabipa. He also translated some works of Christian religion into Tibetan. From here he came to Lahul where he spent two years from 1906-08, at Kyelang.

For the benefit of the residents the missionaries introduced many new and useful activities by opening a school and a dispensary. Dorje, it is said, was the first boy to enter the school. A church too was constructed in Leh.

A newspaper named *La.daks Phonya* was started, perhaps the first newspaper in the region of Ladakh. The publication continued till 1953. And then another paper named *sNang.gsal* was brought out. In 1937, Aesbo brought Radio in this area for the first time, bringing the residents of Leh a little closer to the modern world. During the War time the people would flock to the mission compound to hear the war news. The batteries of the machine were charged by the windmill at Choglamsar (Rizvi, 2001: Preface, vii). They opened a Library also. For the benefit of the farmers they brought from Germany many agricultural implements and vegetable seeds which were not known to the people here. The Ladies of the mission taught the women knitting of socks, gloves, sweaters, and other handicraft works. They also demonstrated the use of smokeless iron hearth.

Peter was at the mission in Leh and Kyelang between probably 1930 and 1940, and was interned at the outbreak of World War II at Yule Camp in Kangra. Dr. Marx died at Leh in 1891 due to Typhus. Some other important dates connected with the mission are as under:

Schlaginweit visited Leh in 1856.

Rechler joined in 1868.

Ribback joined in 1896 and died in Germany in 1940.

Francke lived here from 1896 to 1914.

Peter was in Leh and other places between 1930 and 1940, and according to one source, he was here since 1908.

Smith was at Leh in 1909.

G. Reichel was in Leh, at the time of Francke or after him.

Dr. Shawe collaborated with Francke in 1903 in the archaeological undertaking of excavation of the graves in Leh.

Dr. K. Marx collected the manuscripts of the history of Ladakh in Ladakhi and published with translation in *JASB* in 1891, 1894, and 1902, the last script was translated by Mrs Francke. Marx died in 1891.

Leh office was closed in 1948 or in 1956.

Visitors to the missionaries never fail to appreciate their helping attitude. They admire their capabilities, and their role in the advancement of numerous activities in the area. Biscoe, for instance, commenting on the works of the missionaries residing at Leh lauds them profusely: "The mission at Leh has been blessed with some very fine missionaries. They have to be a very whole-hearted lot, for their pay is a mere pittance, and until lately they did not return home on furlough, but died at their post like Dr. Marks and Dr Redslop, but I am glad to say that in these days there is a wiser and more humane policy, for surely it is wiser that a missionary's life should be lengthened by periods of rest than that he should live a short time and have to be replaced by a novice. It is more humane in that parents may be permitted to see their children now and again, whom they have sent to school in the Homeland. The missions in Srinagar and Leh are able to help one another in various ways. During the war Dr and Mrs Heber were able to come to the help of the Srinagar Mission Hospital at a time of need, and much were their services and presence appreciated. 'Outside the town in the waste of sand is a little oasis; it is the Christian cemetery, in which lies, among other honoured remains, the body of Miss Irene Petrie, a most gifted missionary, who compressed into the short space of three years a most marvelous amount of living work among the women and children of Srinagar. She came up to Ladak on her much-needed holiday, and passed away shortly after her arrival at Leh from typhoid fever, which she had contracted in Srinagar. Her sister, Mrs Ashley Carus-Wilson, has written her life, which is well worth reading, as it tells of a beautiful life spent in the highest service" (Biscoe, 1922: 222-223).

The European visitors to Leh did not forget to pay visit to the mission office. These missionaries guided and assisted the travellers with the information and knowledge about the area, and also with material goods. They were helpful in making arrangements for their stay, medicine, curing of the diseases, and in many other ways.

Sven Hedin, a scientific explorer has noted his experiences with the missionaries: "The Moravian missionaries in Leh rendered me invaluable service. They received me with the same hospitability and kindness as before, and I passed many a memorable hour in their pleasant domestic circle. Pastor Peter had endless worries over my affairs, Dr Shawe, the physician of the mission, was an old friend I had known on my former journey. He died in Leh a year later, after..... a life devoted to suffering humanity. Many of my dearest recollections of long years I have spent in Asia are connected with the Mission stations, and the more I get to know about the missionaries the more I admire their quiet, unceasing and often thankless labours. All the Moravians, I met in the Western Himalayas are educated to a very high standard and came out exceptionally well prepared for the work before them. Therefore it is always very stimulating and highly instructive to tarry among them, and there is none among the Europeans now living who can vie with these missionaries in their knowledge of the Ladak people and their history. I need only mention Dr Karl Marx and Pastor A.H. Francke as two men who are thoroughly at home in strictly scientific archaeological investigation.

'In Leh the missionaries have a Community which they treat with great gentleness and piety, for they know well that the religion inherited from their fathers has sunk deep into the bone and marrow of the natives, and can only be overcome by cautious patient labour. Even the Ladakis who never visit the Mission stations always speak well of the missionaries, and have a blind confidence in them, for apart from their Mission work they exercise an effect by their good example. The Hospital is made great use of, and medical science is some way of access to the hearts of natives.

'During the last days of my stay in Leh I saw my old friends again, Mr. and Mrs Ribbach, in whose hospitable house I had spent many pleasant winter evenings four years ago" (Sven Hedin, 1909: 56-57).

It is not known when exactly the office at Khalatse was opened. Francke was here from 1899 to 1904, and Ribbach joined in 1906 and remained here upto 1913. A European visitor to the place narrates the condition of the missionaries working there in the words, "... hospitality seems to be a Moravian virtue, and it was a very pleasant evening that we spent. My hosts had only recently come to Khalatse which to them seemed quite exciting, populous place after a couple of years on the Lahoul side, where for the six winter months they were entirely and completely cut off and got no mails at all" (Ganpat, 1916: 236-237). The missionaries had come from Lahoul with kids, says Ganpat.

At Khalatse the mission had constructed a large house with several rooms and a big courtyard. In 1931 a traveller's lodge of three storeys high was constructed at Leh which benefited the residents of Leh also. The upper floors were made residence and the ground floor was kept for the cattle.

A.H. Francke joined at Leh in 1896 and remained in India till 1914. 'Pastor Francke was stationed chiefly at Leh, and his work as historian and writer of folklore stands out above that of any other student of Western Tibet'. Francke says, I travelled in Ladakh, Spyiti etc. between 1896 and 1914. In between he stayed at Khalatse in Ladak and was also stationed at Kyelang between 1906 and 1908. In 1908 Francke sent G. Hettasch of Kyelang alongwith his Munshi Bzod-pa bde-chen to Zanskar with the purpose of searching if any chronicle existed regarding the kings of Zanskar. Hettasch was successful in finding a manuscript of two pages and Zodpa copied it which Francke published it later on. Francke kept himself always engaged in the study of language, literature, folklore, archaeology, etc. of the region and has produced a vast hoard of valuable material. Studying the skeletons in a mass grave in Leh, Francke remarks, "there are several ancient graves on which the late Dr Shawe and myself did some excavation work in 1903 at Leh". Some of the results on this subject can be found published in his monumental work. In 1909 Francke conducted a tour of the borders of the Western Tibet, the regions lying along the Tibetan border between Kinnaur and Ladak on behalf of the Archaeological Survey of India, Government of India, proposing to study the archaeological aspects of the area. During this occasion he gathered a number of valuable articles and data. The results of his labour are published in his renowned work, *Antiquities of Indian Tibet,* in two volumes. More materials has been published in various journals in India and Germany in English and German language. F.W. Thomas, while writing a Foreword to the Francke's work in 1925 remarks on the point: "The printing of Dr. Francke's work was commenced in 1913. It was practically suspended during the war years, and the difficult period which followed: and since the resumption in 1920 it has been retarded by several circumstances, among which may be mentioned the supply of Tibetan type and the author's residence in Germany, entailing a vast amount of correspondence. The work has undergone considerable revision both prior to being submitted to the press and subsequently".

Francke also expressed his desire to visit Guge in the Western Tibet, but he was prevented from doing so. He, however, dispatched some resourceful and capable local persons who were able to gather and bring home some important documents concerning the history etc. of the region on the Indian side, but unfortunately failed to come to light.

In the First Volume of the work Francke gives the narration of his journey which includes the description of the places, important monuments, numerous objects, documents and his observations and comments on them. The second Volume of the work covers mainly the Ladags rGyal-rab (History of Ladak) in original and its English translation. Genealogies, and other minor documents regarding various smaller states surrounding Ladak together with their English rendering and commentaries of the translator are also added.

On the capabilities of the translator, the scholars comment that, 'As regards the difficulties of the texts, it may be said that the edition and translation have been rendered possible only by Dr. Francke's personal acquaintance with the language, people and topography of Ladakh and the neighbouring territories, and by the help which he was able to obtain in the country itself. There remain many points of reading, rendering, and explanation in regard to which certainty has not been attained. Francke has collected documents in the book coming from many of the small states in the Western Himalayas which do not have much connection with each other. Therefore each of the state has its own way of writing a word which renders extremely difficult to understand the meaning of the word for an outsider'.

Francke was the first scholar to edit the Chronicles of Ladakh (*La-dvags*) in full and render its translation into English. The work on the manuscript was begun before him by Schlaginweit, who visited Leh in 1856. Marx worked on the subject thereafter and published it in three parts in the *JASB,* out of which the last part was translated by Mrs Francke. Csoma de Koros, who lived in Zanskar and Kinnaur between 1820 and 1830 is said to have been the first European, to hear the existence of a continuous historical narrative in Western Tibet, but he did not have opportunity to see the book. Alexander Cunningham who visited Ladak in 1846-47 was perhaps the first scholar who was successful to dig out a copy of the rare document. He got it copied into Urdu which contained the history of Ladak starting from the sixteenth century A.D. till the Dogra War (A.D.1834), and utilized it in his book *'Ladak'* in the chapter entitled 'Under Native Rulers.' Francke felt on comparison that Cunningham's source varied from the matter he utilized in the chronicle that he translated himself.

Francke utilized the assistance received from the native Christian scholars like Bzod-pa phun-tshogs of Khalatse and Joseph Tshe-brtan of Leh in the preparation of his numerous works.

Emil von Schlagintweit edited a translation of a version of the *Ladags Gyalrabs* in 1866. "The first to bring a copy of such an original document to Europe was Hermann v. Schlagintweit, who visited Leh in 1856. It was a copy specially prepared for him by three lamas. This copy was published by Emil v. Schlagintweit, with a German translation, *in Abhandlungen der kgl. bayerischen Akodemie der Wissenschaften,* vol. x, 1866." Francke supposes that 'a copy of the *Lad-dvags rgyal-rabs,* very similar to that of Schlagintweit, must have been in the hands of the Rev. H.A.Jaeschke when he made his collections of Tibetan words for his Tibetan-English dictionary. He also finds Jaeschke's rendering often different from that of Schlagintweit. "Dr. K.Marx, a Moravian missionary at Leh, soon observed the insufficiency of Schlagintweit's translation of the *Ladags Gyalrabs.* At the same time he discovered at Leh two manuscripts, which contained fuller accounts of the times subsequent to A.D. 1620. He even induced a Ladakhi nobleman, Munshi dPal-rgyas to write the story of the Dogra war, as such an account did not yet exist. Basing on this new material, Dr. Marx proposed to edit a History of Ladakh (of the West Tibetan empire, beginning with King Nyima-mgon in the tenth century) in three parts. The first part was to contain the history of Ladakh from Nyima-mgon to Senge-rnamrgyal (beginning of seventeenth century); the second part, the history from Bde-ldan-rnam-rgyal down to the Dogra wars (A.D. 1834); and third part, that of the Dogra wars. The first part of his work appeared in the *JASB,* 1891, consisting of text, translation, and notes, exactly as intended by the author, who had died a few weeks before its publication. Of the second part, the Tibetan text being lost, an English translation only, with a few notes, was published by Dr. K. Marx's brother, Professor G. Dalman. It appeared in the *JASB,* 1894. The third part, with a translation appeared in *JASB,* 1902. This was the state of things when Dr. Vogel, officiating Director General of ASI, asked Francke to bring out a complete edition of the Ladvags rgyal rabs" (Francke 1926-II: 1-2).

Francke obtained the manuscripts of the second part of the Marx's work for the period covering 1620 to 1834, which contained, besides a chapter on the history of Ladak, a write up on the Dogra War from Munshi Pal-ge through Rev. G. Reichel of Leh. He translated it at once into German. This German translation, together with a note on the relationship of the three different accounts of the Dogra War, was published in the *ZDMG,* vol. lxiv. Thus began the work of writing of the fuller version of the history of Ladak.

Another commendable work that Francke did is that he was the first scholar to make thorough study of the Tabo monastery in Spiti and bring the important historical monument on the international map. It soon attracted an unceasing row of national and international scholars. He also initiated researches into the life and works of Rinchen Zangpo and his master who sponsored him for studies to Kashmir in India alongwith twenty companions.

John Bray spent two years teaching in India, before joining at the Moravian school in Leh, Ladakh. He has published research papers on Ladakh and now works as an Asian affairs analyst in London and is still in regular contact with Ladakh. He translated the work named *Dogpa Namgyal* into English, written by Samuel Ribbach in German.

Samuel Ribbach has made a great contribution towards the culture of the residents of Ladakh by creating the work entitled *Drokpa Namgyal* (Culture and Society in Ladakh). It is a complete document on the life of a Ladaki and his society. Originally written in German language, it was translated into English by John Bray, one of his colleagues, who is also his biographer. Bray reports that alongside the work as a missionary he conducted extensive research into Ladakhi culture and contributed material to a Ladakhi grammar and a collection of local folk-songs. Ribbach after his return to Germany worked as a research scholar at the Hamburg Museum of Ethnology and continued language work for the Moravian mission. He died in 1940.

Dogpa Namgyal makes an interesting, absorbing and educative reading. The work is a detailed and in depth study of the Ladakhi society, its culture and tradition. The story is woven around the life of Dokpa Namgyal, head of a family in a village in Ladak. In truth it a story of the part of the life of the household named *'Dragshos'*, covering the span of the proprietorship of Namgyal's lifetime. Household is an unchangeably continuing nucleus social organization of the Ladakhi and similar other societies. The author traces, in the description of Namgyal's life, the lives of his former and the latter generations. His relations with the villagers and others, all his roles as head of the household and as a member of the societal world, are other threads weaving the plot. Ribbach's intention as regards the manner of presentation of the work was twofold. He wrote it in the form of a semi-fictional biography in order to make it more entertaining to the general audience, although the requirement of the scholars was also in his mind. Originally published in German in1940, it was translated into English which appeared in 1986 in India.

The book has now become a part of history. The translator accepts that the author's ambition has been fulfilled. The book has come through the dark dungeons of Hitler's hard hand. Bray remarks further in the Introduction of the book: 'This book is a study of the life of a farmer from Ladakh or, as European scholars have often called it, Western Tibet. It is a semi-fictional biography of Drogpa Namgyal, a leading villager from Kalatse, who lived in the early years of the twentieth century.

'Kalatse, now often known as Khalsi, is a village familiar to any traveller approaching Ladakh from Kashmir. It is the first village one comes to in the Indus valley after descending several miles of hair-pin bends from the desicated mountains of Lamayuru. Noted for its green fields and walnut trees, Kalatse is an oasis in the arid mountains that surround it on all sides.

'It was always on the main trade route from Kashmir to Leh, the capital of Ladakh, and from there to Sinkiang or Great Tibet, but it is only a generation since the only means of transport was by foot. Today in summer, when the passes are open, regular convoys of military and civilian trucks and buses rumble through on their way to Leh.

'Influences are at work which are changing the society. There are now more schools and wider work opportunities. ..Improved means of communication have brought new ideas and new fashions so that many of the old traditions are no longer followed. It is therefore particularly valuable to have a detailed account of life in Ladakh as it was seventy or eighty years ago before these changes began to take effect'.

John Bray, giving the background of the life of Ribbach, writes: 'Samuel Ribbach was a German missionary of the Moravian Church who spent more than twenty years in the Indo-Tibetan borderlands. He first came to India in 1892 to the Moravian mission station at Kyelang, Lahul. There he served under Wilhelm Heyde who had already spent nearly half a century in Lahul. Heyde was an accomplished Tibetan scholar; he was later to work in Darjeeling on a revised version of the Tibetan New Testament (the original translation having been the work of another Moravian scholar, H.A. Jaeschke) and he acted as co-editor of a Tibetan dictionary produced by the Bengali scholar, Sarat Chandra Das. In Heyde Ribbach therefore had a masterly Tibetan teacher.

'Having served his apprenticeship in Lahul, Ribbach moved in 1896 to Leh, Ladakh, at about the same time as another young missionary A.H. Francke, later Professor of Tibetan at Berlin University, who had been sent to Ladakh in order to continue the work of Bible translation. Ribbach himself was a man of several talents. He was skilled in engineering and building but he also collaborated in the translation of the Old Testament into Tibetan and contributed to a collection of Ladakhi songs and a Ladakhi grammar, both edited by Francke. Throughout the time in Ladakh Ribbach collected information on the life and customs of the local people. In this he was assisted particularly by Ga Phuntsog who provided much of the information on which Ribbach based his account of Ladakhi marriage in this book.

'In 1906 Ribbach moved to Kalatse and worked there until 1913 when he returned home to Germany on leave. When war broke out between Britain and Germany in August 1914 he was still in Europe and was unable to return to India either during the war or after it because the British authorities imposed a ban on all German missionaries. For a time he found alternative work as a research scholar at the Hamburg Museum fur Volkerkunde where he wrote a monograph about the Buddhist teacher Padmasambhava. Subsequently he taught in a Moravian college and continued Tibetan language work for the Moravian mission'.

'In Ribbach's retirement the project closest to his heart was the writing of Drogpa Namgyal. Parts of the book were published in a Moravian magazine, *'Kampf und Sieg'* but the full text was not published until 1940 by which time the Second World War had broken out. It was published (in German) by an anthroposophist firm which was suppressed by Hitler soon afterwards.

'Ribbach intended the book to be a scholarly contribution to Tibetan studies but thought that it would be more readable and hence acceptable to a wider audience if it were presented as a biography with a strong story line. The story is fictional in that events and conversations did not take place exactly as described here but it is nonetheless closely based on fact. The local house names and all the details of local geography are authentic. The Dragshos family, to which the hero belongs, plays an important role in Kalatse life to this day and, although there has never been a member of the Dragshos family called Dropgpa Namgyal, some of the minor characters of the story, such as Tsetan the hermit are recognizable from accounts of Kalatse published in Moravian mission magazines. One imagines that the anonymous missionary in the final chapters of the book is based on Ribbach himself" (John Bray, 1986: Introduction iv-vi).

The Converts and Native Scholars

The Moravians had opened many schools where native students were educated. They imparted better education and training to some more able boys. A few native scholars in Ladakh and Kinnaur took lead and assisted the missionaries and other European scholars in their investigative studies by doing interpretations and translation of many difficult works.

Hooper makes reference to two lamas who came into contact with the Moravians in the early phase of their establishment. Nono Tshetan Phuntsogs from Ladakh, transcribed the works like *sTon.pa'i mdsad.pa bchu, kun.tu.dga.ba'i ka.bshad,* explanations on *sum.rtags* and the reader books from first to the fourth class. In 1957 a wall painting (*zhal-thang*) containing the twenty-four deeds of the Christ was prepared.

Yoseb Gergan, a scholar from Ladakh, was widely read and highly knowledgeable. He assisted the Moravian scholars in their investigations in the fields of language, history, archaeology, social customs, etc. Joseph Gergan was his religious name and in short in his own language he was known commonly by Yoseb. His full name was bSod-nams tshe-brtan yo-seb dge-rgan. He met Rahul Sankritayayan at Leh in 1933. Rahul says that there is only one person i.e. Joseph in whole of Ladakh who can write in pure Bhoti language. He was then of about sixty years or above. He had spent whole of his life in the study of Bhoti literature. He could not study Buddhist philosophy since he was converted into Christianity since his childhood. But in respect of secular literature he was very well conversant. They both felt that after him there would be no scholar left like him. Gergan is so old yet he has not seen a rail. He says, "I have seen in the picture" (Rahul, 1956 b: 4).

Perhaps it was the same person, Yoseb Gergan, whose childhood incident is narrated by one of the visitors to Leh in the following words: "I went to the Moravian missionaries, who had kindly invited Dr. E. F. Neve and myself to stay with them. They have been doing a great and useful work here for many years, by means of hospital, schools, and visiting the people in their homes. They had then a congregation of about thirty Christians.

'The history of one of them with whom I was connected for some years is interesting. A certain monk in a monastery in Nubra was dying, and he sent for one of the missionaries whom he knew to visit him. Nubra Valley is some fifty miles from Leh over the other side of the Kardang Pass, 17,400 feet high.

'The missionary went at once, and was in time to see him before he died. The monk told him that he heard the gospel through the preaching of the missionaries, and believed in Christ as his Saviour, but had not been bold enough to confess openly on account of the persecution which would follow, but as he had failed to do the first thing he would do the second, and that was to give his son to the missionaries to be brought up a Christian. The monk passed away like the dew drop off the lotus leaf, let us hope, and his son was taken to the mission at Leh, and remained with them until the age of fourteen, when he was sent to the Mission School at Srinagar. The missionaries took the opportunity of some friendly Tibetans going down to Srinagar on business and delivered Joseph, for that was his Christian name, to their safe keeping. I remember the interest and pleasure it was welcome this quiet and stolid Ladakhi to the school. He arrived in his Tibetan costume, looking most quaint, for I had seen few Tibetans up to that time. I am glad to say he was proud of his national dress and wore it all the time he was at school.

'Joseph had a hard time of it among the Brahman boys, who laughed at his dress, which, as a matter of fact, was far more becoming than theirs, and also tormented him on the quiet because he was a Christian.

'Joseph never allowed himself to be drawn by his tormentors, he never retaliated, nor did he show the least fear of them, but I did not see why his persecutors should have it all their own way. I believe in a boy managing his own affairs among the boys without help from outside if possible, so I set to work to teach him to box. He became an apt pupil, as he started fair, without any lee-way to make up in the matter of cowardice or weakness of any kind, so in a short time he became thoroughly respected, notwithstanding the difference in religion or dress, and before he left school was the most respected and, I might say, popular boy in the school. As he was preparing to return to his own country, I asked him what profession he would choose. Would he care to join the State service, as very few Ladakhis were educated and all posts were filled by Kashmiri Brahmans and Indian? It would be good for the country if some of these officials were natives of Ladakh. I pointed out that if he took that line he would have power and influence later on, which he could put to good use. His answer was: 'I do not want power or riches. All I want is that I may have opportunities of preaching Christ to my people. I would prefer to be a missionary.

'He returned to Leh, and in course of time became headmaster of the Mission School, which post he has held for many years, where he is training his own country-men, and preaching Christ to them by life as well as by words. I am glad to say that his education has not given him any ideas of being a babu, and therefore too much of a gentleman to do manual labour, for in the vacations he is to be seen driving his yoke of oxen and carrying manure on his back in a basket very similar to those used in Switzerland for the same purpose. His education has not unmanned him, as it has done so many in Kashmir and India.

'So the dying monk in the monastery at Nubra did well for his country, though it seems odd to those who do not know the way of monks that they should have sons bequeath" (Biscoe, 1922: 220-222).

Yoseb Gergan who died on 11 August, 1946, wrote a valuable book in Bhoti, the crux of the labour of his whole life, on the history of Ladakh, entitled *'Ladags Rgyalrabs Chhimed gTer'* which was published by his son, S.S. Gergan (bSod-nams skyabs-ldan dge-rgan), posthumously in 1976.

Marco Pallis in his work *'Peaks and Lamas'*, has recorded a memorable incident in the appreciation of Joseph Gergan bringing forth another aspect of his character, in the words: "Another friend in Leh, of whose generous help we cannot speak too gratefully, was a Christian called Joseph Gergan who, however, in spite of his change of religion, had not attempted to become like a European, as is too often the case with converts. He was a man who truly deserved the name of Christian; for never have I come across anyone in whom the love of Christ and the imitation of His life were more manifest. There was no attempt to slur over the inconvenient portions of Christ's teaching; in him was seen the simplicity of a child, side by side with the wisdom of a cultivated, well-read mind. When very young he came into contact with missionaries and felt impelled to embrace the Christian faith. At that time his brother, in un-Buddhist fashion, had attempted to bully him. When Joseph reached the age of full discretion he decided that so serious a step required to be taken with open eyes, so he proceeded to devote some years to a careful study of the other two traditions possible for him, namely, the Mussulman and the Buddhist. After three years he decided against the first but it took him eight years fully to make up his mind about the second. His Christianity, as may well be imagined, had both justified itself and remained free from bitterness: for a man who so impartially tried to weigh up alternatives and to find out the good in them all, was not of the stuff that bigots and made of. We always spoke of him as 'Gergan the Translator,' borrowing the term from St. Marpa and the other eleventh century importers of sacred books into Tibet, for Joseph too was a man who only tried to impart to others a doctrine which he had first practiced himself. He had been occupied for years on the tremendous task of turning the Bible into colloquial Tibetan and had actually reached the end of St. John's Gospel" (Marco Pallis, 1936: 291-292).

Marco Pallis, a celebrated explorer appears to avoid to make reference to any fact connected with the Moravians. He could have in no way remained ignorant of this fact and even the presence of any European there, while staying at Leh and also at Poo, in Kinnaur. Gergan, indeed, was inducted into the faith by the Moravians and he presently belonged to Moravian mission. It seems that Marco Pallis showered all his generosity and appreciation for the Moravians also on the unassuming Yoseb Gergan.

Presently Leh Mission School, headed by Gergan Sonam Dava, is functioning well and is progressing. There are about 1200 students on roll and is one of the excellent schools in the region, observes a keen Ladakpa` (Phuntsog, 2000: 178-180).

5.
Translation of Bible in the Western Trans-Himalayan Languages

Moravian missionaries worked in the Western Himalaya and Western trans-Himalayan regions. Since they wanted to teach the good sayings of the Bible to the natives in their own language, they studied the languages of these areas as one of the essential components of their work. They selected a script for each of the unwritten language, which suited it best and was conventionally nearest to it, such as Tibetan, *tankri,* etc. Thereafter they translated small sections of the scriptures into them. Besides, they collected and preserved a number of local literature, documents and inscriptions. The missionaries involved in this project were highly educated. This was one of the great moments in the history of these regions.

Tibetan and Ladakhi: Hooper has collated the history of translation of the Bible into various dialects of the western Himalayan states including the Tibetan language. After A.W. Heyde and E. Pagell settled in Kyelang, H.A. Jaeschke, who had been commissioned to devote himself to the task of translating the Bible into Tibetan, joined them in 1857. He was a great scholar and was well versed in several languages, including Sanskrit, Persian and Arabic. He was then forty years of age and was endowed with all the qualifications essential for accomplishing the assigned task.

After joining the mission at Kyelang, Jaeschke soon proceeded to Ladakh for familiarizing himself with the atmosphere of the society there and learning the Tibetan language. There he lived with a family at sTok, near Leh, for three months. Joining his colleagues in Kyelang, he was delighted to make acquaintance of educated lamas who helped him with his Tibetan studies. Hooper makes reference specially of two lamas. "Following the death of Tashi Lama in 1854, a suspected case of poisoning, they with others had been summoned to Peking. They preferred to become refugees, and making their way westward they settled in Ladakh and became friends of the Moravian missionaries. Gergan Sodnam Wangyal, the elder of the two, was never baptized. The other Lama Zodpa Gyaltsan, was the first lama to become a Christian and received the name Nathanael". Nathanael appears to have been associated with the missionaries for much longer period and had been of much help to them, occasionally. Sodnam Wangyal, although he had not been converted, also assisted them.

Jaeschke set about his task with great thoroughness and he compiled the Tibetan-German dictionary, of which an English translation was published at the expense of the Government of India, in 1881. He also prepared a Tibetan grammar, and a number of books and tracts for children as well as adults. All these were first lithographed and then printed on a small hand machine at Kyelang. The first portion of Scripture, a harmony of the Gospels, was printed in this manner in 1860. Other portions were printed in succeeding years by the same method. Jaeschke was responsible for translation of whole of the New Testament, with the exception of Hebrews and Revelation. He remained in touch with the work until his death in Berling in 1883. The translation was completed by Redslob and Nathanael, and in 1885 an edition of the Epistles and Revelation was printed at Ghum, Darjeeling, where the Scandinavian Alliance Mission had its headquarters. This was followed by the first edition of the New Testament of which 5000 copies were printed. The original specimen of letters for the type face was made by a man of the Zangskar district and it had been a source of pleasure to Tibetans for long time.

Redslob and Nathanael began translation of the Old Testament, and in the later stages they completed the Pentateuch, which was again printed on the mission's hand press. Redslob's last work was the Psalms, in the translation of which he was assisted by Gergan Sodnam Wangyal, now a married farmer in Ladakh. He intended to retire in 1891, but before he could begin the long journey home, he died at Leh, six years after the Mission station had been opened there. In 1896 the Moravian Mission asked for a new edition of the New Testament, but because of criticisms which had been expressed concerning the difficulty of the language in Jaeschke's translation, negotiations led to the setting up of a representative committee in 1898. This met at Ghum, to which place A.W. Heyde was transferred as chairman of the committee. Other members were J.F. Fredericksen of the Scandinavian Alliance (till his death, when E. Amundsen took his place), J.R. MacDonald and his son David MacDonald, who were successively government trade agents at Gyantse in Tibet, the latter being an Anglo-Tibetan, and Graham

Sandberg. The New Testament thus revised was issued in 1903, the first edition being printed at Shanghai. Unfortunately only the four Gospels and the Acts were dealt with thoroughly, and this revision was never completely acceptable to the Ladakhi Christians who continued to prefer Jaeschke's translation. Heyde retired to Herrnhut in 1903, after an absence of fifty years from the land of his birth. At his request, the printing of the Pentateuch was begun in Berlin. The translation had been revised by A.H. Francke. Psalms meanwhile were printed in Calcutta, the work of Redslob and Nathanael. It is of interest to note that this was in metrical form, in metre that was familiar in classical Tibetan. Apart from seeing the Pentateuch through the press, his other activities were the correction of Redslob's version of Joshua up to Chapter 10, and reading the proofs of a reprint at Oxford of the New Testament in new medium type – a task that was continued by Mrs Heyde after his death.

Meanwhile, others were continuing translation of the Old Testament, among them F.E. Peter and Yoseb Gergan, the son of Sodnam Wangyal. S. Ribbach and David MacDonald of Gyantse undertook the preparation of the rest of the Old Testament, the Bible Society at the request of the Moravian Mission making a contribution towards Dr. Francke's salary. In 1914 Dr. Francke travelled to India by way of Russia and Chinese Turkistan, to carry out scientific investigation on the Tibetan borders on behalf of the Royal Ethnological Museum of Munich. He had hoped to visit the eastern and western frontiers and to confer with Mr. MacDonald about the Old Testament translation; but with other German missionaries, he was interned during the 1914-18 war and at the end of it he was repatriated.

In 1919 Yoseph Gergan assumed the main burden of the task, helped first by Bishop F.E. Peter of Leh and later by the Rev. Norman Driver. Yoseph was only twelve when his father died in 1890. He went to the missionaries and begged to be allowed to become a Christian. He was educated at Canon Biscoe's famous school at Srinagar. For many years he worked at the translation, his work being checked by others. The Old Testament was completed by 1934, after which Gergan revised Jaeschke's New Testament and re-translated the Psalms. His name will always stand high in the roll of those who gave themselves to the work of Tibetan translation. Although he knew no Hebrew, he used several English versions and the revised Urdu Bible. He was also widely read in Tibetan literature. When he died in 1946, the manuscript was not entirely ready for the press, and now the mantle fell on his son-in-law, Eliya Tsetan Phuntsok. He was another remarkable convert from Buddhism, a Tibetan scholar and poet, who took leave from government service and later devoted his whole time to Christian work. The story of how the Bible was printed at Lahore amid all the difficulties of the post-partition period, of Gapel's journey from Leh with the manuscript, and the Rt. Rev Chandu Ray's efforts to get safe passé for Gapel and his precious manuscript through the lines of the Indian and Pakistani armies then fighting each other in Kashmir, is one of outstanding courage, devotion and ingenuity, and before the end of 1948 the Bible was in print in one volume.

The main story revolves round the mission at Leh, because it is there that there has been a sustained effort extending over many years. But other work among Tibetans has been done in the Darjeeling district, and until the advent of the Communist regime, on the eastern frontier of Tibet proper with the rest of China. In these areas the version of 1903 has been more widely used than the 'Ladakh' version, and later on more attempts were made to prepare a New Testament that would be acceptable to all. The draft has been prepared by Eliya Tsetan Phuntsok, and Pierre Vittoz, who spent twelve years in Ladakh. They lived at Landour and gave their whole time to the work, but they have received valuable help from the Rev. G. Tharchin, a scholar well versed in the Lhasa dialect, who was the pastor of the Tibetan congregation in Kalimpong and editor of a newspaper in Tibetan. Although the prosecution of the task had been hindered by many difficulties, it had been helped indirectly by the influx of Tibetan refugees and by consultation with missionaries who worked for many years on the eastern Tibetan frontier (Hooper, 1963: 140-144).

Chambiali: Chambiali is the language of the Chamba state, one of the hill states now a district in Himachal Pradesh. 'It is written in *Tankri* script, which is used for all ordinary correspondence in the hills and in the Chamba state, and is the medium for all state correspondence between the capital and the officials in the interior. It is a very ancient character, one of the oldest in northern India, and was at one time (more than a thousand years ago) in use everywhere in Chamba on the plains as well as in the hills'. Three of the Gospels were translated and published by the Church of Scotland Mission in 1882. In 1910 a revised translation of all the four Gospels, prepared by Dr. Hutchison of the Church of Scotland Mission in Chamba, with the help of the Rev. Sohan Lal, was ready; the Gospels were published by the Punjab Auxiliary of the Bible Society.

In Chamba one of the outstanding characters among the missionaries, Rev. H.A. Hutchison, is known to us through his number of unforgettable works. He had been associated with H.A. Rose who was in charge of compilation of the Census Report of the Punjab, which then comprised most of the northern and north-west India. A valuable work of historical and sociological significance encompassing the whole region of the present states of Himachal Pradesh, Haryana and Punjab and Pakistan was also compiled by him. Hutchison was also associated with another renowned scholar, J. Ph. Vogel. The *History of Punjab Hill States* in two volumes, which till today is not only the authoritative work, but the only work known of this kind and stature were also prepared by them. Hutchison also assisted H.A. Rose since 1903 in the preparation of the *Gazetteer of the Chamba state.* However, after 1906 he worked mostly alone and the Gazetteer was published in 1910 at Lahore. Similarly the British government authorities were dependent on the contributions from the learned missionaries of Kyelang for the preparation of the gazetteer of the district and many other publications and official reports on these areas.

Kulluvi: This is a dialect spoken in parts of the Kangra district of the Punjab, now a district in the state of Himachal Pradesh, then by about 100000 people. St. John's Gospel was printed in the language of Kulu in 1932. The translation was prepared under the supervision of an officer of the Forest Service and the whole cost of the edition was borne by him.

Zangskari: St. John's Gospel which was translated by the Rev. H.M. Mazzoni, a Swiss missionary of the Central Asian Mission residing at Kargil, was printed in the dialect of Zanskar in 1951. The translation had been completed in 1946, but the printing was delayed owing to the difficulties which arose in 1947.

Purigskad: Purig was a district in northern Kashmir, formerly under the rule of Dogras from Jammu. The Scripture Gift Mission issued a small edition of St. John's Gospel, The Acts of the Apostles and Paul's Letter to the Romans in 1938. Translator of the works was Mr. David Berger of the Central Asian Mission.

Balti: Balti is a language spoken by the Muslim population of Baltistan in north-west Kashmir. It is identified by Dr. Grierson with Bhotia, and belongs to the Himalayan and Trans-Himalayan group of the Tibeto-Burman family. St. Matthew was published by the Punjab Auxiliary of the Bible Society in 1903 in this language. The translation was the work of the Rev. F. Gustafson of the Scandinavian Alliance Mission. At that time 2000

Baltis are said to be able to read. A second edition was issued in 1906, and St. John, by the same translator, appeared in 1907. In 1919 a tentative edition of Acts was prepared by the Rev. H.C. Robertson of the Central Asian Mission with the help of the *munshi* who had assisted Mr. Gustafson, and St. Luke was also published, translated by a Punjabi Christian under Mr. Robertson's supervision.

Shina: Gurezi dialect, spoken in the valley of Kishenganga, Kashmir, is known as Shina. St. Mark's Gospel, translated by a Christian teacher in Gurez, where there is a small Christian Dard community, was published by the Bible Society in 1930 at the request of the Central Asian Mission.

Lahuli: Kyelang had gained an advantageous position, since the Moravians had installed printing machine here which catered to the needs of the other centres in the region viz Leh and Poo. Largest number of sacred literature in local languages were printed and published from here.

St. Mark's Gospel is in three dialects. In Punan, spoken by 2000 people, some verses were translated by A.W. Heyde in anticipation of a whole Gospel being translated. In 1908 A.H. Francke had completed a version of St. Mark, and he struck off forty copies of it, which were circulated among the people. After this test and after careful revision, it was lithographed at Herrnhut in 1911 at the expense of the Bible Society. At the same time, in the Manchad dialect, Dr. Francke similarly circulated a version made by himself and the Tibetan evangelist and former Lama, Zodpa. This was printed by lithography in 1914. No other Gospels have been issued.

Dr. Francke and Zodpa, whose expenses were met by the Bible Society during the time that he was released by the Moravian Mission for this work, were also responsible for a version in Tinan, which after a similar process of testing was published in 1915. None of the versions in the dialects mentioned above are now in print, and Hooker says, it seems unlikely that they will be required in the future.

Kinnauri: Mrs and Mr J.T. Bruske of the Mission reduced the Kinnauri language to writing and translated St. Mark's Gospel into it. The work was published in 1908 by the Bible Society at Lahore. The cost was met by the Church of England congregation at Simla as their centenary offering. The work at Chiné was subsequently taken over by the Salvation Army, and in 1918 a translation of St. John prepared by F. Mortimer was issued in the Tankri script.

Here are given the dates of the first publication of a part of the Scripture in various languages of the Western Himalayan region:

Language	*Year of publication*
Urdu	1743
Hindi	1806
Tibetan	1860
Full Bible in Tibetan was published (for the first time)	1948
Chambiali	1882
Balti	1903
Ladakhi	1905
Lahuli:	
a) Punan	1907
b) Manchad	1908
c) Tinan	1914
Kanauri	1909
Kullu	1932
Shina: Gurez	1929
Purigskad	1938
Zangskari	1951

APPENDICES

Appendix I

Titles of the inscriptions and other documents, original in German with English rendering in the brackets and facsimiles of original texts

A. *First Collection of Tibetan Historical Inscriptions on Rock and Stone from West Tibet by A.H. Francke, 1906 (Erste Sammlung tibetischer historischer Inschrift auf Felsen und Steinan in West Tibet Von A.H. Francke, 1906)*

1. Inschrift yon Balukhar, *circa* 800 AD (Inscription from Balukhar, *circa* 800 AD).
2. - do -
3. - do -
4. Felsen in der (Stone inscription from).
5. Alchi Khargog, circa 800-1000 AD.
6. Inschrift von Sadpur, Baltistan, circa 1000.
7. - do -
8. - do -
9. Inschrift von Rongdo, Baltistan c. 1000 AD (Inscription from Rongdo, Baltistan, c. 1000 AD).
10. Inschrift on Konig Skyid Ide Nyima mgon c. 975 AD Sheh, wahrscheinlich. (Inscription of King Skyid Ide Nyima mgon, c. 975 AD).
11. Inschrift von Alchi Khargog, c.l 000-1400 AD (Inscription from Alchi Khargog c. 1000-1400 AD).

12. to 28. - do -

29. Auf..inem (?) Maitreya in Leh, c. 1000 AD. (Upon the Maitreya statue at Leh, c. 1000 AD.)
30. Bruckenbau in Khalatse von Konig Naglug wahrecheinlich c. 1150 AD. (Inscription near the bridge at Khalatse, king Naglug, c. 1150 AD).
31. Vassall en furst Shirina von Khalatse c. 1150-1200 AD.(Vassal prince Shirima from Khalatse c. 1150-1200 AD).
32. Vassall en furst rGyashin von Khalatse c. 1150-1200 AD. (Vassal prince rGyashin from Khalatse c. 1150-1200 AD).

33. Votivinschrift von Khalatse fort c. 1200 AD. (Votive inscription from Khalatse fort, c. 1200 AD).
34. Inschrift seine Bruckenwartes von Khalatse, c. 1200AD. (Inscription from the bridge from Khalatse, c. 1200 AD).
35. Inschrift auf dem Vajrapani ber Daru von Konig Kunga rNamrgyal c. 1250 AD (Inscrption on the statue of Vajrapani from Daru, King Kunga Namgyal, c. 1250 AD.)
36. Edikt von Konig Bumlde in Mulbe c. 1430 AD (Edict of king Bumlde in Mulbe c. 1430 AD.).
37. Inschrift von Mulbe, bezuglich (Inscription from Mulbe.)
38. Votiv inschrift von Tingmogang, Konig Lha dbang rnam rgyal, c. 1550-1580 AD. (Votive inscription from Tingmogang, King Lha dbang rNam rgyal, c. 1550-1580 AD).
39. Hymn an Tsongkhapa und seine Schuler, Diskyid, Nubra, c. 1400-1500 AD (Hymn on Tsongkhapa and his school, Diskyid, Nubra, c. 1400-1500 AD).
40. Votivtafel von Hundar, Nubra c. 15-1600. vasallen Konig Tshebang brtanpa (Votive inscription from Hundar, Nubra, c. 15-1600, vassal king Tsebang brTanpa).
41. Votivtafel von Hundar, Nubra, Vassllen Konig, Bhagmir, c. 15-1600 (Votive inscription from Hundar, Nubra, Vassal king, Bhagmir, c. 15-1600).
42. Votivinschrift von Mulbe Vassal konig Khri rGyal von Khartse c. 1500 (Votive inscription from Mulbe, vassal king Khri rGyal, from Khartse c. 1500).
43. Inschrift von Chigtan Ruinen Kloster, Vasallen ,c. 1500 AD (Inscription from Chigtan, a ruined monastery, vassal kings Tashi and Joboje, c. 1500 AD). (Additional title in Tibetan reads *chig-tan mgon-pa'i nangsli-tsag pai'i khar 'di ltar 'bris yod.* Inside the monastery, on the Li-tsar (?) of the Chigtan monastery, it is written like this.)
44. Wegebau bericht, Konig, Tshedbang rnam rgyal c. 1580-1600. Hanubeg (?). (On the way, about King Thse dbang rnam rgyal, c. 1580-1600 AD Hanugeg (?).
45. Hochzeitswunch an konig 'aJam dbyang rnam rgyal, c. 1600-1620 (King 'aJam dbyang rnam rgyal, on marriage, c.1600-1620).
46. Votivtafel Vassallen Konig von Zangskar c. 1600-1650, sPadum (Votive inscription of a vassal king from Zangskar, c.1600-1650), Spadum.
47. Votivtafel Vassallen Konig von Zangskar c. 1600-1650, (Ating?) (Votive inscription of a vassal king from Zangskar on a slate) (Ating ?).
48. Votivtafel Schlapwart in sPadum, Zanskar c. 1650. (Votive Inscription on slate from Spadum, Zanskar, c. 1650).
49. Votivtafel Vassallen Konig von Zangskar, wahrscheinlich, 1650 in 1800 AD. (Votive inscription, vassal king from Zangskar, 1650 or 1680).
50. Brucken bau bericht Konig Sengge rnam rgyal, c. 1620-1650 AD, Saspola (Regarding King Sengge rNarngyal, c. 1620-1650, from Saspol).

51. Hymne un Konig Sengge rNamgryal c. 1620-1650., Basgo (Hymn for King Sengge rNamrgyal, c. 1620-1650, from Basgo).
52. Votivtafel. KonigSengge rnamgyal, c. 1620-1650. Lingshed. (Votive inscription on slate for king Sengge rnamrgyal c. 1620-1650, Lingshed).
53. Verlassene Stein in Tagmacig Duhalt nach Angabau von Zenlen, diedem gabaen (reading doubtful) Waben Sengge rnam rgyal, c. 1620-1650 (Stone inscription from Tagmacig, Sengge rnam rgyal, c. 1620-1650.)
54. Hymne on Korng Sengge rnam rgyal, c. 1620-1650 AD Skyurbuchan. (Hymn on King Senge rNamgyal, c. 1620-1650AD. Skyurbuchan).
55. Inschrift wen (bie?) der verlassene ... Kharbu, konig Sengge rnam rgyal c. 1620 (Inscription from a ruin from Kharbu for king Sengge rnam rgyal, c. 1620).
56. Votivinscrift von Rongdo, Nubra(?), konig Sengge rnam rgyal, c. 1620-1650. (Votive Inscription from Rongdo, Nubra, king Sengge rnam rgyal, c. 1620-1650).
57. Votivinschrift von Hundar, Nubra, Konig Sengge rnamrgyal, c. 1620-1650). (Votive inscription from Hundar, Nubra, Konig Sengge rnamrgyal, c. 1620-1680).
58. Votivtafel Saspola, Konig Sengge rnamrgyal, c. 1620-1650. (Votive inscription on slate from Saspola, King Sengge rnamrgyal, c. 1620-1650.).
59. Votivtafel Daru,konig bDeldan rnamrgyal,c.1650-1680 (Votive inscription on slate from Daru, king bDeldan rnamrgyal, c. 1650-1680).
60. Votivtafel. Daru, konig bDeldan rnamrgyal, c. 1650-1680. (Votive inscription on slate from Daru, king bDeldan rnamrgyal, c. 1650-1680).
61. Votivtafel, Tagmacig Konig bDeldan rnamrgyal, c. 1650-1680. (Votive inscription on slate, from Tagmacig, king bDeldan rnamrgyal, c. 1650-1680).
62. Votivtafel. Spithug. Konig bDeldan rnamgyal, c. 1650-1680. (Votive inscription from Spithug, king bDeldan rnamgyal, c. 1650-1680).
63. Stein... Edikt von Khalatse konig bDeldan rnamrgyal (reading doubtful) (Edict from Khalatse king bDeldan rnamrgyal).
64. Skyurbuchan Hymne an bDeldan rnamrgyal, c. 1650-1680 (Hymn from sKyurbuchan for king bDeldan rnam rgyal, c. 1650-1680).
65. Votivtafel. Phe. Konig bDe ldan rnam rgyal, c. 1650-1680 (Votive inscription on slate from Phe, for king bDeldan rnam rgyal, c. 1650-1680).
66. Votivtafel, Tagmacig, Konig Nyima rnam rgyal, c. 1700-1730 (Votive inscription on slate, from Tagmacig, king Nyima rnam rgyal, c. 1700-1730).
67. Saspola. Hymn on Konig Nyima rnam rgyal, c. 1700-1730 (Hymn of king Nyima rnam rgyal, from Saspola, c. 1700-1730).
68. sKyurbuchan. Hymn on Konig Nyima rnam rgyal c. 1700-1730 (Hymn of king Nyima rnam rgyal, from SKyurbuchan, c. 1700-1730).
69. Wegebau zarischan Achinathang u. Hanu, Nyima rnam rgyal, c. 1700-1730 (from village Achinathang, Hanu, on a way, Nyima rnam rgyal, c. 1700-1730).

70. SKyurbuchan, Votivtafel. Konig Nyima rnam rgyal, c. 1700-1730 (Votive inscription king Ṅyima rnam rgyal, c. 1700-1730).
71. Deskyid in Nubra. Hymn on Konig Nyima rnam rgyal... c. 1700-1730 (Hymn for king Nyima rnam rgyal, from Deskyid in Nubra, c. 1700-1730).
72. Domkhar. Votivtafel. Konig bDes Kyong rnam rgyal, c. 1730-1745 (Votive inscription from Domkhar, king bDe sKyong rnam rgyal, c. 1730-1745).
73. Deskyid in Nubra. Hymn an bDe skyong rnam rgyal, c. 1730-1745 (Hymn for king Nyima rnam rgyal, from Deskyid in Nubra, c. 1730-1745).
74. SKyurbuchan, Votivtafel, Konig Phuntsog rnam rgyal, c. 1745-1760 (Votive inscription on slate from SKyurbuchan, for king Phuntsog rnam rgyal, c. 1745-1760).
75. SKyurbuchan, Votivtafel, Konig Phuntsog rnam rgyal, c. 1745-1760 (Votive inscription from SKyurbuchan for king Phuntsog rnam rgyal, c. 1745-1760).
76. Patogsa. Votivtafel, Konig Tse dbang rnam rgyal, c. 1760-1780 (Votive inscription from Patogsa, king Tse dbang rnam rgyal, c. 1760-1780).
77. Hanupata, Konig Tse dbang rnam rgyal I, c. 1580-1600, Bunckenbau (?). (From Hanupata, King Tse dbang rnam rgyal I. c. 1580-1600).
78. Domkhar, Votivtafel. Tse dbang rnam rgyal II, c. 1760-1780 (Votive inscription on slate from Domkhar, king Tse dbang rnam rgyal II, c. 1760-1780).
79. Skyurbuchan, Tse dbang rnam rgyal II, Votivtafel. c. 1760-1780 (Votive inscription from Skyurbuchan, for king Tse dbang rnam rgyal II, c. 1760-1780).
80. Skyurbuchan, Tse dbang rnam rgyal II, Votivtafel. c. 1760-1780 (Votive inscription from Skyurbuchan, king Tse bstan rnam rgyal II, c. 1760-1780).
81. Skyurbuchan, Tse bstan rnam rgyal, Votivtafel. c. 1780-1790 (Votive inscription from Skyurbuchan, king Tse bstan rnam rgyal, c. 1780-1790).
82. Skyurbuchan, Tse bstan rnam rgyal, Votivtafel. c. 1780-1790 (Votive inscription from Skyurbuchan, king Tse bstan rnam rgyal, c. 1780-1790).
83. Nubra Deskyid, Tse bstan rnam rgyal, Votivtagel (votive inscription on slate from Deskyid, c. 1780-1790).
84. Zarischan Domkhar u Skyurbuchan Tse dpal don grub rnam rgyal, c. 1790-1841 (From Domkhar in Skyurbuchan for king Tse dpal don grub rnam rgyal, 1790-1841).
85. Hundar in Nubra. Votivtafel. Tse dpal don grub rnam rgyal, 1790-1841 (From Hundar in Nubra. Votive inscription for Tse dpal don grub rnam rgyal, 1790-1841).
86. Spithug. Votivtafel. Tse dpal don grub rnam rgyal, 1790-1841 (Spithug. Votive inscription for Tse dpal don grub rnam rgyal, 1790-1841).
87. Daru. Vativtafel. Minister Tse dbang dongrub c. 1800 (From Daru. Votive inscription Minister Tse dbang don grub c. 1800).
88. Khalatse, Votiv inschrift 1852. (Votive inscription from Khalatse, 1852).
89. Wegebau in der Yuru schlucht. 1902 (From Lama Yuru, on the way in a ravine, 1902).

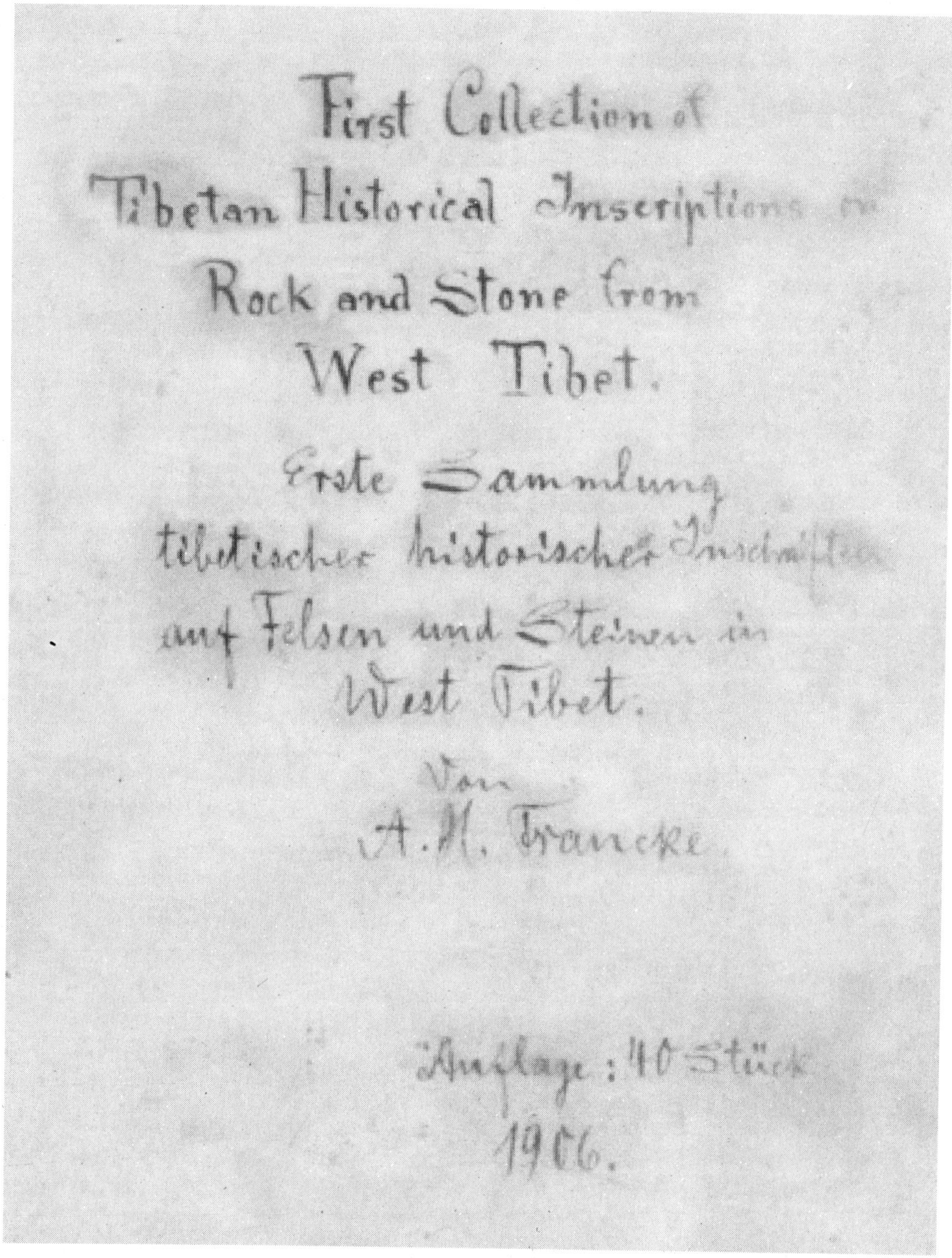

First Collection of
Tibetan Historical Inscriptions on
Rock and Stone from
West Tibet.

Erste Sammlung
tibetischer historischer Inschriften
auf Felsen und Steinen in
West Tibet.

Von
A. H. Francke

Auflage: 40 Stück
1906.

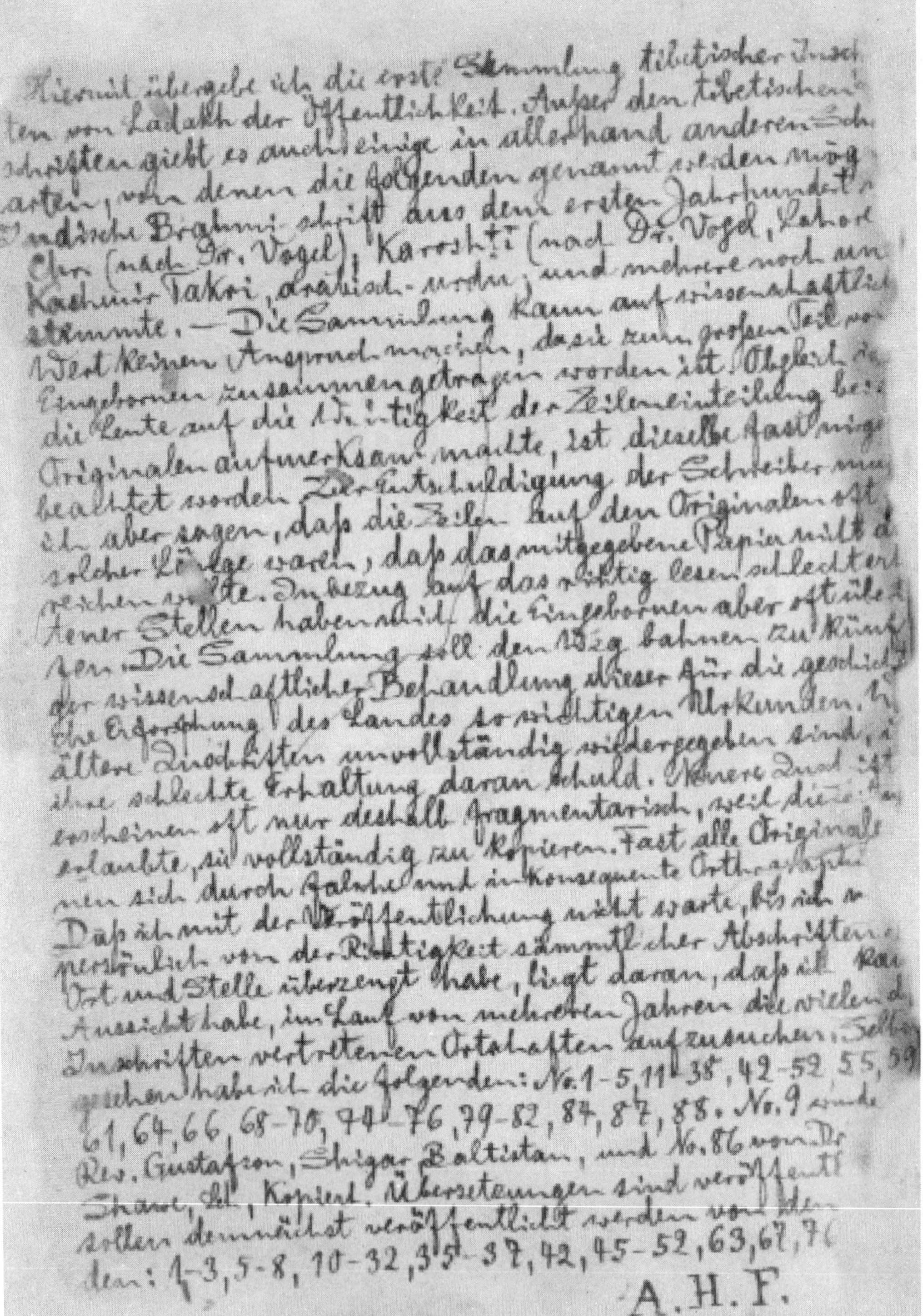

Hiermit übergebe ich die erste Sammlung tibetischer Inschrif-
ten von Ladakh der Öffentlichkeit. Außer den tibetischen In-
schriften giebt es auch einige in allerhand anderen Schrift-
arten, von denen die folgenden genannt werden mögen:
Indische Brahmi-schrift aus dem ersten Jahrhundert n.
Chr. (nach Dr. Vogel), Karoshti (nach Dr. Vogel, Lahore)
Kashmir Takri, arabisch-urdu, und mehrere noch unbe-
stimmte. — Die Sammlung kann auf wissenschaftlichen
Wert keinen Anspruch machen, da sie zum großen Teil von
Eingebornen zusammengetragen worden ist. Obgleich ich
die Leute auf die Wichtigkeit der Zeileneinteilung bei
Originalen aufmerksam machte, ist dieselbe fast nirgends
beachtet worden. Zur Entschuldigung der Schreiber muß
ich aber sagen, daß die Zeilen auf den Originalen oft
solcher Länge waren, daß das mitgegebene Papier nicht aus-
reichen wollte. In bezug auf das richtig lesen schlecht erhal-
tener Stellen haben sich die Eingebornen aber oft über-
[illegible]. Die Sammlung soll den Weg bahnen zu künf-
[tiger] wissenschaftlichen Behandlung dieser für die geschicht-
liche Erforschung des Landes so wichtigen Urkunden. Wenn
ältere Inschriften unvollständig wiedergegeben sind, ist
ihre schlechte Erhaltung daran schuld. Neuere Inschriften
erscheinen oft nur deshalb fragmentarisch, weil die [illegible]
erlaubte, sie vollständig zu kopieren. Fast alle Originale [zeich-]
nen sich durch Fehler und inkonsequente Orthographie [aus.]
Daß ich mit der Veröffentlichung nicht warte, bis ich mich
persönlich von der Richtigkeit sämmtlicher Abschriften an
Ort und Stelle überzeugt habe, liegt daran, daß ich keine
Aussicht habe, im Lauf von mehreren Jahren die vielen durch
Inschriften vertretenen Ortschaften aufzusuchen. Selbst
gesehen habe ich die folgenden: No. 1-5, 11-38, 42-52, 55, 59,
61, 64, 66, 68-70, 74-76, 79-82, 84, 87, 88. No. 9 wurde [von]
Rev. Gustafson, Shigar, Baltistan, und No. 86 von Dr.
Shawe, Leh, kopiert. Übersetzungen sind veröffentlicht [und]
sollen demnächst veröffentlicht werden von den [Inschrif-]
ten: 1-3, 5-8, 10-32, 35-37, 42, 45-52, 63, 67, 7[illegible]

A.H.F.

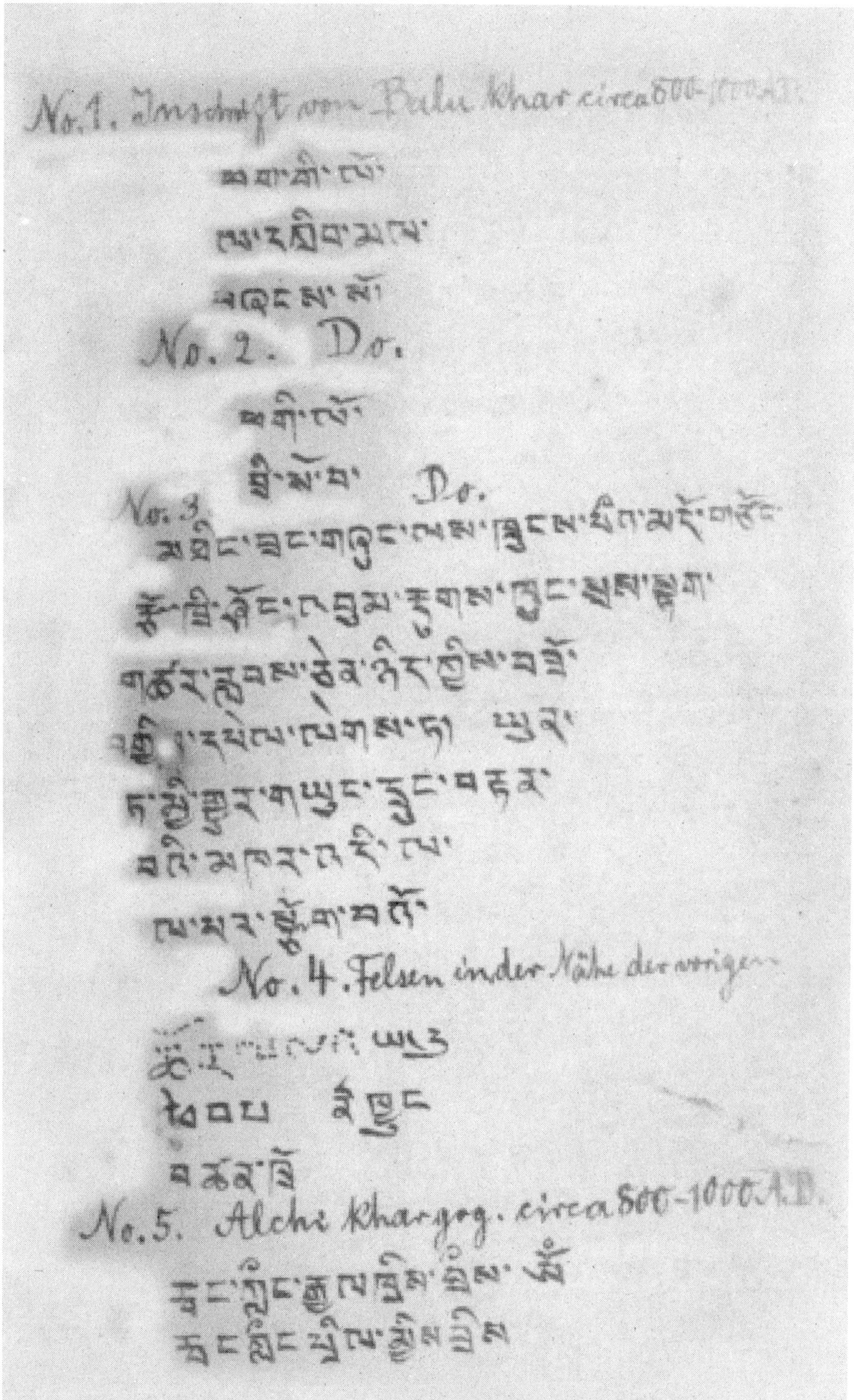
No. 1. Inschrift von Bulu Khar circa 800-1000 A.D.

No. 2. Do.

No. 3. Do.

No. 4. Felsen in der Nähe der vorigen

No. 5. Alchi Khargog. circa 800-1000 A.D.

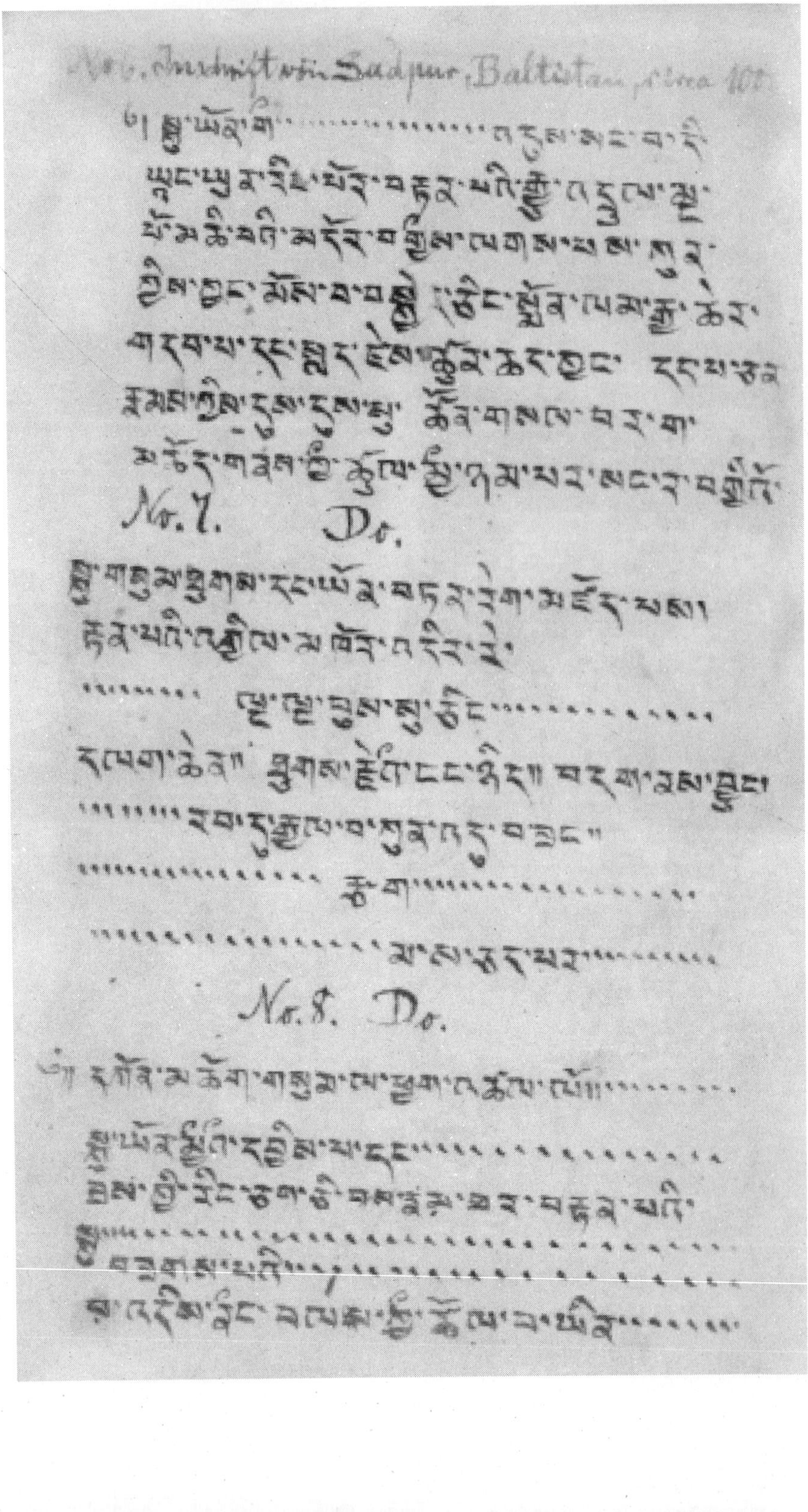
No. 6. Inschrift von Sadpur, Baltistan, circa 100

No. 7. Do.

No. 8. Do.

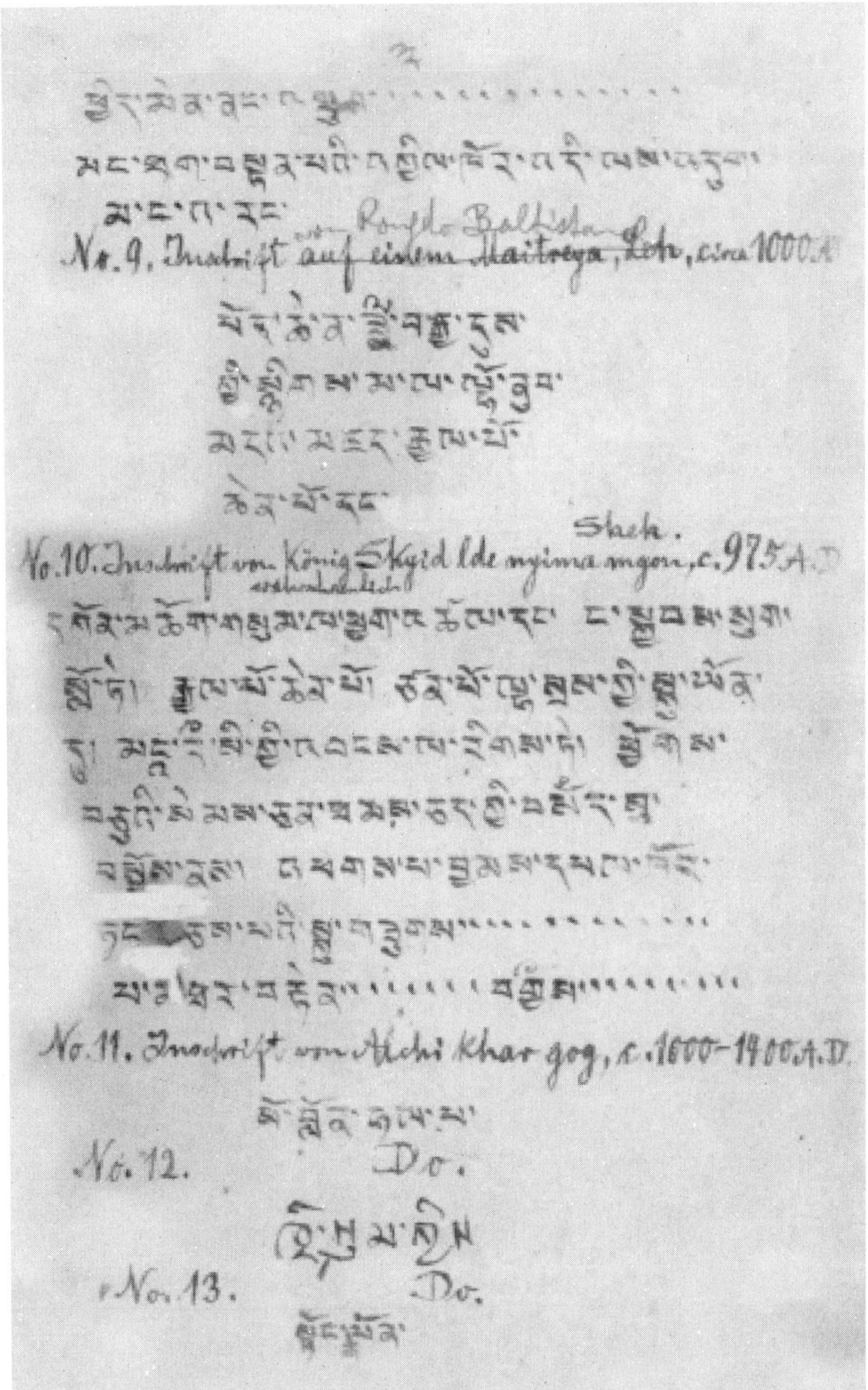

No. 9. Inschrift ~~auf einem Maitreya, Leh~~ von Rongdo Baltistan, circa 1000 A.D.

No. 10. Inschrift von König Skyid lde nyima mgon, c. 975 A.D. Sheh.

No. 11. Inschrift von Alchi Khar gog, c. 1000–1400 A.D.

No. 12. Do.

No. 13. Do.

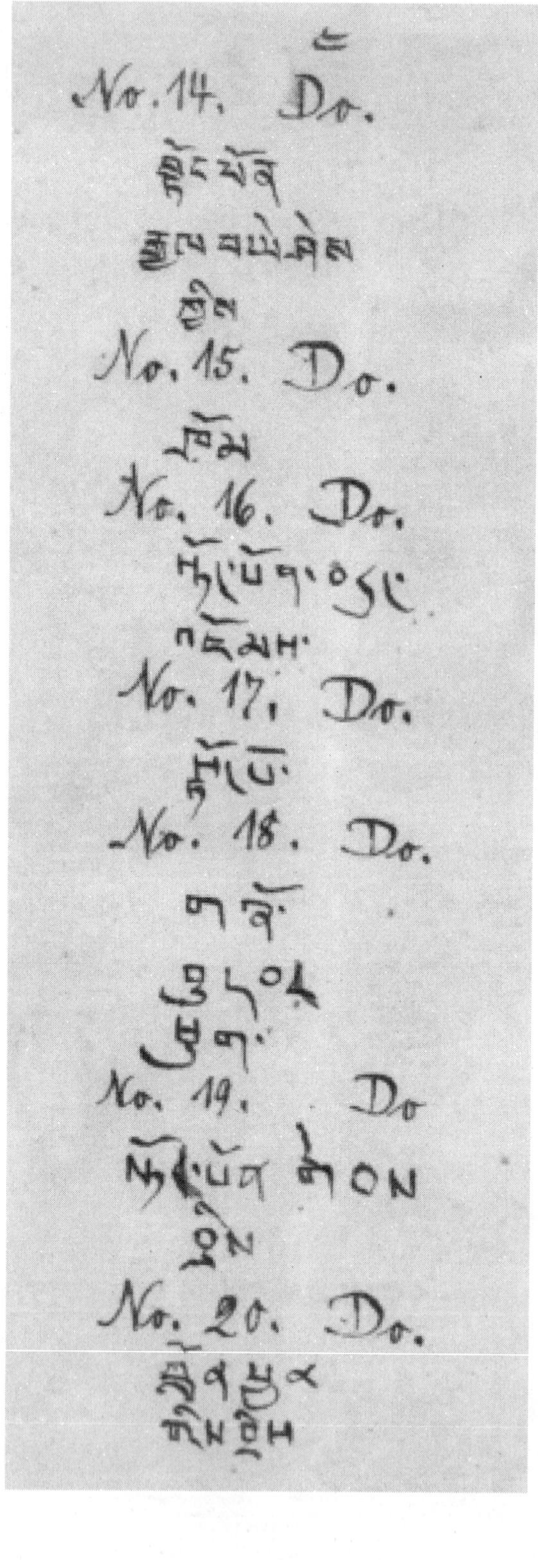
No. 14. Do.

No. 15. Do.

No. 16. Do.

No. 17. Do.

No. 18. Do.

No. 19. Do

No. 20. Do.

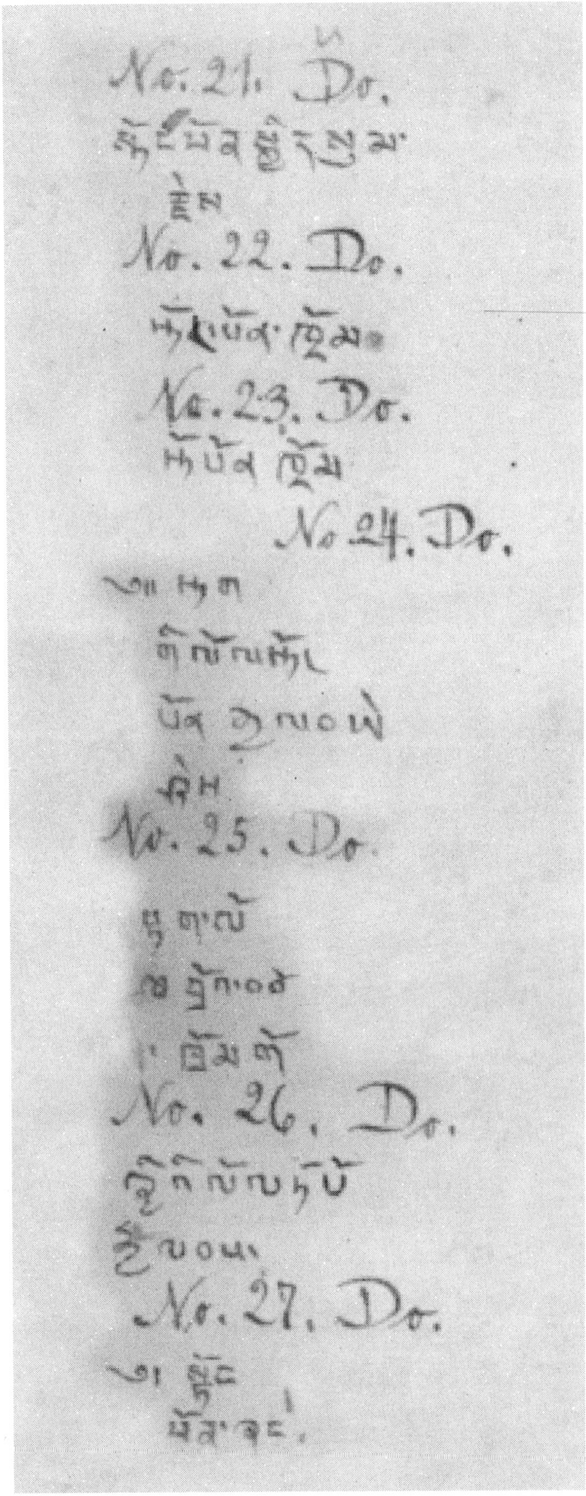
No. 21. Do.

No. 22. Do.

No. 23. Do.

No. 24. Do.

No. 25. Do.

No. 26. Do.

No. 27. Do.

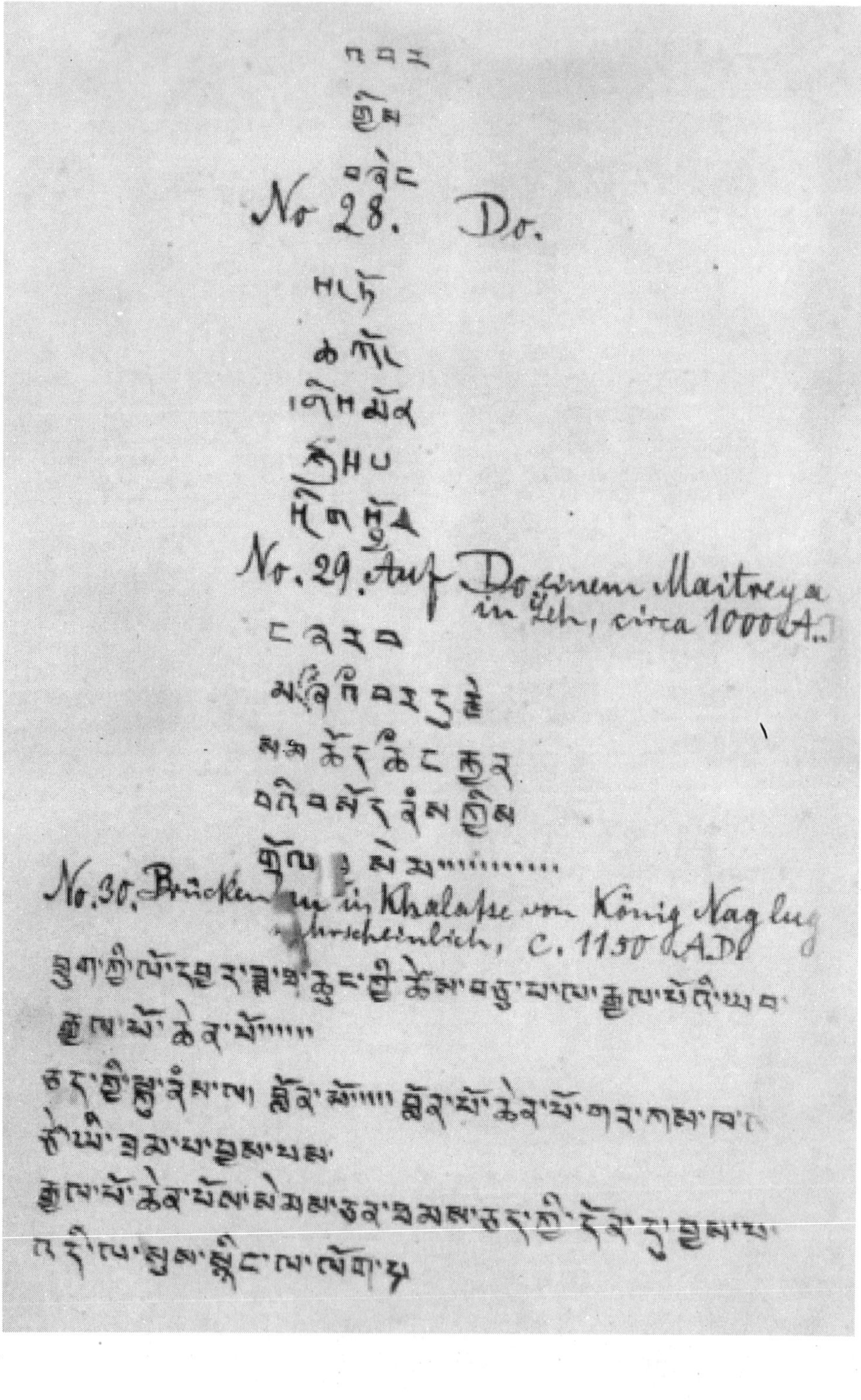

No 28. Do.

No. 29. Auf Do einem Maitreya in Leh, circa 1000 A.D.

No. 30. Brückenbau in Khalatse von König Naglug wahrscheinlich, c. 1150 A.D.

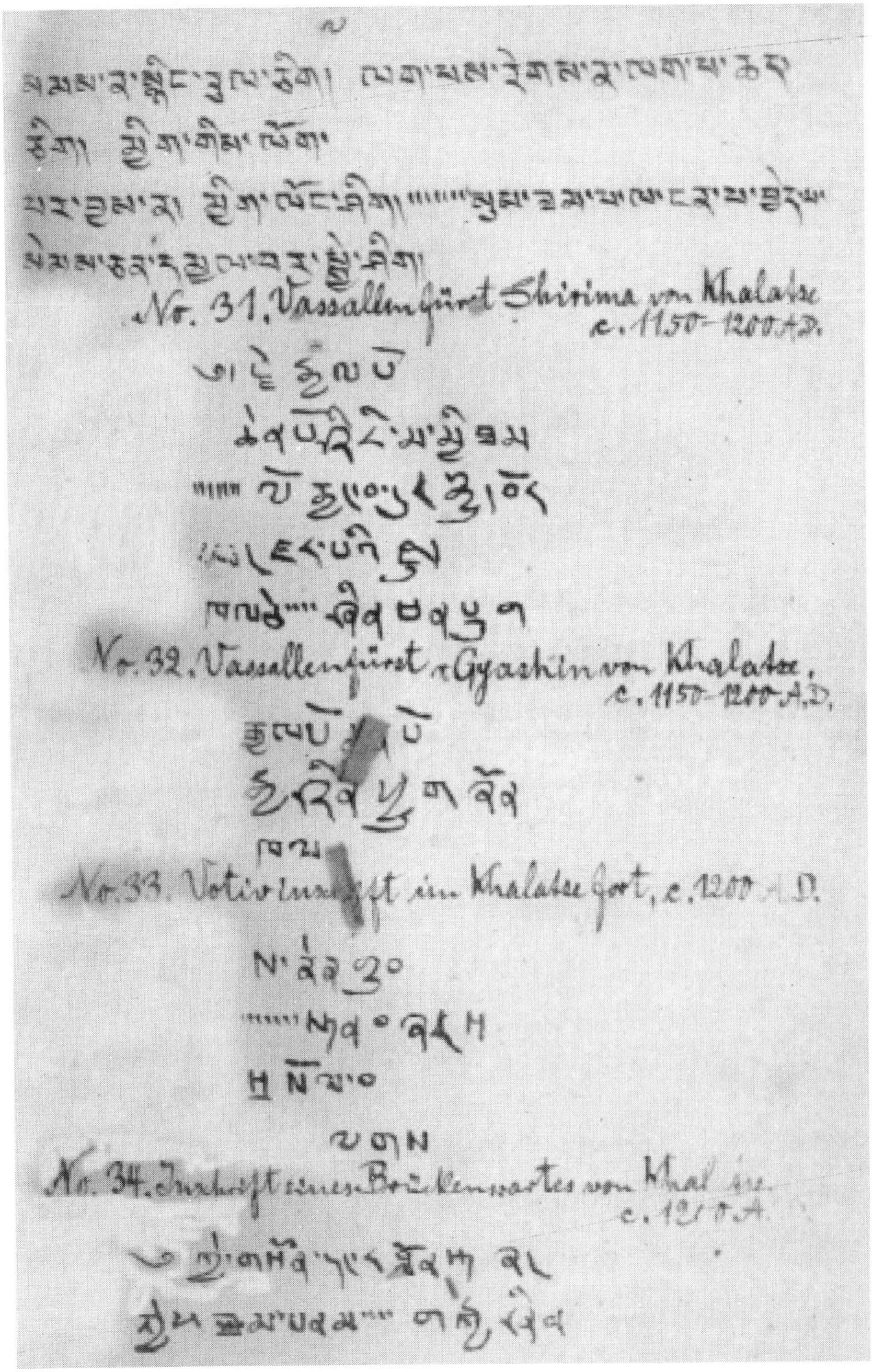

No. 31. Vassallenfürst Shirima von Khalatse c. 1150–1200 A.D.

No. 32. Vassallenfürst rGyashin von Khalatse, c. 1150–1200 A.D.

No. 33. Votivinschrift im Khalatse fort, c. 1200 A.D.

No. 34. Inschrift eines Brückenwartes von Khalatse. c. 1200 A.D.

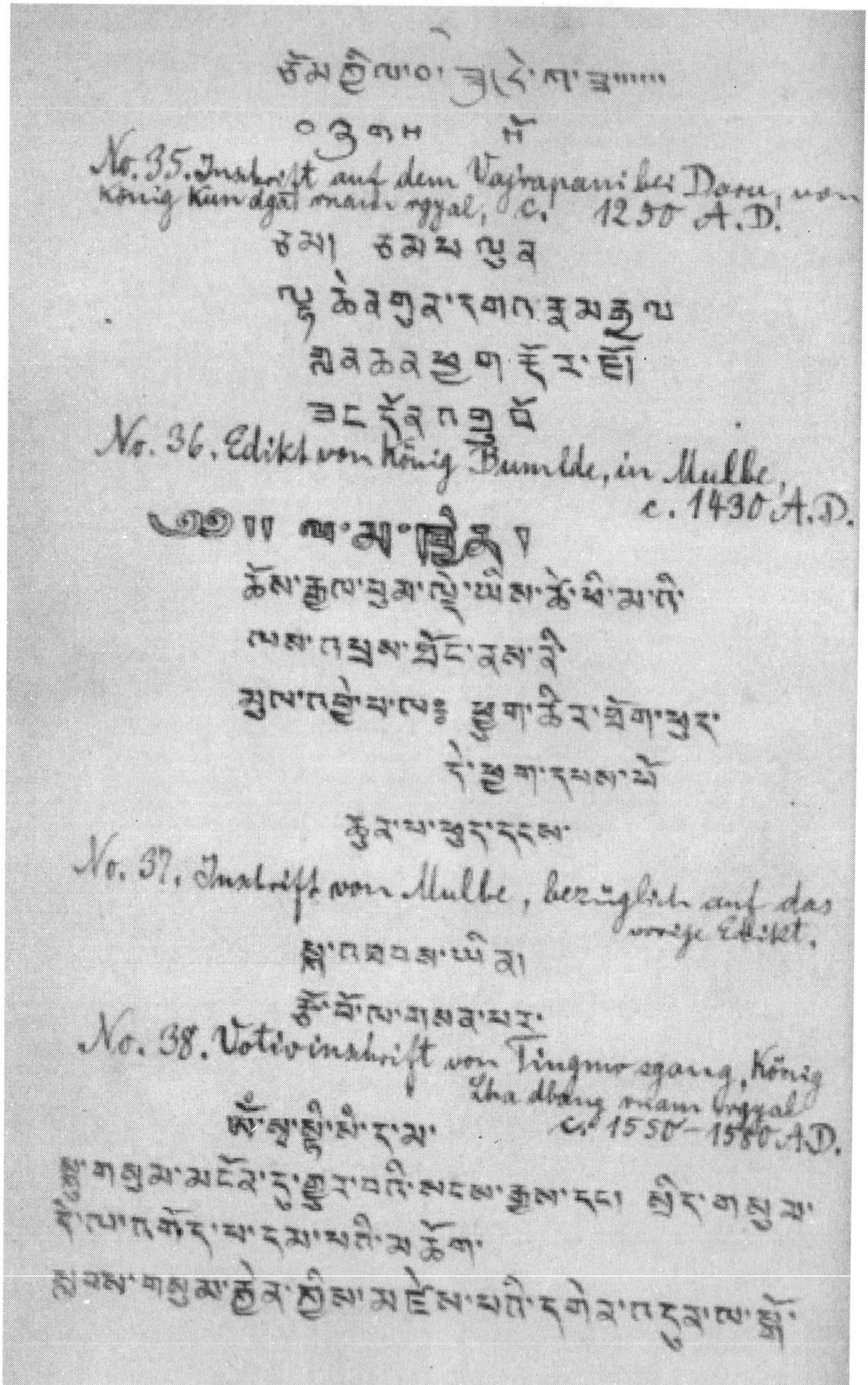

No. 35. Inschrift auf dem Vajrapani bei Dom, von König Kun dgaʼ rnam rgyal, c. 1250 A.D.

No. 36. Edikt von König Bumlde, in Mulbe, c. 1430 A.D.

No. 37. Inschrift von Mulbe, bezüglich auf das vorige Edikt.

No. 38. Votivinschrift von Tingmo sgang, König Lha dbang rnam rgyal c. 1550–1580 A.D.

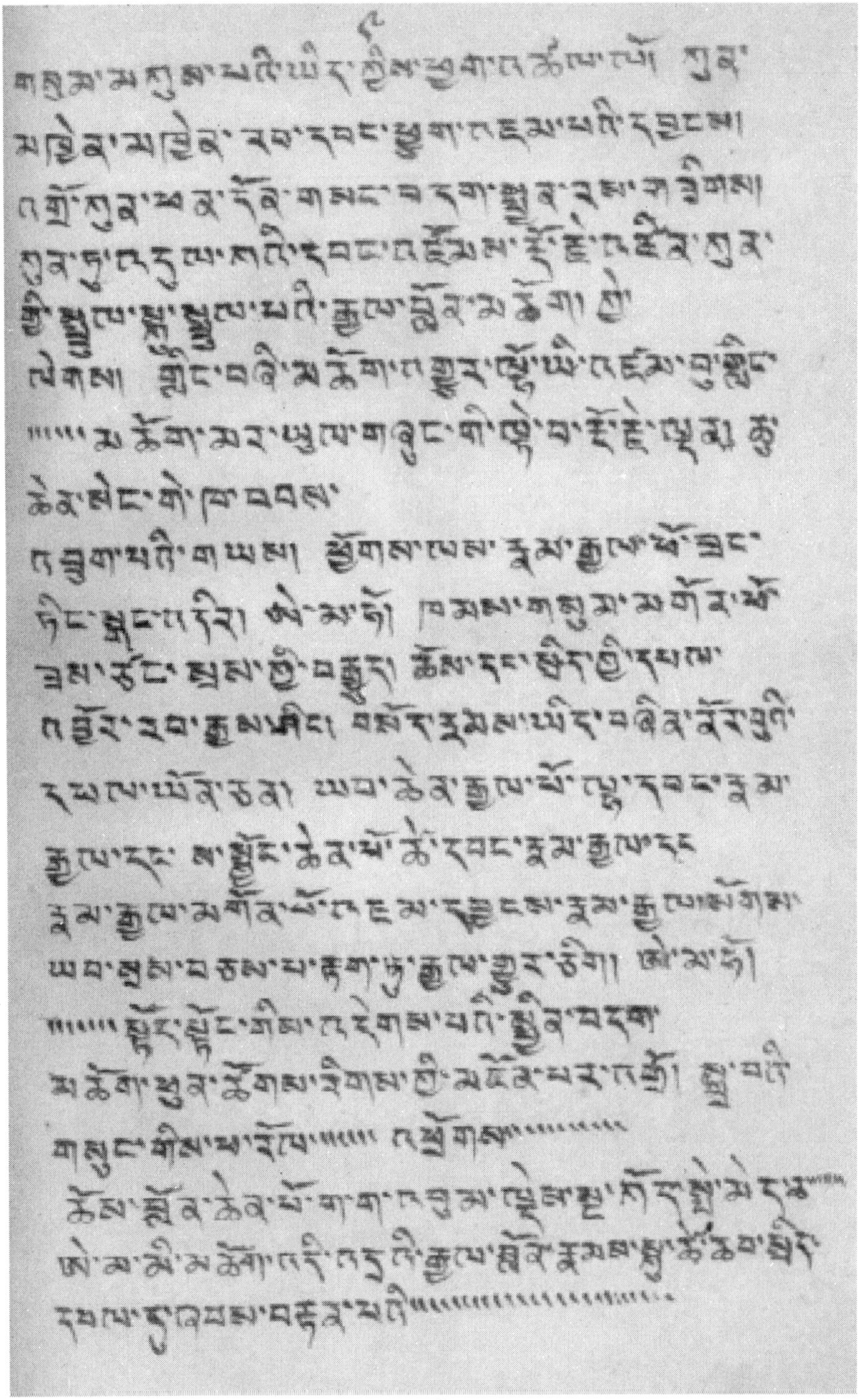
གསུམ་མཁྱེན་པའི་ཡིད་ཀྱིས་ཕྱག་འཚལ་ལོ། ཀུན་
མཁྱེན་མཁྱེན་ནམ་དབང་ཕྱུག་འཇམ་པའི་དབྱངས།
འགྲོ་ཀུན་ཕན་དོན་གསང་བ་དག་སྒྲུབ་ནས་གཟིགས།
ཀུན་ཏུ་འདུལ་བའི་དབང་འཇོམས་རྡོ་རྗེ་འཛིན་ཀུན་
གྱི་སྤྲུལ་སྐུ་སྤྲུལ་པའི་རྒྱལ་བློན་མཆོག །
ལེགས། སྐྱིད་བཞི་མཆོག་འགྱུར་ལྡོ་ཡི་འཛམ་བུ་གླིང་
......མཆོག་མར་ཡུལ་གཞུང་གི་ལྡོ་བ་རྡོ་རྗེ་ལྡན། ཆུ
ཆེན་སེང་གེ་ཁ་བབས་
འབྲུག་པའི་གཡས། ཕྱོགས་ལས་རྣམ་རྒྱལ་པོ་བཟང་
ཉིང་སྐྱོང་འདེར། ཨེ་མ་ཧོ། ཁམས་གསུམ་མགོན་པོ
ཟས་ཙོང་སྲས་ཀྱི་བརྒྱུད། ཆོས་དང་སྲིད་ཀྱི་དཔལ་
འབྱོར་རབ་རྒྱས་པའི། བསོད་ནམས་ཡིད་བཞིན་ནོར་བུའི་
དཔལ་ཡོན་ཅན། ཡབ་ཆེན་རྒྱལ་པོ་ལྡེ་དབང་རྣམ་
རྒྱལ་དང་། སྲས་སྒྲོན་ཆེན་པོ་ཚེ་དབང་རྣམ་རྒྱལ་དང་
རྣམ་རྒྱལ་མགོན་པོ་འཇམ་དབྱངས་རྣམ་རྒྱལ་སོགས་
ཡབ་སྲས་བཅས་པ་རྟག་ཏུ་རྒྱལ་གྱུར་ཅིག། ཨེ་མ་ཧོ།
......སྐྱོད་སྡོང་གིས་འདྲེགས་པའི་སྐྱིན་བདག
མཆོག་སྦྱིན་ཚོགས་རིགས་ཀྱི་མཐོང་བར་འགྱོ། སྐུ་བའི
གསུང་གིས་པ་རོལ་...... འགྲོགས..........
ཆོས་སྐྱོན་ཆེན་པོ་གགའ་བསུམ་ལྡེམ་སྦྱོ་ཀོད་སྤྲོ་མི་དཔ
ཨེ་མ་ཧི་མཆོག་འདི་འདུའི་རྒྱལ་བློན་རྣམས་སྐུ་ཚེ་བ་སྲིད
དཔལ་ཏུ་འཕེལ་བརྟན་པའི...........

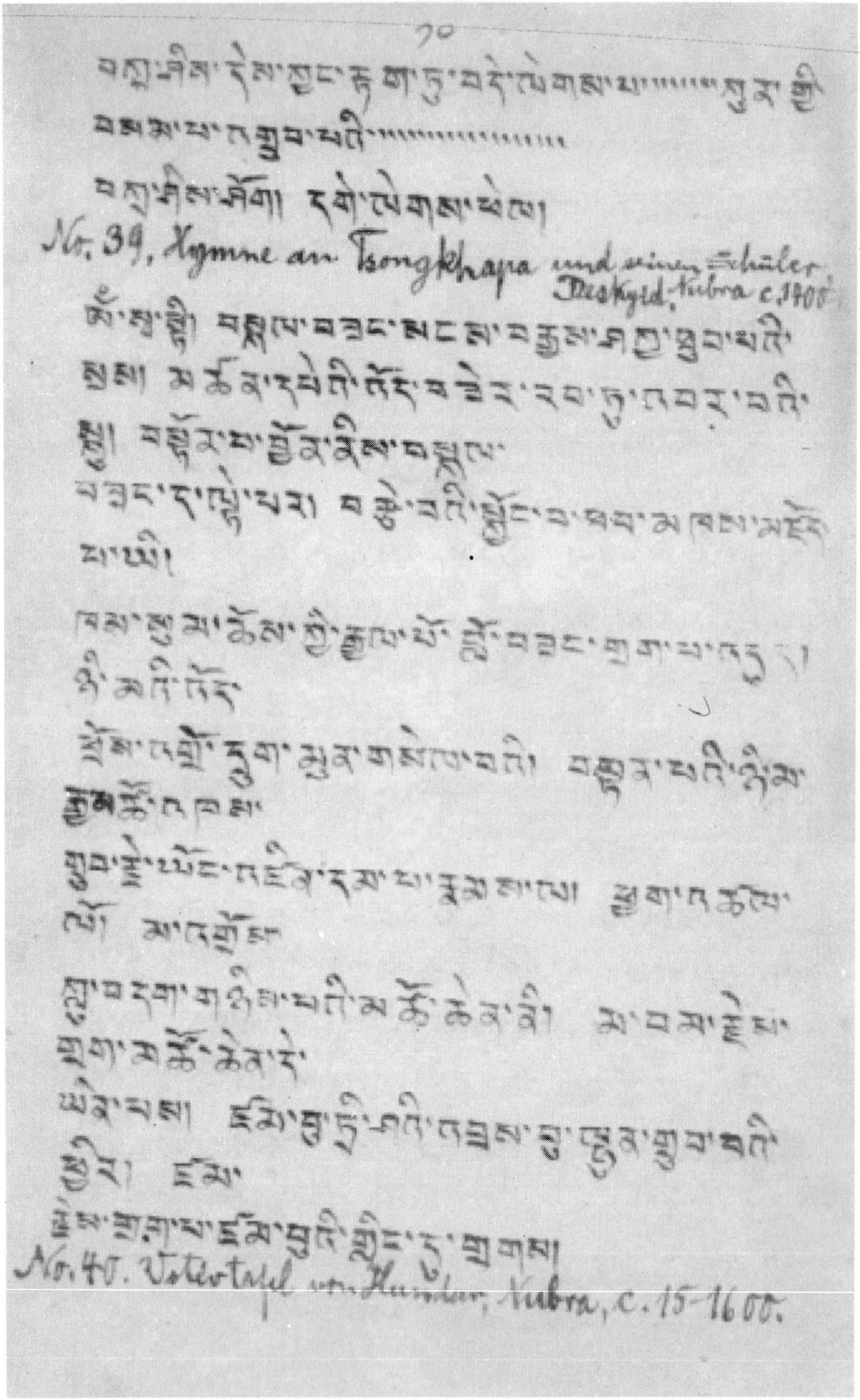
70
No. 39, Hymne an Tsongkhapa und seinen Schüler
Deskyid, Nubra c. 1400
No. 40. Vatertafel von Hundar, Nubra, c. 15-1600.

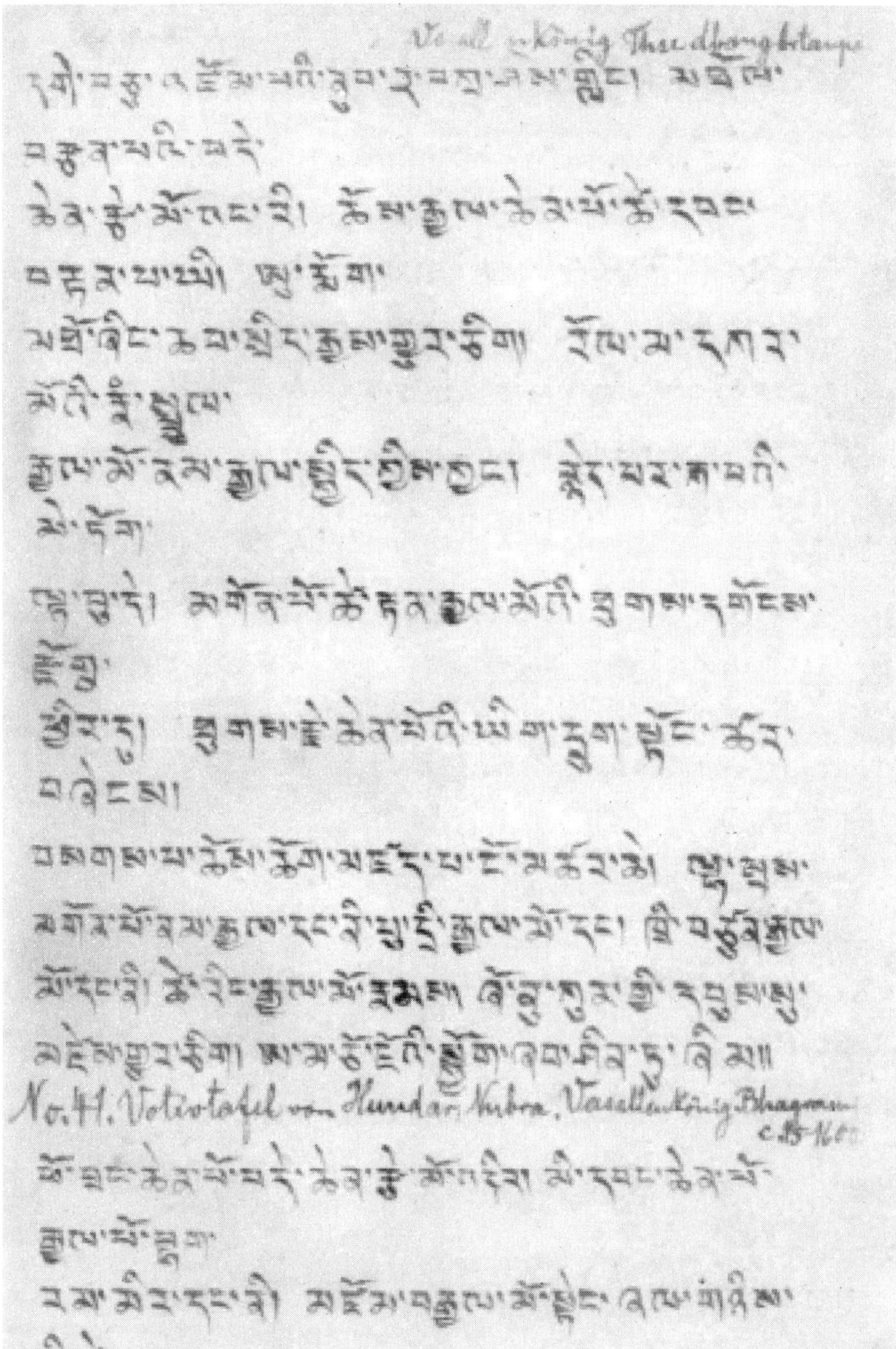
No. 41. Votivtafel von Hundar, Nubra, Vasallenkönig Bhagan

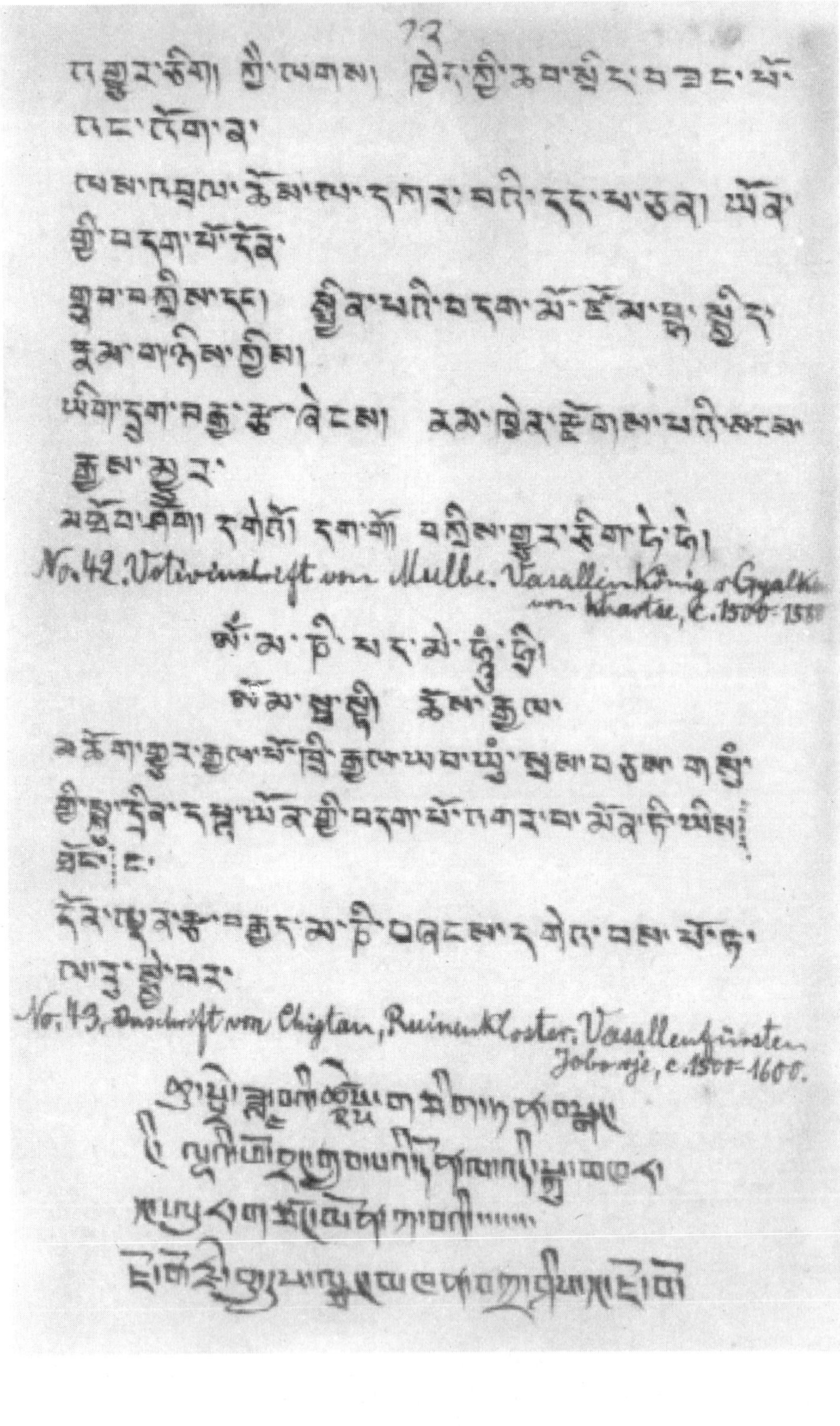

No. 42. Votivinschrift von Mulbe. Vasallenkönig o. Gyalpo von Khartse, c. 1500–1600

No. 43. Inschrift von Chigtan, Ruinenkloster. Vasallenfürsten Jobrogje, c. 1500–1600.

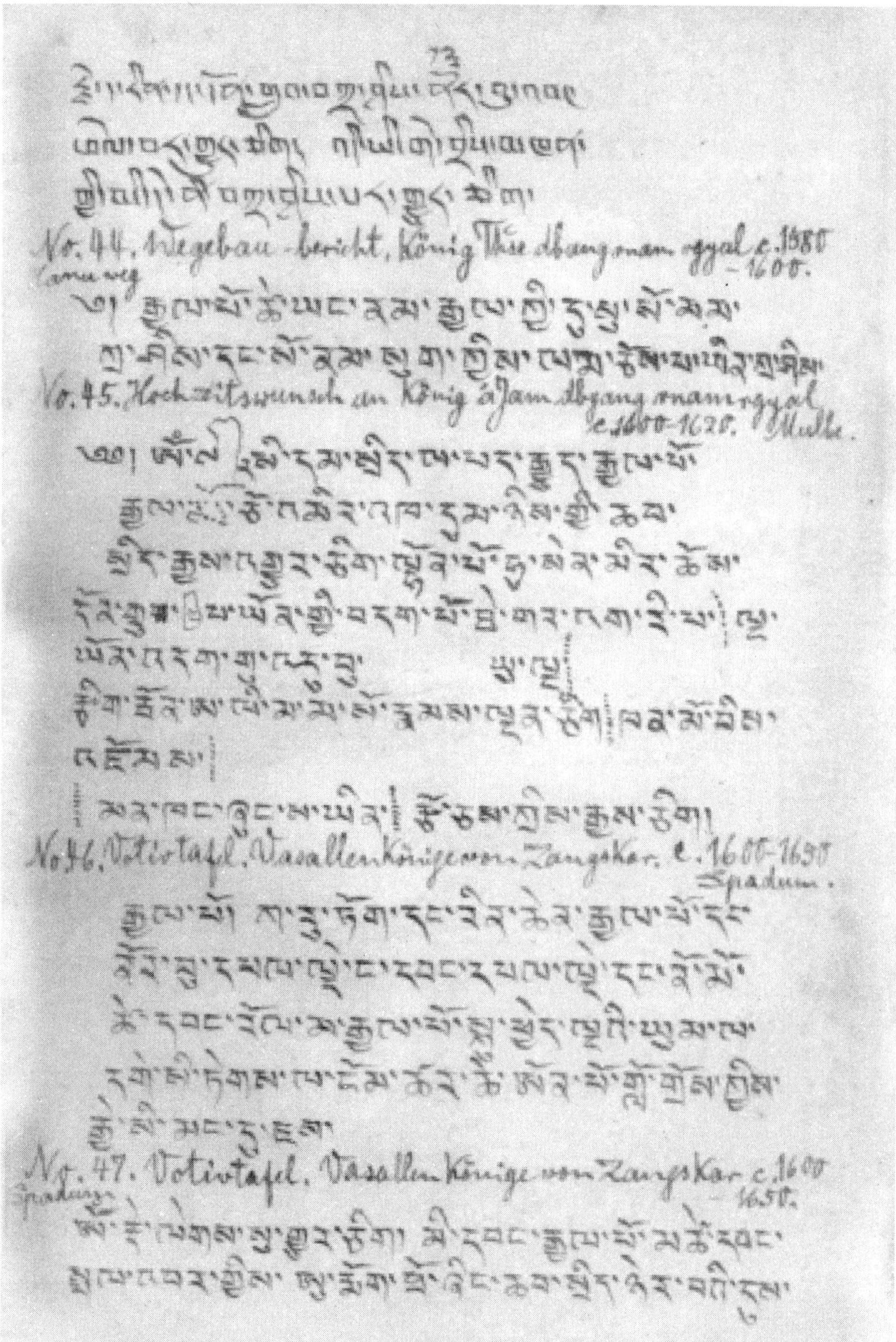

No. 44. Wegebau-bericht, König Thse dbang rnam rgyal c. 1580 – 1600.
Lamayurg

No. 45. Hochzeitswunsch an König àJam dbyang rnam rgyal c. 1600-1620. Mulbe.

No. 46. Votivtafel. Vasallenkönige von Zangskar. c. 1600-1650 Spadum.

No. 47. Votivtafel. Vasallen Könige von Zangskar c. 1600 1650.
Spadum

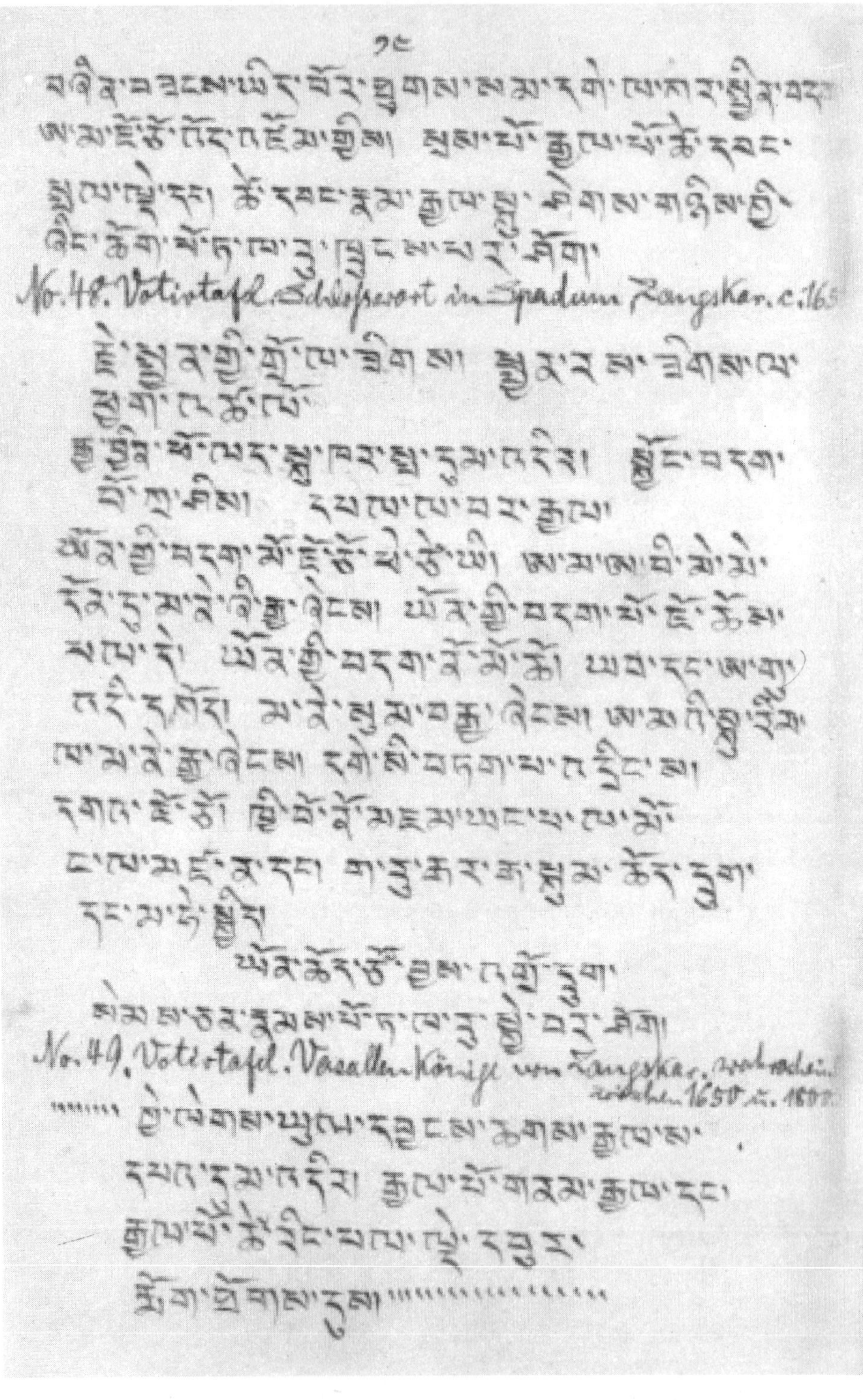
No. 48. Votivtafel. Schlossrest in Spadum Zangskar. c. 165
No. 49. Votivtafel. Vasallen-Könige von Zangskar, wahrschein[lich] zwischen 1650 u. 1800

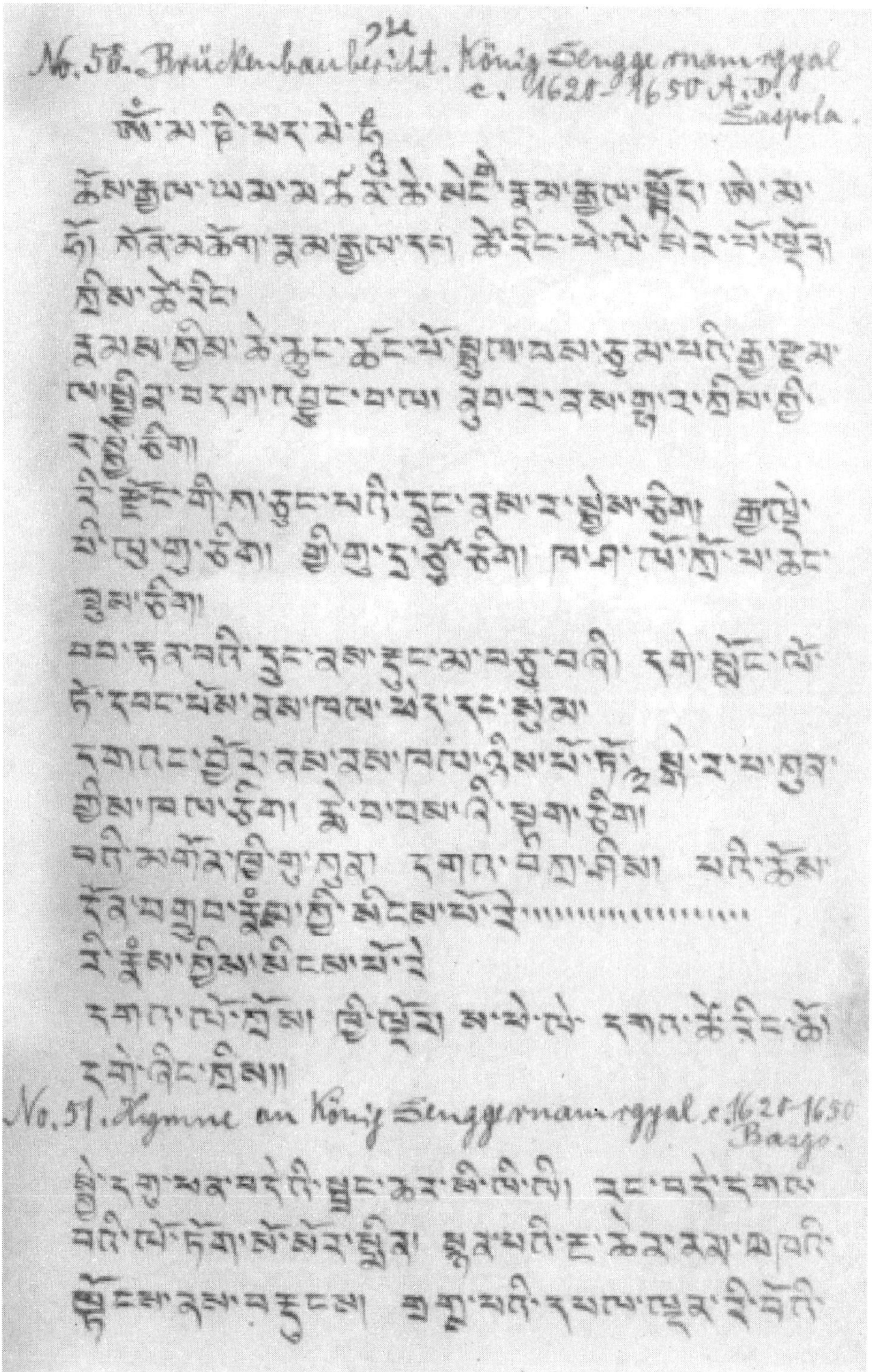

No. 50. Brückenbaubericht. König Sengge rnam rgyal c. 1620–1650 A.D. Saspola.

ཨོཾ་མ་ཎི་པད་མེ་ཧཱུྃ

ཆོས་རྒྱལ་ཡབ་མ་མ་ཚོ་ཐུ་ཆེ་སེངྒེ་རྣམ་རྒྱལ་སྐྱོང་། ཡེ་ས་
ཧོ། ཀོན་མཆོག་རྣམ་རྒྱལ་དང་། ཚེ་རིང་ལེ་ལེ་མེར་པོ་ལྡེར།
ཁྲིམས་ཚོ་རིང་

རྣམས་ཀྱིས་ཆེ་རྒྱུང་ཚང་པོ་སློབ་བས་རྒྱམ་པའི་རྒྱ་རྣམ
ལ་སྒྲིན་པ་དག་འབྱུང་བ་ལ། ཟུབ་ར་ནས་གླ་ར་ཁྲིམས་ཀྱི
ར་སྒྲུ་ཅིག

དེ་རྗོང་གི་ཀ་ཐུང་པའི་ཟུང་ནས་ར་སློམ་ཅིག རྒྱ་ལྡེ་
མི་ལྡེ་ཀུ་ཅིག ཀྱི་གུ་དུ་ཐུ་ཅིག ཁ་ཕ་ལོ་ཀོ་མ་ཚང་
ཟུམ་ཅིག

བང་ཧྲན་པའི་ཟུང་ནས་ཟུང་མ་བརྒྱུ་བཞི། དགེ་སློང་ལོ་
ཧེ་དབང་པོས་ནས་ཁལ་སེད་དང་སུམ།

དཀའ་འགྱུར་ནས་ནས་ཁལ་འཇིམ་པོ་ཧེ་ སྨེ་ར་པ་ཀུན་
ཀྱིས་ཁལ་ཅིག སྐྱེ་བ་བས་འི་སྒྱུག་ཅིག

པའི་ཨ་གོན་ཡི་གུ་ཀུན། དཀའ་བཀྲ་ཤིས། པའི་ཆོས་
དོན་བསྒྲུབ་རྣམས་ཀྱི་མིངས་སོ་ནི.....................

ནི་རྣམས་ཀྱིས་མིངས་སོ་ནི

དཀའ་ལོ་ཀྱིས། ཡི་ལྡེར། ས་ལེ་ལ་ དཀའ་ཚེ་རིང་ཧོ།
དགེ་ཤིང་ཁྲིམས།།

No. 51. Hymne an König Sengge rnam rgyal c. 1620–1650 Bazgo.

སྦྱི་དགུ་མན་པདེ་ཀི་སྦྱང་ཆར་མི་ལི་ལི། ནང་བདེ་དཀའ
པའི་ལོ་ཏོག་སོ་སོར་སྨིན། སྨན་པའི་ཛ་ཆེར་རས་མཁའི
སྤྲིངས་ནས་བརྟངས། གྲགས་པའི་དཔལ་ལྡན་རི་བོའི

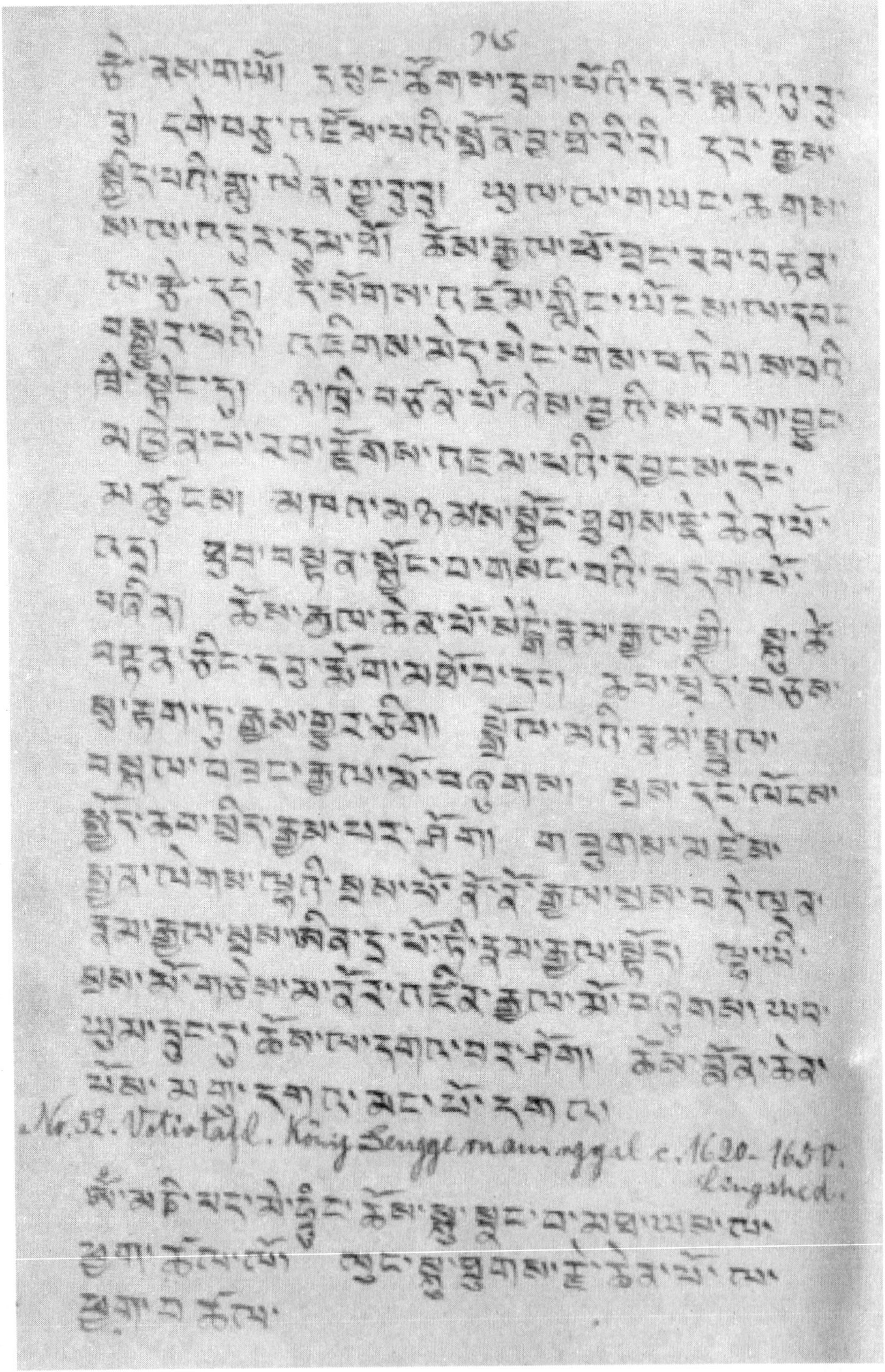
No. 52. Votivtafel. König Sengge rnam rgyal c. 1620–1650.
Lingshed.

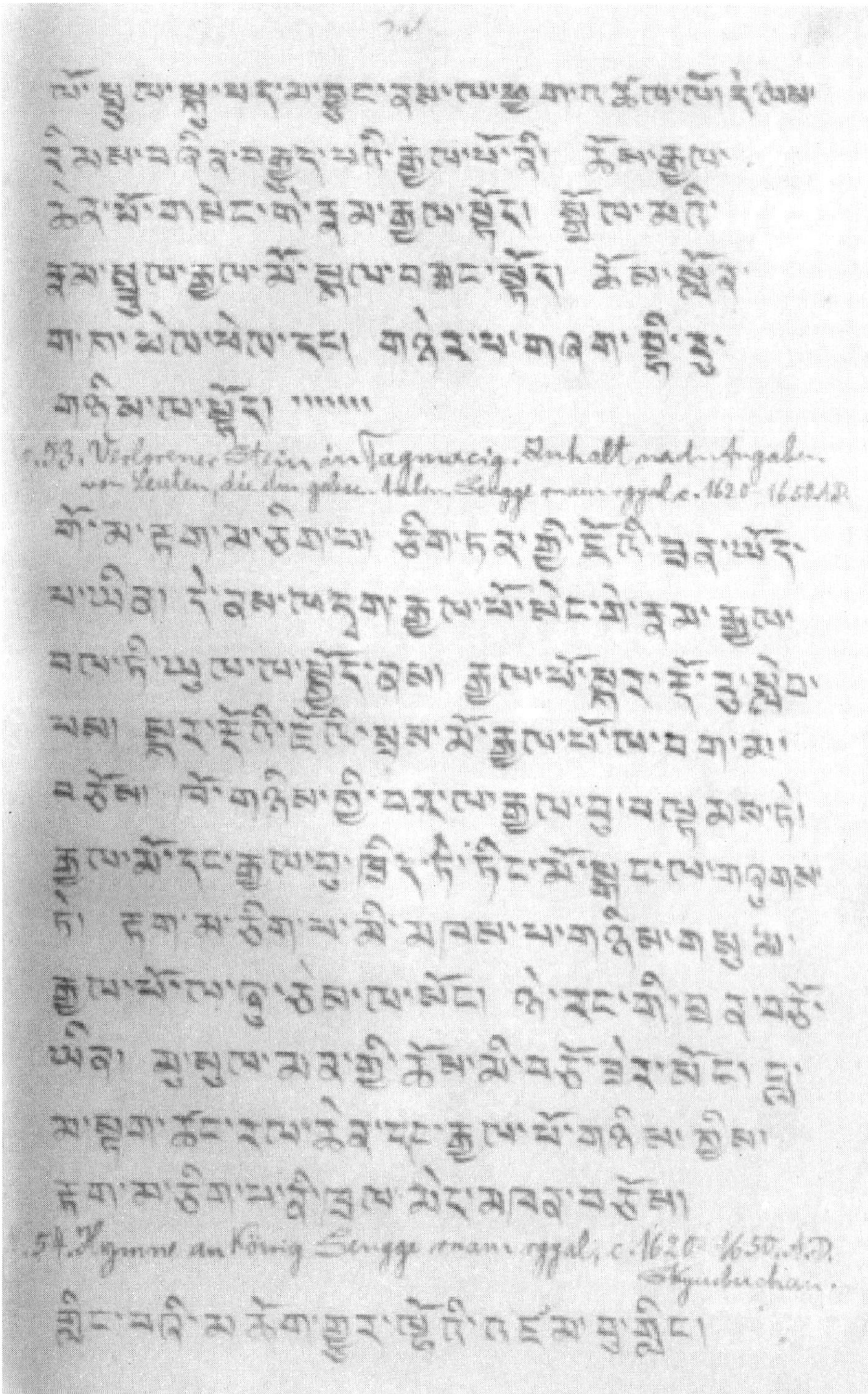
53. Vorlorener Stein in Tagmacig. Inhalt nach Angaben von Leuten, die den gehen Halten. Sengge rnam rgyal c. 1620–1650 A.D.
54. Hymne an König Sengge rnam rgyal, c. 1620–1650 A.D.
Khyunbuchan.

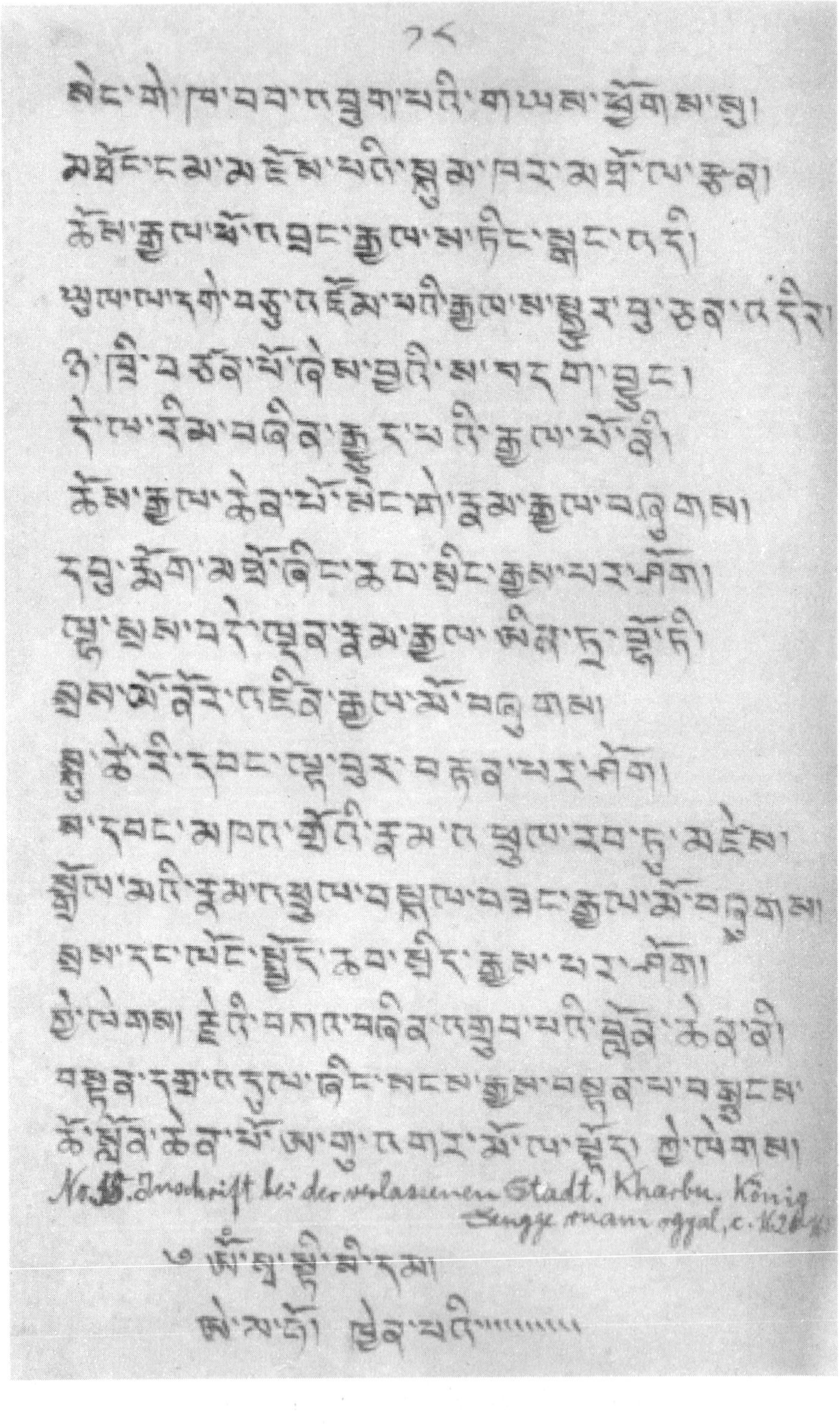

༧༨

སེང་གེ། ཁ་བབ་འབྲུག་པའི་གཡས་ཕྱོགས་སུ།
མཐོང་ངམ་མཛེས་པའི་སྤྲུམ་ཁར་མགོ་ལ་རྒྱན།
ཆོས་རྒྱལ་སོ་འབྲང་རྒྱལ་ས་ཉིང་སྣང་འདི།
ཡུལ་ལ་ལ་དགེ་བཅུ་འཛོམ་པའི་རྒྱལ་ས་སྤུར་བུ་ཅན་འདིར།
ཉི་ཁྲི་བཙན་པོ་ཞེས་བྱའི་ས་བདག་བྱུང་།
དེ་ལ་རིམ་བཞིན་རྒྱུད་པའི་རྒྱལ་པོ་ནི།
ཆོས་རྒྱལ་ཆེན་པོ་སེང་གེ་རྣམ་རྒྱལ་བཞུགས།
དབུ་རྨོག་མཐོ་ཞིང་ཆབ་སྲིད་རྒྱས་པར་ཤོག།
ལྷ་སྲས་བདེ་ལྡན་རྣམ་རྒྱལ་ཞེས་བྱ་ཉིད།
སྲས་ཨོ་ནོར་འཛིན་རྒྱལ་མོ་བཀུགས།
སྐུ་ཚེ་རི་དབང་ལྷ་བྱུར་བརྟན་པར་ཤོག།
ས་དབང་མཁའ་འགྲོའི་རྣམ་འཕྲུལ་རབ་ཏུ་མཛེས།
སྒྲོལ་མའི་རྣམ་འཕྲུལ་བསྐལ་བཟང་རྒྱལ་མོ་བཀུགས།
སྲས་དང་ལོང་སྤྱོད་ཆབ་སྲིད་རྒྱས་པར་ཤོག།
ཕྱི་ལེགས། རྗེའི་བཀའ་བཞིན་འགྲུབ་པའི་བློན་ཆེན་ནི།
བསྟན་དགྲ་འདུལ་ཞིང་སངས་རྒྱས་བསྟན་པ་བསྐྱངས།
ཚེ་སྨོན་ཆེན་པོ་ཨ་གུ་འགར་མོ་ལ་སྨོན། ཕྱི་ལེགས།

No. 35. Inschrift bei der verlassenen Stadt. Kharbu. König Sengge rnam rgyal, c. 1620.

༄ ཨོཾ་སྭ་སྟི་སི་དྷམ།
ལེ་ལ་ཏོ། ཕྱིན་པའི་..........

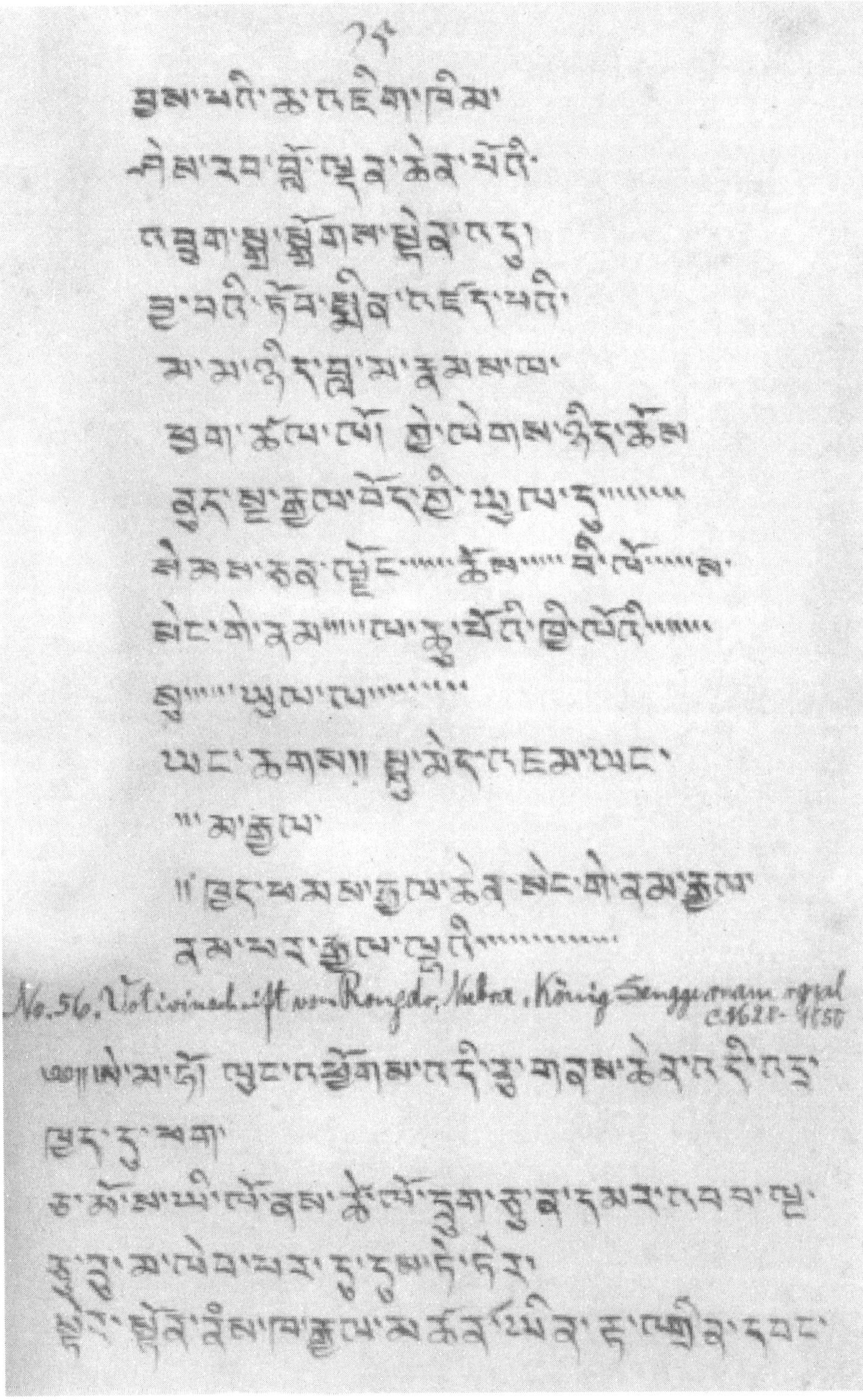
No. 56. Votivinschrift von Rongdo, Nubra, König Sengge rnam rgyal c. 1620-1650

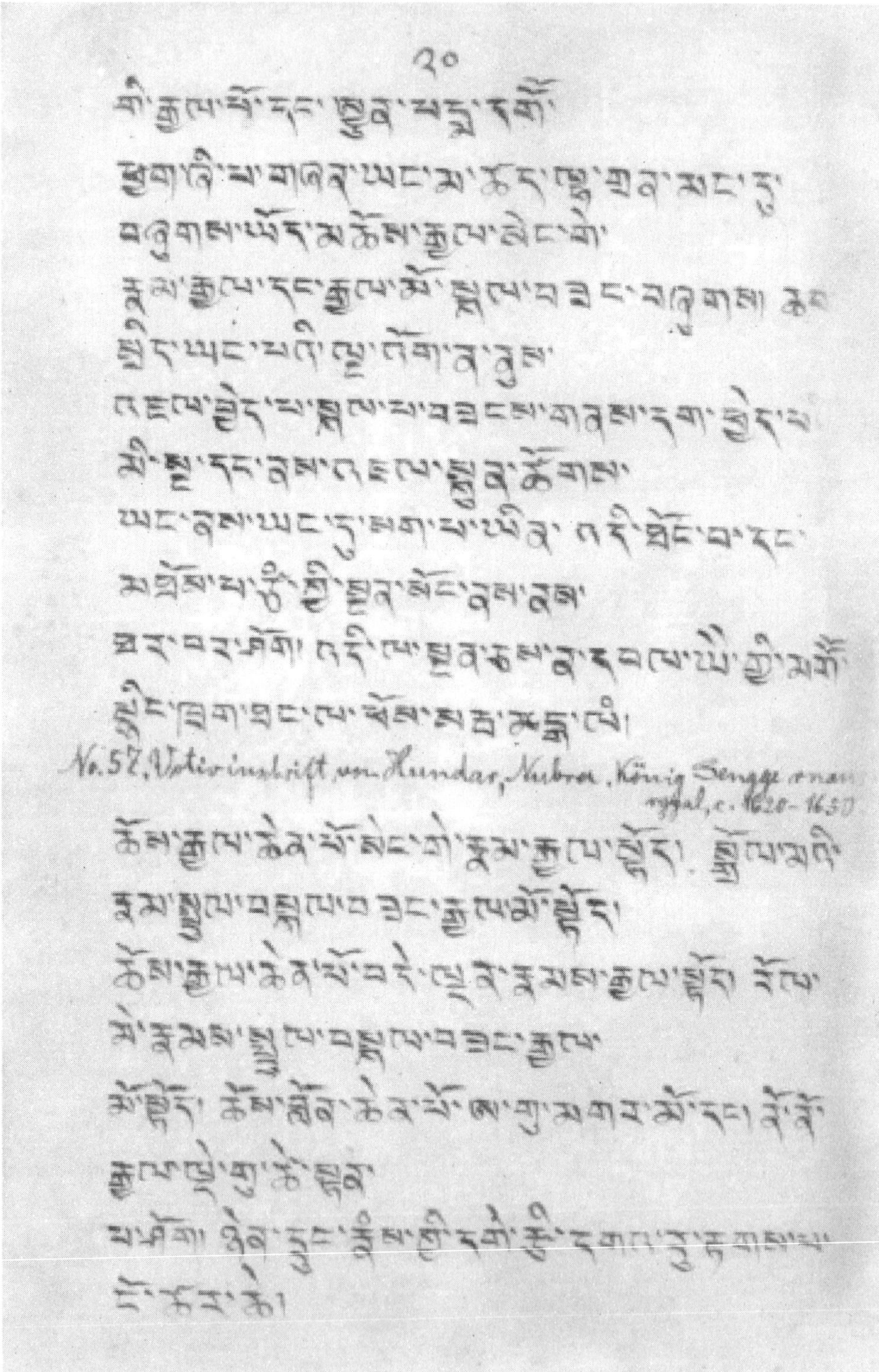

༢༠

གི་རྒྱལ་པོ་དང་། ཕྱུན་པདྨ་དགོ

ཕྱག་ཐེ་ས་གཞན་ཡང་མ་ཆད་ལྷ་གྲུན་མང་དུ

བཞུགས་ཡོད་མཆོས་རྒྱལ་སེང་གེ

རྣམ་རྒྱལ་དང་རྒྱལ་མོ་སྐལ་བཟང་བཞུགས། ཆེ

སྲིད་ཡང་པའི་ལྷོ་ཁོག་ན་ཐུས

འཛམ་གླིང་སྐལ་པ་བཟངས་གནས་དག་ཕྱེད་པ

མི་སྤྱི་དང་ནས་འཛམ་ཕྱུན་ཚོགས

ཡང་ནས་ཡང་དུ་སག་པ་ཡིན་ འདི་ཕྱོང་བ་དང

མཐོས་པ་ཧུྃ་ཀྱི་ཕྱིན་སོང་ནས་ནས

ཟར་བར་ཤོག། འདི་ལ་ཕྱིན་རུས་ན་རབ་ལ་ཡི་ཀྱི་མགོ

སྙིང་ཁྲག་ཐང་ལ་སོས་སུ་བ་སྒྲུ་ལི།

No. 57, Votivinschrift von Hundar, Nubra, König Sengge rnam rgyal, c. 1620–1650

ཆོས་རྒྱལ་ཆེན་པོ་སེང་གེ་རྣམ་རྒྱལ་སྡེར། སྐྱེ་ལ་མའི

རྣམ་སྐྱེལ་བསྐལ་བ་བཟང་རྒྱལ་མོ་སྡེར།

ཆོས་རྒྱལ་ཆེན་པོ་བདེ་ལྡན་རྣམས་རྒྱལ་སྡེར། རོལ

མ་རྣམས་སྐྱེལ་བསྐལ་བ་བཟང་རྒྱལ

མོ་སྡེར། ཆོས་སློབ་ཆེན་པོ་ཨ་གུ་མཁར་མོ་དང་། ནོ་ནོ

རྒྱལ་ཕྱེ་གུ་ཚེ་སྡན

པ་ཤོག། ཉེན་རྡུང་རྣམས་ཀྱི་དགེ་རྒྱུ་དཀའ་དུ་རྟགས་པ

ང་ཚར་ཆེ།

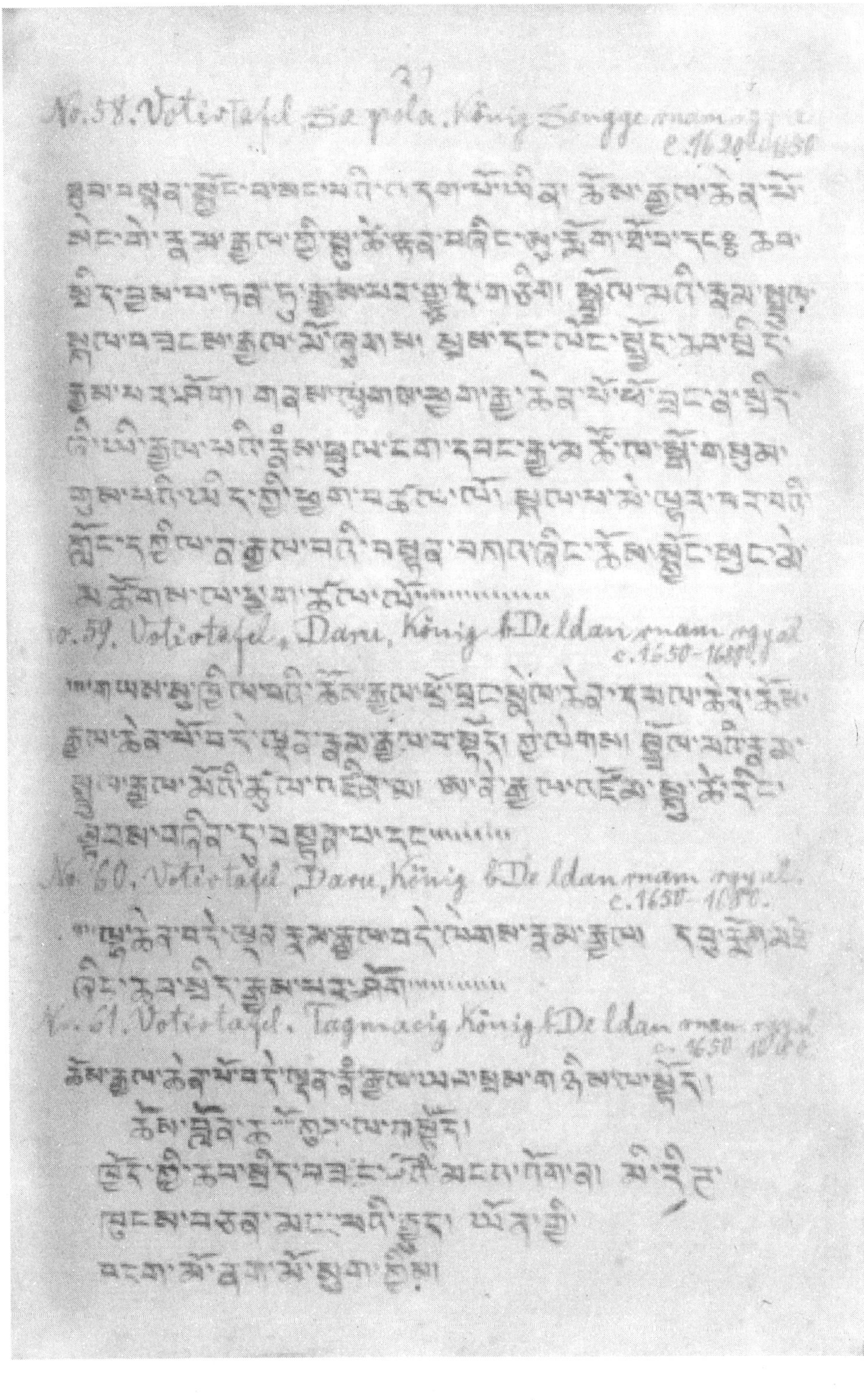
21

No. 58. Votivtafel Sa pola. König Sengge rnam rgyal c. 1620 bis 1650

No. 59. Votivtafel, Dam, König bDe ldan rnam rgyal c. 1650–1680.

No. 60. Votivtafel, Dam, König bDe ldan rnam rgyal c. 1650–1680.

No. 61. Votivtafel. Tagmacig König bDe ldan rnam rgyal c. 1650–1680.

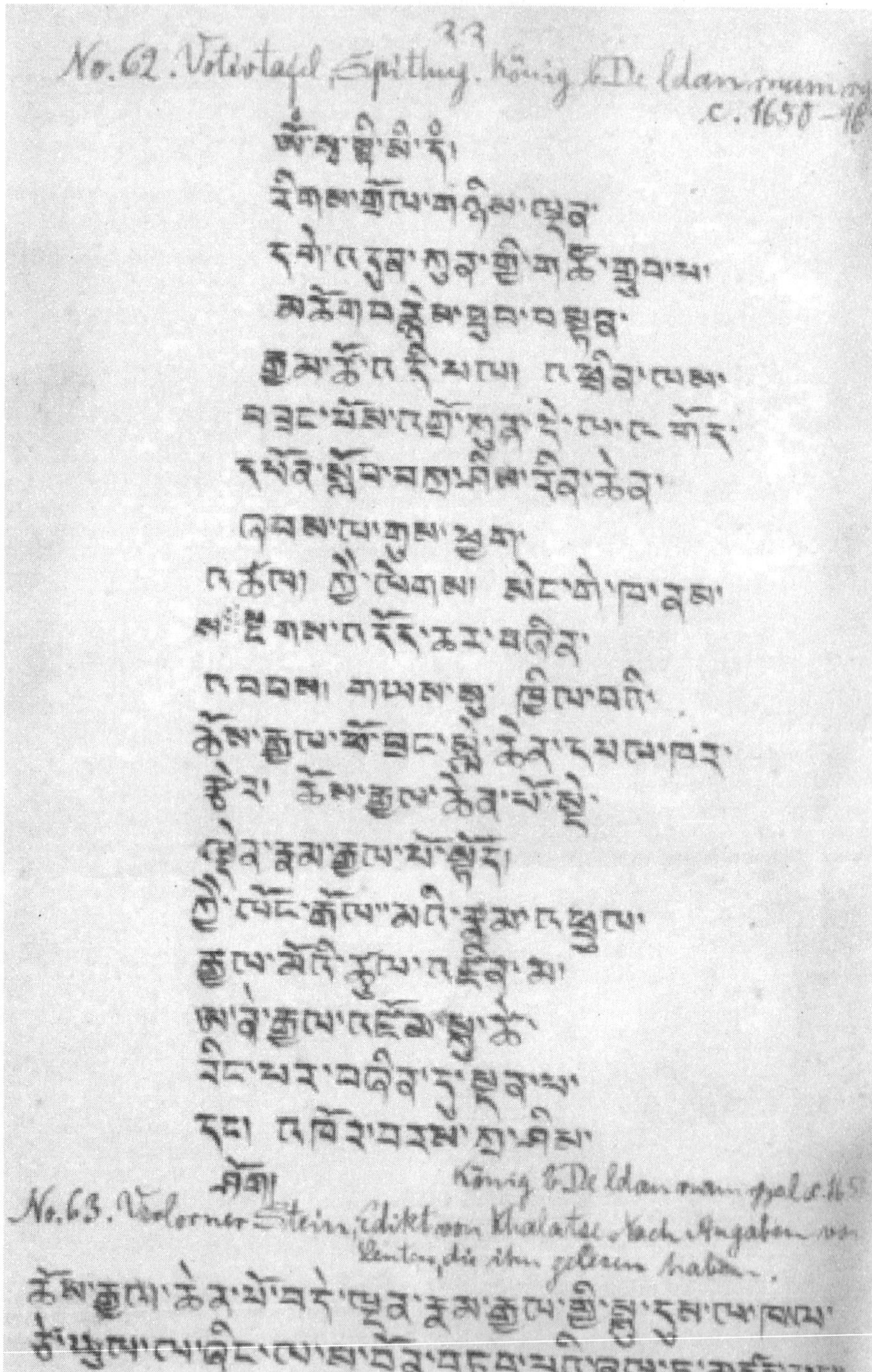

No. 62. Votivtafel, Spithug. König bDe ldan rnam rgyal c. 1650–16[..]

ཨོཾ་སྭ་སྟི་སི་དྷཾ།
རིགས་ཀྱི་ལ་གཉིས་ལྡན་
དགེ་འདུན་ཀུན་གྱི་གཙོ་རྒྱལ་བ་ལ་
མཆོག་བརྙེས་རྒྱལ་བ་བསྟན་
རྒྱ་མཚོ་འདི་ས་ལ། འཕྲིན་ལས་
བཟང་མོས་འགྲོ་ཀུན་དེ་ལ་འགོད་
དཔོན་སློབ་བཀྲ་ཤིས་རིན་ཆེན་
ཞབས་ལ་གུས་ཕྱག་
འཆོལ། ཕྱི་ལོགས། མང་ཐེ་ཁ་ནས་
ས་ཛཱ་གས་འདོད་ཆར་བཞིན་
འབབས། གཡས་སུ་ཕྱི་ལ་བའི་
ཆོས་རྒྱལ་སོ་ཐང་སྐྱེ་ཆེན་དཔལ་ཁར་
རྗེ་ར་ ཆོས་རྒྱལ་ཆེན་པོ་སྐྱེ་
ལྡན་རྣམ་རྒྱལ་པོ་སྐྱོང་།
ཕྱི་ལོང་ཆོ་ལ་མའི་རྣམ་འཕྲུལ་
རྒྱལ་མོའི་རྟུལ་འཛིན་མ།
ཨ་ན་རྒྱལ་འཛོམས་སྐྱུ་ཚེ་
རིང་པར་བཞིན་དུ་སྨོན་ལ་
དང་། འཁོར་བཅས་སྐུ་ཤིས་
ཤོག།

König bDe ldan rnam rgyal c. 165[.]

No. 63. Verlorner Stein, Edikt von Khalatse. Nach Angaben von Leuten, die ihn gelesen haben.

ཆོས་རྒྱལ་ཆེན་པོ་བདེ་ལྡན་རྣམ་རྒྱལ་གྱི་སྐུ་དུས་ལ་ཁལ་མ
ཙེ་སྤྱལ་ལ་ཞིང་ལ་ས་བོན་བཏབ་པའི་ཞལ་ཏ་མཛད་པས

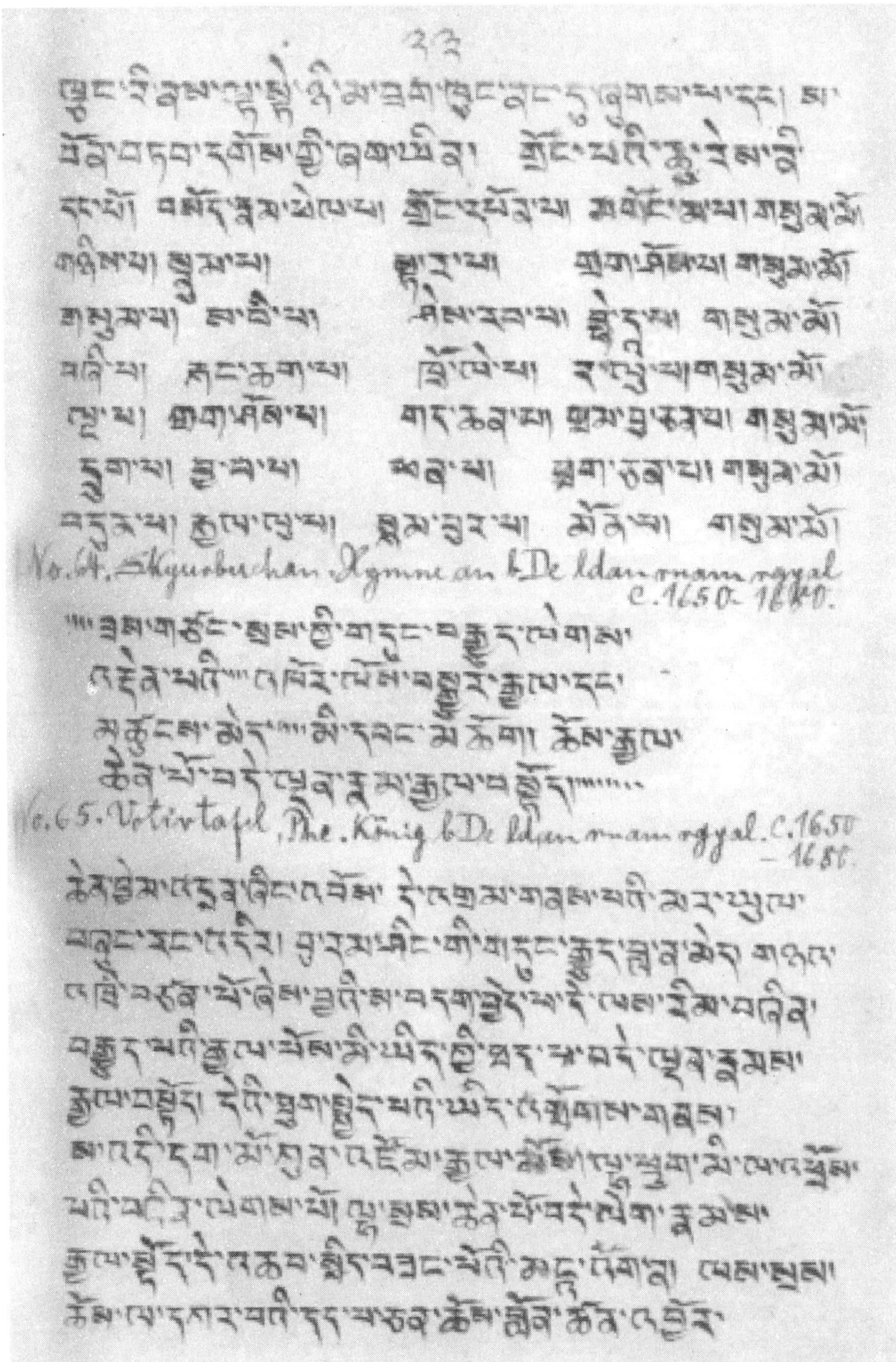

No. 64. Skyurbuchan Hymne an bDe ldan rnam rgyal
c. 1650–1680.

No. 65. Votivtafel, Phe. König bDe ldan rnam rgyal. c. 1650
– 1680.

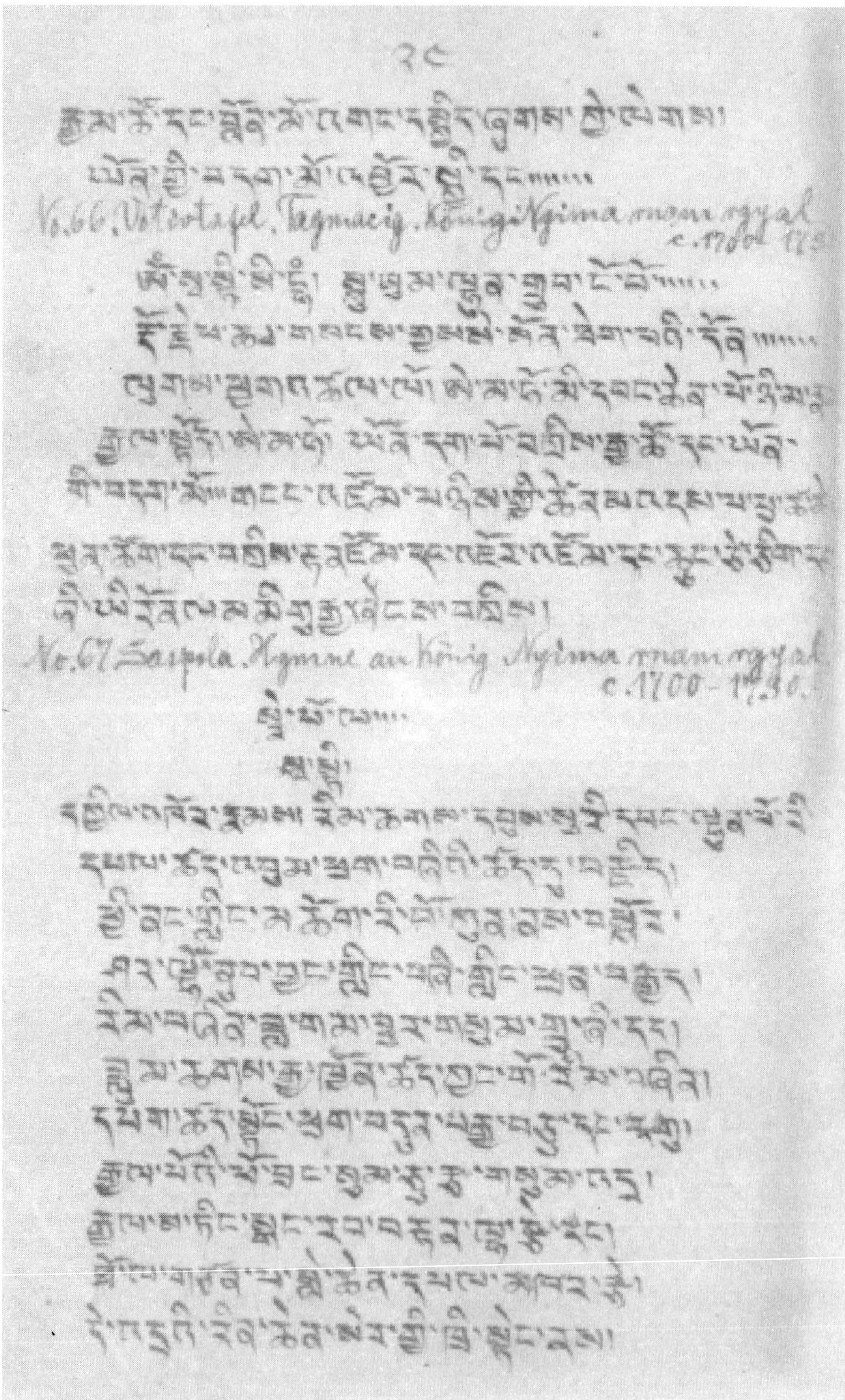
No. 66. Votivtafel, Tagmacig. König Ngima rnam rgyal
c. 1700
No. 67 Saspola. Hymne an König Ngima rnam rgyal
c. 1700 –

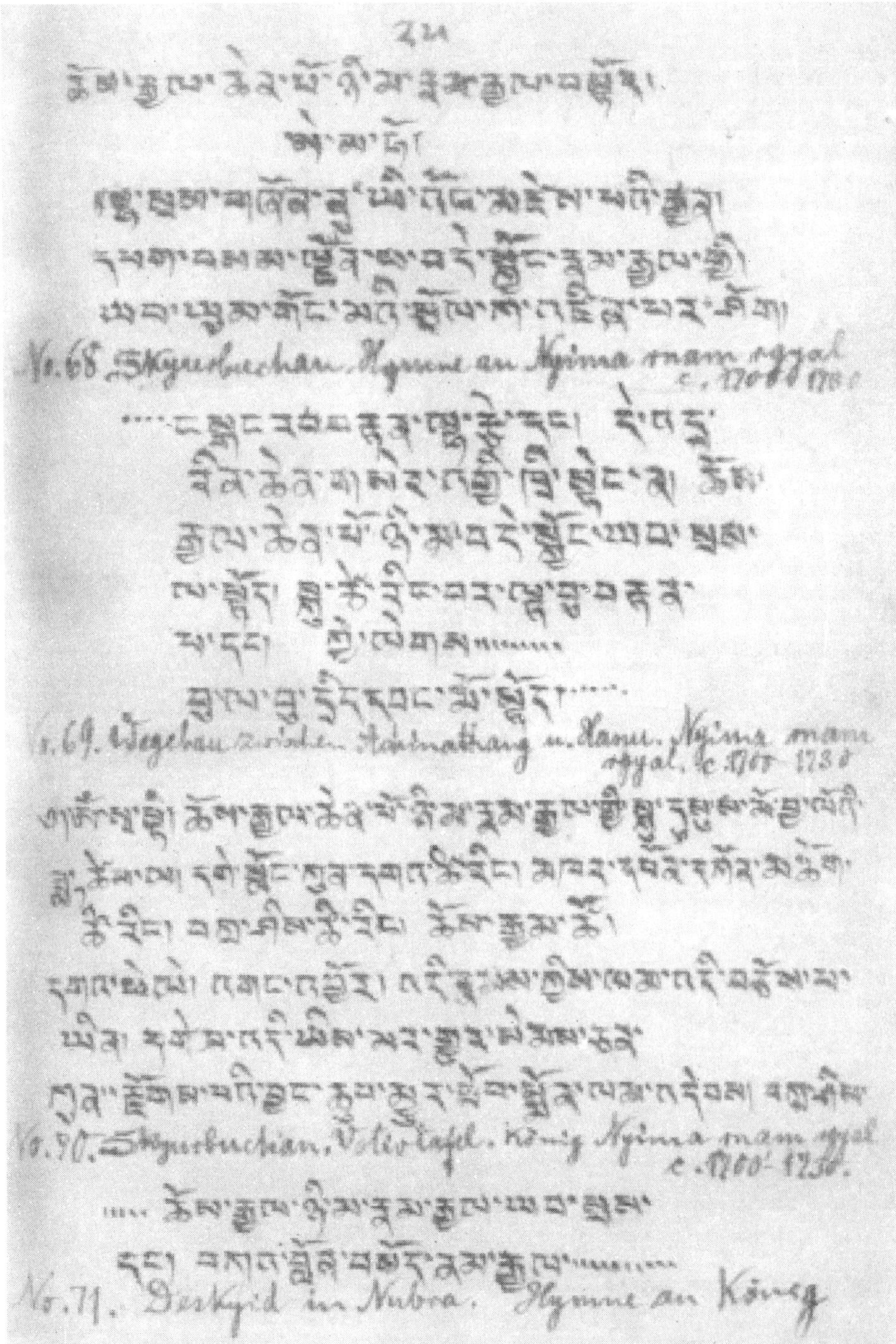
No. 68. Skyurbuchan, Hymne an Nyima rnam rgyal c. 1700 bis 1730

No. 69. Wegebau zwischen Achinathang u. Hanu. Nyima rnam rgyal. c. 1700–1730

No. 70. Skyurbuchan, Votivtafel. König Nyima rnam rgyal c. 1700–1730.

No. 71. Deskyid in Nubra. Hymne an König

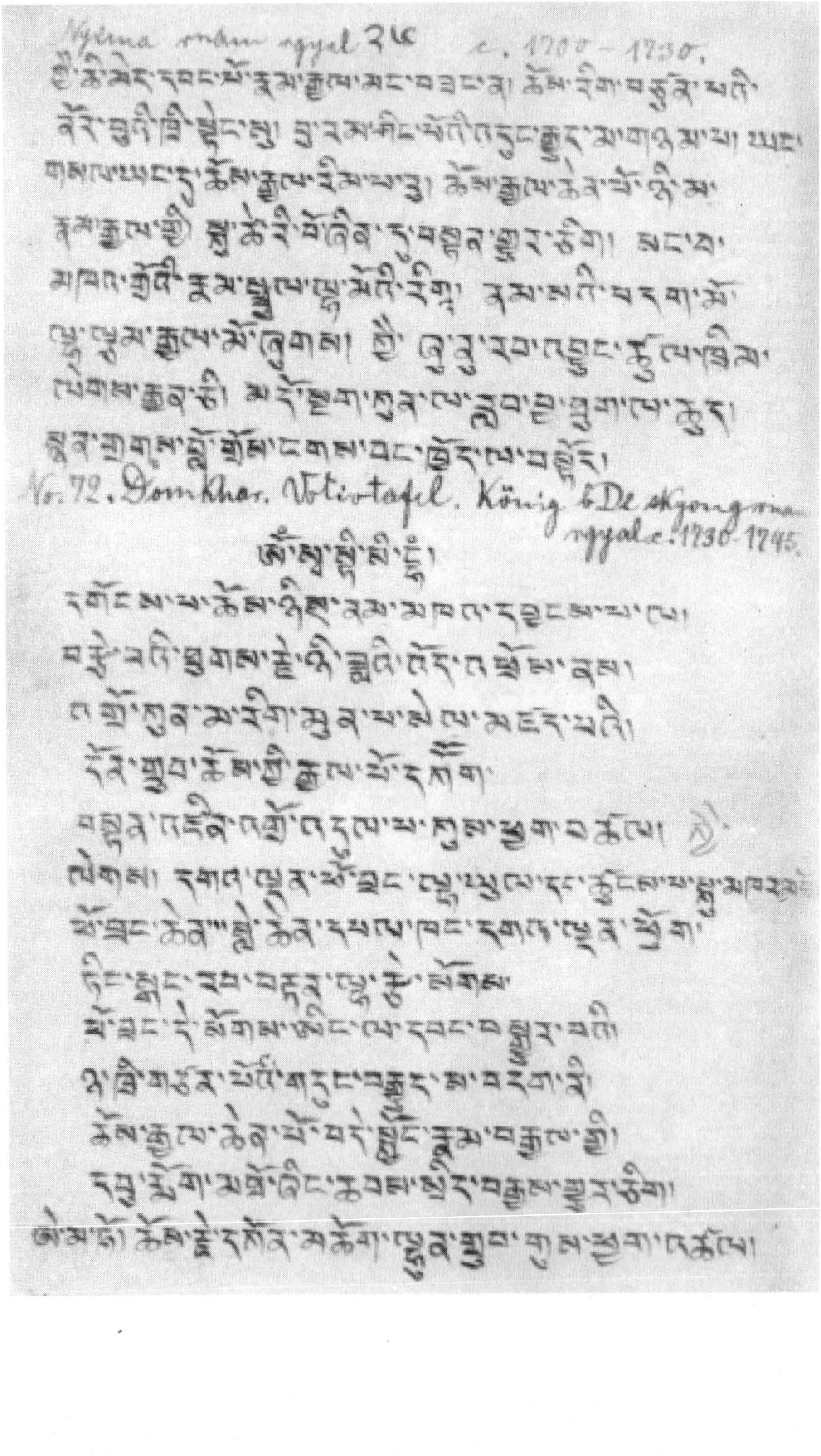
Nyima rnam rgyal 26 c. 1700–1730.

No. 72. Domkhar. Votivtafel. König bDe skyong rnam rgyal c. 1730–1745.

ཨོཾ་སྭ་སྟི་སིདྡྷཾ།

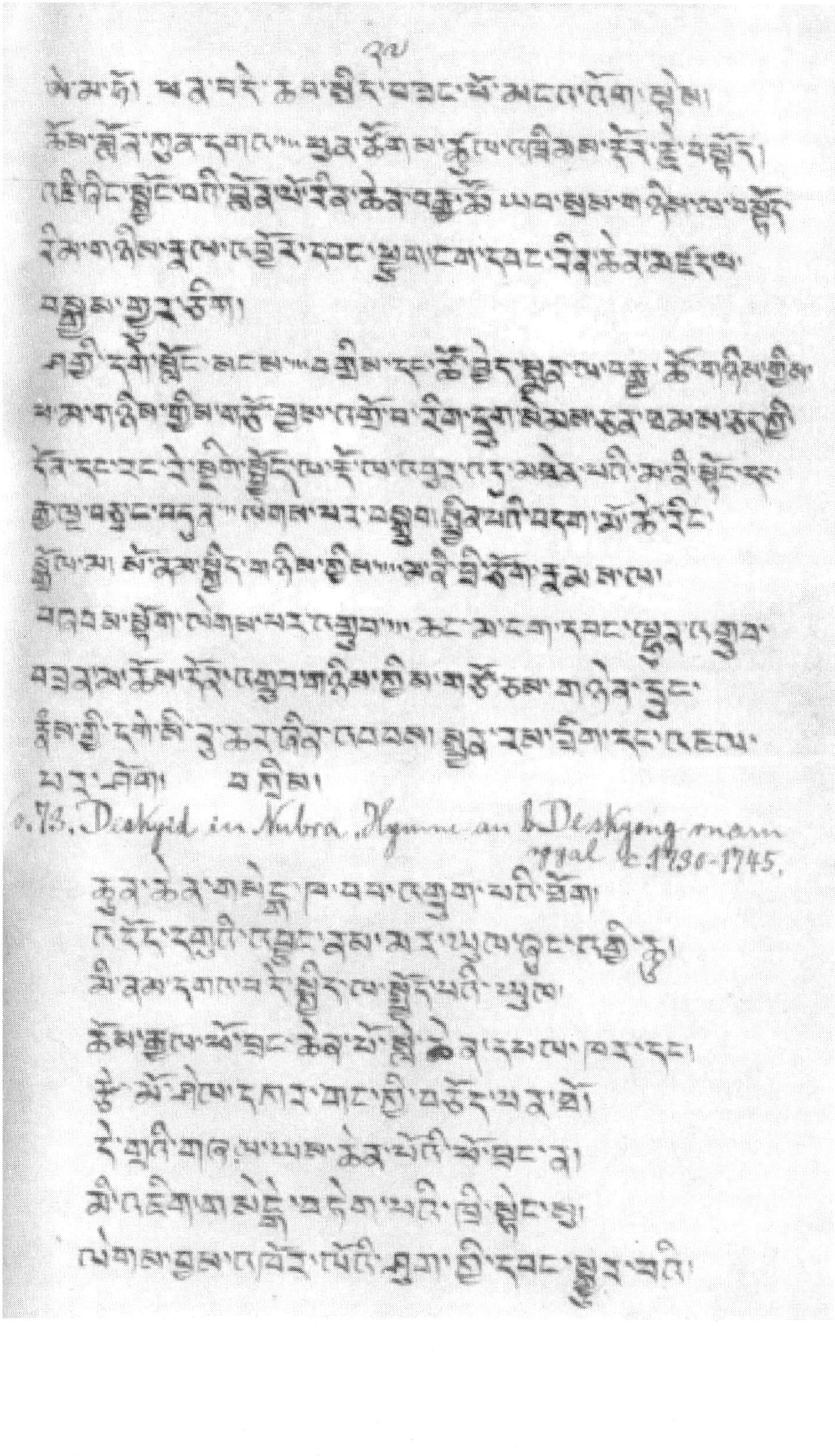
c. 73, Diskyid in Nubra, Hymne an bDeskyong rnam rgyal c. 1730-1745,

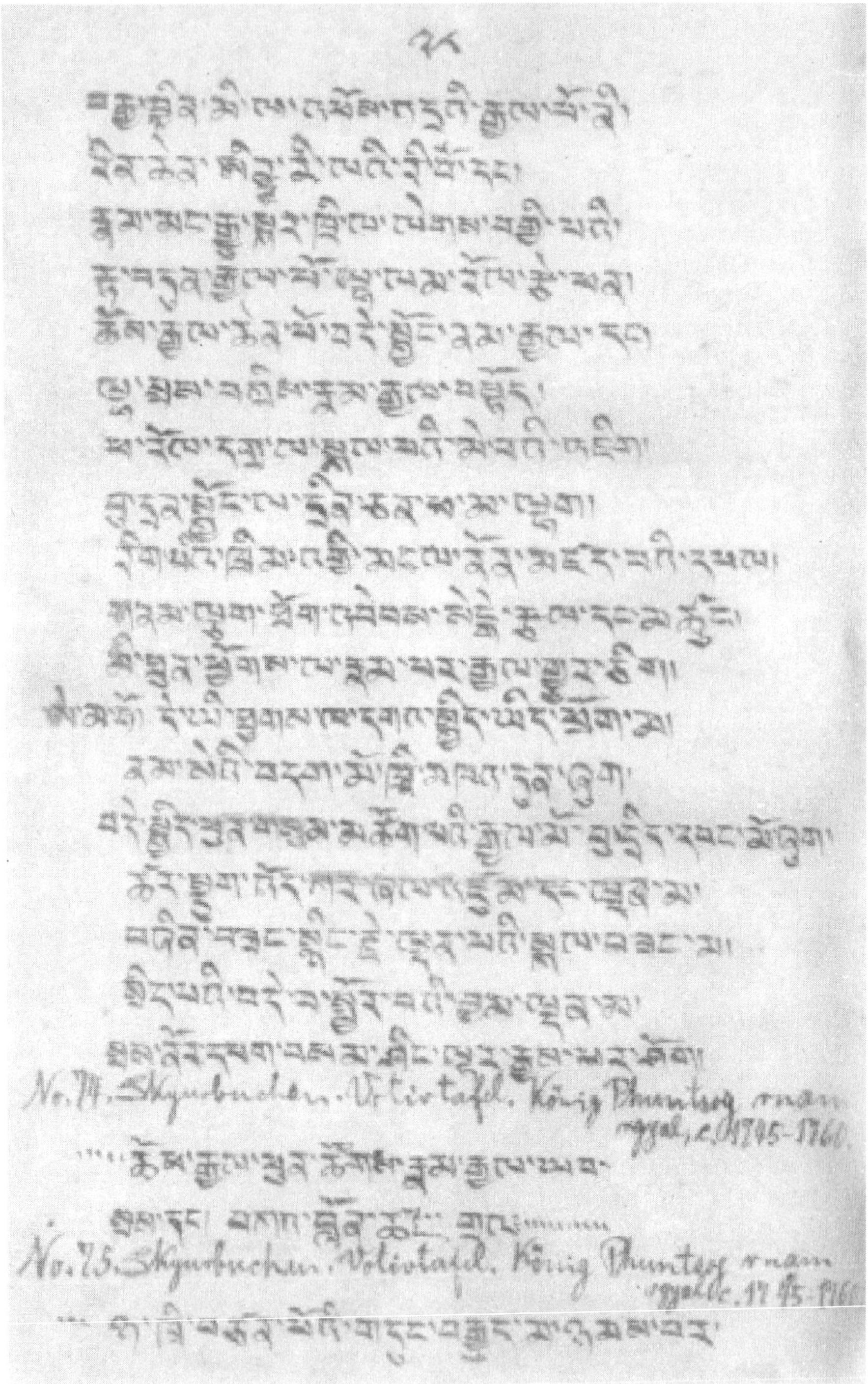
No. 74. Skyurbuchen. Votivtafel. König Phuntsog rnam rgyal, c. 1745-1760.
No. 75. Skyurbuchen. Votivtafel. König Phuntsog rnam rgyal c. 1745-1760

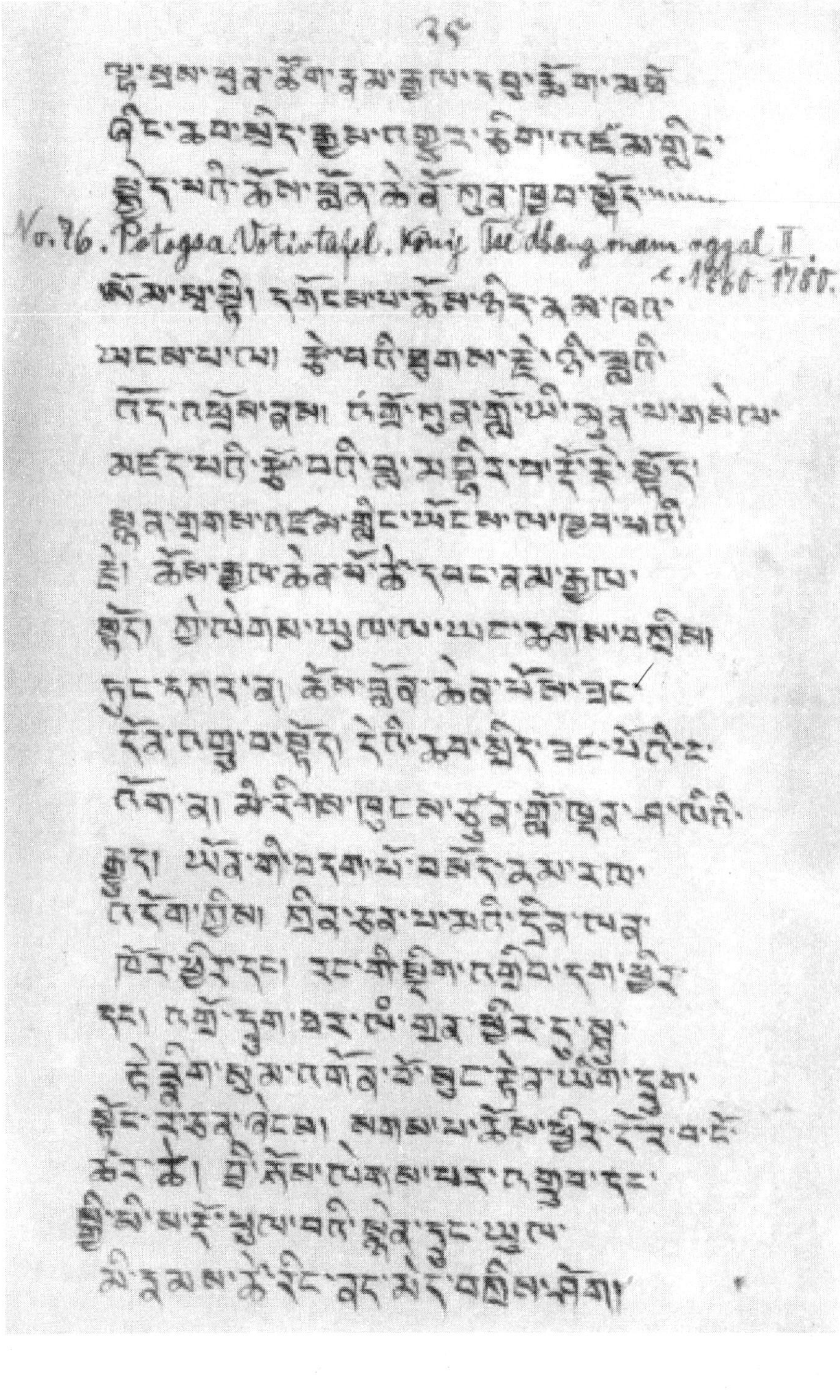

No. 76. Potogsa Votivtafel, König Tse dbang rnam rgyal II c. 1760-1780.

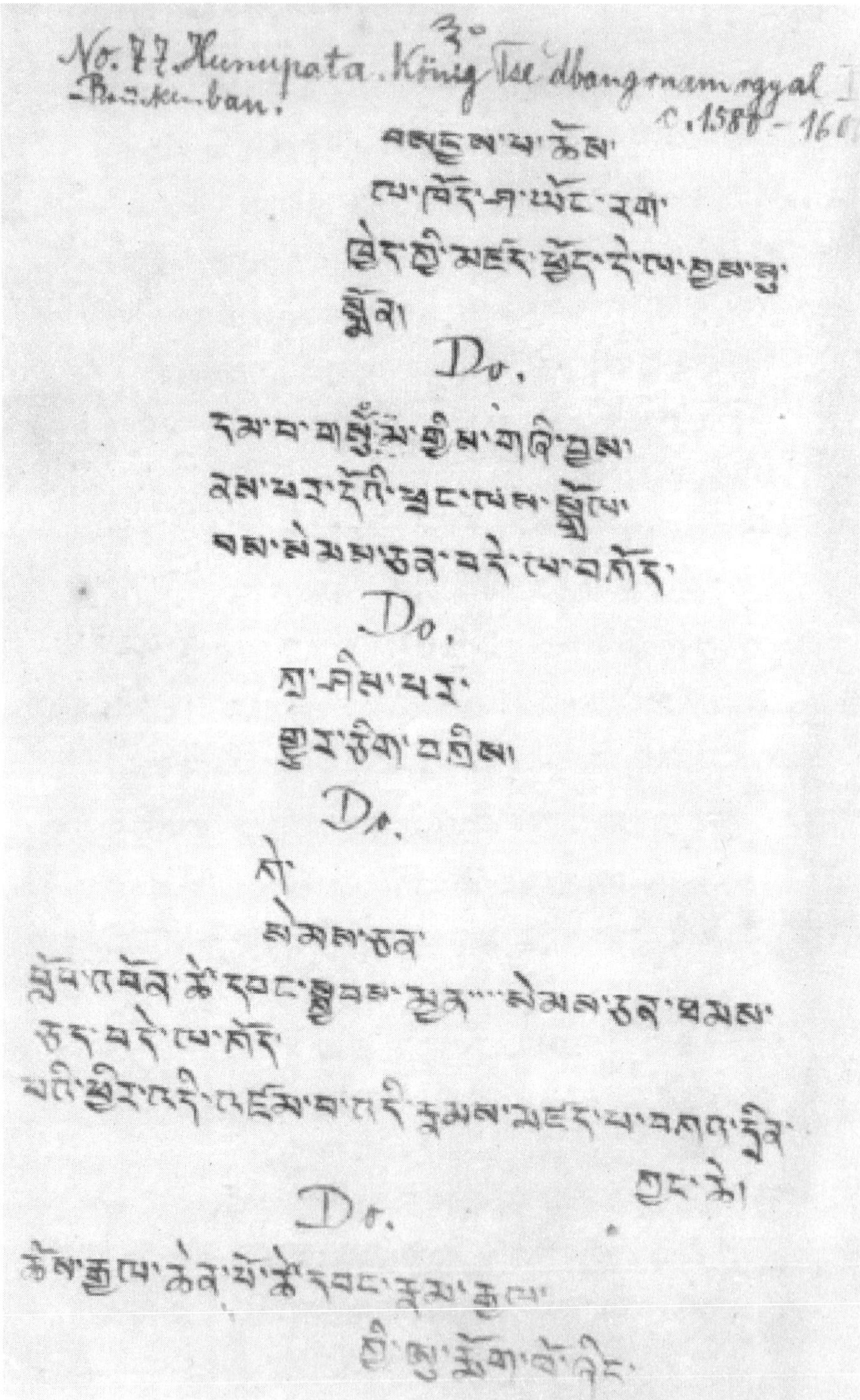

No. 77 Hunupata. König Tse dbang rnam rgyal I
-Bu... ban. c. 1588 - 160[illegible]

བཙྲམ་པ་ཆེས་
ལ་ཁྲིད་ཀ་ཡོང་ནག་
ཕྱེད་ཀྱི་མཛད་སྤྱོད་དེ་ལ་ཕྱུག་ཏུ་
སྨིན།

Do.

དམ་པ་གསུམ་གྱི་མ་གཞི་བྲམ་
ནམ་པར་དགེའི་སྤང་ལས་སྐྱེ་
བས་སེམས་ཅན་བདེ་ལ་བཀོད་

Do.

ཀུ་ཤིས་པར་
སྤྲུར་ཅིག་བགྲིས།

Do.

ཀེ་
སེམས་ཅན་
སྤྲུལ་འཁོན་ཚེ་དབང་སྤྱན་ཞུན་... སེམས་ཅན་ཐམས་
ཅད་བདེ་ལ་བཀོད་
པའི་ཕྱིར་འདི་འཛམ་གླིང་འདི་རྣམས་མཛད་པ་བཀའ་དྲིན་
ཀྱང་ཆེ།

Do.

ཆོས་རྒྱལ་ཆེན་པོ་ཚེ་དབང་རྣམ་རྒྱལ་
ཤི་ལུ་ཚོགས་ལོ་ཞིང་

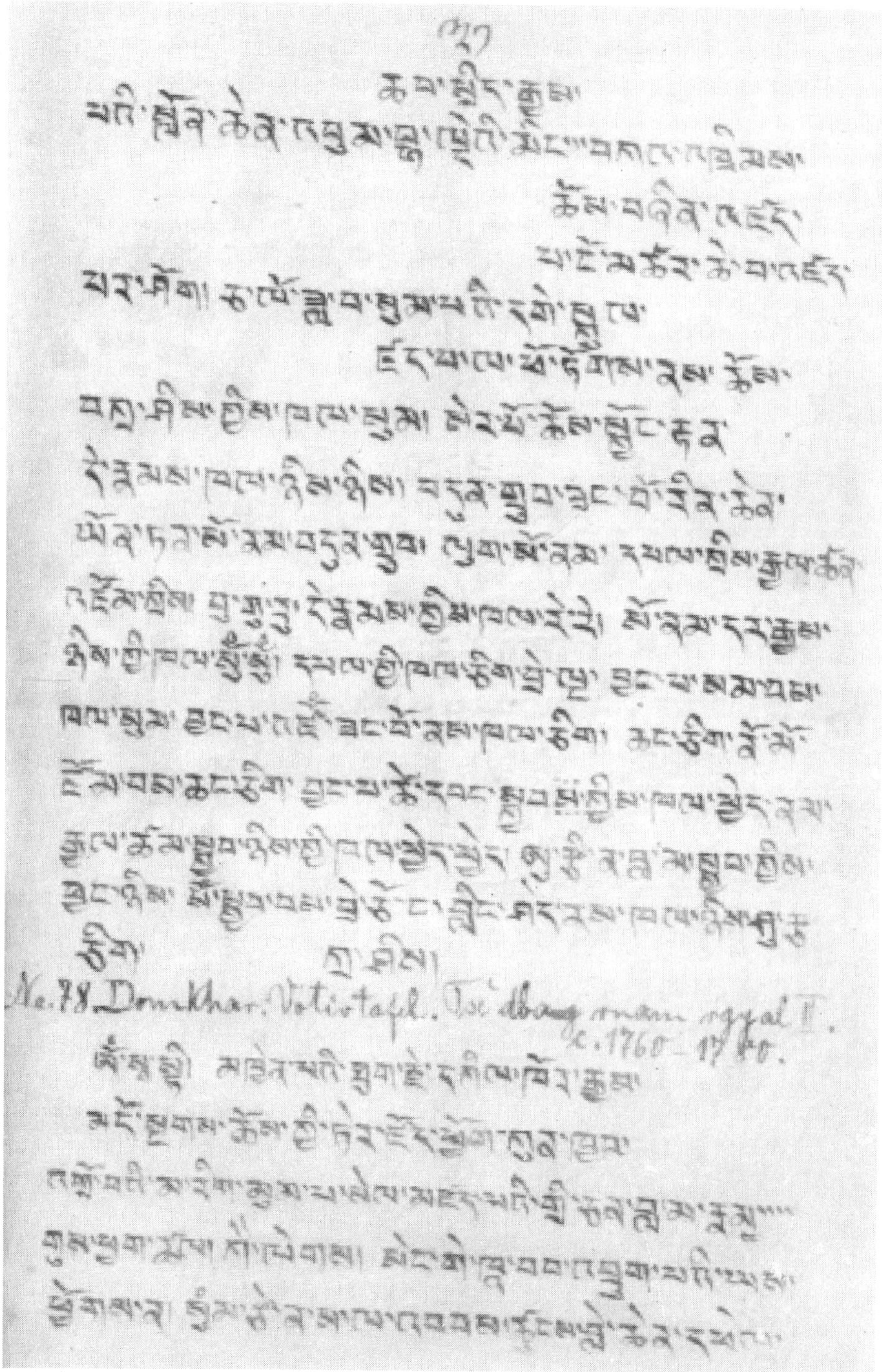
No. 78 Domkhar. Votivtafel. Tse dbang rnam rgyal II.
c. 1760–1780.

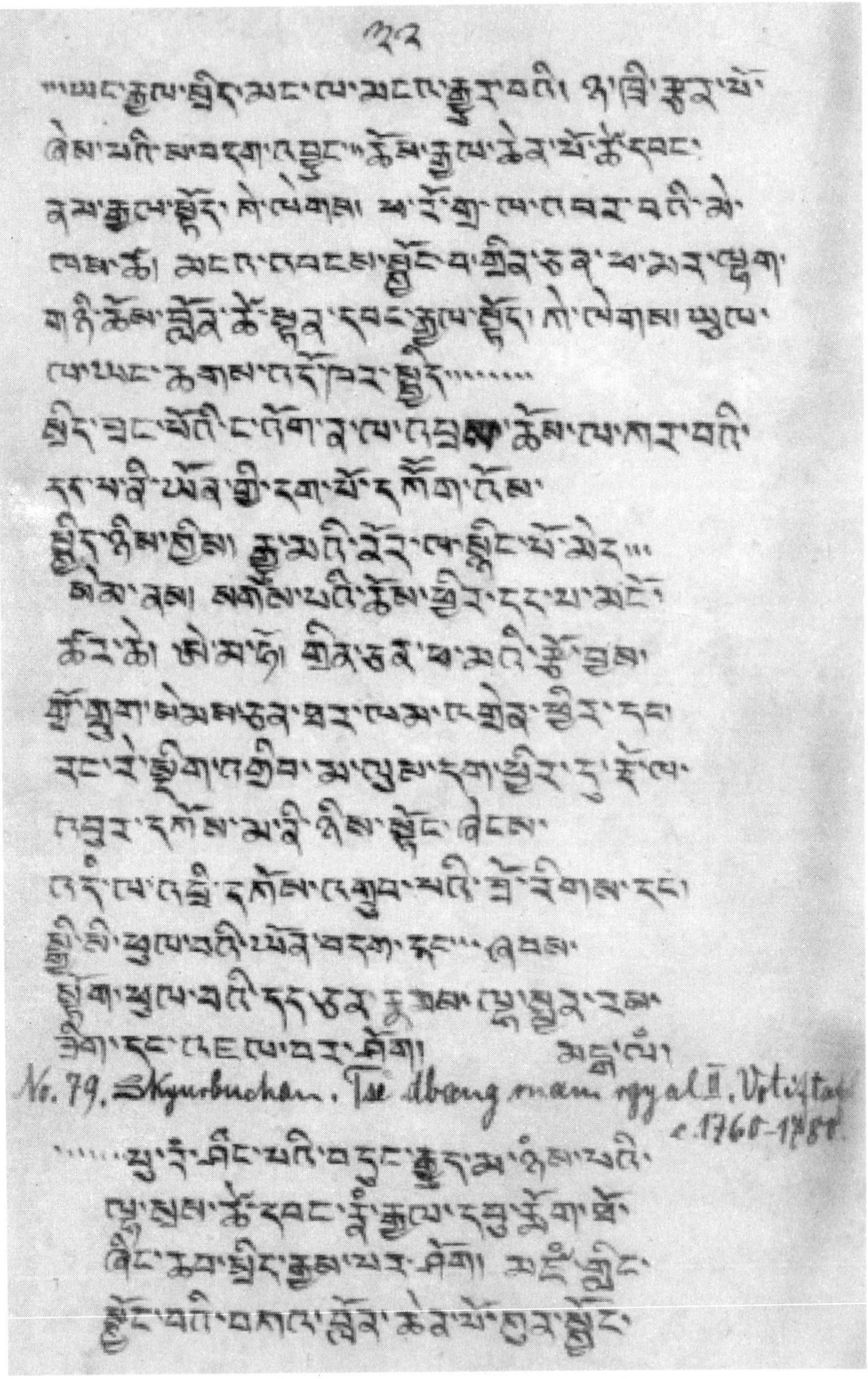
No. 79. Skyurbuchan. Tse dbang rnam rgyal II.
c. 1760-1781

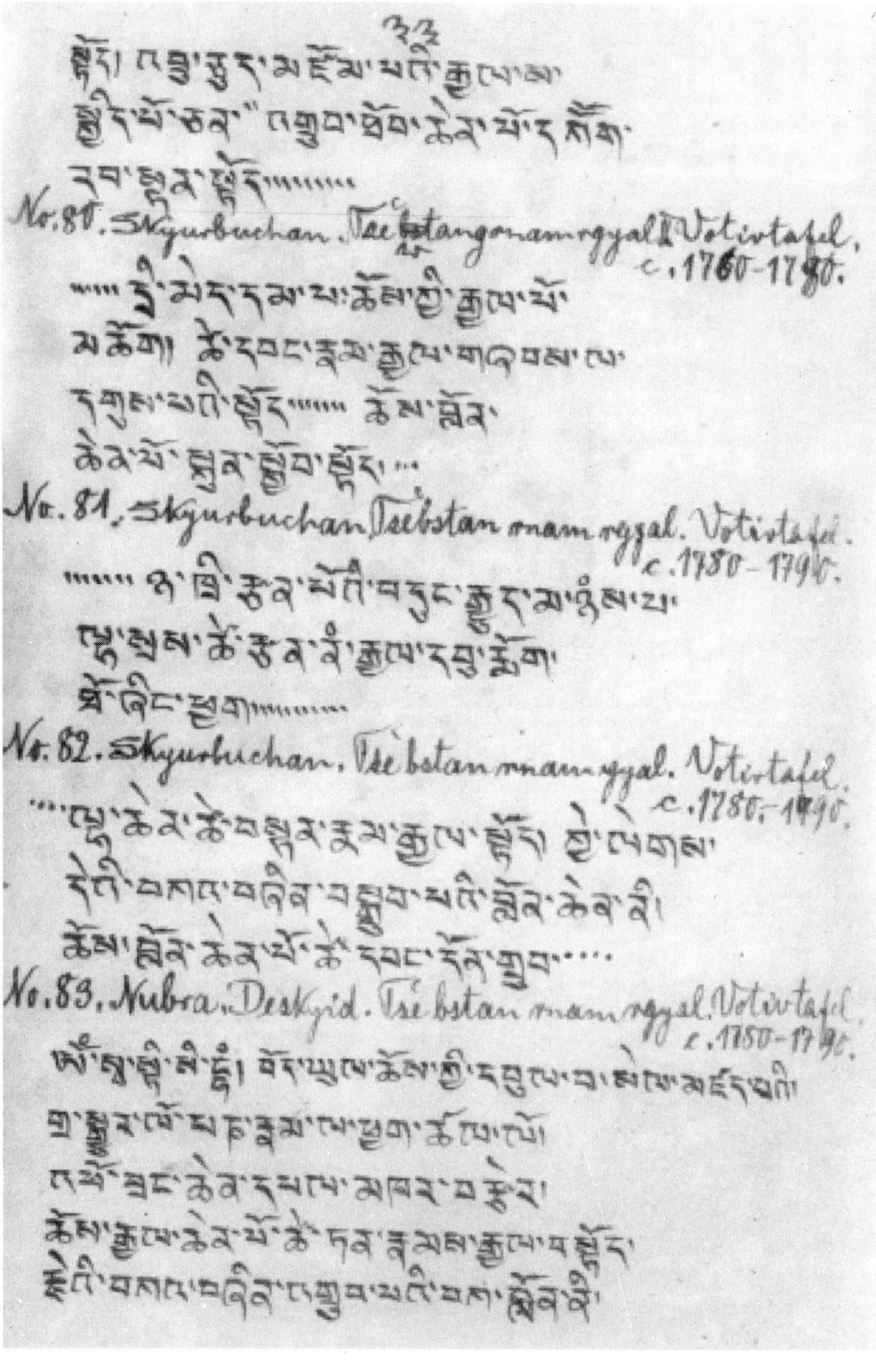
No. 80. Skyurbuchan. Tsebstan rnam rgyal. Votivtafel.
c. 1760-1790.
No. 81. Skyurbuchan Tsebstan rnam rgyal. Votivtafel.
c. 1780-1790.
No. 82. Skyurbuchan. Tse bstan rnam rgyal. Votivtafel.
c. 1780-1790.
No. 83. Nubra. Deskyid. Tse bstan rnam rgyal. Votivtafel.
c. 1780-1790.

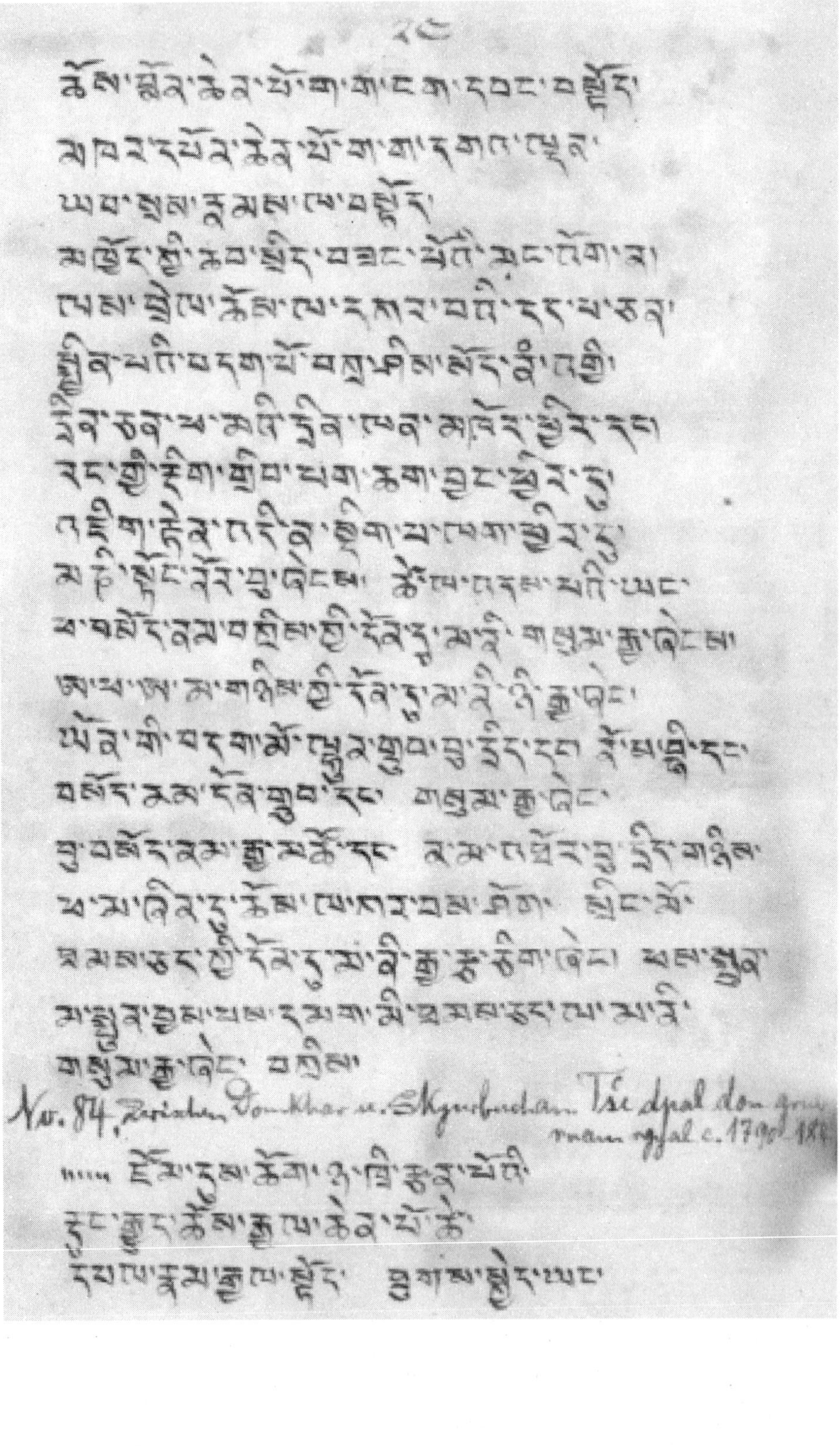
Nr. 84, Zwischen Domkhar u. Skyurbuchan. Tse dpal don grub rnam rgyal c. 1790–18..

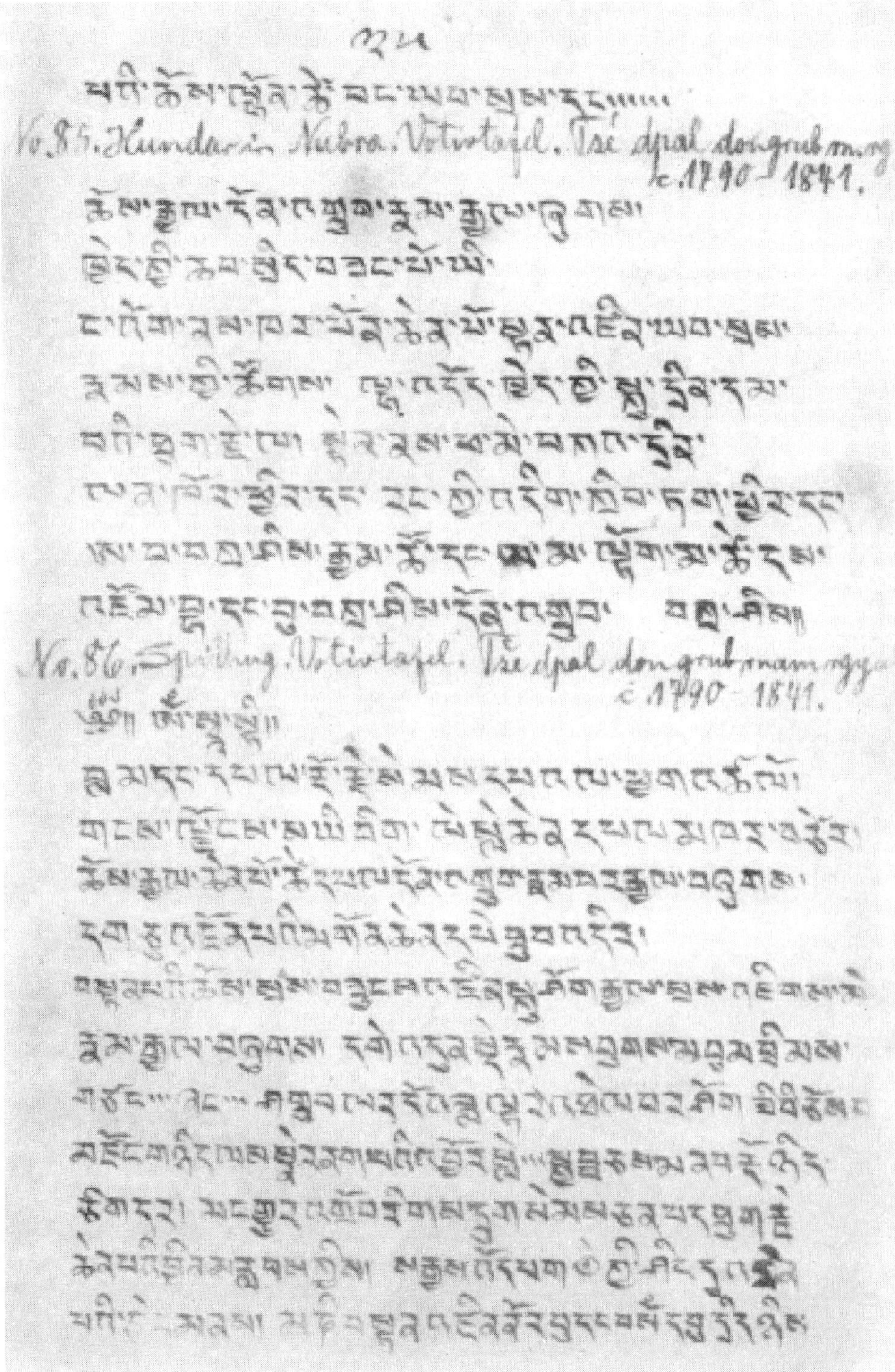

No. 85. Hundar in Nubra. Votivtafel. Tsé dpal don grub rnam rgy
c. 1790–1841.

No. 86. Spituk. Votivtafel. Tsé dpal don grub rnam rgya
c. 1790–1841.

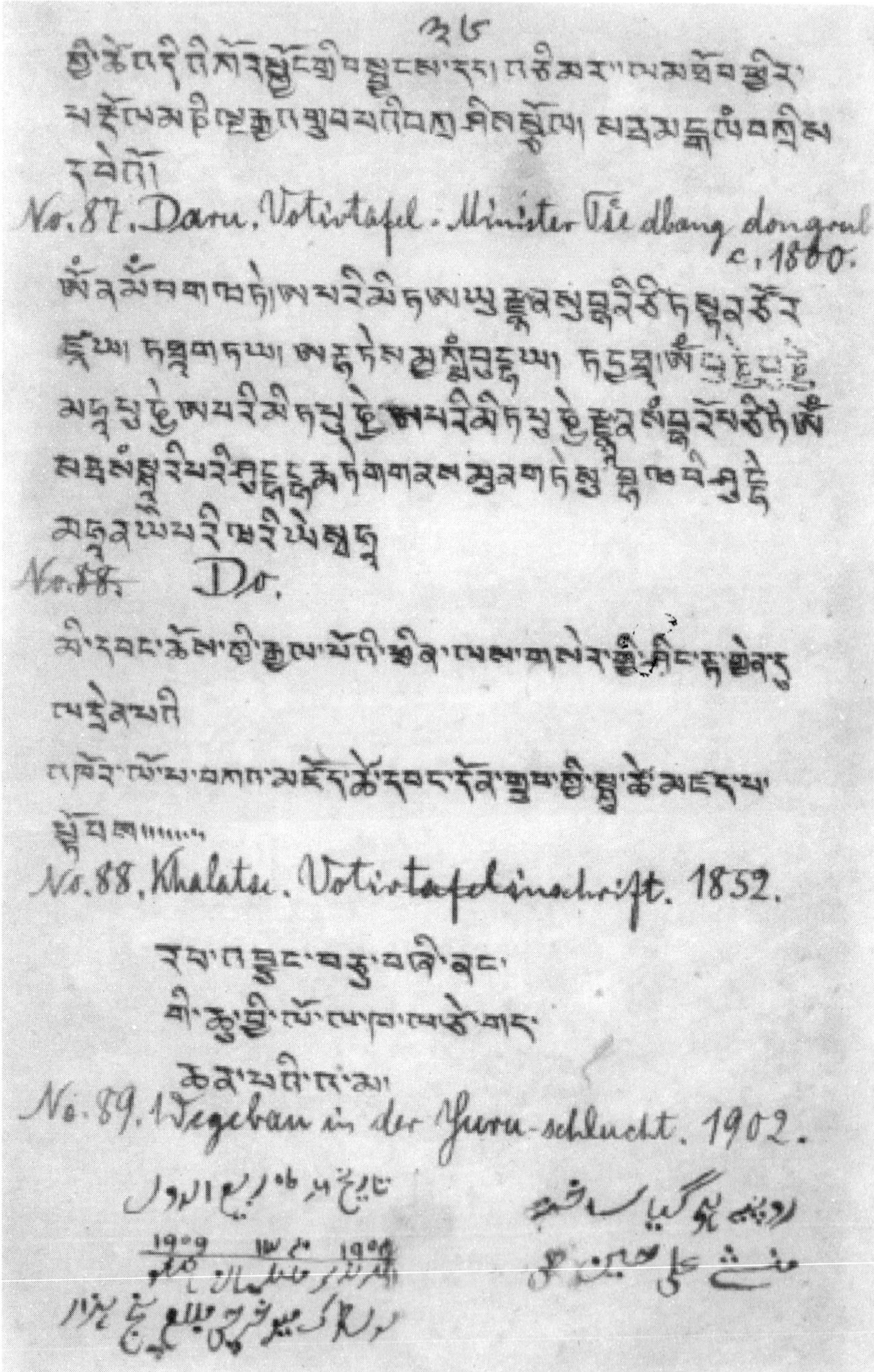
No. 87. Daru. Votivtafel. Minister Tse dbang dongrub c. 1800.
No. 88. Do.
No. 88. Khalatse. Votivtafelinschrift. 1852.
No. 89. Wegebau in der Yuru-schlucht. 1902.

B. *Second Collection of Tibetan Historical Inscriptions on Rock and Stone from West Tibet by A.H. Francke, 1907 (Zweite Sammlung tibetischer historischer Inschriften auf Felsen und Steinen in West Tibet von A.H. Francke, 1907)*

90. bTsanpo inschrift von Sheh unten Schleh(?) Wahrscheinlich Zeit Nyima mgon 975-1000 AD (bTsanpo Inscription from Sheh, King Nyima mgon, c. 975-1000 AD).

91. bTsanpo inschrift von Sheh beim Sman bla wabrscheinlich Zeit Nyima mgon c. 975-1000 AD (bTsanpo Inscription from Sheh near Sman bla, Nyima mgon c. 975-1000 AD).

92. Inschrifteines Tusken bKrashis(?) von Drangtse (Inscription of prince Tusken b Krashi (?) from rDranktse).

93. Alte Inschrift beim Goldbergwerk, Nyurla (Ancient inscription on gold bangle from Nyurla).

94. Alte Inschrift gegennber Hibti vielleichtc 1000 AD (Old inscription from opposite to Hibti, 1000 AD).

95. Bild inschrifter alten Kashmir kloster, Alchi c. 900-1200 AD (From Alchi, 900-1200 AD).

96. sTong pon inschrift von Alchi mkhargog wahrscheinlich 1000-1400 AD (Inscription from Alchi mkhar gog, i.e. ruined castle c. 1000-1400 AD).

97.-101. Desgleichen. (- do -)

102. Aufdem Vajrapani fels bei Daru, Konig Lhachen Kunga Namgyal, brilleicht der Lha rnam rgyal des rgyal rabls c. 1250 AD. Verbesserte Lesung(?) (From stone image of Vajrapani from Daru, King Lhachen Kunga Namgyal, Lha rnam rgyal, c. 1250 AD).

103. Konig rNamgyal mgonpo und ' aJam dbyangs rnamrgyal von Domkhar. c. 1560 AD (King rNamrgyal mgompo and 'aJambdyangs rnamrgyal from Domkhar, c. 1560 AD)

104. Unbekannter Konig Od den (Udden?), Mulbe (An unknown King Odde (Udden?), from Mulbe).

105. Votivinschrift der Adelsfamlie Skyab .. in Khalatse wabrscheinlich Zeit Sengge rNamrgyal (Votive inscription from Skyab Khalatse, probably of the time of Sengge rnamrgyal).

106. Votivinschrift auf Felsen Domkhar Konig bDe ldan rnam rgyal, c. 1620-1640 (Votive inscription on stone from Domkhar, king bDe ldan rnam rgyal, c. 1620-1640).

107. Votivinschrift Mani-mauer von sKyurbuchan. bDelegs rnam rgyal als Prinr c. 1640. (Votive inscription on Mani mural from Skyurbuchan, prince bDelegs rnam rgyal, 1640).

108. ...? Lama Mepham mgon an konig Statt zeit bDelegs rnam rgyal c. 1650. Nyrula (?, Lama Mepham of the period of Delegs rnam rgyal, c. 1650, Nyrula).

109. Votivinschrift Unbekannter Furst Rinchen rnam rgyal Skyurbuchan (Votive inscription, prince Rinchen rnam rgyal, Skyurbuchan).
110. Aus der wan inschrift im alten Basjos (?) Schlop, zeit Sengge rnamrgyal c. 1590-1620 (Inscription of the period of Sengge rnamgyal, c. 1590-1620).
111. Votivinschrift Mani mauer in Khalatse Konig Nyima rnamgyal c. 1680-1720 AD (Votive inscription from mani mural in Khalatse, King Nyima rnam rgyal, c. 1680-1720 AD).
112. Votivinschrift Mani mauer in Skyurbuchan. Konig Nyima rnam rgyal. c. 1680-1720 AD (Votive inscription from Mani mural, Skyurbuchan, King Nyima rnam rgyal, c. 1680-1720).
113. Hymne (?) an Phunthsog rnamrgyal Mani mauer in Mangyu c. 1740-1760 (Hymn, Phuntsog rnam rgyal, on mani in Mangyu, c. 1740-60).
114. Votivinzchrift von Skyurbuchan Mani mauer Konig Phuntsog rnamrgyal c. 1740-1760 AD. (Votive inscription from Skyurbuchan on mani, king Phuntsog rnam rgyal, c. 1740-60).
115. Votivinschrift Mani-mauer in Skyurbuchan, Konig Thse dbang rnam rgyal II, c. 1760-80 (Votive inscription, mani in Skyurbuchan, king Thse dbang rnam rgyal II, c. 1760-80).
116. Aus der votivinschrift Mani-mauer in Nyurla. Konig Tshe bstan rnam rgyal c. 1780-90 (Votive inscription from Nyurla, on Mani, king Thse bstan rnam rgyal, c. 1780-90).
117. Votivinschrift Mani-mauer in Skyurbuchan, Konig Tshe bstan rnam rgyal c. 1780-90 (Votive inscription from Skyurbuchan, on Mani, king Thse bstan rnam rgyal, c. 1780-90).
118. Votivinschrift von Domkhar, Konig Thsedpal dongrub Dorje rnam rgyal c. 1790-1841. (Votive inscription, from Domkhar, king Thsedpal dongrub Dorje rnam rgyal, c. 1790-1841).
119. Votivinschrift Mani mauer in Skyurbuchan. Konig Tshe dpal dongrub dorje rnam rgyal, c. 1790-1841. (Votive inscription on Mani in Skyurbuchan, king Tshe dpal don grub rdorje rnam rgyal, c. 1790-1841).
120. Wegebau inschrift in der Lama Yuru schlucht, 1902 (Inscription from Lama Yuru, concerning battle of 1902).
121. Votivinschrift der noch umbe Kannten Minister bSod rnams dpal ‘abyor, Sheh bei...mchod ten (Votive inscription from near Stupa, Minister bSod rnam dpal abyor, from Sheh).
122. Inschrift uber Baumpflanrung (?) der Dogra offiziers Farman Khalatse.. 1905. (Orders of the Dogra Officers, Khalatse 1905).

Die folgenden Inschriften sind von Lahoul und Chamba bis Triloknath (Inscriptions on stone from Lahoul and Chamba, from Triloknath).

123. Inschrift auf den Felsskulpturen von Khardang. Wahrscheinlich 12 tes Jahrhundert Konig Lhachen Utpala (?) {Inscription on stone sculpture from Kardang of 12th century, king Lhachen Utpala (?)}.

124. Uberrest der Inschrift auf der linien Skulptur von Kyelang Wahrscheinlich 12 tes Jahrhundert (Inscription on a sculpture from Kyelang, about 12th century).

125. Alte buddhistsche Inschriften auf den Felsen von Yurnad (An ancient Buddhist inscription from village Yurnad).

126. Alte Inschrift bei den verlassenen Dorf oberhalb Kyor (Ancient inscription from an abandoned place above Kyor).

127. Inschrift der Fursten. Hayar von Lahoul. Zeitgenesle des Lahoul Tshedbang rnamgyal und des Konigs von Kulu Parbad Sing c. 1700-1730 AD bei zhugnur (Inscription from Hayar in Lahoul about prince Tshedbang - rnamrgyal of Lahoul, and king from Kulu Parbat Singh, 1700-1730 AD).

128. Besbrichsigle (?) aber nicht ausgefuhrt votiv inschrift Bauines mchod rten. ......Besitz desen Fursten Amar Chand von Lahoul. Zeit des Fortens Thsedbang rnamgyal, und des Konigs von Kulu Parbad Singh c. 1700-1730 (Prince Tshedbang rnamgyal of Lahul and king Parbat Singh of Kullu, c. 1700-30).

129. Anrufung des Lama Ngag dbang rnam rgyal (c. 1650) Mani mauer bei Gandola (Lama Ngabang rNam rgyal, c. 1650, Mani inscription from Gandola).

130. Anrufung des unbekaunten Lama Padma siddhi. Mani mauer bei Dubchling (Mani inscription from Tubchiling, Lama padma siddhi).

131. Grup an den Lama Ngag dbang rnamgyal (c. 1650) Mani mauer Bei Tangti (Lama Ngabang rNam rgyal, c. 1650, Mani inscription from Tangti).

132. Anrufung des Lama Ngagdbang rnamrgyal (c. 1650) alter mchod rten bei Gandola (Lama Ngabang rnam rgyal, c. 1650, from Gandola).

133. Grupan den umbekaunten Lama Rinchen dpal bzang Mani mauer bei Biling (Lama Rinchen dPal bzang, Mani inscription from Billing).

134. Inschrift der Unbikamten Konig in (von Kulu?) Dzivanti – beim Gandola – Kloster Fels (Inscription on rock from Gandola, Rani Zivanti from Kullu).

135. Aus der Votivinschrift auf der Mani mauer bie Khangsar tse. Prinz Pritim (Riddhi – Partem?) Sing von Kulu (Wahrocheninlich 17 tes Jahrhundert) (Votive inscription for king Pritim Singh from Kullu 17th century).

136. Anrufung (?) des Lama bDeba rgyamtsho. Mani mauer maner bei Gozang (Inscription on Mani stone from Gozan of Lama bDeba rgyamtsho).

137. Aus der Inschrift bei dem Mani in Lod. Unbekunnter Minister ... Tshering. (Inscription on Mani in Lot, Minister Tshering).

138. Inschrift des Furshen d Ngos drub rnam rgyal (von Zanskar) am Wegenach Triloknath, bei Margul, Mani mauer, Vielleicht 18 tes Jahrhunderte (Inscription Ngos drub rnam rgyal (Zanskar) on way to Triloknath 18th century).

139. Inschrift des Brahmanen Ganga Ram in Hobzdadi von Triloknath Villeicht 18 tes Jahrhunderte (Inscription, brahman Ganga Ram from Triloknath 18th Century).

140. Votivinschrift Mani mauer bei Bog. Kulu Konig Bhirkhyim (Bakermant) Sing (c. 1790-1810) [Votive inscription on Mani stone from village Bog, Kullu king Vikram Singh, c. 1790-1810].

141. Votivinschrift Mani mauer bei Bog. Lahoul furst Dharma – Sengge Wahrscheinlich c. 1790-1810 (Votive inscription on Mane stone from village Bog, Lahoul, Dharma Sengge, c. 1790-1810).

142. Votivinschrift bei Tangti. Wahrscheinlich 19 tes Jahrhunderte (Votive inscription from Tangti 19th century).

143. Felsinchrift auf der Tangti eben. 18 tes oder 19 tes Jahrhunderte (Inscription from Tangti, 18th-19th century).

144. Inschriften von Triloknath pilgrim aus She-chushod u Lahoul (Halb Bunan) Oberhalb der Barik Wahrscheinlich 19 tes Jahrhunderte (Inscription from Triloknath by a pilgrim from Sheh-Chushood).

145. Inschrift eines Triloknath pilgrims. Bei Triloknath 19 tes Jahrhunderte (Inscriptions by the pilgrims to Triloknath, near the village Triloknath, 19th century).

Second Collection of
Tibetan Historical Inscriptions
on
Rock and Stone from
Western Tibet.

Zweite Sammlung
tibetischer historischer Inschriften
auf Felsen und Steinen in
West Tibet.

Von
A. H. Francke.

Auflage: 40 Stü
1907.

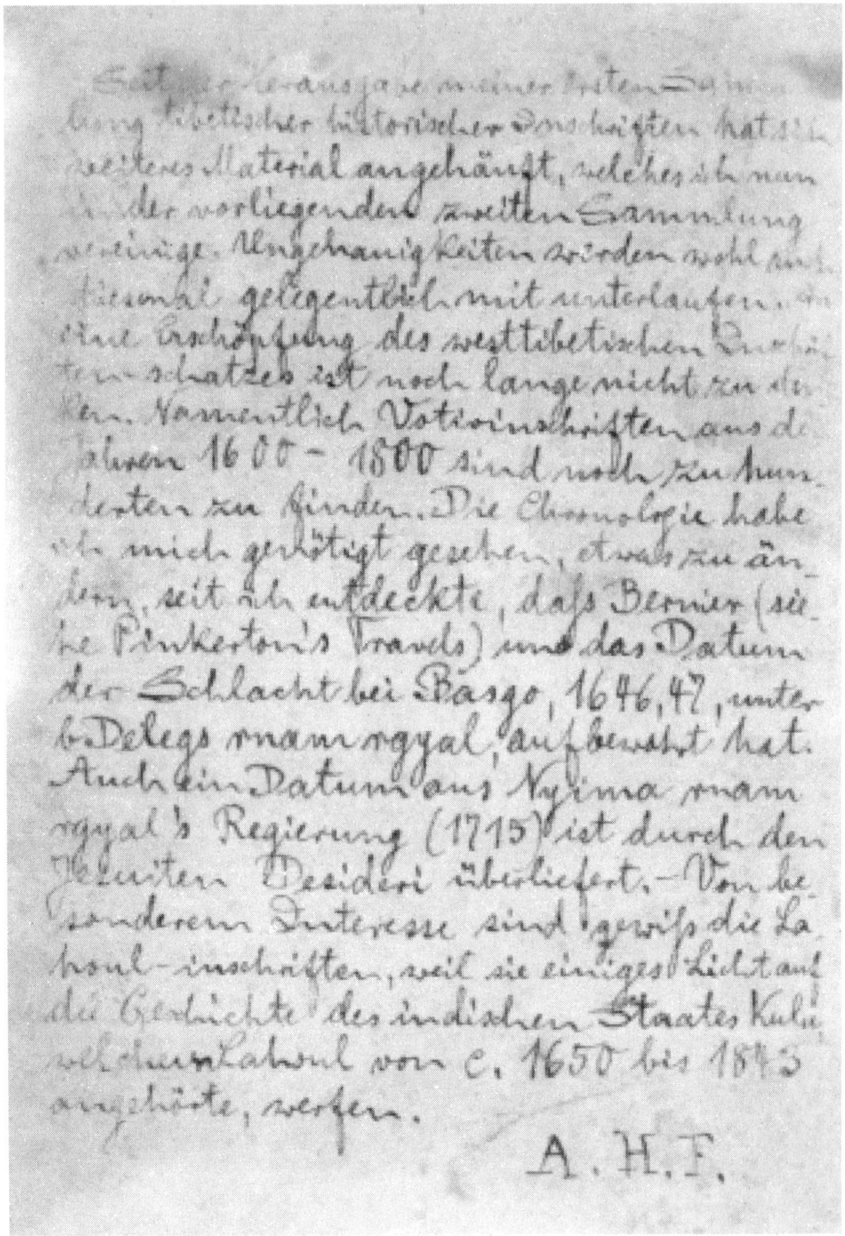

Seit der Herausgabe meiner ersten Sammlung tibetischer historischer Inschriften hat sich weiteres Material angehäuft, welches ich nun in der vorliegenden zweiten Sammlung vereinige. Ungenauigkeiten werden wohl auch diesmal gelegentlich mit unterlaufen. An eine Erschöpfung des westtibetischen Inschriftenschatzes ist noch lange nicht zu denken. Namentlich Votivinschriften aus den Jahren 1600 – 1800 sind noch zu hunderten zu finden. Die Chronologie habe ich mich genötigt gesehen, etwas zu ändern, seit ich entdeckte, daß Bernier (siehe Pinkerton's Travels) uns das Datum der Schlacht bei Basgo, 1646,47, unter bDelegs rnam rgyal, aufbewahrt hat. Auch ein Datum aus Nyima rnam rgyal's Regierung (1715) ist durch den Jesuiten Desideri überliefert. – Von besonderem Interesse sind gewiß die Lahoul-inschriften, weil sie einiges Licht auf die Geschichte des indischen Staates Kulu, welchem Lahoul von c. 1650 bis 1843 angehörte, werfen.

A. H. F.

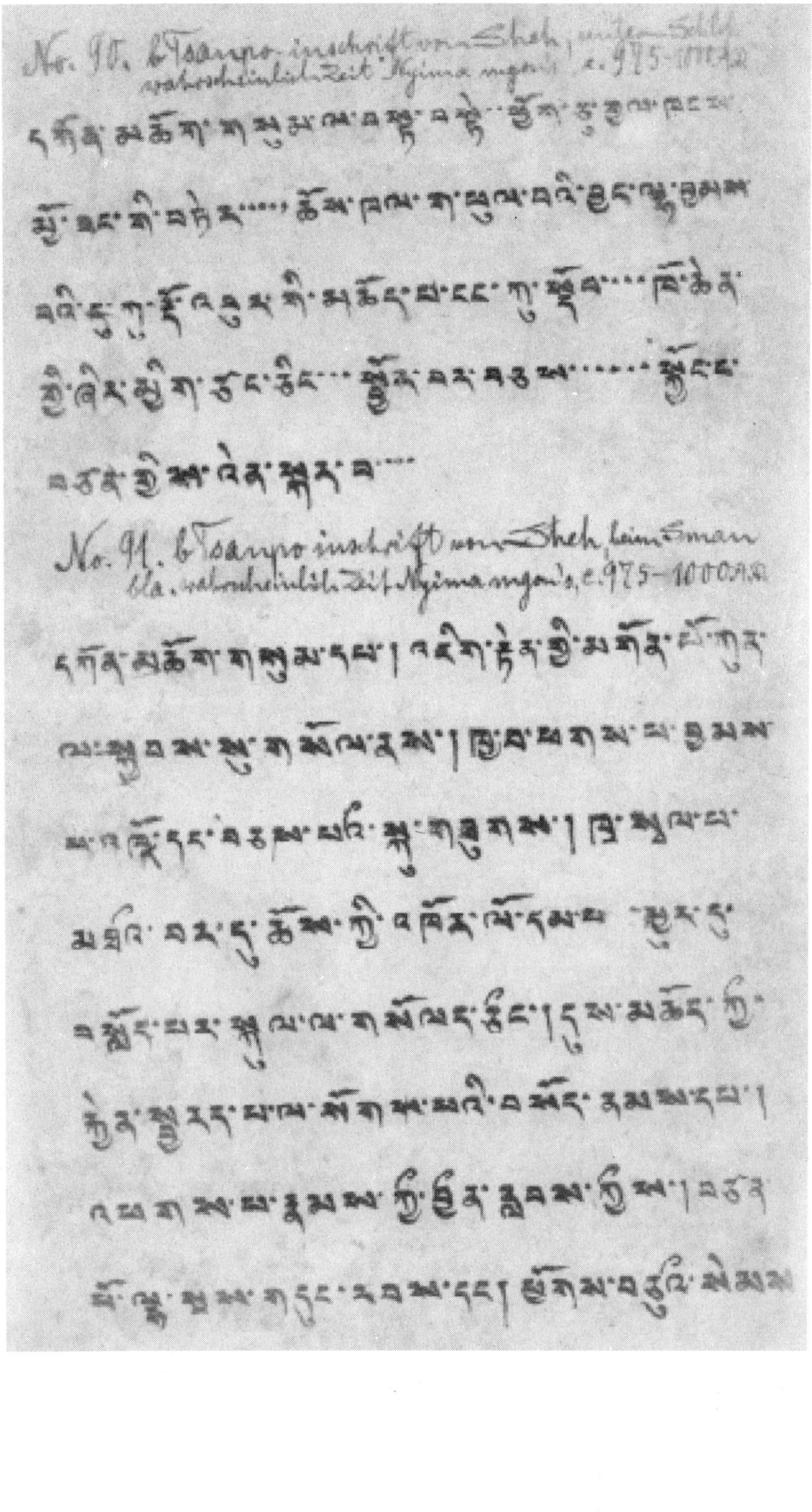

No. 90. bTsanpo-inschrift von Sheh, unterm Schloss wahrscheinlich Zeit Nyima mgon's, c. 975-1000 A.D.

དཀོན་མཆོག་གསུམ་ལ་བསྟོད་བསྔོ་... སྒྲོག་ཏུ་རྒྱལ་ཁང་ལ

སྦྱོ་ཞང་གི་བཏེར·····, ཆོས་ཁལ་གི་སྤྱལ་བའི་ཕྲེང་ལྷ་ཐམས

ཞའི་ཧྭ་ཀྱ་རྗེ་འབྱུར་གི་མཆོད་པ་ངང་ཀུ་སྟོབ····ཁྲི་ཆེན

ཀྱི་ཞིར་སྤྱི་ག་ཙང་རྩིང···སྤྱོར་བར་ཞུ་ཙས······སྤྱང་ང

བཙན་གྱི་ཟས་འཞེན་སྐྱར་བ····

No. 91. bTsanpo inschrift von Sheh beim Sman bla. wahrscheinlich Zeit Nyima mgon's, c. 975-1000 A.D.

དཀོན་མཆོག་གསུམ་དཔལ། འཇིག་རྟེན་གྱི་མགོན་པོ་ཀུན

ལ་སྐྱབས་སུ་གསོལ་ནས། ཁྲོ་བོ་མཁས་པ་ལ་ཐམས

ས་བརྗོད་དང་ཞུ་ཙམ་པའི་སྐུ་གཟུགས། ཁྲི་སྐུལ་ལ

མཐའ་བར་དུ་ཆོས་ཀྱི་འཁོར་ལོ་དམ་པ་ སྐུར་དུ

བསྒོད་པར་སྐྱ་ལ་ལ་གསོལ་བ་རྩིང། དུས་མཆོད་ཀྱི

རྐྱེན་སྐྱེ་རིད་པ་ཁལ་སོག་ས་མའི་བསོད་ནམས་དཔལ།

འཕགས་པ་ཐམས་ཀྱི་ཐྲིན་རླབས་ཀྱིས། བཙན

པོ་ལྷ་སྲས་གདུང་རབས་དང། ཕྱོགས་བཅུའི་སེམས

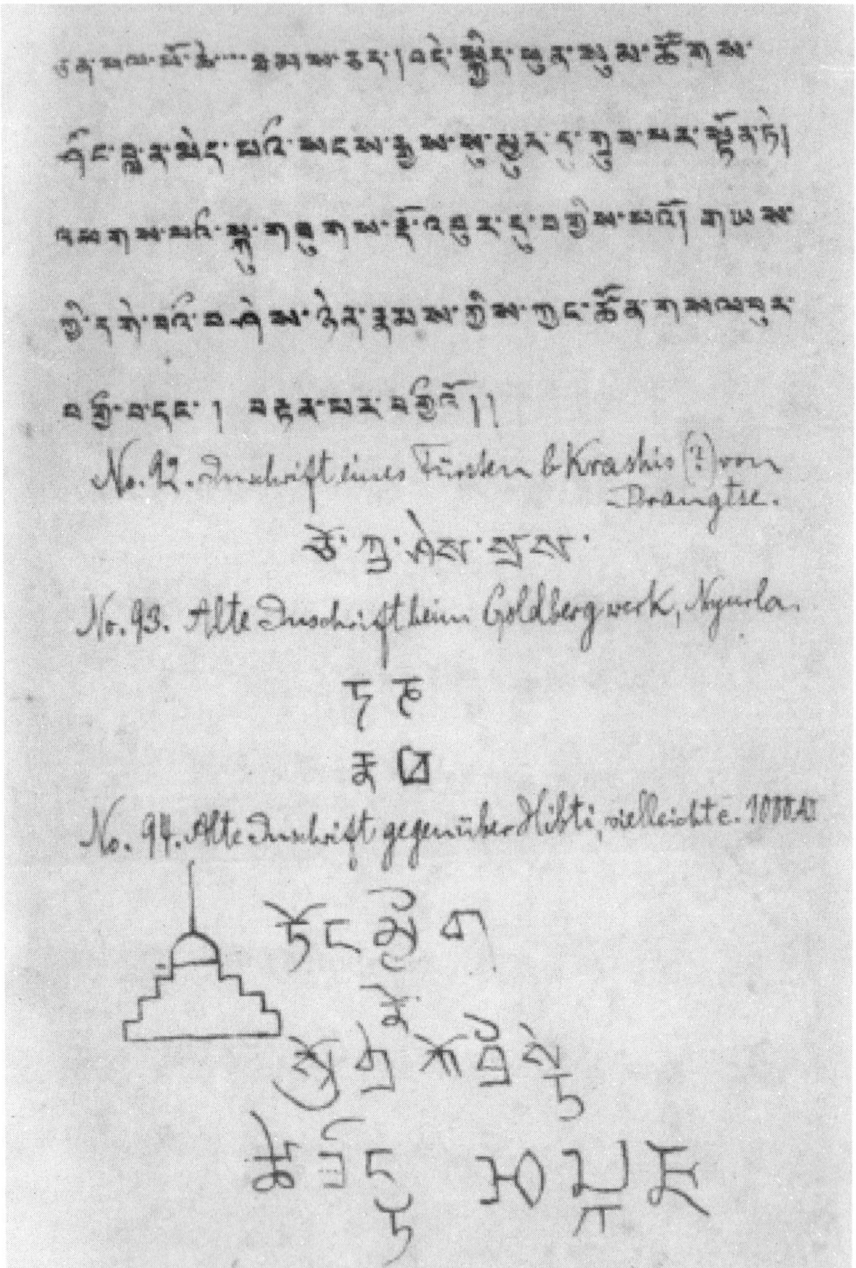

No. 92. Inschrift eines Fürsten b Krashis (?) von Drangtse.

No. 93. Alte Inschrift beim Goldbergwerk, Nyurla.

No. 94. Alte Inschrift gegenüber Hilti, vielleicht c. 1000 AD

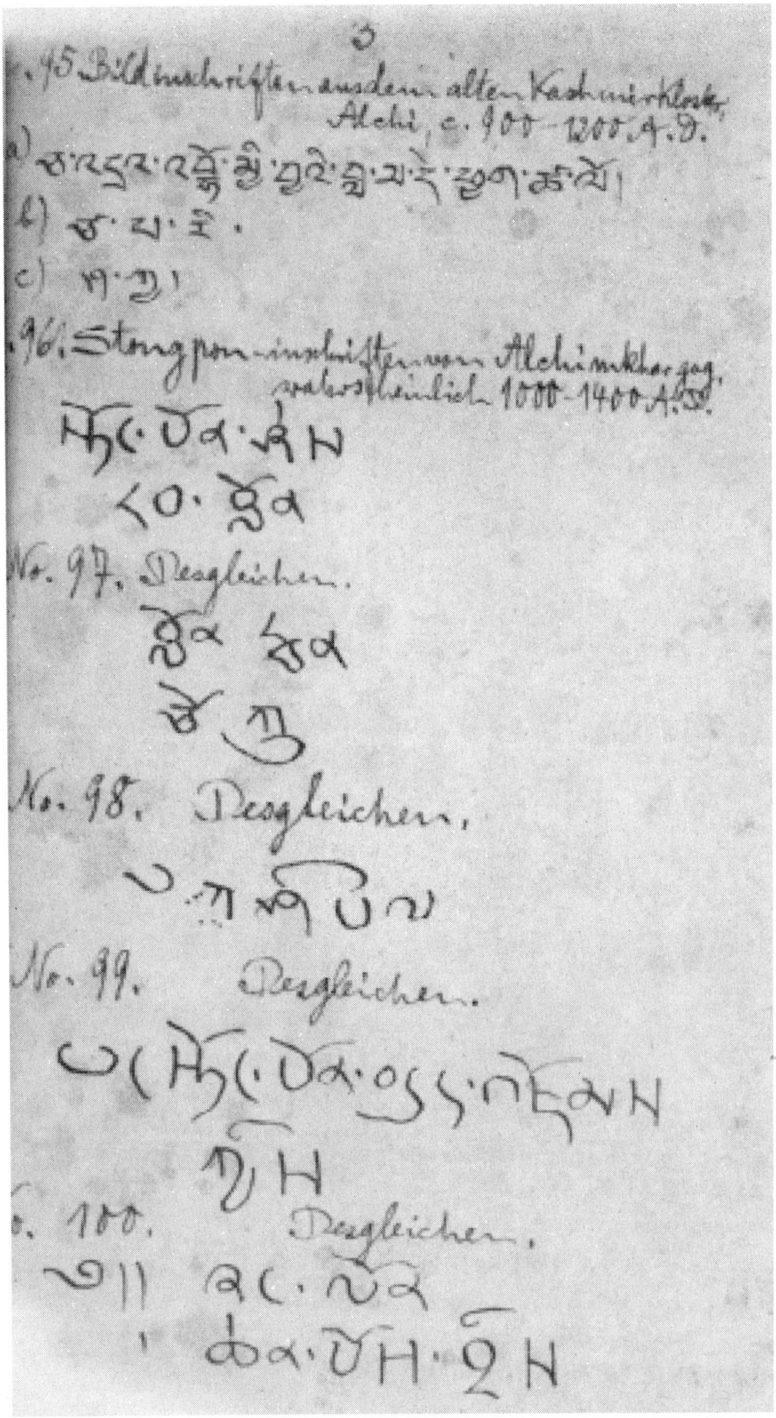

3

[No]. 95. Bildinschriften aus dem alten Kaschmirkloster, Alchi, c. 900–1200 A.D.

a) [illegible]

b) [illegible]

c) [illegible]

[No]. 96. Stongpon-inschriften von Alchi mkhar gog, wahrscheinlich 1000–1400 A.D.

[illegible]

No. 97. Desgleichen.

[illegible]

No. 98. Desgleichen.

[illegible]

No. 99. Desgleichen.

[illegible]

[N]o. 100. Desgleichen.

[illegible]

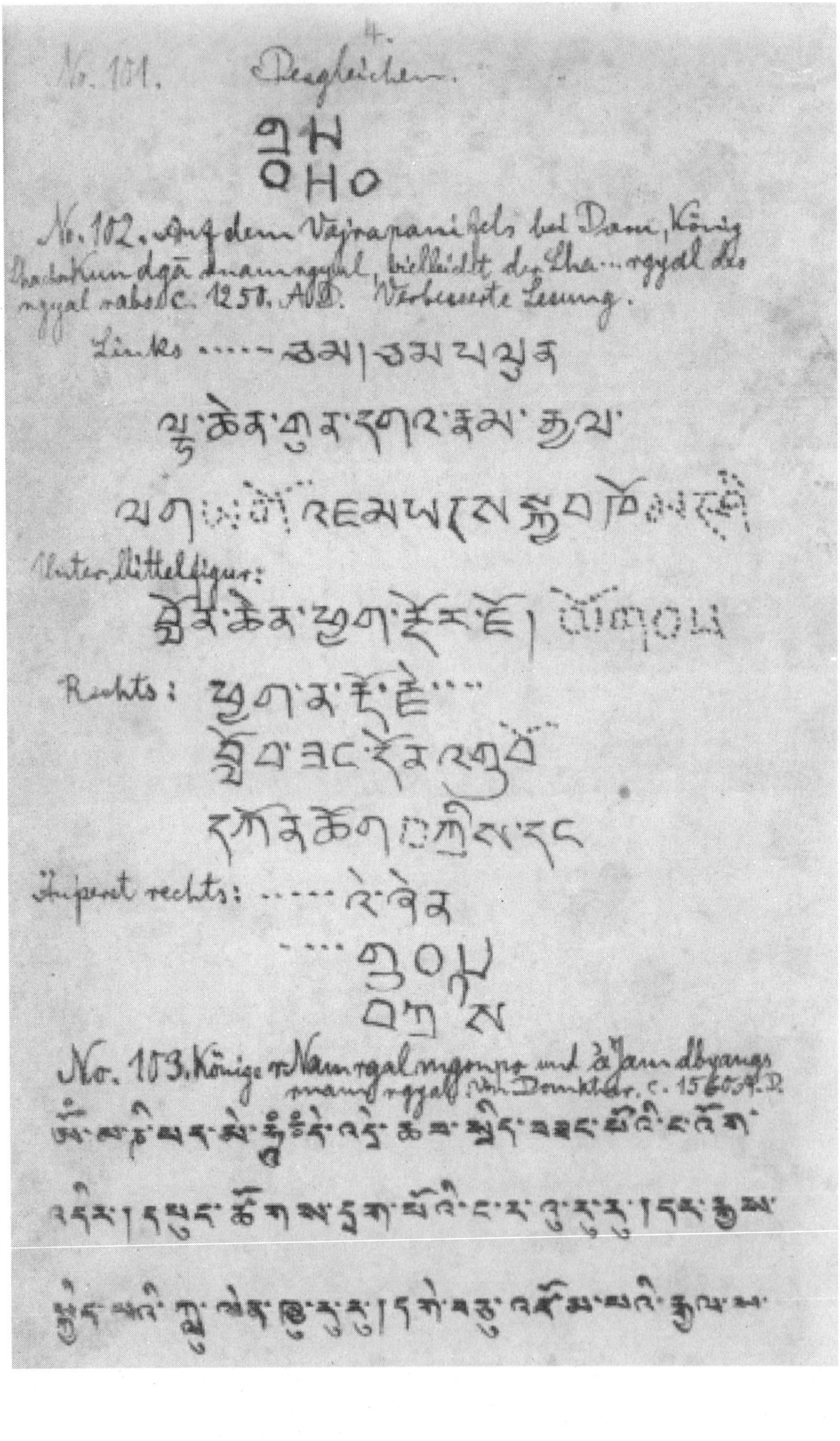

4.

No. 101. Desgleichen.

No. 102. Auf dem Vajrapanifels bei Dom, König ... Kun dgā rnam rgyal, vielleicht der Lha ... rgyal des rgyal rabs c. 1250 A.D. Verbesserte Lesung.

Links .....

ལྷ་ཆེན་ཀུན་དགའ་རྣམ་རྒྱལ་

Unter Mittelfigur:

Rechts:

Äußerst rechts: .....

No. 103. Könige ... Nam rgyal mgon po und Jam dbyangs rnam rgyal ... Domkhar. c. 1560 A.D.

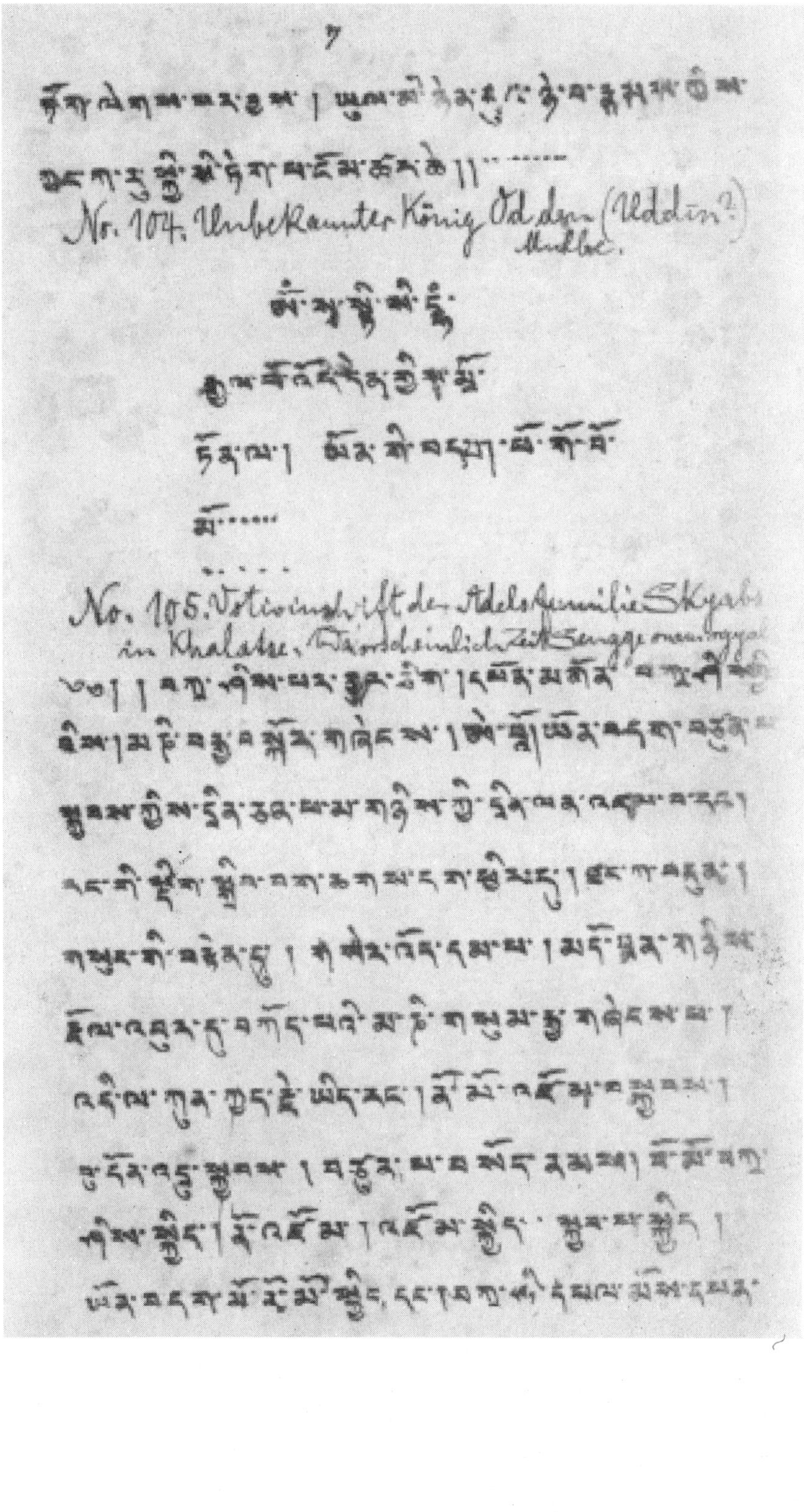

7

No. 104. Unbekannter König Od dun (Uddun?) Mulbe.

ཨོཾ་མ་ཎི་པདྨེ་ཧཱུྃ

No. 105. Votivinschrift der Adelsfamilie Skyabs in Khalatse. Wahrscheinlich Zeit Sengge rnam rgyal

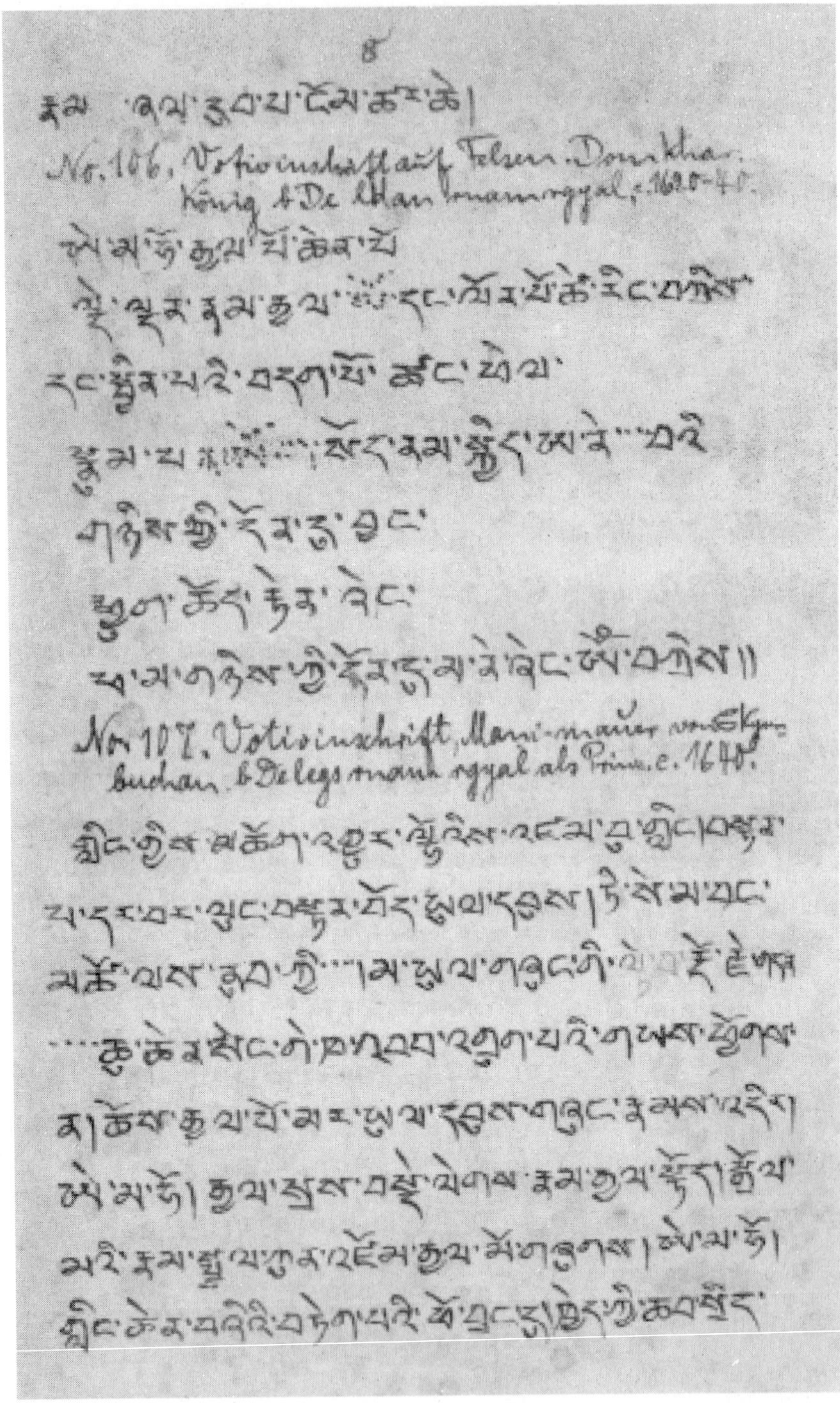
8

No. 106, Votivinschrift auf Felsen. Donkhar.
König bDe ldan rnam rgyal, c. 1620-40.

No. 107. Votivinschrift, Mani-mauer von Skyu-buchan. bDe legs rnam rgyal als Prinz. c. 1640.

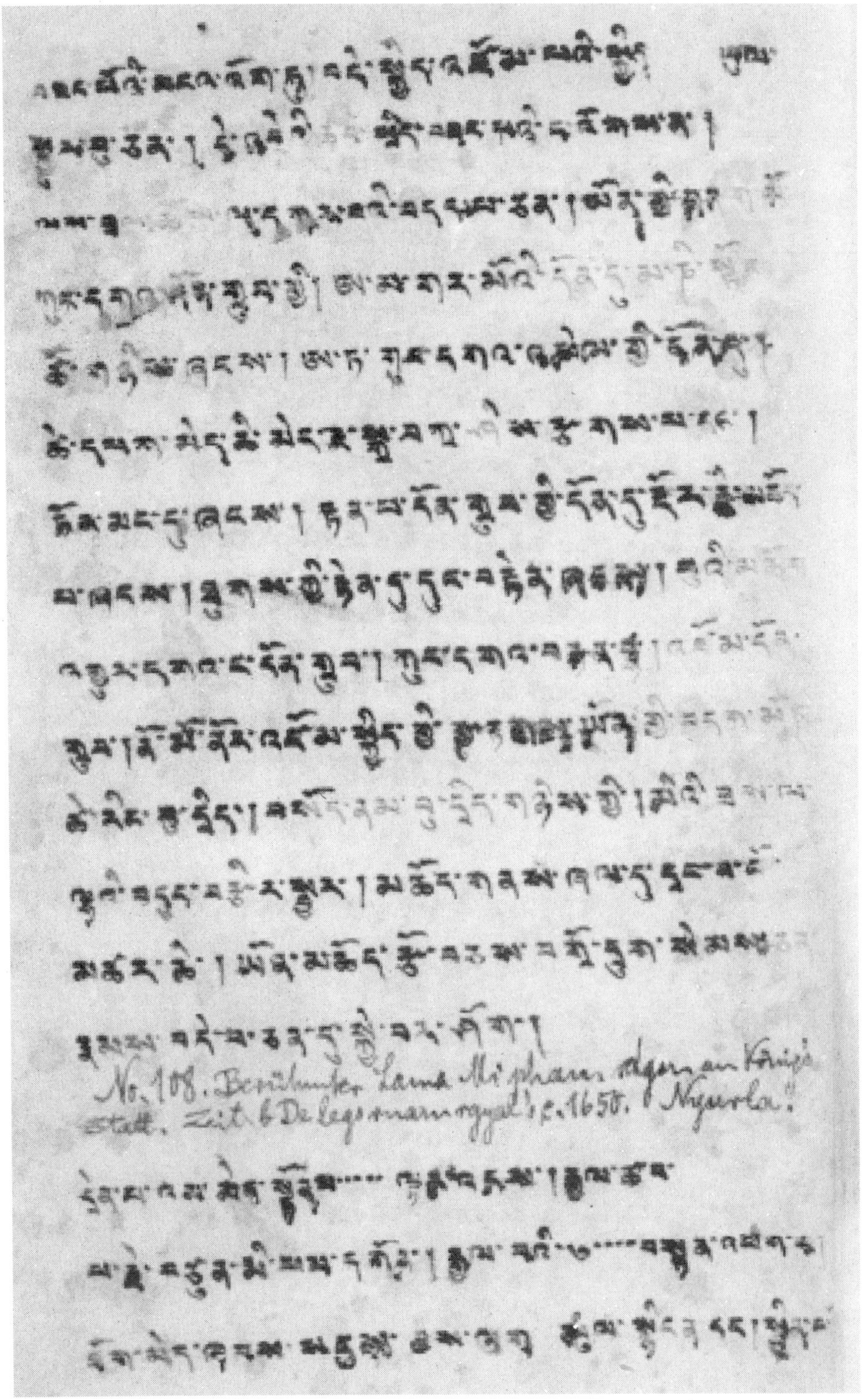
No. 108. Berühmter Lama Mi pham dgon an Kriegs-
statt. Zeit d. De legs rnam rgyal's, c. 1650. Nyurla!

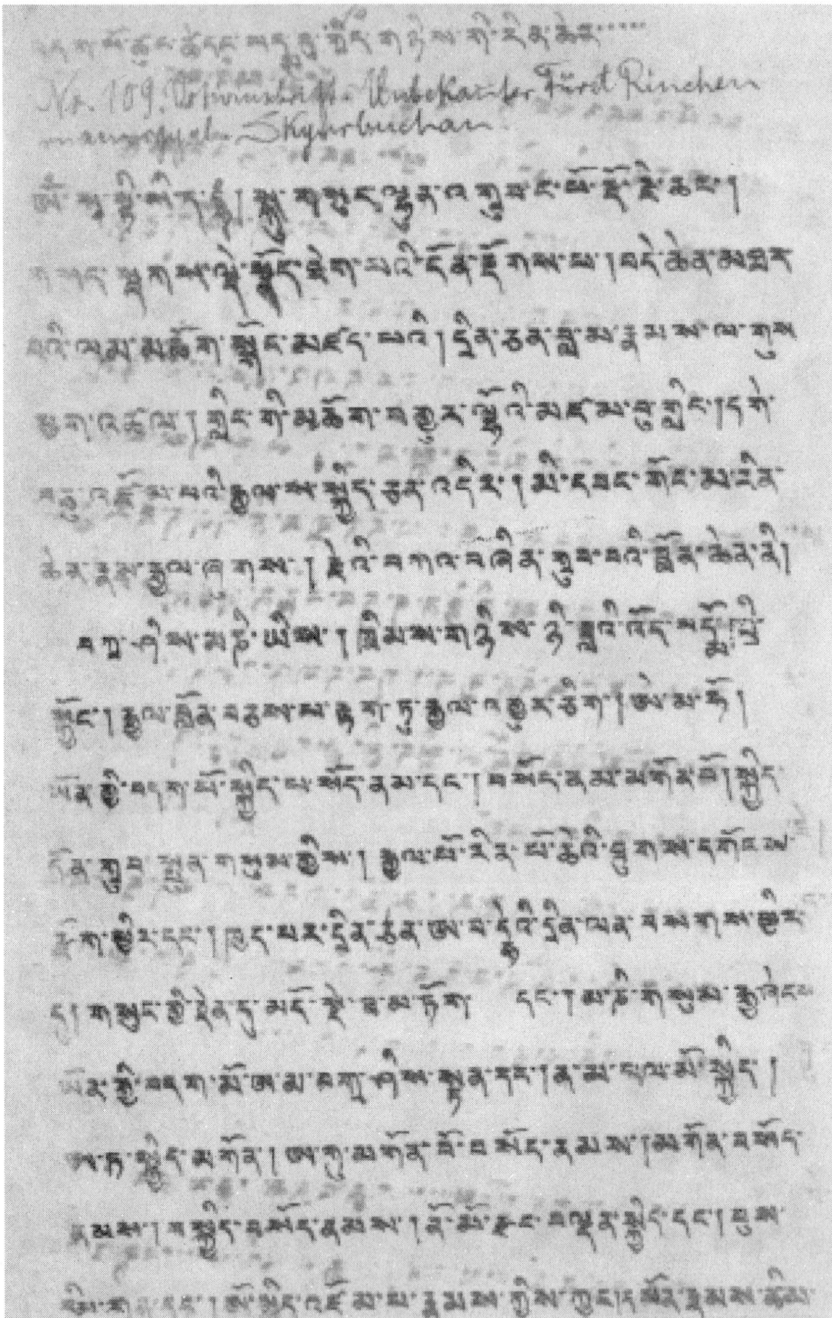

འདམ་དཀར་འདེར། ཕྱིན་ཡིན་ལག་བརྒྱུད་ཕྱིན་ཆུ་བོ་འབབ།
མདུན་སྟེ་ཞིང་ནག་མ་ཚལ་ལོ་འདབ་རྒྱས། བར་ནི་འབྲུ་བཅུད་མི
སྨིན་ཀང་ཡང་མེད། དེ་འདྲའི་སྐྱིད་ལ་དབང་བའི་སྨོན་ཆེ་ན་ནི།
མ་ཚོལ་དགུ་དགྱེང་འཛོམས་པའི་ནམ་ལ་ཀམ་ཡིན། ལ་མོར་འདང་མ
བུ་བཞིན་སྐྱོང་བའི་ཡབ་ཅིག་ཡིན། རིགས་མ་བཟང་ཁྱུང་བཙུན
རྒྱལ་པོ་སྲུའི་རྒྱུད། མདངས་རྒྱས་བསྟན་པའི་སྨིན་བདག་ཆེན་པོ
བཀྲ་ཤིས་རྒྱལ་མཚན་གྱིས། ཆོས་རྒྱལ་ཆེན་པོ་ནམ་རྒྱལ་མགོན
པོ་དང་ འཇམ་དཔལ་དབྱངས་ནམ་རྒྱལ་ཕྱག་ན་དགོངས་རྡོ་གསུམ་ཕྱིར
དུ། ཧོ་རྗེ་འཆང་རྗེ་བླ་མ་ སྐུ་འདྲ་བཞེངས། ཡབ་ཆེན་ཨ་ཕ་ཀུ
ཀི་མདང། ཨ་མ་ཁྱུ་མེ་དང་། ཨ་ཇོ་བཀྲ་ཤིས་ཚེ་རིང་། ཚེ་རིང
ཏོན་འགྲུབ། མ་མ་པ་པ་ཏོན་འགྲུབ། མམ་ཀ་བཀྲ་ཤིས།
བཀྲ་ཤིས་བརྒྱ་མཚོ། བཀྲ་ཤིས་ལྷུན་འགྲུབ། ཚེ་རིང་འཕེལ
ནི་མ་མ་དགོངས་བརྡ་གམ་ཕྱིར་མ་ཏོ་ལྷ་བརྒྱ་ཞེངས། ཨེ་མ
ཞི་མཛོ་མ་དགོངས་པ་ཆོས་ཀྱི་དབྱངས་ ཀ་ཀེ་གས་པ་ལ་མཆི
སྟོང་རྒྱ་ཅན་ཁྲངས། བསམ་གས་པ་ཆོས་ཕྱིར་བཏོད་མ་ངོམས་

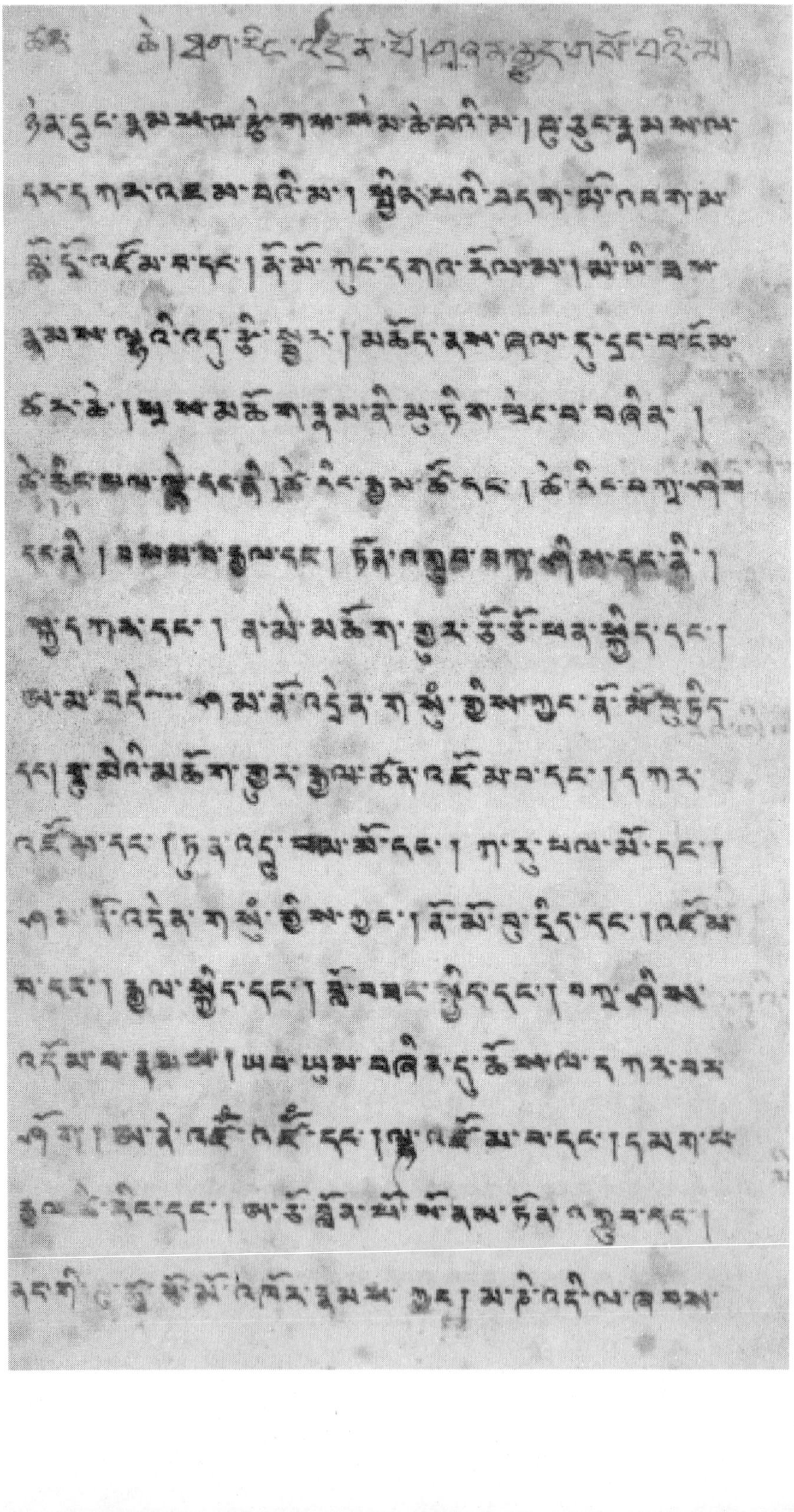

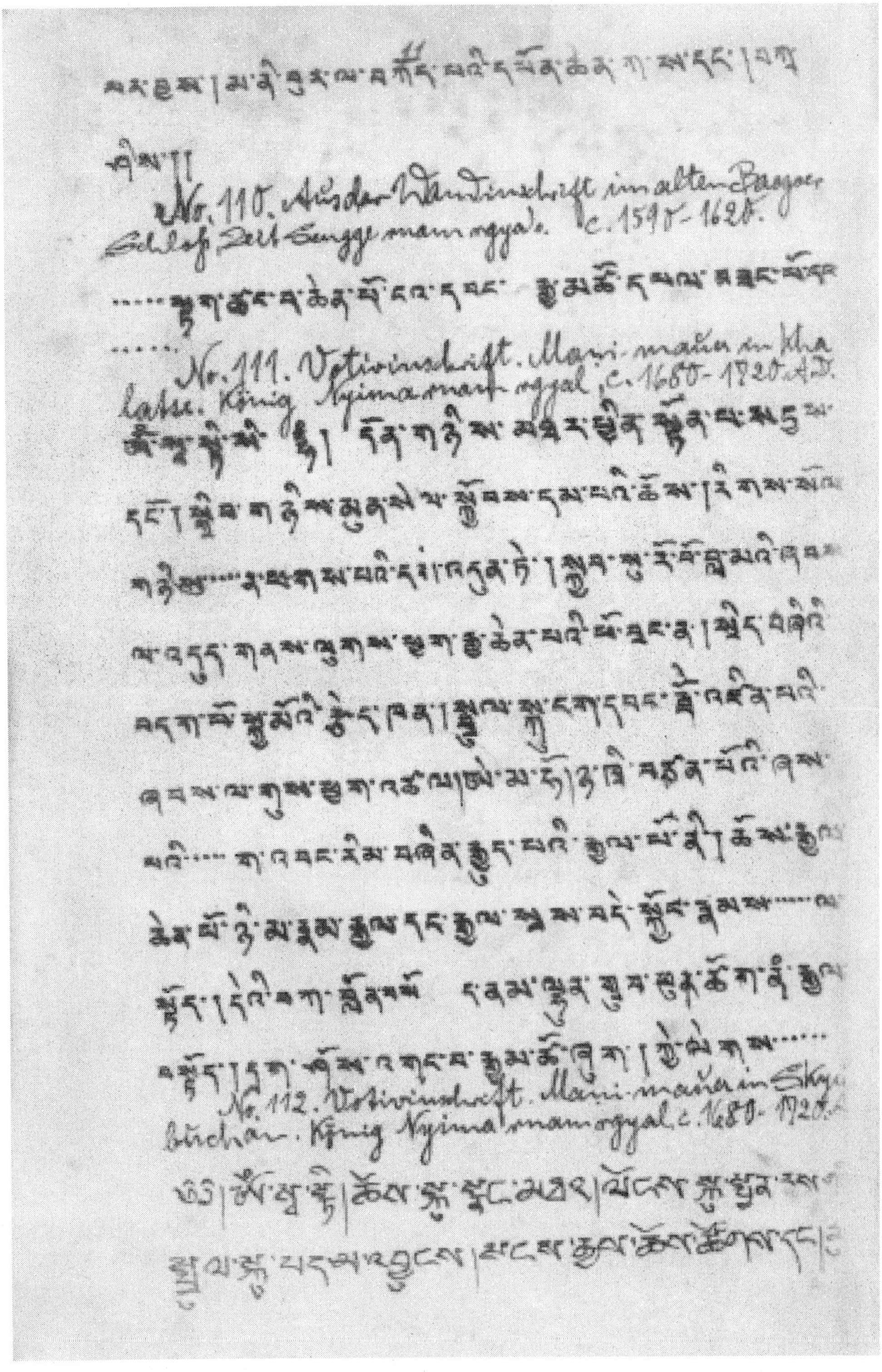

No. 110. Aus der Wandinschrift im alten Bagoer Schloß. Zeit Sengge rnam rgyal. c. 1590–1620.

No. 111. Votivinschrift. Mani-mani in Kha latse. König Nyima rnam rgyal, c. 1680–1720 A.D.

No. 112. Votivinschrift. Mani-mani in Skyubuchan. König Nyima rnam rgyal c. 1680–1720 A.D.

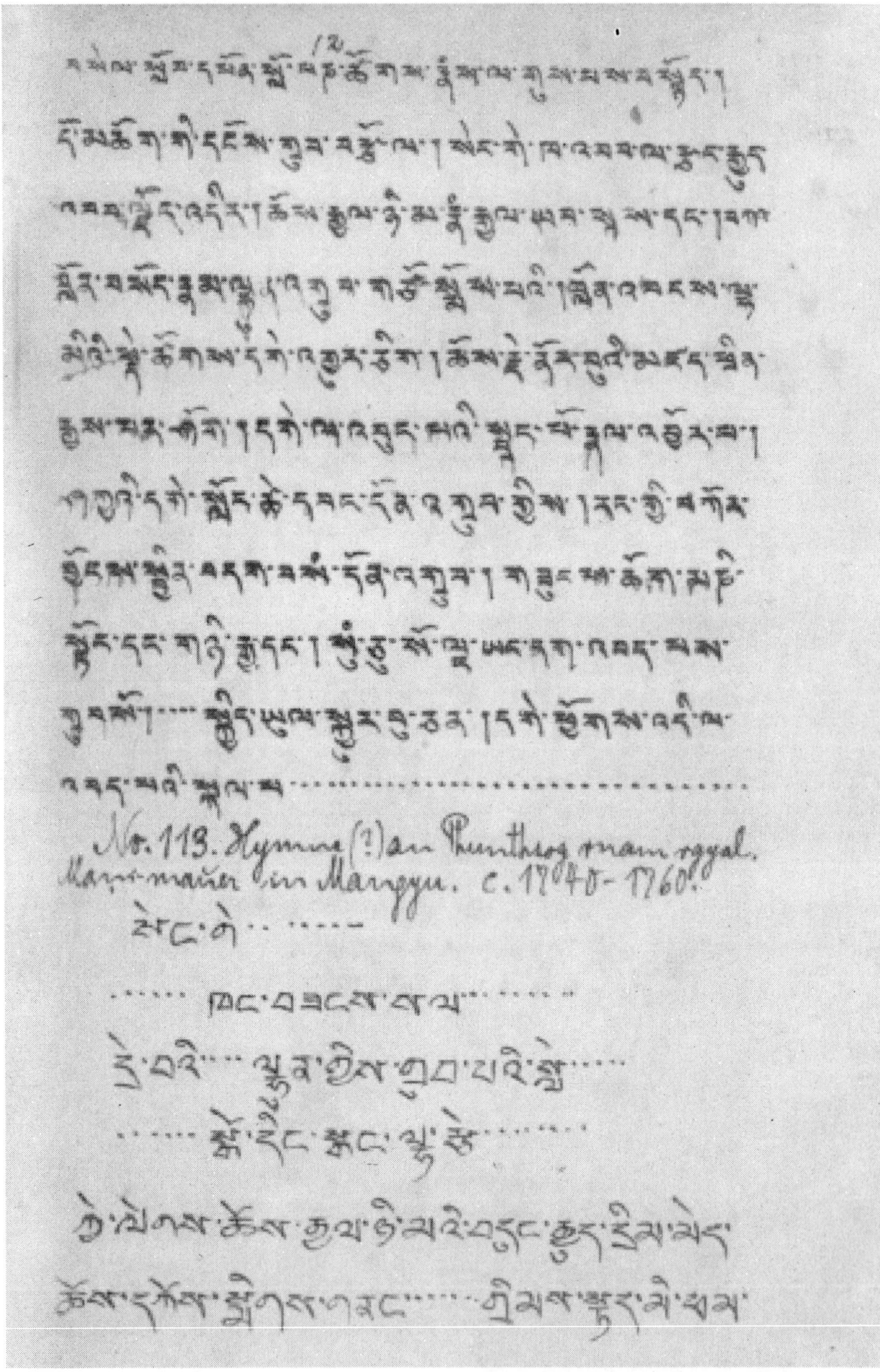
No. 113. Hymne (?) an Phun thsog rnam rgyal.
Mani-mauer in Mangyu. c. 1740-1760.

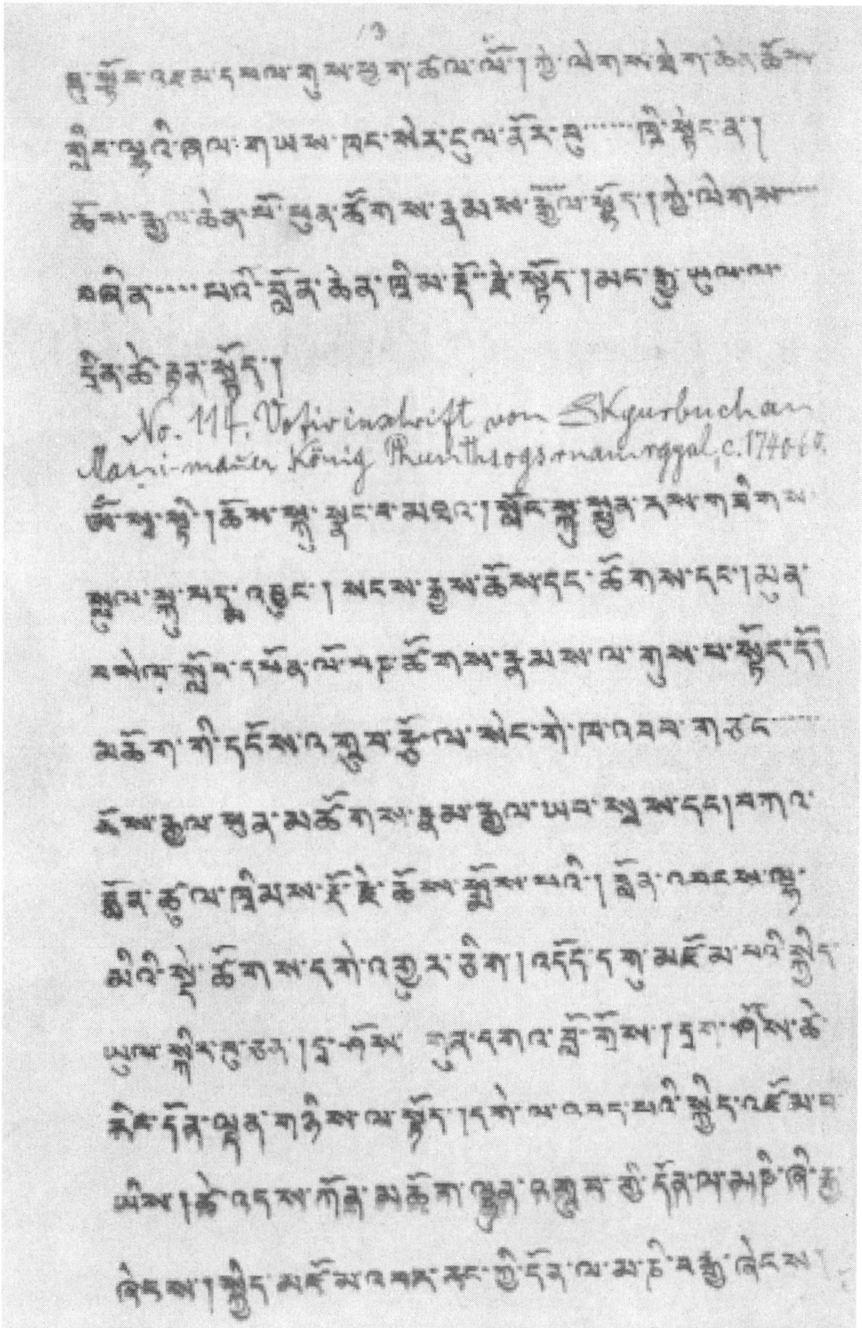
No. 114. Votivinschrift vom Skyurbuchan Mani-mauer König Phunthsogsrnamrgyal, c. 1740 n. Chr.

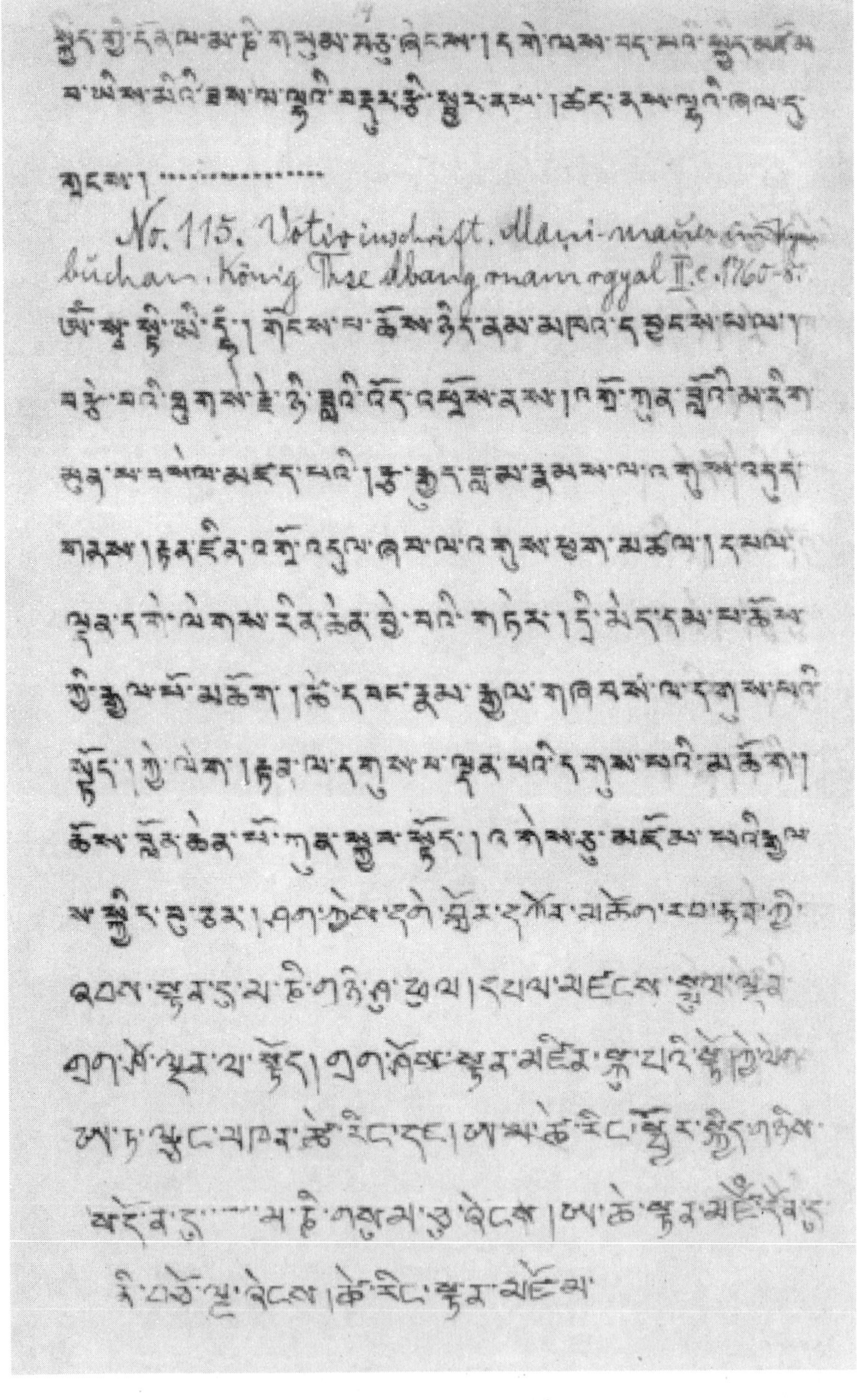

No. 115. Votivinschrift. Mani-mauer … büchan. König Thse dbang rnam rgyal II. c. 1760-81.

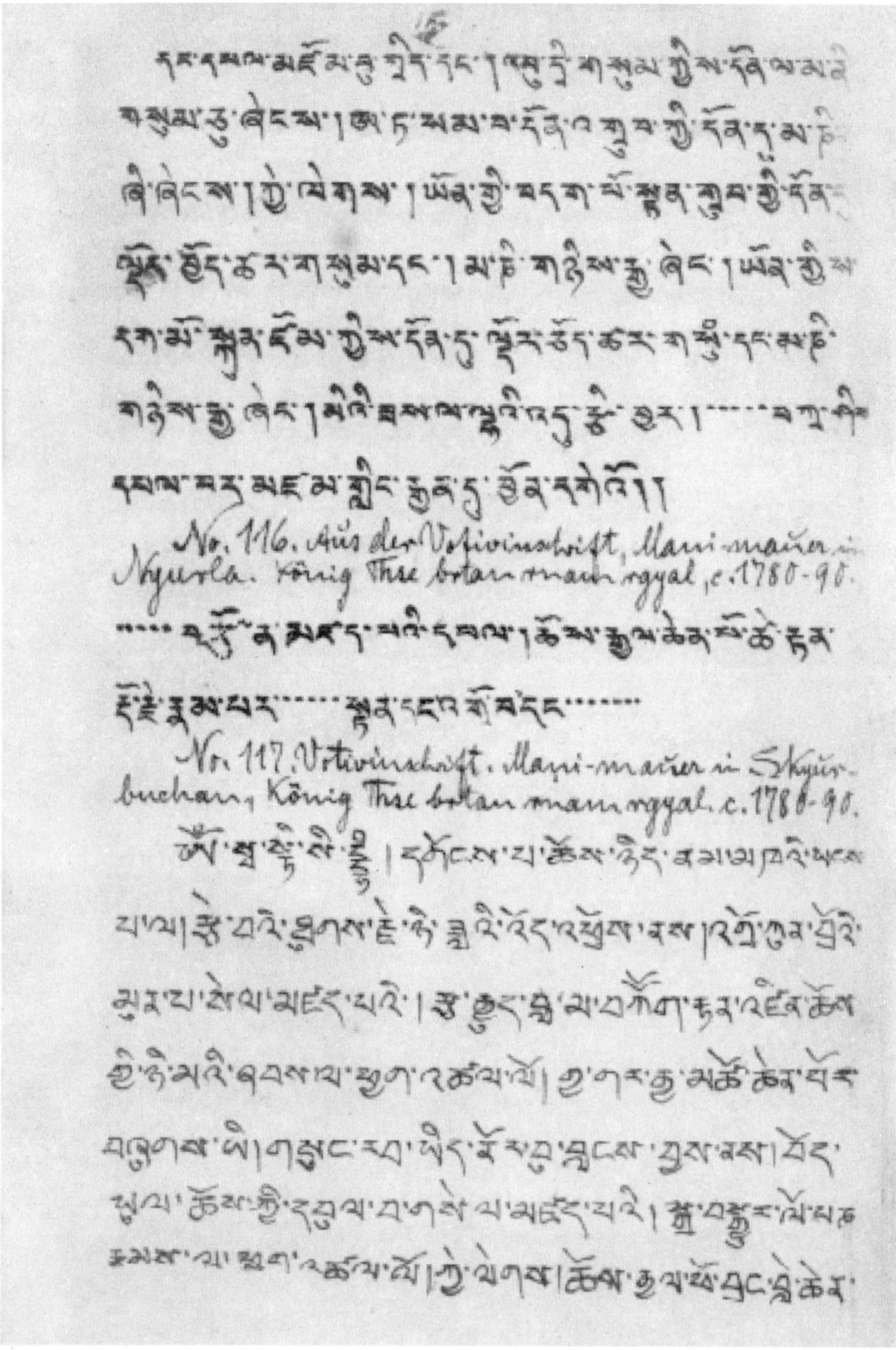
No. 116. Aus der Votivinschrift, Mani-mauer in Nyurla. König Thse brtan rnam rgyal, c. 1780-90.

No. 117. Votivinschrift. Mani-mauer in Skyurbuchan, König Thse brtan rnam rgyal. c. 1780-90.

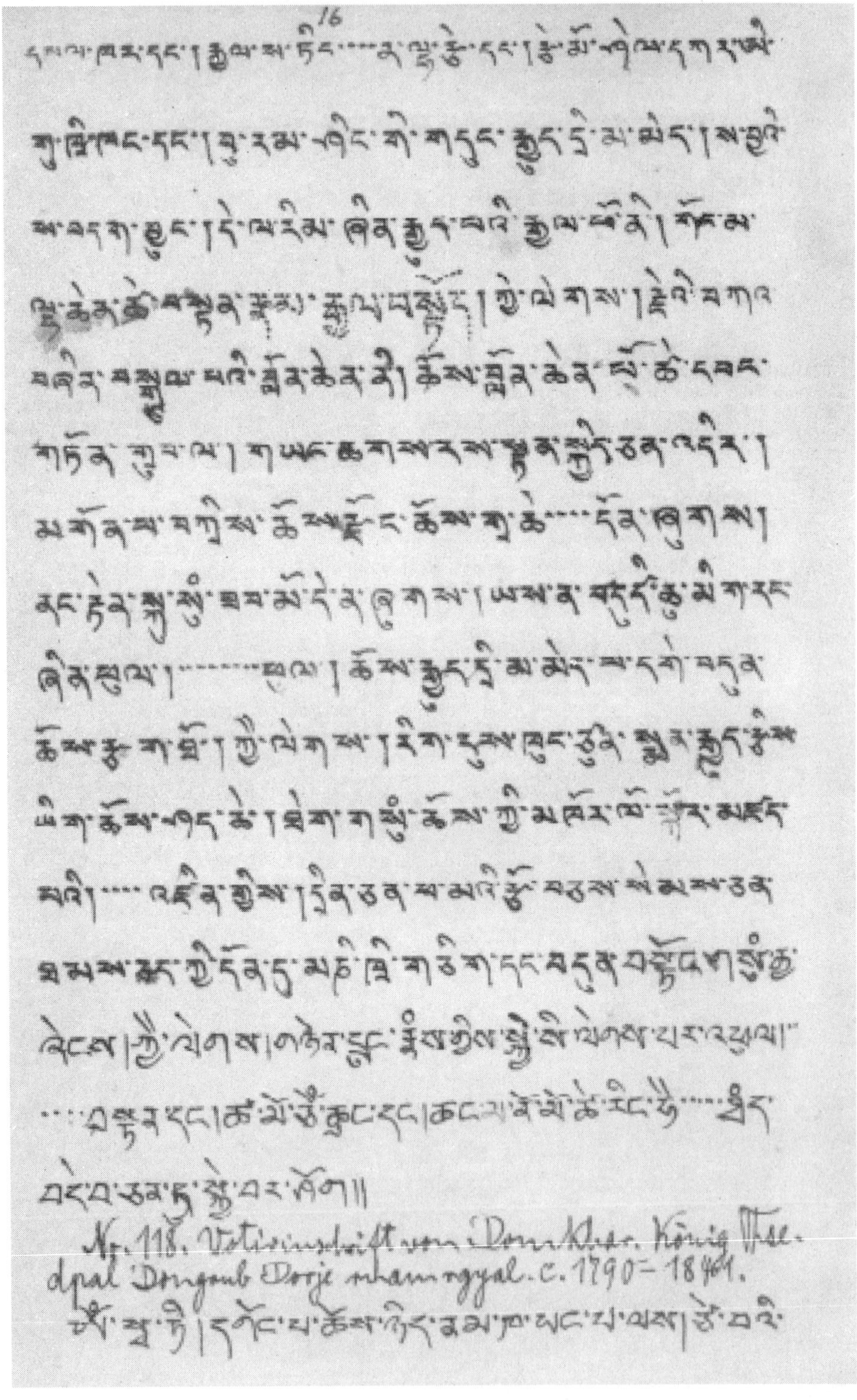

Nr. 118. Votivinschrift von Domkhar. König Thse-dpal Dongrub Dorje rnamrgyal. c. 1790–1841.

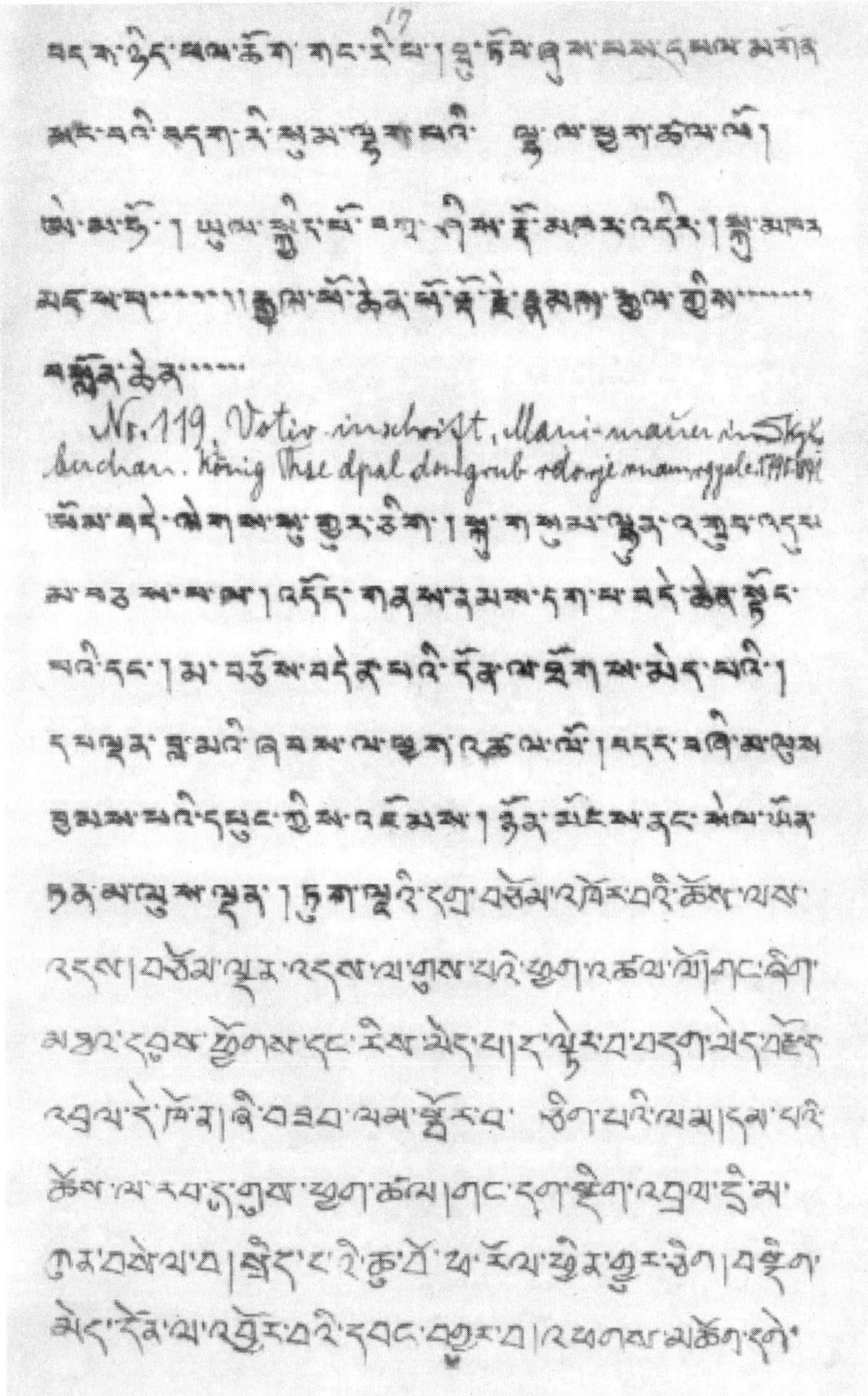

Nr. 119, Votivinschrift, Mani-mauer in Skyibuchan. König Thse dpal don grub rdorje rnam rgyal. 1790–1841

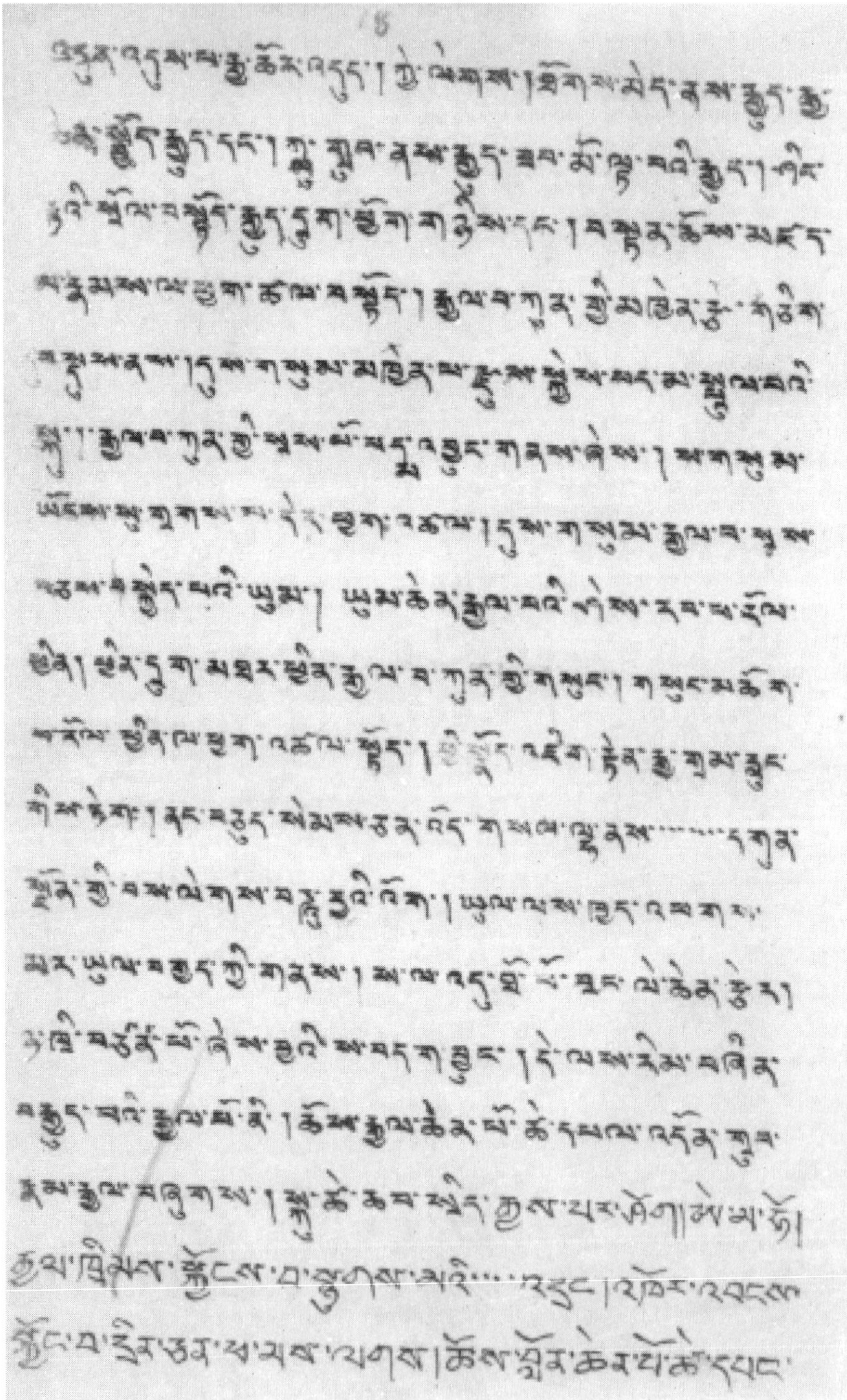

19

ངོ་ཚ་ཁྲུས་བསྐྱེད། ཨེ་མ་ཧོ། ལྷ་ནས་སྤང་རི་མདངས་དཀར་ཡོལ་བས
སྐྱངས། མ་རིག་ནད་ཀྱིས་འཛིན་བུ་ཚོས་ཡུམ་གོས་མ་གོན། ཕར་ན
མ་གོན་པ་བཀྲིས་ཆོས་རྫོངས་བཞུགས་པས། འདི་སྤྱོད་འཁོར་བའི་རྒྱ
ས་སྒྲིད་བྲེ་ཅན། ཡུལ་གྱིས་དཔོན་པོ་གྲུབ་ཀྱི་སྐྱབས་བསོད་ནམས
མ་སྐྱིད་ཤ་ཀ་འབྲིན་ཆེ་བའི་འབྲིན་ཅན་པ་མ་ལག་སྤྲ། མཁར་དཔོན
ཆེན་པོ་དཀོན་མཆོག་ཚེ་རྟན་བསྐྱེད། ནོ་མོ་བསྐྱེ་འཛིན་བསྐྱེད། །
ཡོན་གྱི་བདག་པོ་……དང་། དཀོན་མཆོག་མཐར་ཕྱིན་གྱིས
འབྲིན་ཅན་པ་མ་ག་ཉིས་གྱི་འབྲིན་ལན་འཛལ་བ་དང་། རང་གི་སྐྱེ
གྲིབ་ས་བག་ཕྱག་བདག་ཕྱིར་དུ། ཨ་མའི་ཡང་སེམས་གྱི་འདོན་དུ
ཀའི་སྙིང་པོ་རིན་རྗེ་ག་ཅིག་པ་ཚར་ཅིག་དང་། འབུར་དུ་ཞིན་པའི
མཎི་ལྷ་བརྒྱ་བཞེངས། ཨ་མ་སྒྲུམ་སྐྱིད་ཀི་དོན་དུ་རི་རྗེ་མཆོད་པ
ཐང་ག་ཅིག་དང་མ་ཎི་ལྷ་བརྒྱ་བཞེངས། དགེ་སློང་དཀོན་མཆོག
མཐར་ཕྱིན་རང་གི་དོན་དུ་ཀའི་སྙིང་པོ་རྗེ་རྗེ་མཆོད་པ་མཆར
ག་ཅིག་དང་། མཎི་སྟོང་བདུན་དང་རྒྱ་རྒྱ་བརྒྱ་ཞངས། གཞན་ཡང
སྙན་དུང་རྣམས་ཀྱི་སྐར་མཚམས་ཀི་སྐྱེ་སེ་ཀ་རྒྱ་འཕྲུལ་པའི་དོན
དུ་མཎི་སྟོང་བཞེངས། མཎི་འདི་ལ་ས་ཞབས་རྟག་འགྲུལ་བའི་ལམ
མི་ཐམས་ཅད་འདིའ་ཕན་ཐོ་སྐྱེ་ཡར་ཤོག། འབྲིས།།

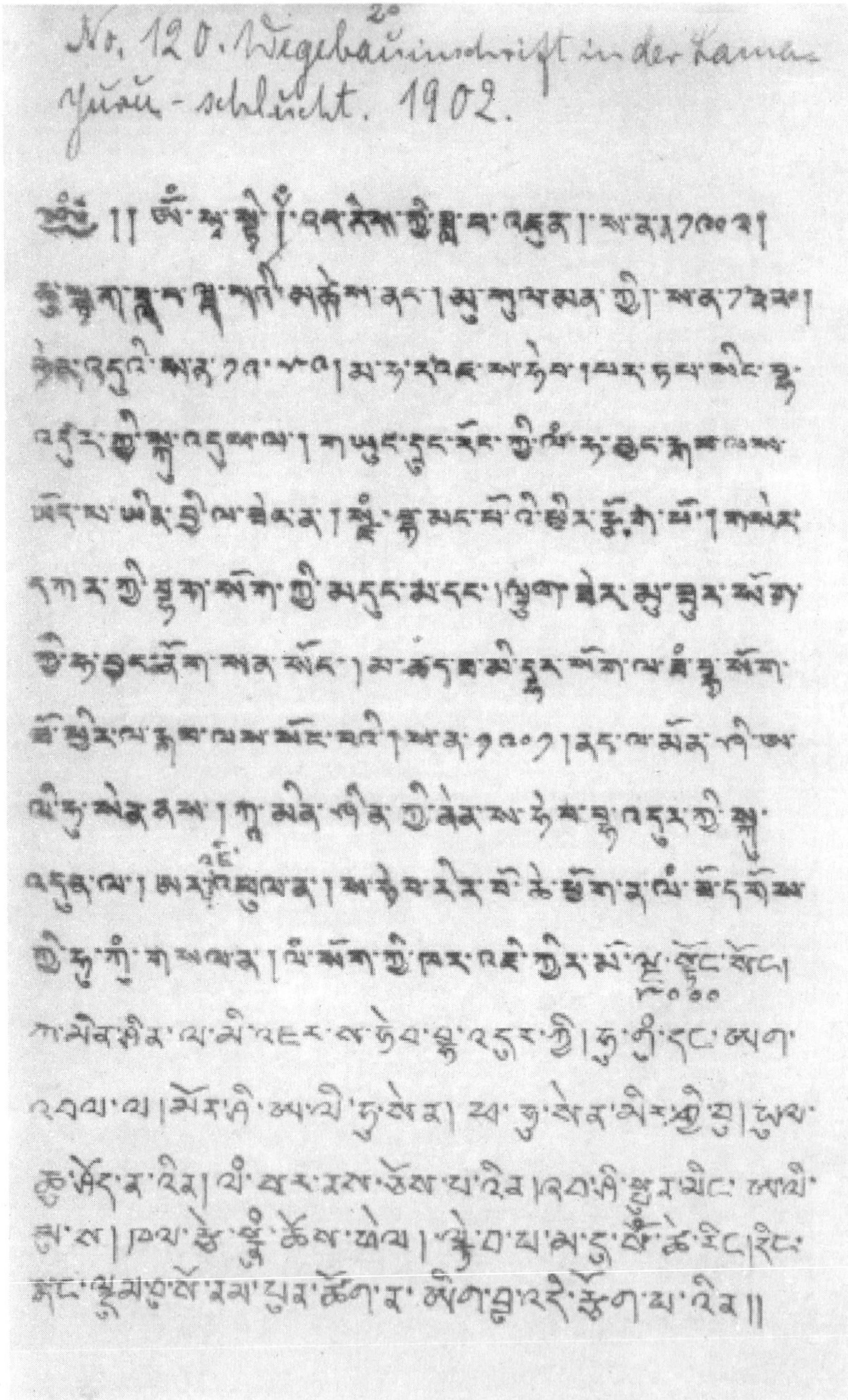
No. 120. Wegebauinschrift in der Kamaa-
yüru-schlucht. 1902.

21

No. 121. Votivinschrift des noch unbekannten Ministers bSod nams dpal ʼbyor, Sheh, bei zwei mchod rten.

[illegible]

དཔལ་འབྱོར་ཞིང་དཔོན་སྐྱོ་བ་བཟང་བཀྲིས ||

No. 122. Inschrift über Baumpflanzung des Dogra-offiziers Farman. Khalatse-brücke. 1905.

فرمان حوال دار

[illegible]

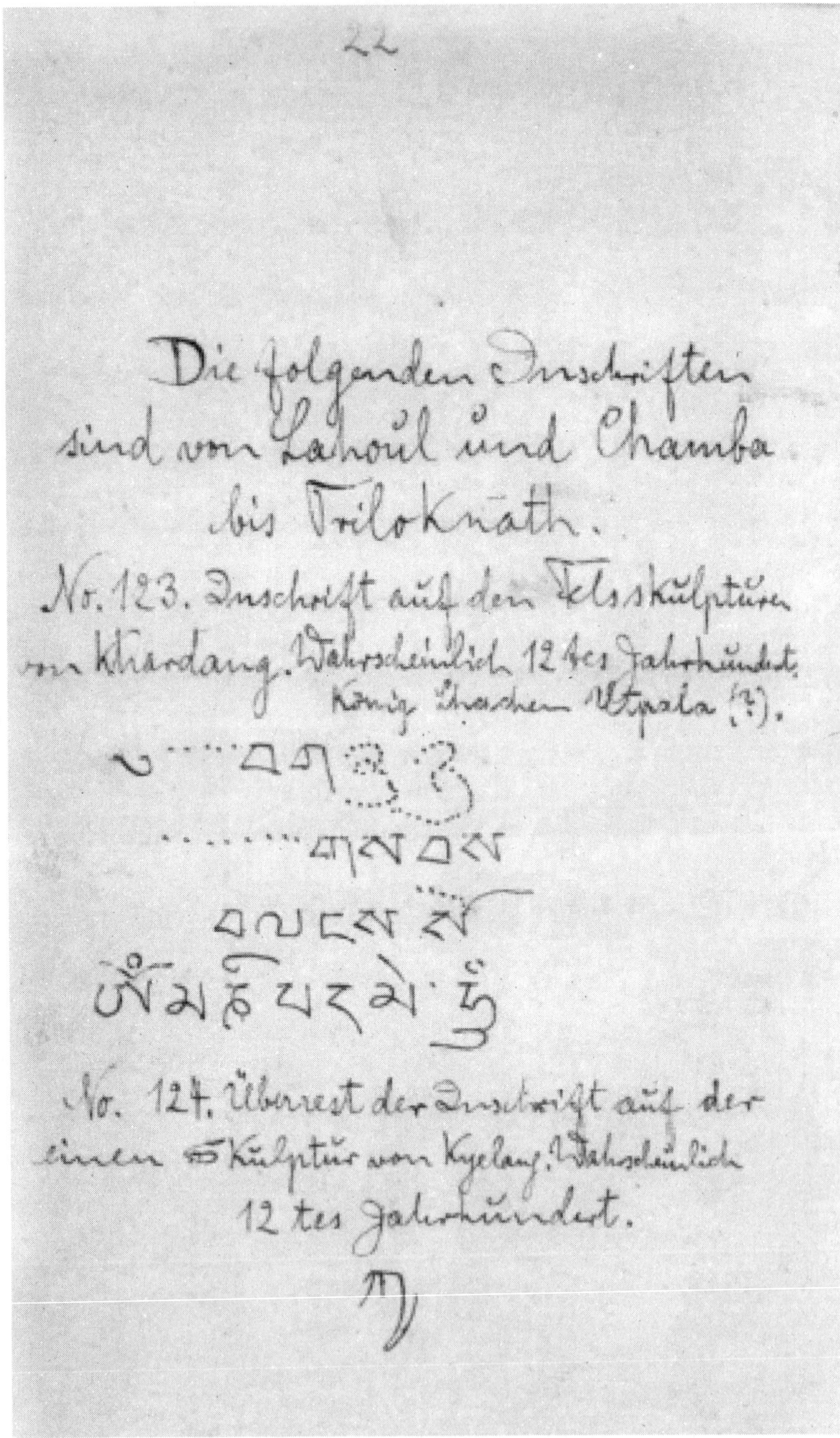

22

Die folgenden Inschriften sind von Lahoul und Chamba bis Triloknath.

No. 123. Inschrift auf den Felsskulpturen von Khardang. Wahrscheinlich 12tes Jahrhundert. König Lhachen Utpala (?).

ཨོཾ་མ་ཎི་པདྨེ་ཧཱུྃ

No. 124. Überrest der Inschrift auf der einen Skulptur von Kyelang. Wahrscheinlich 12tes Jahrhundert.

ཀ

23

No. 125. Alte buddhistische Inschriften auf dem Felsen von Gurnad.

ཨོཾ་ཨཱ་ཧཱུཾ་བཛྲ་གུ་རུ་པདྨ་སིདྡྷི་ཧཱུཾ

སྐམ་ལྡན

ཨོཾ་ཝཱ་གཱི་ཤྭ་རི་ཧཱུཾ

ཨོཾ་མ་ཎི་པདྨེ་ཧཱུཾ

ཨོཾ་བཛྲ་པཱ་ཎི་ཧཱུཾ

ཨོཾ་སྭ་བྷ་ཏ་[illegible]བཛྲ་ཡོ་ཤུ་ཧཱ།

ཨོཾ་ཨཱ་མི་དྷེ་ཝ་ཧྲཱིཿ

No. 126. Alte Inschrift bei dem verlassenen Dorf oberhalb Kyor.

ཕྱུ་ཤུན་ཁྲིན།

No. 127. Inschrift des Fürsten Hayar von Lahoul. Zeitgenosse des Lahoul-Fürsten Thse dbang rnam rgyal und des Königs von Kulu Parbad Sing c. 1700–1730 A.D. bei Zhugmur.

༄། ཨོཾ་སྭ་སྟི་སིདྡྷཾ།

ཞི་ལ་ཇེད་སྐྱོང་རྒྱུང་བའི་གྲངས་ལ

ཀཱ་ར་ང་ཞས་རོ་སྐྱ་བརྩན་རྡེང་ཞལ་གཞིས

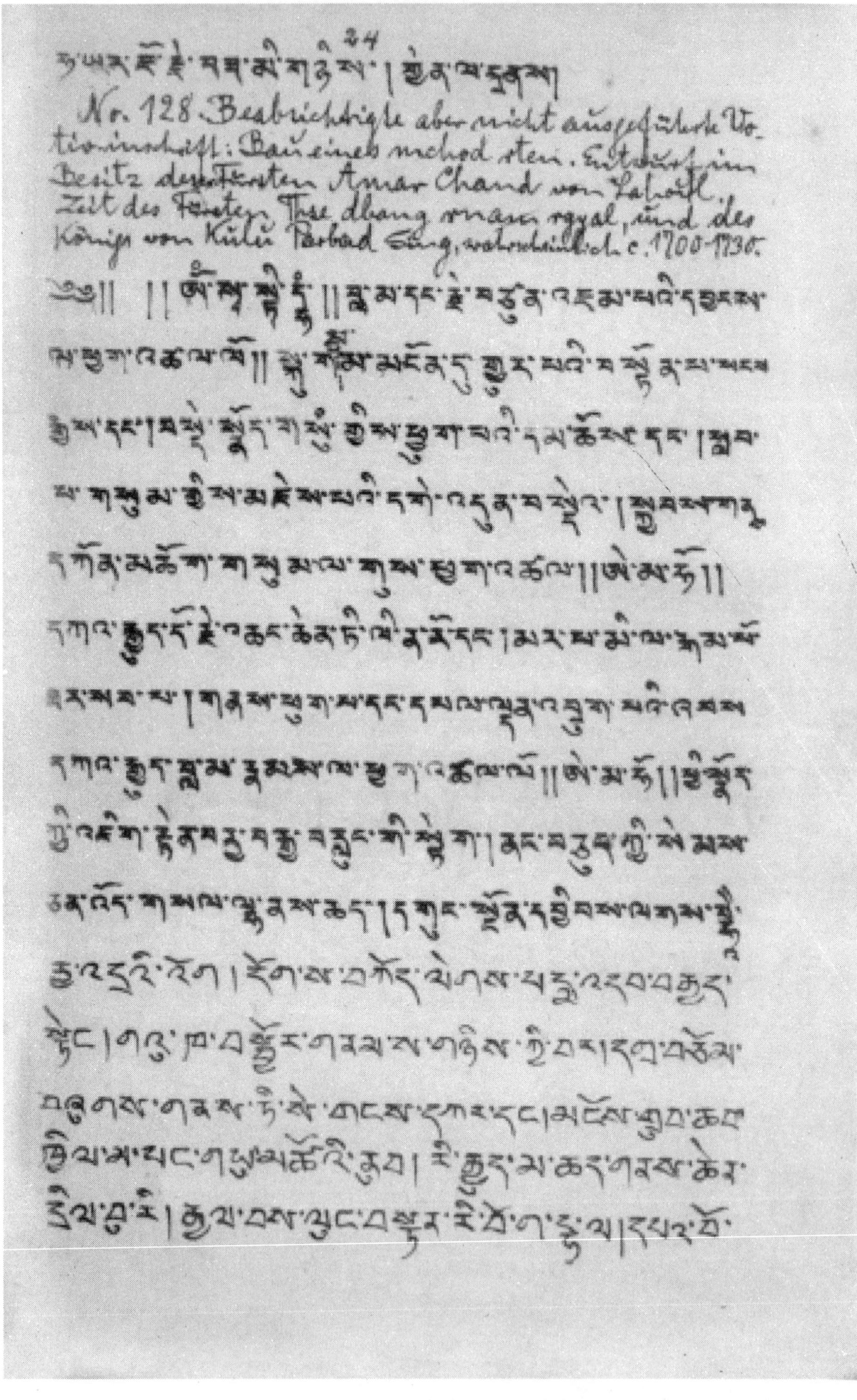
No. 128 Beabsichtigte aber nicht ausgeführte Votivinschrift: Bau eines mchod rten. Entwurf im Besitz des Fürsten Amar Chand von Lahoul. Zeit des Fürsten Tshe dbang rnam rgyal, und des Königs von Kulu Parbad Sing, wahrscheinlich c. 1700-1730.

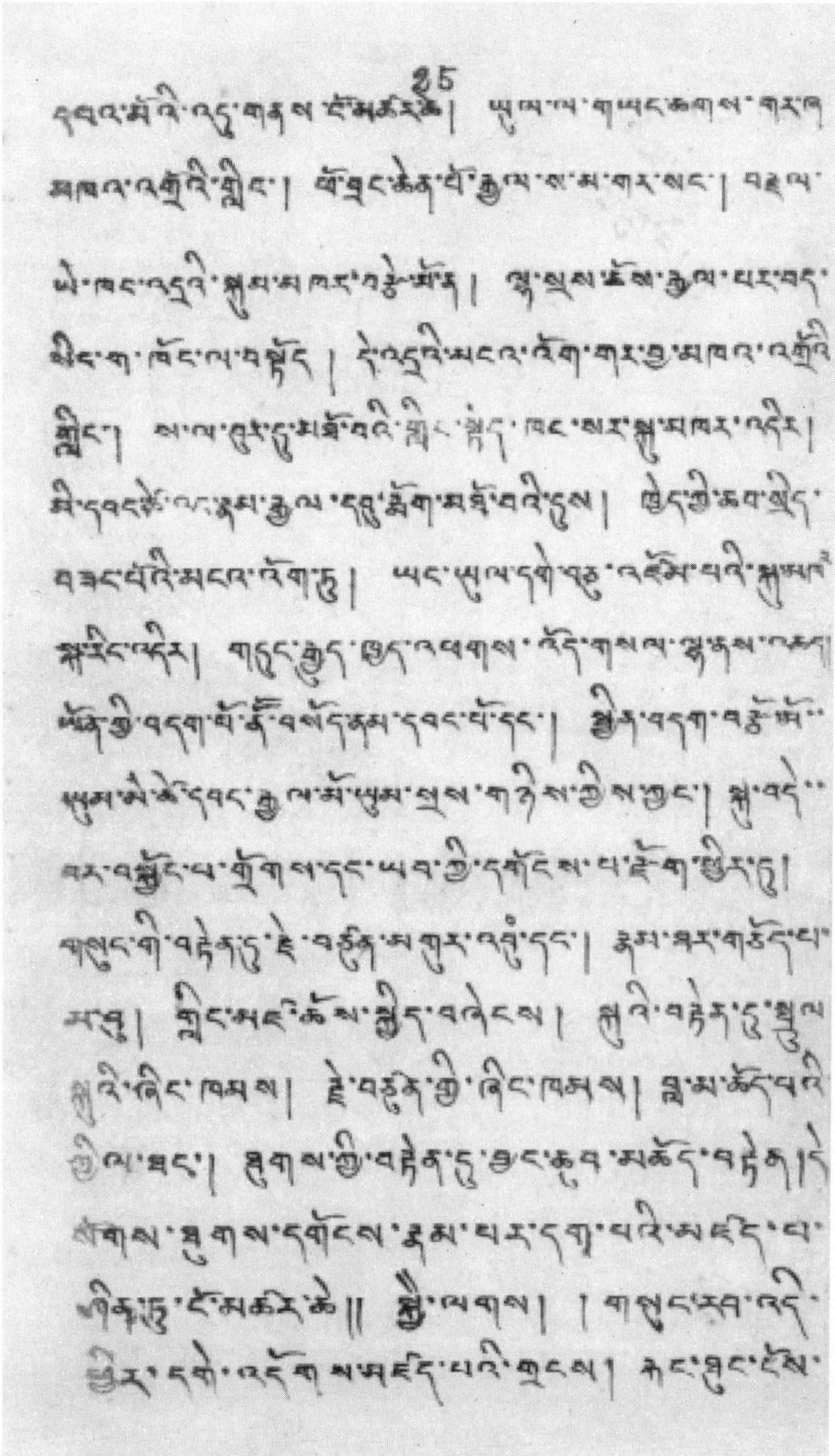

༣༥

དཔའ་མོའི་འདུ་གནས་ངོ་མཚར་ཆེ། ཡུལ་ལ་གཡང་ཆགས་གནས
མཁའ་འགྲོའི་གླིང་། ཕོ་བྲང་ཆེན་པོ་རྒྱལ་ས་མ་གར་ལང་། བཞལ་
ཡེ་ཁང་འདུའི་སྐུ་མ་ཁར་བརྩེ་མོན། ལྷ་ལུས་ཆོས་རྒྱལ་པར་བད་
མིང་ག་ཁོང་ལ་བསྟོད། དེ་འདྲའི་མངའ་འོག་གར་ཞ་མཁའ་འགྲོའི
གླིང་། ས་ལ་ཤུར་དུ་མཚོ་བའི་སྐྱི་སྐྱོད་ ཁང་ལར་སྐུ་མཁར་འདིར།
མི་དབང་ཚེ་ལ་རྣམ་རྒྱལ་དགྲ་ཚོགས་མནོ་བའི་དུས། ཁྱེད་ཀྱི་ཆབ་སྲིད་
བཟང་པོའི་མངའ་འོག་ཏུ། ཡང་ཡུལ་དགེ་བཅུ་འཛོམ་པའི་སྐུ་མཁར
སྐར་རིང་འདིར། གདུང་རྒྱུད་ཁྱད་འཕགས་འདི་གསལ་ལྷ་ནས་འཆག
མཆན་ཀྱི་བདག་པོ་ཚོ་བསོད་ནམས་དབང་པོ་དང་། སྐྱིན་བདག་བཙོ་མོ
ཡུམ་མི་ཚེ་དབང་རྒྱལ་མོ་ཡུམ་སྲས་གཉིས་ཀྱིས་ཀྱང་། སྐུ་བདེ
བར་བསྐྱོད་པ་གྲོགས་དང་ཡབ་ཀྱི་དགོངས་པ་རྫོགས་ཕྱིར་དུ།
གསུང་གི་རྟེན་དུ་རྗེ་བཙུན་མ་གུར་འབུམ་དང་། རྣམ་ཐར་གཅོད་པ་
མ་བུ། གླིང་མཛེ་ཚོས་སྐྱིད་བཞེངས། སྐུའི་རྟེན་དུ་སྤྱལ
སྐུའི་ཞིང་ཁམས། རྗེ་བཙུན་ཀྱི་ཞིང་ཁམས། བླ་མ་མཆོད་པའི
ཀྱིལ་ཐང་། ཐུགས་ཀྱི་རྟེན་དུ་བྱང་ཆུབ་མཆོད་རྟེན། དེ
ཚོགས་ཐུགས་དགོངས་རྣམ་པར་དག་པའི་མཛད་པ་
ཡིན་ཏུ་ངོ་མཚར་ཆེ།། སྐྱེ་ལགས། །གསུང་རབ་འདི་
ཕྱིར་དགེ་འདོག་མ་མཛད་པའི་གྲངས། ཉང་བྱང་ངོས་

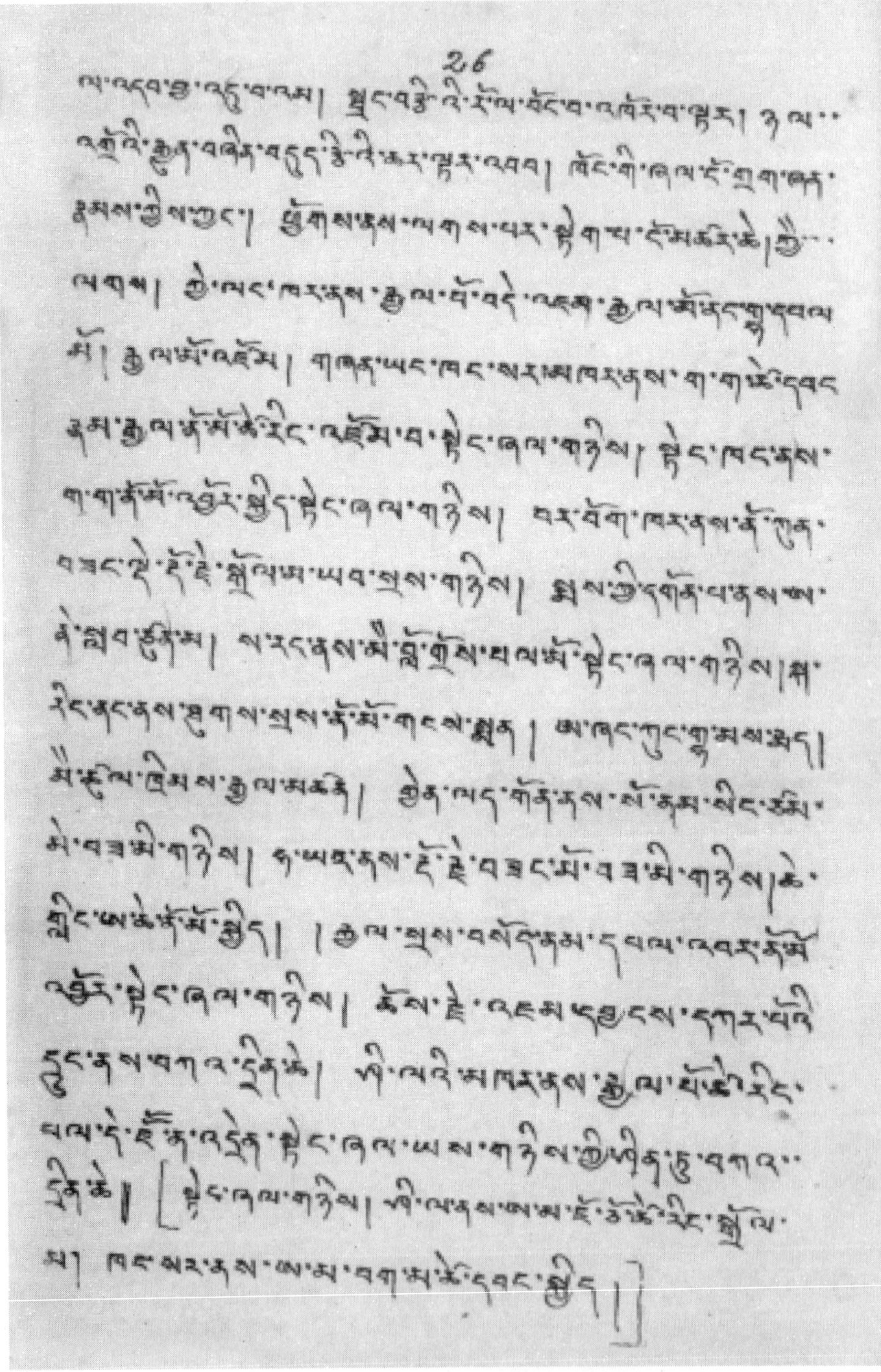

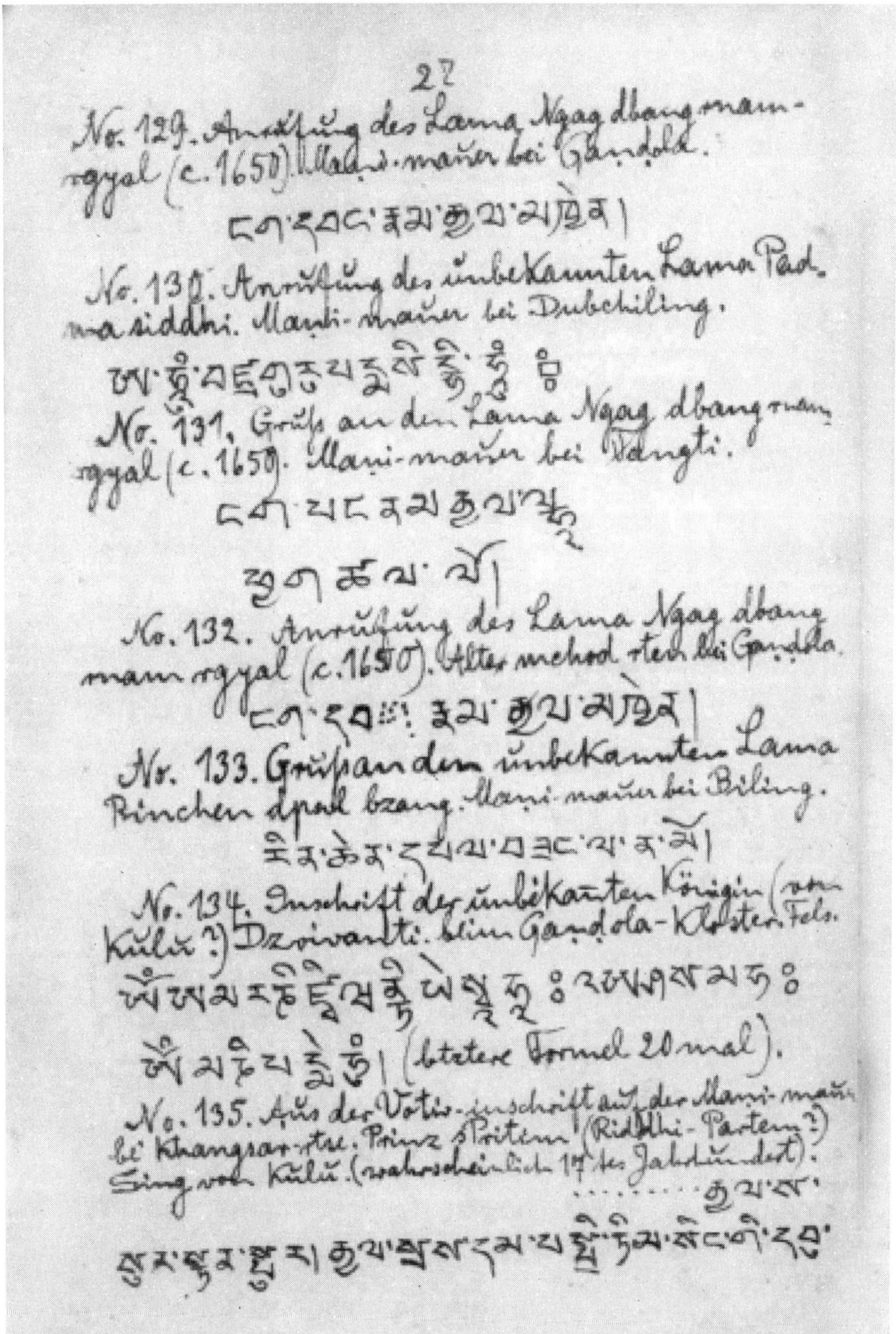

27

No. 129. Anrufung des Lama Ngag dbang rnam-rgyal (c. 1650). Mani-mauer bei Gandola.

ངག་དབང་རྣམ་རྒྱལ་མཁྱེན།

No. 130. Anrufung des unbekannten Lama Padma siddhi. Mani-mauer bei Dubchiling.

ཨཿཧཱུྃ་བཛྲ་གུ་རུ་པདྨ་སིདྡྷི་ཧཱུྃ་ཧྲཱིཿ

No. 131. Gruss an den Lama Ngag dbang rnam-rgyal (c. 1650). Mani-mauer bei Wangti.

ངག་དབང་རྣམ་རྒྱལ་[illegible]

ཕྱག་འཚལ་ལོ།

No. 132. Anrufung des Lama Ngag dbang rnam rgyal (c. 1650). Alter mchod rten bei Gandola.

ངག་དབང་རྣམ་རྒྱལ་མཁྱེན།

No. 133. Gruss an den unbekannten Lama Rinchen dpal bzang. Mani-mauer bei Biling.

རིན་ཆེན་དཔལ་བཟང་ལ་ན་མོ།

No. 134. Inschrift der unbekannten Königin (von Kulu?) Dzoiwanti. beim Gandola-Kloster Fels.

ཨོཾ་ཨ་མ་ར་ཎི་ཛཱི་ཝན་ཏྱེ་ཡེ་སྭཱ་ཧཱ༔ ཨཱ་ཡུར་ཛྙཱ་ན་མ་ཏ༔

ཨོཾ་མ་ཎི་པ་དྨེ་ཧཱུྃ། (letztere Formel 20 mal).

No. 135. Aus der Votiv-inschrift auf der Mani-mauer bei Khangsar-rtse. Prinz Pritam (Riddhi-Partam?) Sing von Kulu. (wahrscheinlich 17tes Jahrhundert):

……… རྒྱལ་པོ་

ཕྱུར་ལྡན་སྤྲུ་ར། རྒྱལ་སྲས་དམ་པ་སྤྲི་ཏམ་སེང་གེ་[illegible]

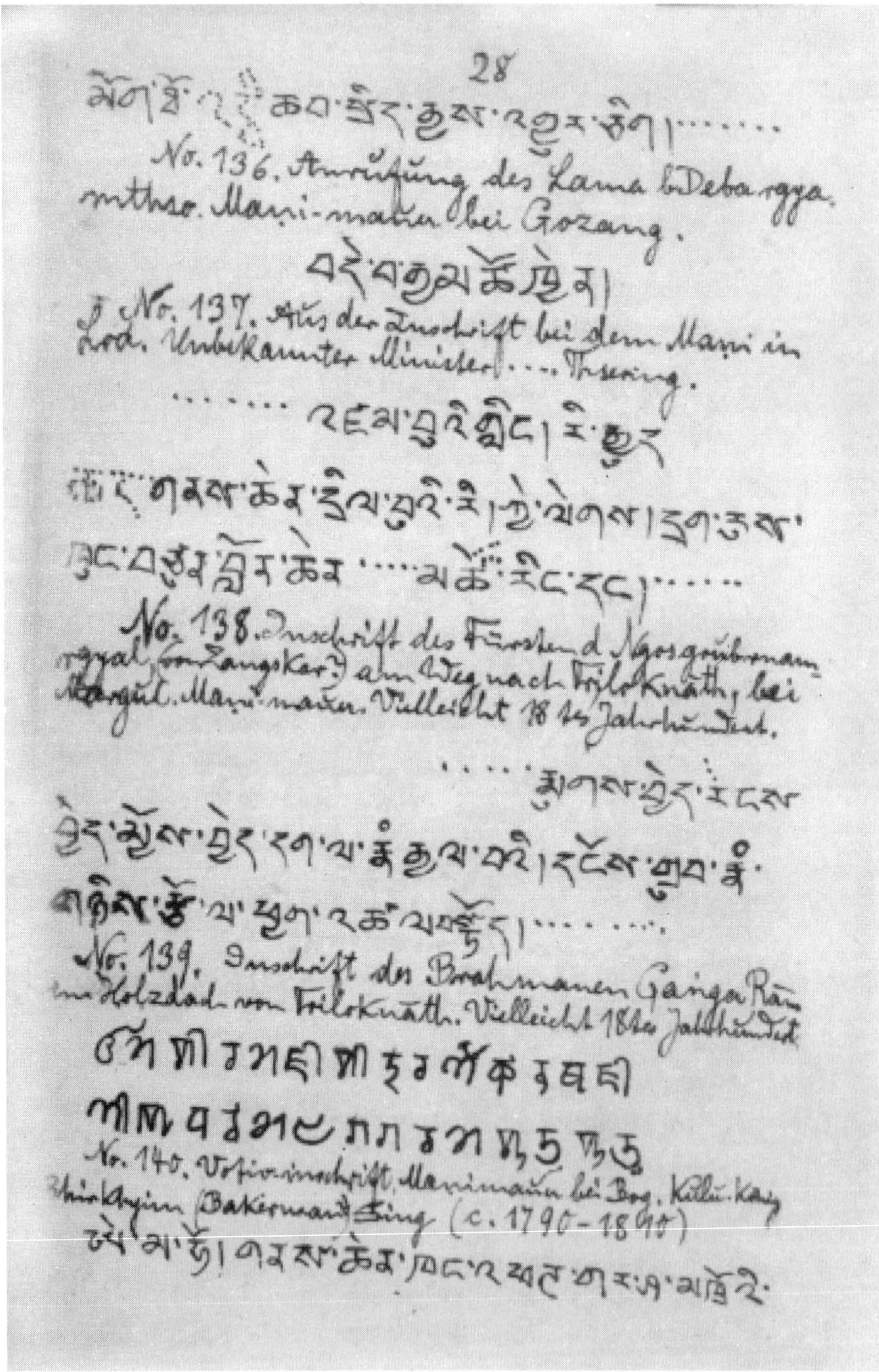
28

No. 136. Anrufung des Lama bDeba rgya mtsho. Mani-mauer bei Gozang.

No. 137. Aus der Inschrift bei dem Mani in Lod. Unbekannter Minister ..... Thsering.

No. 138. Inschrift des Fürsten d Ngos grub rnam rgyal von Zangskar am Weg nach Triloknath, bei Margul. Mani-mauer. Vielleicht 18 tes Jahrhundert.

No. 139. Inschrift des Brahmanen Ganga Ram im Holzdach von Triloknath. Vielleicht 18tes Jahrhundert

No. 140. Votivinschrift, Manimauer bei Bog, Kullu. Kay Shin Khyim (Bakermand Sing (c. 1790–1840)

༢༩

གནས། རྡོ་གཅན་…རྫོངས་རི་བོ་སྐྱིན་དྷྱ་ལ། ཡ་མཚན་སྣང་བྱུང་

དཔལ་གྱི་དྲི་ལ་བུའི་རི། མཚམས་རྣམས་སུ་གྱི་ཕྱིན་གྱི་སྐྱ་བ་པའི་གནས།

མཁར་རི་དཀར་པོ་དཀར་ཏི་རྫི་འདྲ། རི་གསུམ་འདུས་པ་གནས་ཆེན་

ལབ་སྐྱི་འདྲ། རྩེ་གསུམ་འདུས་…པ་དཔལ་གྱི་རྒྱུ་བར་འདྲ། ཞིང་

རྫོང་པ་རྩི་རི་རྩི་སྔོང་…འདྲ། གནམ་ས་ལ་ཀྲ་ལམ་ཚ་འཁོར་རྩི་བས་

བརྒྱད་འདྲ། ས་ལ་ཀྲ་ལམ་ཚ་པདྨ་འདབ་བརྒྱད་འདྲ། ལོགས་ལ་

ཀྲ་ལམ་ཚ། བཀྲལ་ཏྲེ་བརྒྱད་འདྲ། ལོ་སྐྱལ་ཞིང་བྲོ་བའི་ཆ་བྱུང་

འདྲ། སྐྱེལ་ཞིང་ཁྲོའི་ཅ་ཅར་འདྲ། མཁར་རིའི་མི་ཀ་ལོ་རྩི་རྩིའི་

འདྲ། ཡུལ་ལུའི་མི་འདྲ་རྒྱ་བོད་འདྲེ་པ་འདྲ། ཆ་ལུགས་མི་

འདྲ་ཁྲིམས་པའི་གྱིན་ཆ་འདྲ། ཕུན་འདོད་ཁང་ལྷ་མོ་ཕུའི།

ཀུ་ཨུ་ཏ་རང་ཅན་ཟླུའི་ཆེན་པོ་ཞུགས། དེ་རྫུ་ཡི་དི་རྡེ་ཁག

མོ་ཞུགས། ལོ་བྲང་ཆེན་པོ་ཕུར་ཏན་ཕུ་རི་ཡི། རྒྱལ་པོ་ཚེ

པོ་གླིར་ཁྱིམ་ལེགས་ཀྱི་དགུ་རྫོག་བོ་བའི་འདུས། ཡུལ་ལ་དགེ

ཆག་གར་ཕག་མཁྲོའི་གླིང་། མི་དབང་ལོ་བྲང་ཁྱད་པར་ཁང་ལར

ན། དྷརྨ་ལེགས་ཡུམ་སྨལ་དགུ་མོག་མདོ་ཞིང་། ཆབ་སྲིད་དར

བའི་དུས། དགེ་བཅུའི་ཁྲིམས་ཀྱི་ལ་བོར་འབངས་འདྲུ

མཛད། ཕྱིག་བཅུ་གཏན་ནས་བཀག་བའི་དཔལ་བོའི།

མཆོག། དེའི་མངའ་འོག་འབོག་གི་གཡུ་ལ་མཚོ་གན།

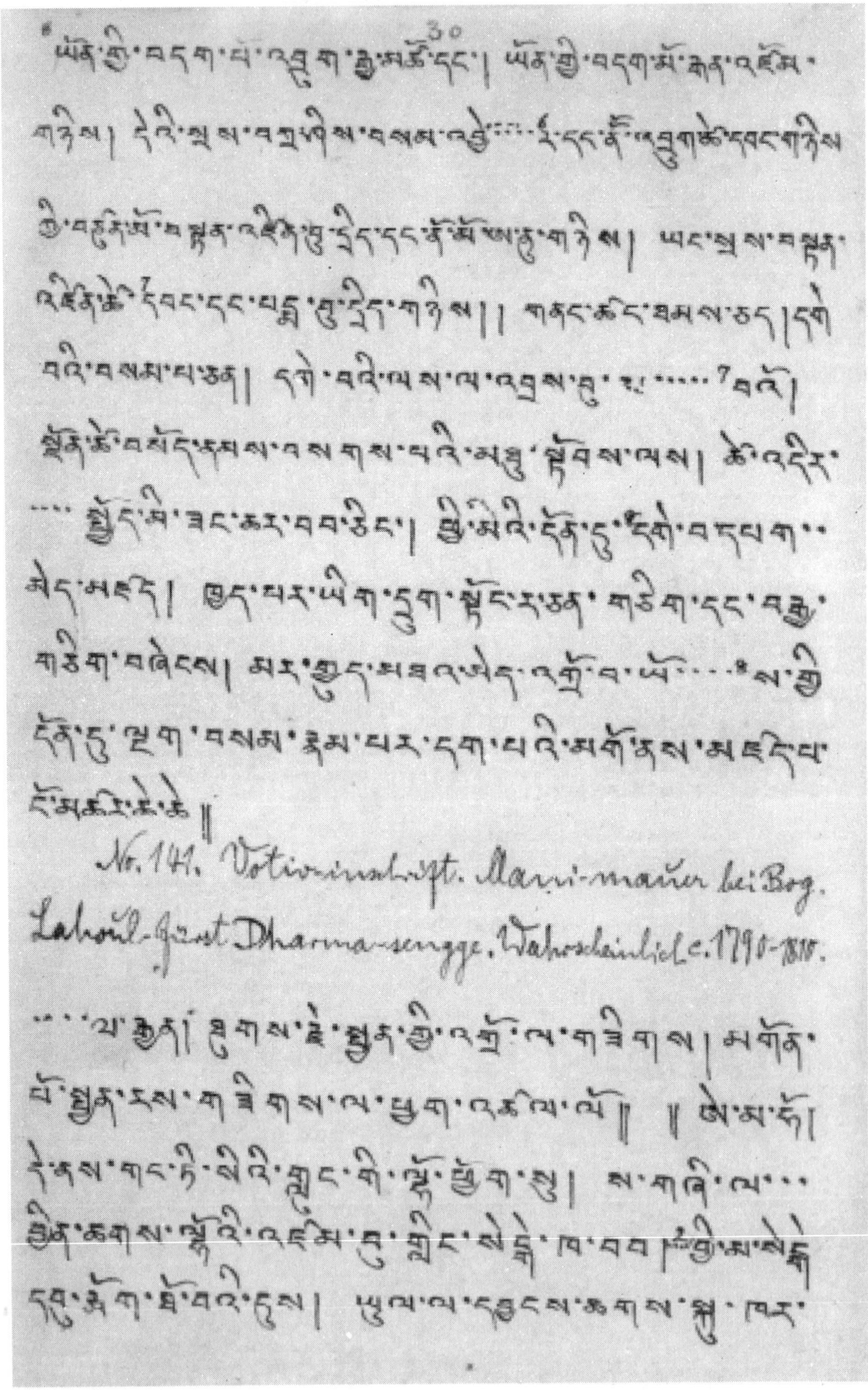
Nr. 141. Votivinschrift. Mani-mauer bei Bog.
Lahoul. Fürst Dharma-sengge. Wahrscheinlich c. 1790-1810.

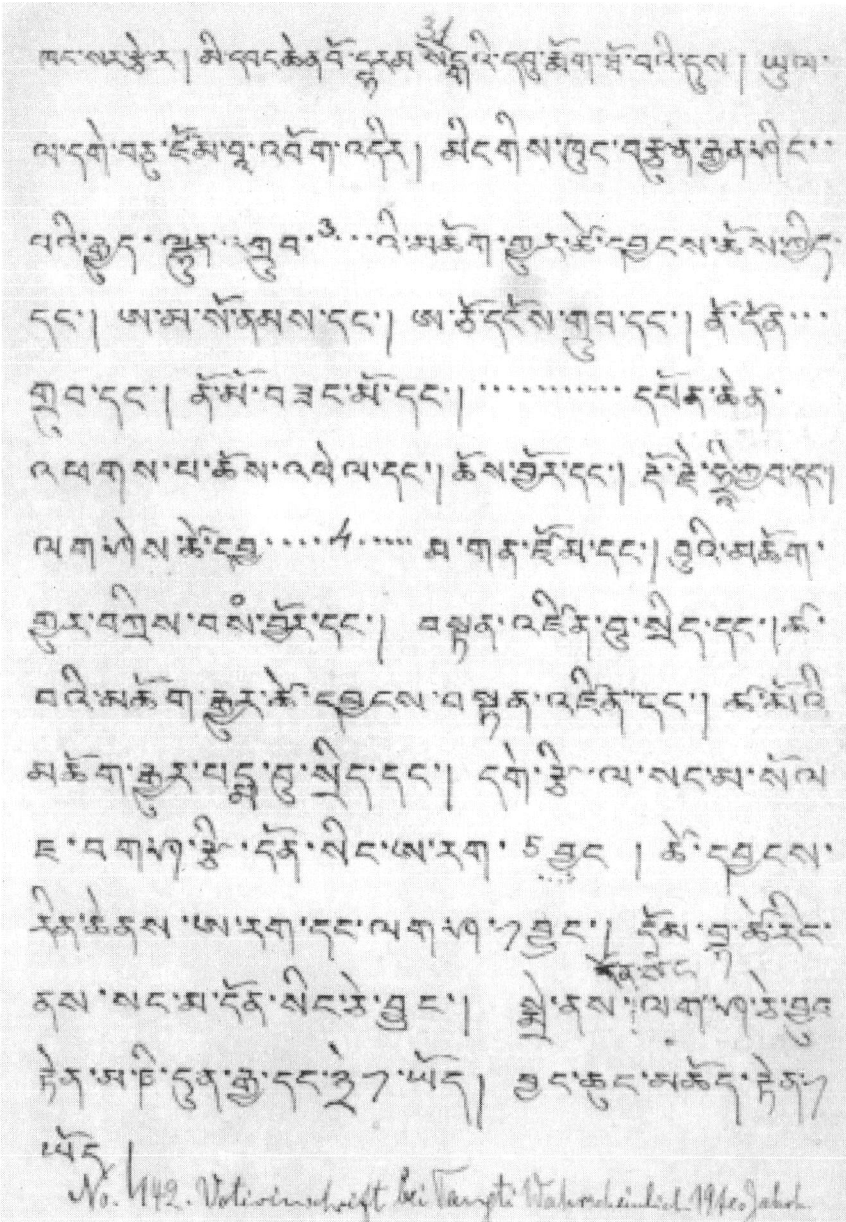
No. 142. Votivinschrift bei Tangti Wahrscheinlich 19te Jahrh.

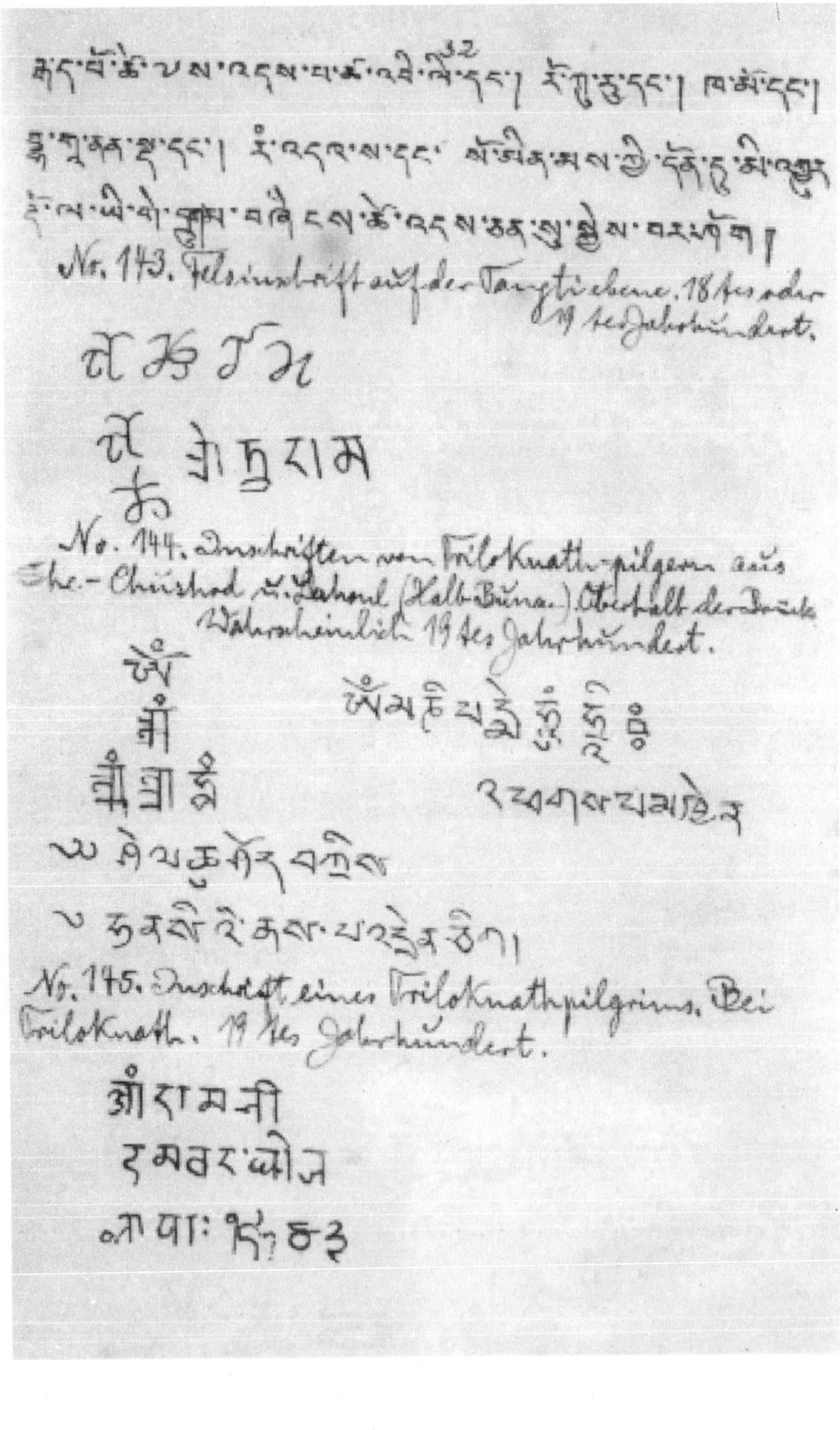
No. 143. Felsinschrift auf der Tangtiebene. 18tes oder 19tes Jahrhundert.

No. 144. Inschriften von Triloknath-pilgern aus ...-Chirshod i. Lahoul (Halb-Büna.) Oberhalb der Brücke. Wahrscheinlich 19tes Jahrhundert.

No. 145. Inschrift eines Triloknathpilgrims. Bei Triloknath. 19tes Jahrhundert.

C. *Ancient folklores in the memory of the people of Lahul (Sngan ma'i dus kyi lo rgyus gar zha pa rnams la yid du rtsam lus pa bzhin bzhugsso||Die historischen und mythologischen Erinnerunger der Lahouler Gesammelt von A.H. Francke, 1907)*

1. Di Saje von der Einfuhrung der Getreide und der Schmiede aus Indien nach Lahoul. Sprache: Bunan (Narration about how the cereals and smiths were brought from India to Lahul, told by Saje. Language : Bunan).
2. Alte religiose Hymne. Beim Feuer aufdem Schnee (wintersonnen wende?) grungen. Sprache Altes Bunan (Ancient religious Hymn sung near the fire or in the sun perhaps in the spring time or end of winter, Language: Ancient Bunan.)
3. Das letzte Menschenopfer in Bar, ober half Kyor. Sprache: Bunan (Story as to how the custom of human sacrifice at Kyor was abolished. Language: Bunan).
4. Gebetslied. Sprache: Bunan (A Prayer. Language: Bunan).
5. Gebetan sPyan ras gzigs. Sprache: Bunan (Prayer for Can ras zigs. Language: Bunan).
6. Das letzte Menschenopfer in Kyelang. Sprache: Bunan (The story of end of the Human Sacrifice at Kyelang. Language: Bunan).
7. Gebetslied. Sprache: Bunan (A Prayer. Language: Bunan).
8. Gebetan sPyan ras gzigs. Sprache: Bunan (A Prayer to the Can ras zigs. Language: Bunan).
9. Der Handel zwischen der Konigen von Kulu und Ladakh, der bis 1843 wahote. Nach dem Bericht eines Augen zeugen. Sprache: Bunan (Commerce conducted between the kings of Kulu and Ladakh, upto 1843, as told by a man from sKyor who in his younger years was in the service of the Rajas. Language: Bunan).
10. Gebetslied. Sprache Bunan (A Prayer. Language: Bunan).
11. Das letzte Menschenopfer in Gus. Tod der Konigin Rupi Rani. Sprache: Manchad (The story of the sacrifice of Rani Rupi in Gus. Language: Manchad.).
12. Grundung von Chod durch Brahmaner von Bandal in Kulu. Sprache Manchad (How the Brahmans came from Bandal village in Kullu and settled near Chod in Lahul. Language: Manchad.).
13. Lied der Musikanten Rokunu und Debunu vor dem Rana von Gus. Sprache: Genisch von Manchad und Pahari (A ballad by the musicians Rokunu and Debunu for the Rana of Gus. Language, late Pahari and Manchad mixture).
14. Lied von der Aufertigung eines Gotzen fin Konig Feti Sing von Kulu durch den Schmied Nandi Ram Phuntshog von Manchad. Sprache, Pahari (Ballad relating the story as to how Nandi Ram Phuntsog from Lahul manufactured a parasol for the god of the Raja Fati Singh of Kullu. Language: Pahari).

15. Die Schlacht bei Bajora. Wegen des von Partem Sing in Sultanpur gebautan Schlos. Kontes zumal Konig mit dem Konig von Mandi der in der Schlacht bei Bajora mit Jhulfe der Lahouler Truppen besiegt wind. Sprache: Pahari und Urdu (Battle at Bajaura, in Kullu, between the Raja of Mandi and Raja Pritam Singh of Kullu whose castle is located at Sultanpur. In this war the Lahoul troups also fought under the banner of Gepang).
16. Die Flucht des Gottes von Marbal. Sprache Manchad (Flight of god Marbal. Language: Manchad).
17. Vertrebung der Ladakher aus Spiti Wahrscheinlich nach der Schlacht bei Basgo c. 1647 AD. Sprache: Westetibetisch (Expulsion of Ladakhis from Spiti in around the war of Basgo, c. 1647 AD. Language: Western Tibetan).
18. Wie die Nagas Tinan mit Quellen versorgten. Sprache: Tinan (How the god Nagas brought the source of water to Tinan. Language: Tinan).
19. Gregs Religiose Hymne der ober Lahouler Tibeter Wintersonnenwende Sprache Lahouler Tibetisch (Gregs. Religious Hymn, sung during the winter in Lahoul. Language: Lahouli-Tibetan).
20. Gregs. Religiose Hymn der Ober Lahouler Tibeter (Wintersonnenwende). Sprache: Lahouler Tibetische. (Gregs Religious Hymn sung during the winter. Language: Lahul-Tibetan).
21. Tod der Prinzessin Paranoli Focher der jo Bali Ram c. 1810 Sprache: Pahari (Song regarding the death of the daughter of Jo Bali Ram, AD 1810. Language: Pahari).

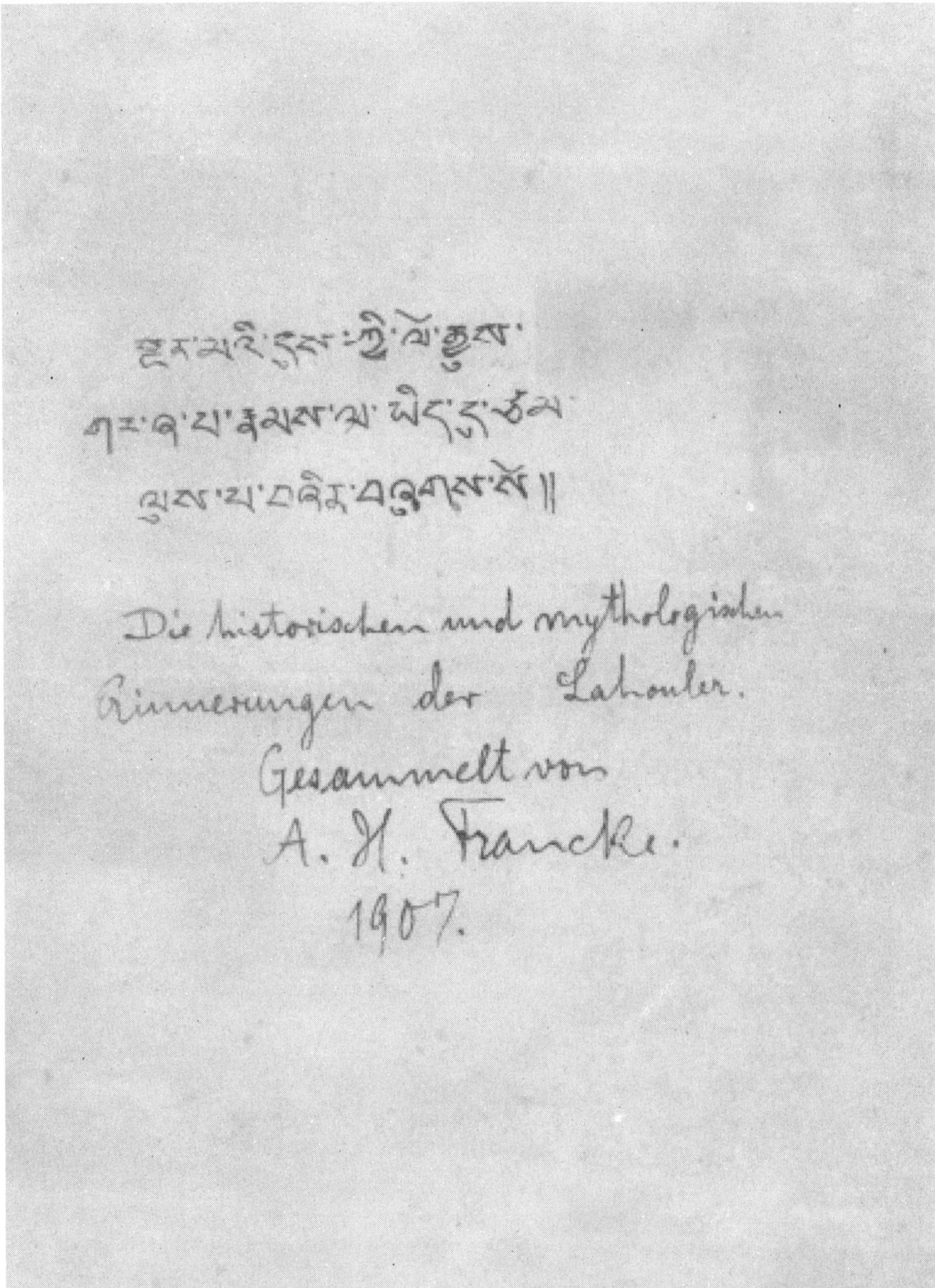

རྒར་ཞའི་དུས་ཀྱི་ལོ་རྒྱུས་
གར་ཞ་པ་རྣམས་ལ་ཡིད་དུ་ཚམ་
ལུས་པ་བཞིན་བཞུགས་སོ ||

Die historischen und mythologischen
Erinnerungen der Lahouler.
Gesammelt von
A. H. Francke.
1907.

Die folgenden Erzählungen und Lieder sind von mir gesammelt worden, um Material zum Studium der 4 Sprachen von Lahoul zu bekommen. Ich muß sagen, daß die Volksstämme von Lahoul, welche jeder kaum mehr als 5000 Seelen zählen, äußerst arm an Volksliteratur sind. Es machte Mühe, nur die folgenden wenigen Erzählungen und Lieder aufzutreiben. Die Lieder No. 4, 5, 7, 8, 10, stammen aus Missionar A. W. Heyde's Sammlung. Die Erzählungen No. 1 und 18 waren von demselben Missionar entdeckt und mir im Abriß deutsch mitgeteilt worden. Ich habe nach diesen Angaben die Originaltexte auffinden können. Erzählung No. 17 ist von Missionar F. E. Peter, S. M. M., entdeckt worden.

A. H. F.

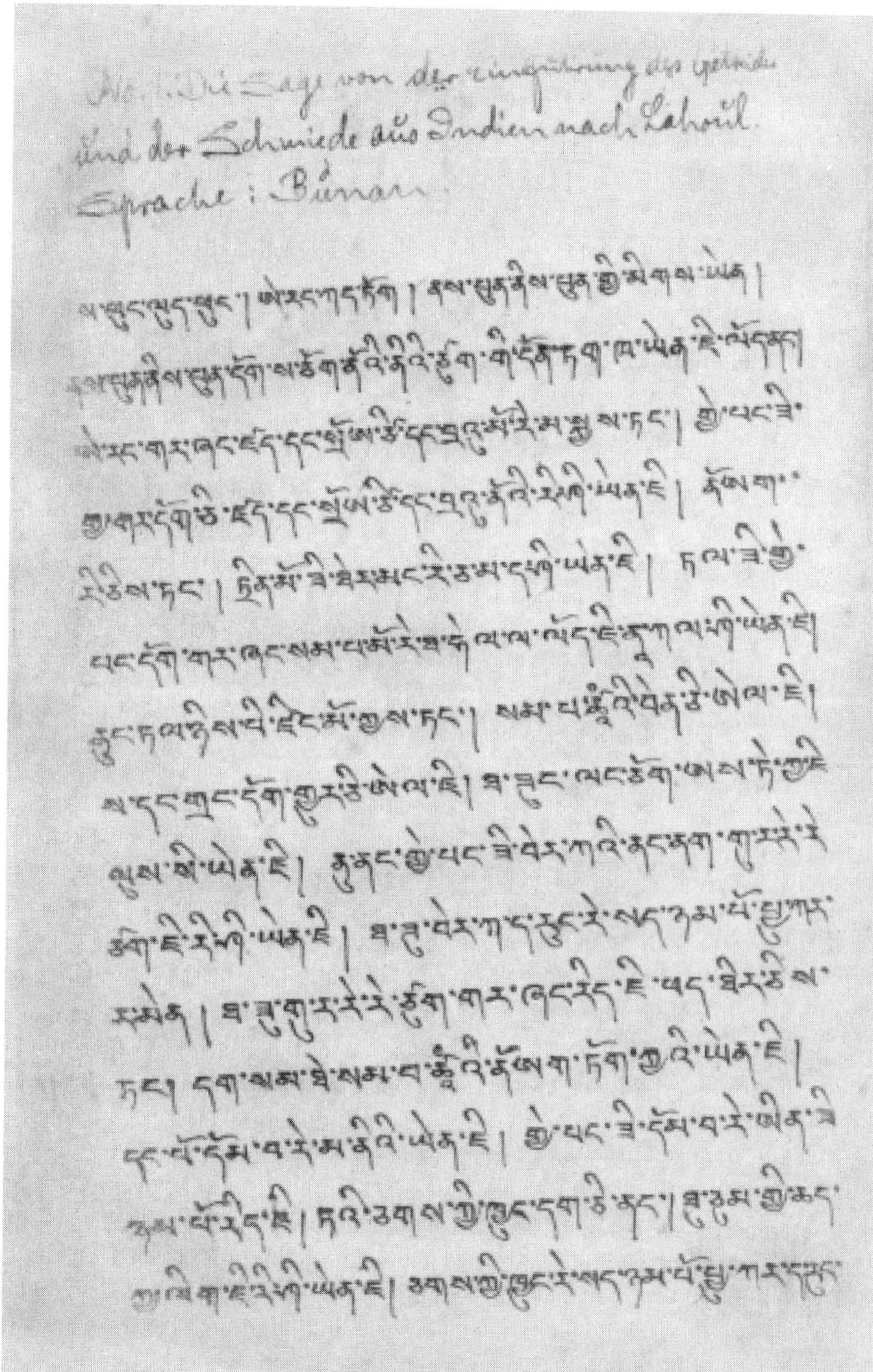
No. 1. Die Sage von der Einführung des Getreides und der Schmiede aus Indien nach Lāhoul.
Sprache: Būnan

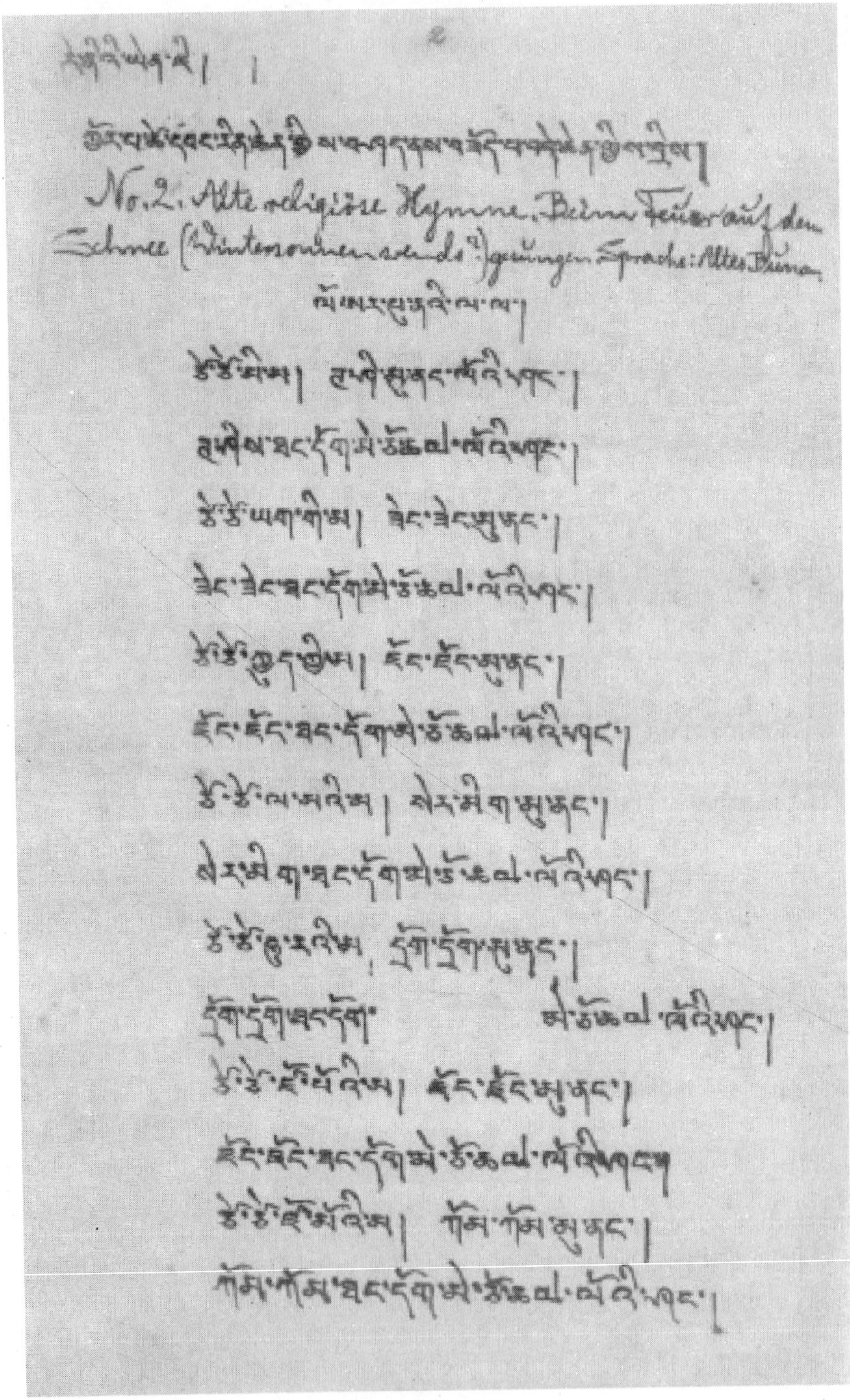

ཆེ་གི་ནི་ལེན་ནི། །

[illegible]

No. 2. Alte religiöse Hymne. Beim Feuer auf den Schnee (Wintersonnenwende?) gesungen. Sprache: Altes Bunan

ལོ་སར་ལྷུ་ནའི་ལ་ལ།

ཧྲི་ཧྲི་མེ་ས། ཉ་ཕྱི་སྤུ་ནང་ལོ་འི་ཡཀ།
ཉ་ཕྱིས་ཐང་དོག་མི་ཙོ་ཚལ་ལོ་འི་ཡཀ།
ཧྲི་ཧྲི་ཡག་གི་ས། ཞེང་ཞེང་སྤུ་ནང་།
ཞེང་ཞེང་ཐང་དོག་མེ་ཙོ་ཚལ་ལོ་འི་ཡཀ།
ཧྲི་ཧྲི་རྒྱུད་གྱིས། རྫོང་རྫོང་སྤུ་ནང་།
རྫོང་རྫོང་ཐང་དོག་མེ་ཙོ་ཚལ་ལོ་འི་ཡཀ།
ཧྲི་ཧྲི་ལ་མ་འི་ས། སེར་མི་ག་སྤུ་ནང་།
སེར་མི་ག་ཐང་དོག་མེ་ཙོ་ཚལ་ལོ་འི་ཡཀ།
ཧྲི་ཧྲི་ཞུ་ར་འི་ས། དྲོག་དྲོག་སྤུ་ནང་།
དྲོག་དྲོག་ཐང་དོག་ མེ་ཙོ་ཚལ་ལོ་འི་ཡཀ།
ཧྲི་ཧྲི་རྫོ་པོ་འི་ས། རྫོང་རྫོང་སྤུ་ནང་།
རྫོང་རྫོང་ཐང་དོག་མེ་ཙོ་ཚལ་ལོ་འི་ཡཀ
ཧྲི་ཧྲི་རྫོ་མོ་འི་ས། ཀོམ་ཀོམ་སྤུ་ནང་།
ཀོམ་ཀོམ་ཐང་དོག་མེ་ཙོ་ཚལ་ལོ་འི་ཡཀ།

3

ཙེ་ཙེ་ཁྱི་ཙེ་འིས། ཐོབ་ཐོབ་སྐྱུ་ནང་།

ཐོབ་ཐོབ་ཟང་སོག་སེ་ཙེ་ཆལ་ལོ་འིཕང་།

ཙེ་ཙེ་ཀ་ར་འིས། ཤུ་ཤུ་སྐྱུ་ནང་།

ཤུ་ཤུ་ཟང་དོག་སེ་ཙེ་ཆལ་ལོ་འིཕང་།

ཙེ་ཙེ་ལྕང་ས་ཀྱིས། ཨོ་ཨོ་སྐྱུ་ནང་།

ཨོ་ཨོ་ཟང་དོག་སེ་ཙེ་ཆལ་ཀོ་འིཕང་།

ཁྱི་འི་སྐྱུ་ནང་ཡམ་ཡེ་ཡ་ཉེང་གོལ་འི་ཆེ།

ཀྱིན་ཡེ་ཏང་ངད་ཡེ་ཏང་།

ཆེན་ཆོ་ལ་ཆེན་ཆེལ་ཉེང་གོལ་འི་ཆེ།

ཀྱི་ཙོ་ནང་ཏམ་པ་གྲོད་ཀྱི་ཡས་ཏོག་པག་ཏུག་ཆལ།

ཤུ་ཙོ་དང་ཙག་དར་གྲོད་ཀྱི་ཡས་ཏོག་ཡར་ཞི་ཆལ།

ཤིར་པེད་དང་ཞལ་ཙོ་གྲོད་ཀྱི་ཡས་ཏོག་ཞིམ་ས་ཏབ་ཆལ།

ཞལ་ཙོ་གྲོད་ཀྱི་ཡས་ཏོག་ཞིམ་ས་ཀྱིར་ཆལ།

དེད་པེང་ཙེ་ཀྱུ་ལ་ཙ་ཡས་ཏོག་ཞོམ་ས་ཀྱེལ་ཀལ།

སྐྱུ་ལི་སྐ་ག་ལི་གྲོད་ཀྱི་ཡས་ཏོག་ཞིམ་ས་སོར་ཆལ།

Nr. 3. Das letzte Menschenopfer in Bar, oberhalb Kyor. Sprache: Bunan.

ཀྱོར་དོག་མི་ཤུར་ཙེ་སད་ཏག་ད་ཙམ་ཙོག་ཁ་ནག་མ་འགྱོ་ཟ་ས་བུ་འི་

སེགས་ཡིན།

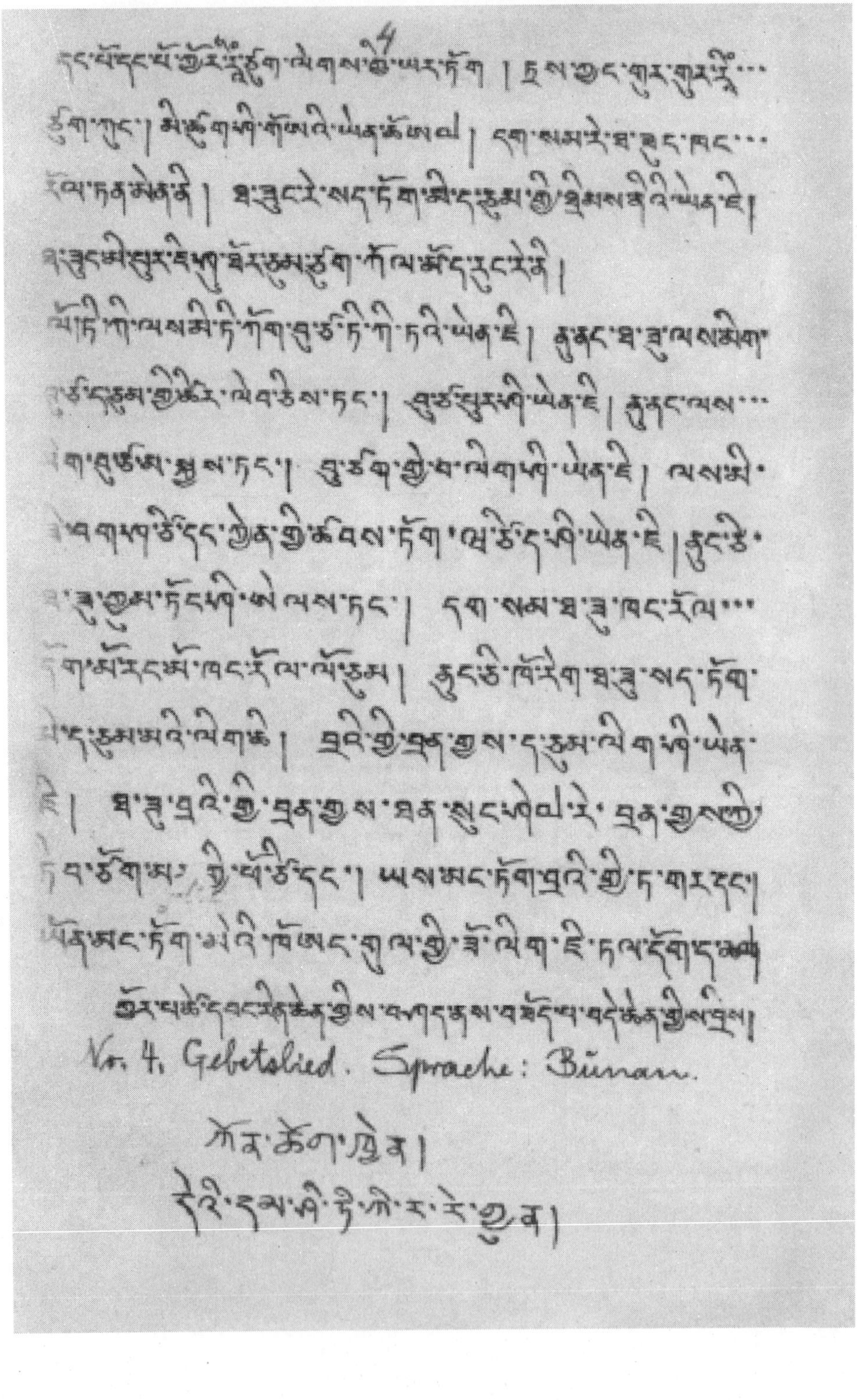

No. 4. Gebetslied. Sprache: Bunan.

རྒྱ་གི་ལ་དེ་རྒྱད།

ཀོན་ཚོག་ཚེན།

No. 5. Gebet an Spyan ras gzigs. Sprache: Bunan.

ཕག་ལ་པ་ཚེན།

ཙི་ཙི་དི་གི་ཐུ་རེ་ད།

དན་ཟེ་སྒྲུག་ཟེ་ལེཨ།

ཕ་དོག་ཀྱི་མཆོད་དི་གི་ཐུལ་ཙེལ།

ཕགས་པ་ ཚེན།

No. 6. Das letzte Menschenopfer in Kyelang. Sprache: Bunan.

དང་པོ་དང་པོ་གར་ཁང་ཐན་ཤུང་ཤི་ག་ ཨད་ཤོ་ག་ལ་མ་ཕྱུར་ཞེ་
དཙི་ཨས་སེ་ཏེ། མི་ཕྱུར་ཞེ་ད་ཧྲུས་ཀྱི་བྲིམས་ནེའི་ཡེན་ཞེ། ཁ་རོག་
རེང་ནང་། ཏེ་ཏེ་མེ་མེ་ཟེའི་པེས་དས་ཀྱི་ནང་ནག་ཀྱི་ཁང་རེ་
བར་ཙིའི་ཞི་ལ་དོག་ཨད་དེ་ཀོག་མི་ད་ཧྲུས་ཀྱི་བྲིམ་ས་ནེན་
ཟ་ལོ་ཤུལ། ལོ་རེ་རེ་དང་ལེ་གས་ཀྱི་ཁུ་རེ་རེ་ཚེ་ཚེར་ལེག་
ག་མི་ད་ཧྲུམ་ལོ་ཤུལ། ཁོ་རེག་ཐ་ཟུ་མི་ད་ཧྲུམ་ཧྲུག་ཁ་ནག་
པའི་ཀྱུ་ཟ་ལོད་ནང་། ལོ་དི་གི་ཨ་པ་ཏེ་ ཀོག་ཚེར་
ལེན་ཤི་ཡེན་ཞེ། ཨ་པ་ཨེན་ཟའི་བུ་ཙ་དི་གི་དའི་
ཡེན་ཞེ། རྒྱས་ཏང་ཨ་པ་ཟེ་ད་ཨེང་གའི་བུ་ཙ་དི་གི་

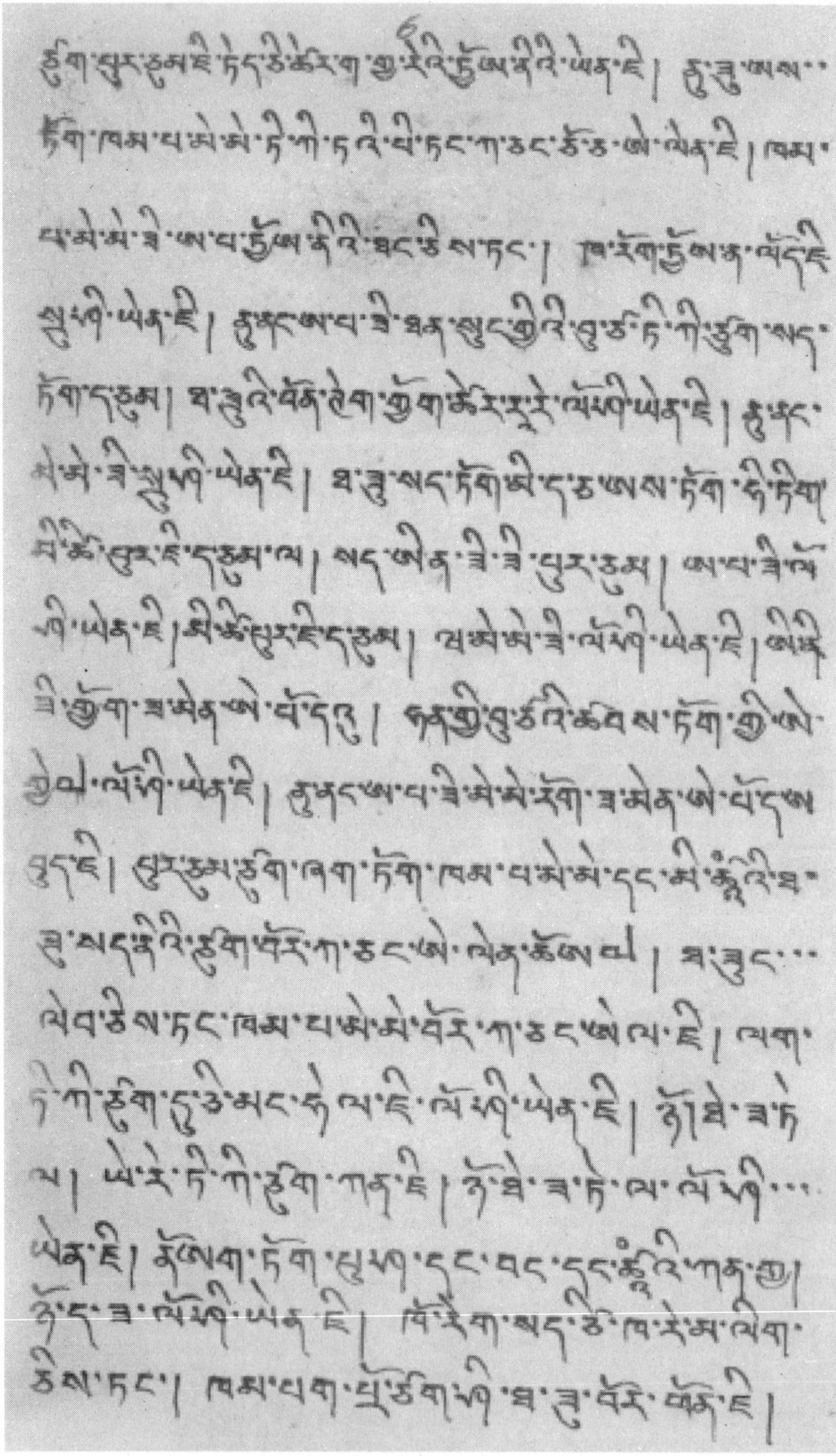

གྲོག་པོའི་ནང་ནག་རྒྱུག་ལ་ཟེར་གྱི་ཡིན་ཧེ།[7] ཝོར་སོ་ཏེ་ཟེ་ཉེ་ལ་ཧེ། ཏེ་ཞིག་སོ་
ཏི་ཟེ་ནོ་ཡིན་པའི་ཡིན་ཧེ། ཏུ་ནང་ག་ཉེ་ཚེ་ཉེ་ལ་ཚེ། མི་མ་དང་རྒྱུམ། ལ་མ་ད་
རྒྱུམ་ལིག་ཚེ། ཀུ་གུ་ཏེ་ལར་ལག་དག་སམ་རེ་ཐ་ཟླ་ཝོར་ནི་ལོ་པགལ། རྒྱུན་
བ་བབས་ཀ་ཡམས་ཏོག། ཏན་ཚང་པའི་ཙུག་མེ་མེ་ཉུ་ནེ་ལོད་ནང་ས་དགྱུར་
ཧེ་པེད་ཆེ་ཡེ་ལ་ཧེ། སད་པེད་ཆེ་ཡེ་ལས་ཏང་སྐྱོན་པ་ཞི་ཧེ་ཡེ་པཱུ་རེ་
ལེ་པགལ། ཟ་རྒྱུ་སད་ཏོག་ག་ཉེ་ཚེ་གྱི་ལང་གི་དེབ་ཏ་ལོ་ཆལ། ཟ་
རྒྱུ་ལི་དོན་ཏག་ཉིད་ང་གྱི་ལང་གི་སད་ཡིན་ཧེ།། གྱི་ལང་པ
༄། ཕྱག་གི་ས་བ་ཕོད་ནས་བཞོད་པ་བདེ་ཚེ་ན་གྱིལ་ཟེལ།

Nr. 7. Gebetslied. Sprache: Bunan.

ཀོན་ཆོག་ཕྱེན།
ཏོག་ཏོག་ར་རེ་ཟད།
རྒྱམ་དོག་ཏབ་པའི་ལེབ་ཙ་ཡམ་ས་ཏོག།
ཡེ་པོ་གྱུ་རེ་ད་ཙ་རྒྱུན།
ཀོན་ཆོག་ཕྱེན།

Nr. 8. Gebet an sPyan ras gzigs. Sprache: Bunan

ཕག་ས་པ་ཕྱེན།
ནད་ར་རེ་ཟ་ད།
ཏིང་ཧོག་གྱབ་ས་ལག་ཧེ་ཡོག་ཙ་རྒྱུན།

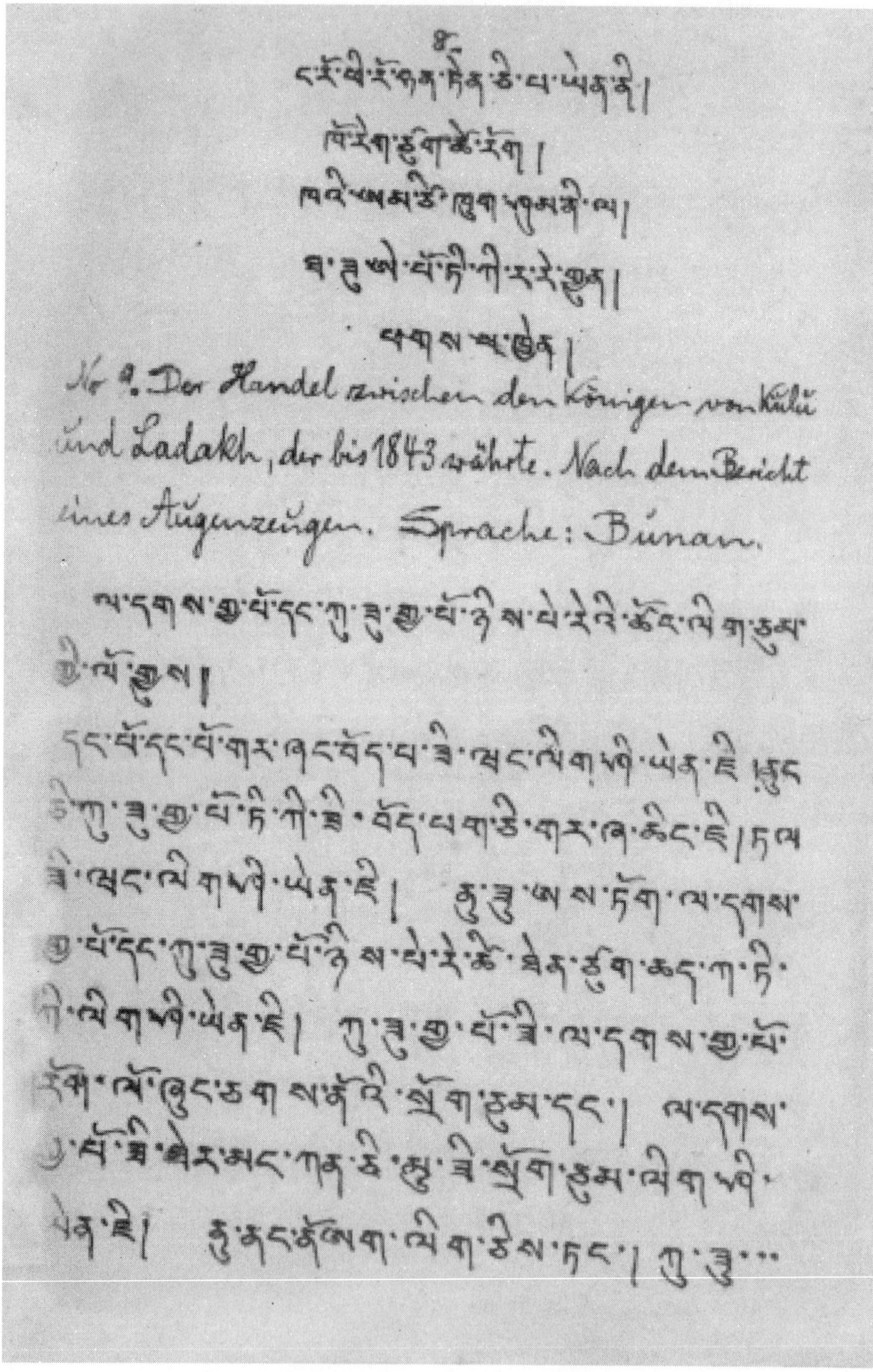
No 9. Der Handel zwischen den Königen von Kulū und Ladakh, der bis 1843 währte. Nach dem Bericht eines Augenzeugen. Sprache: Bunan.

༩

རྒྱ་པོ་ཡི་གར་ཞ་བ་རྩོམ་རིག་དང་གི་ཁྲལ་རྒྱ་ཚབ་ས་ཏོག། ལ་དགས་
རྒྱ་པོ་རྟོག་ཅགས་བ་ཧེ་རེ་རེ་ལོ་ཞུང་དཔྱམ་གྱི་ཧུ་ཀུམ་དཔེ། གར་ཞ་པ་དང་
མི་རྣོག་པའི་ཀུ་ཧུང་ཅི་ཅགས་བཞི་རེ་རེ་ཡིག་ཀར་ཧྱམ། ས་བྲུ་ཅགས་སྐྱོའི
ལ་དགས་མང་ཁ་ནག་ཏེ་ལ་ཚོ་རིང་ནང་། ལ་དགས་མང་ཅི་རྒྱ་པོའི་ལོ་
ཉི་སྒོ་ཏི་ཀི་གར་ཞང་ལས་ཏོག་ཅགས་རྒྱུ་ང་ར་མེད། ཧུ་ཧང་གར་ཞ་
པ་དང་མི་རྣོག་པ་ཡི་སྒོའི་ཅི་ཡིར་མང་སྐྱོའི་ཚོ་ཁྲུ་རེ་རེ་དང་ཅགས་
བ་ཧེ་རེ་རེ་དང་ཅགས་ཙོག་ཅ་བད་ཡུའི་ལས་ཏེ་ས་བྲུ་པོ་ཉའི་ཧུང་
རེད་ཇེ་དཔྱམ། །ཧུ་ཧང་པོ་ཉ་ཡི་གར་ཞ་པ་དང་མི་རྣོག་པ་སྐྱོའི་
དོག་ཅགས་སྐྱོའི་ཀལ་ཇེ་ལིང་ཏི་ལས་ཏོག་ཏེ་ལ་ཧྱམ། ཧུ་ཡྲུ
ལས་ཏོག་ལམ་ཅི་རེ་གྱི་ལང་མང་ཅི་མ་ཉེ་ལ། ཀར་དང་མང་
ཅི་ཉེན་ཟ། ཀུར་ལེབ་ནང་། ཡང་ན་ཁ་ཟིང་གིལ་གྱི་ནད་ར་
སྐྱོའི་ཀར་དང་ཛོམ་མེད། ། ལ་དགས་མང་ཅགས་ལོ་ཞུང་
གྱི་ཀུར་ཟལ་ལེག་ཏེ་ལ་ཕྱི་ཛོད་གྱི་ནི། ལ་དགས་པ་ཡི་
ཀུར་པ་ཛོག་གྲ་ཡང་ན་བཁ་ཕྱི་ཕ་ཁ་ ེ་དཔུམ་མེད། ཟ
བྲུའི་ཚབ་ས་ཏོག་བེར་ཀ་ཤེ་དང་གྱི། རྒྱ་པོའི་ཏིབ་ཀ་ཏེ་ལ་ཧྲུ
ལིང་ཏི་ལས་ཏོག་ཅགས་བྱུ་ཇེ་ད་རེ། ཟ་བྲུང་ཅི་ལགས་
པ་ཚེ་རེ་ཕྱི་ཧྲུག་སྲུ་ཟ་ཀུར་ཅི་གོ་ཡང་མེད། ལ་དགས་པ་
ཇེ་ཅགས་ཀུར་ཅི་ཏབ་ཕྱི་ཡེ་ལ་མེད། །ཧུ་ནང་ཟ་བྲུ་

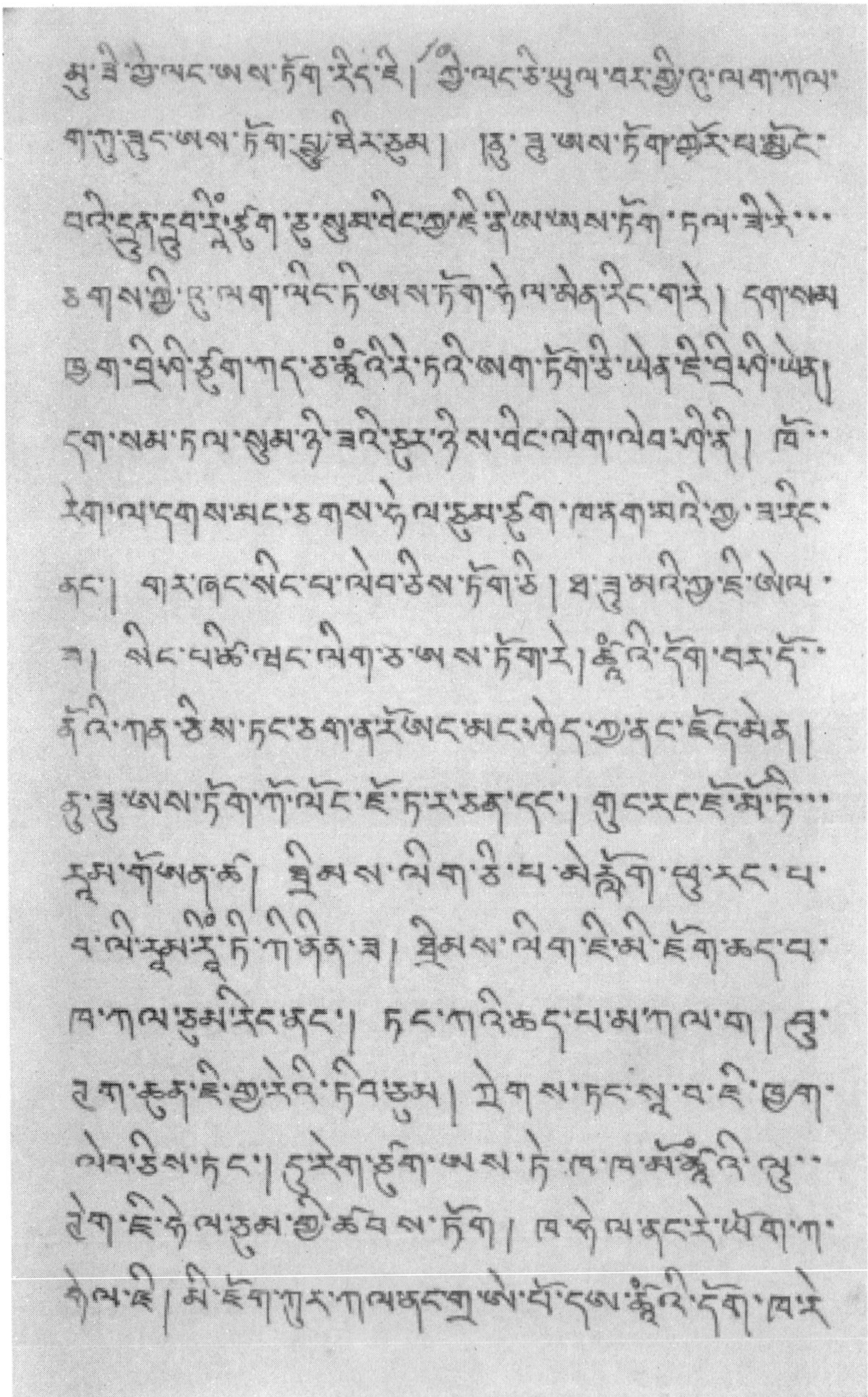

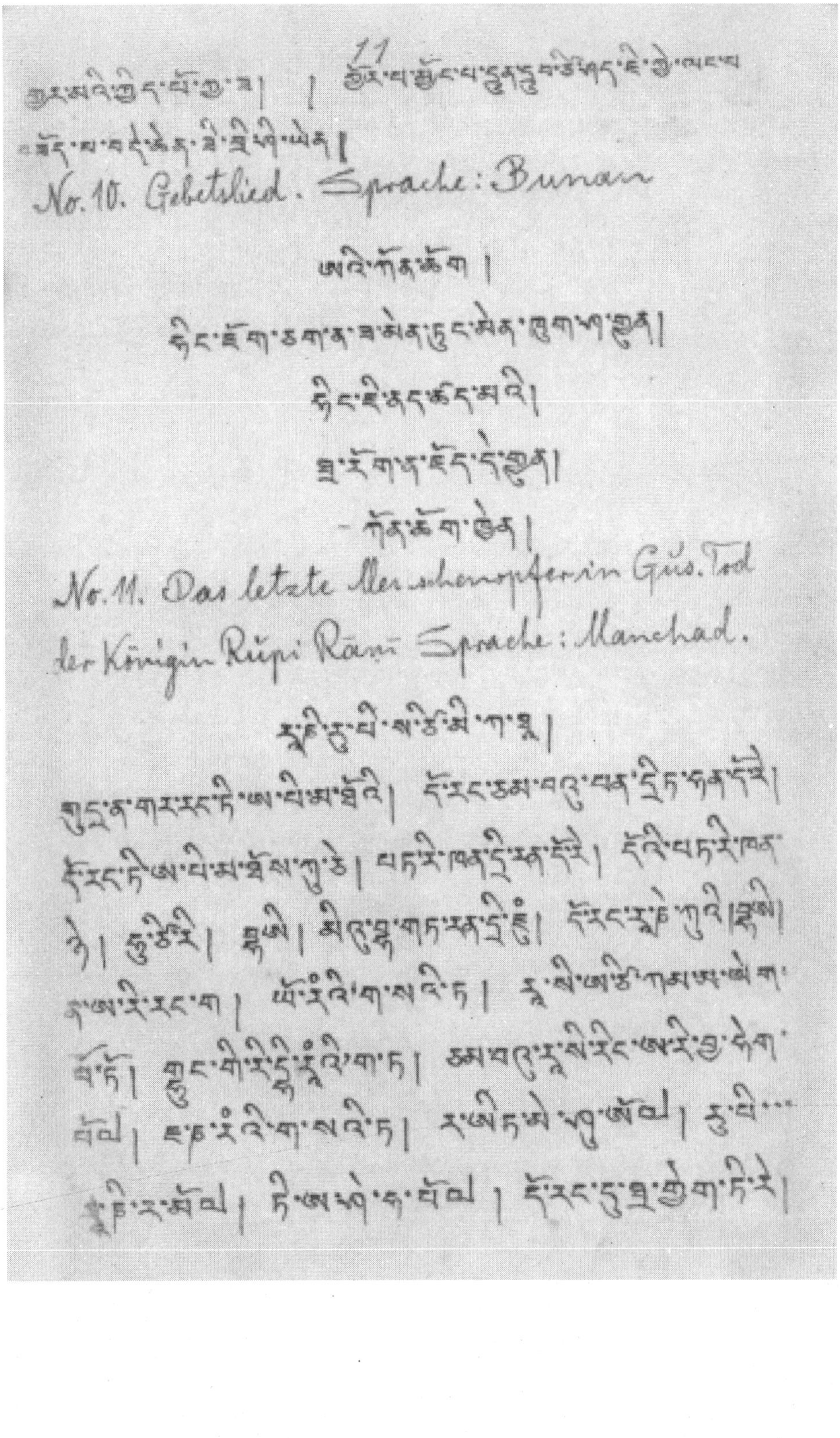

11

No. 10. Gebetslied. Sprache: Bunan

No. 11. Das letzte Menschenopfer in Gus. Tod der Königin Rūpi Rānī Sprache: Manchad.

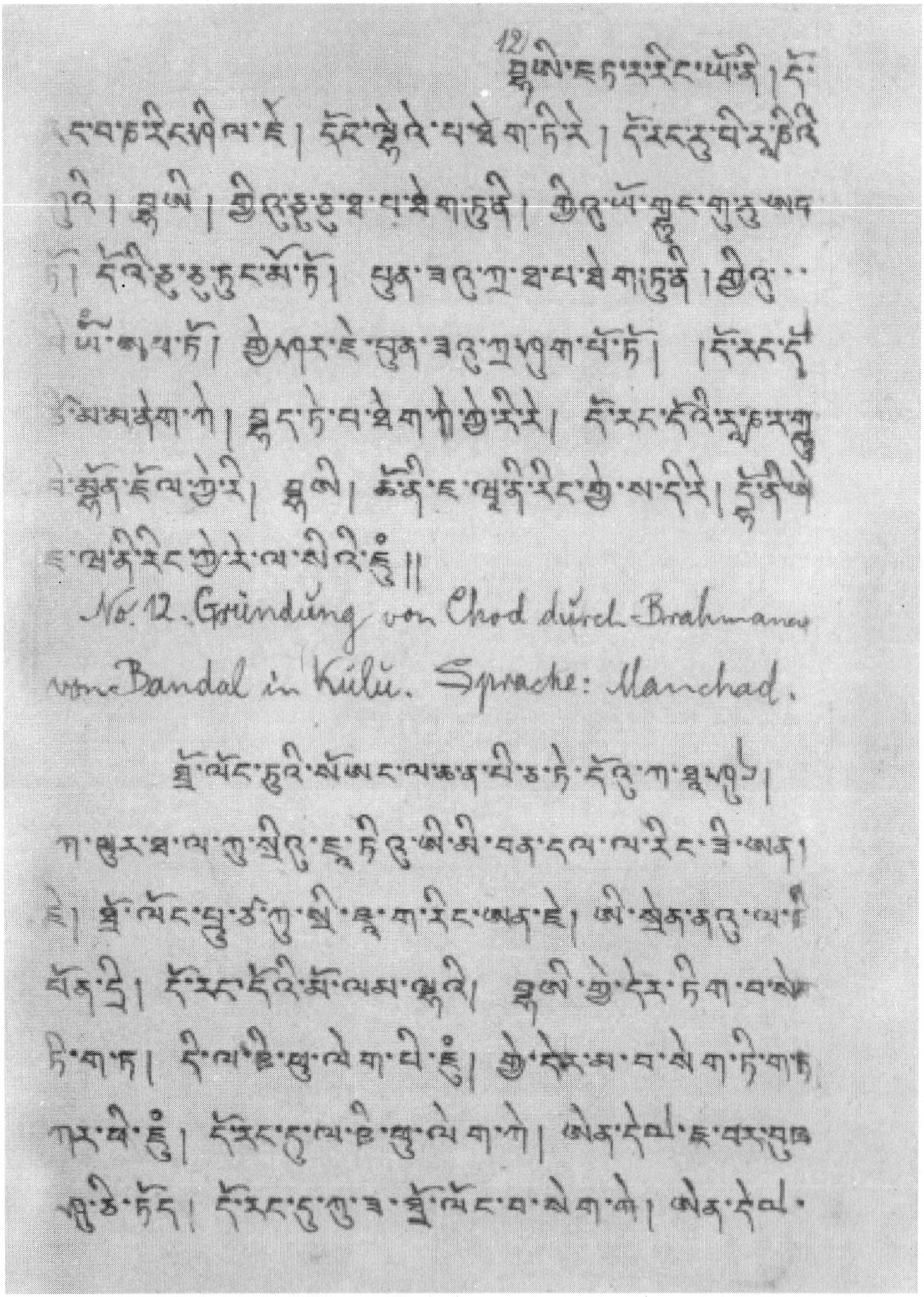

12

No. 12. Gründung von Chod durch Brahmanen von Bandal in Kulu. Sprache: Manchad.

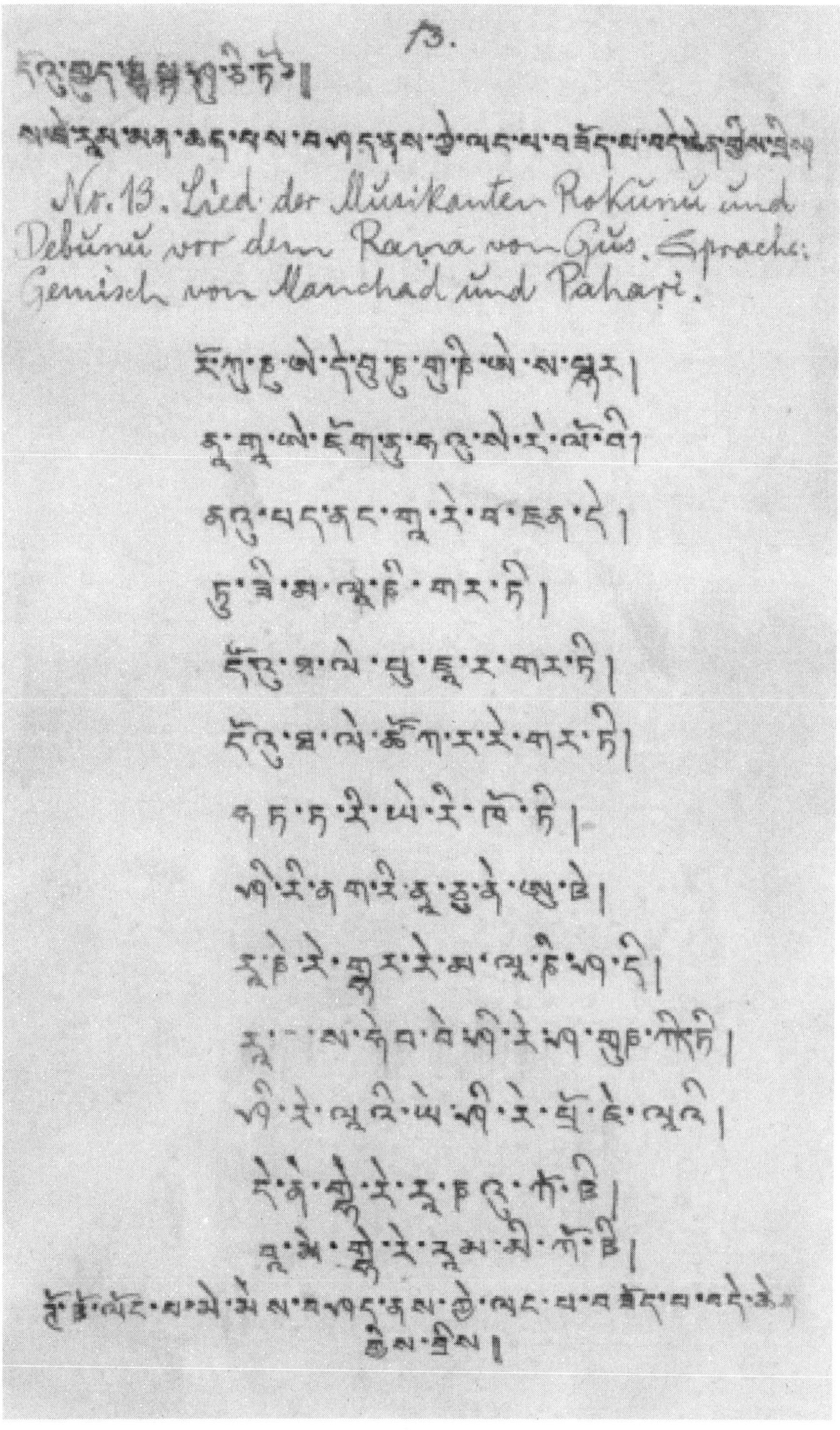

13.

Nr. 13. Lied der Musikanten Rokŭnŭ und Debŭnŭ vor dem Raṇa von Gŭs. Sprache: Gemisch von Manchad und Pahaṛi.

14

No. 14. Lied von der Anfertigung eines Götzen für König Teti Sing von Kulu durch den Schmied Nandi R. Phuntsog von Manchad. Sprache: Pahari.

اندو نروڑا ڈوشنا بہو ے -

پادہا پنڈرا شدھ کاری آنی -

پادہا پنڈیا بو تہی تا ہیرکے

بوتہی تیری نا اندو رہے جہاری رہے ڈوشے -

دیوی ہ گنادھ رہے ڈوشنا ہو ہے -

جو آئی نا جھوڑی سنیارے ری پکیے -

برابی سنیارا شدھ کاری آنی -

برابی سنیارا جہاری گہاڑونے لاگی -

راجا صاحب ہیڑونے آئے -

راجا صاحب ری دِلے نائی گموندا -

برابی سنیارا جہاری گہاڑونے نہ جانی -

جوٹکی جھوڑی سادھو رہے ڈیرے -

سادھو حاکم شادہی کاری آنی -

راجا صاحب بنگلہ نہ بیٹھو رہے -

سادھو حاکما رہے جیدہا کیتی -

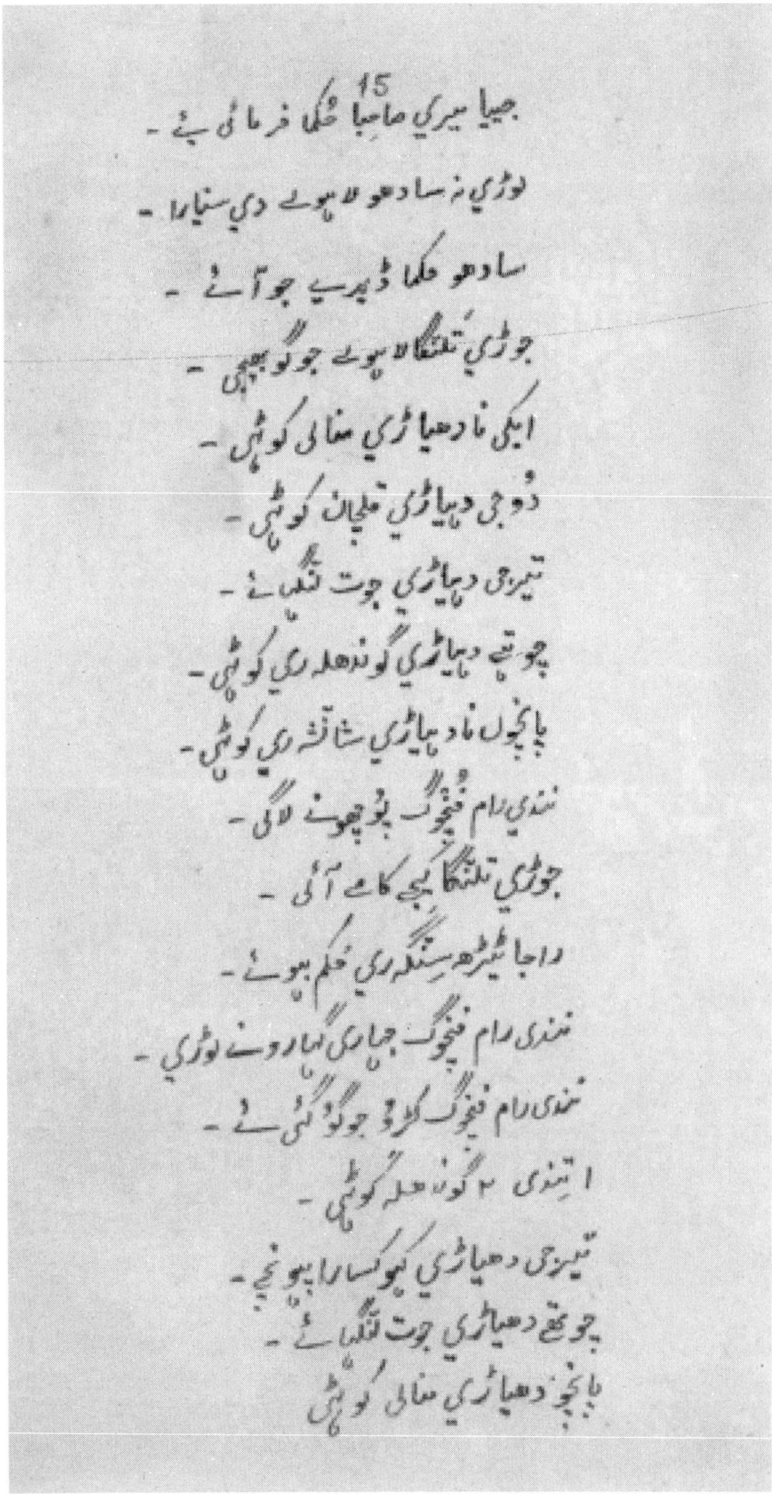
15

جیا میری صاحبا حکم فرمائی ہے -

لوڑی نہ سادھو لاہوے دی سنیارا -

سادھو حکما ڈپرسے جو آئے -

جوڑی تلنگا لاہوے جو گو بھیجی -

ایکی ما دھیاڑی مغالی کوٹھی -

دوجی دھیاڑی تلیاں کوٹھی -

تیجی دھیاڑی جوت لگانے -

چوتھے دھیاڑی گوندھلا ری کوٹھی -

پانچوں ما دھیاڑی شا قشہ ری کوٹھی -

نندی رام فنجوگ پوچھونے لاگی -

جوڑی تلنگا بیجے کامے آئی -

راجا ٹیڑھ سنگھ ری حکم ہوئے -

نندی رام فنجوگ جہاری نہاروے لوڑی -

نندی رام فنجوگ کلاڑو جو گو گئی ہے -

ا نندی ۲ گوندھلا کوٹھی -

تیجی دھیاڑی کپو کسارا پونچے -

چوتھے دھیاڑی جوت لگانے -

پانچے دھیاڑی مغالی کوٹھی

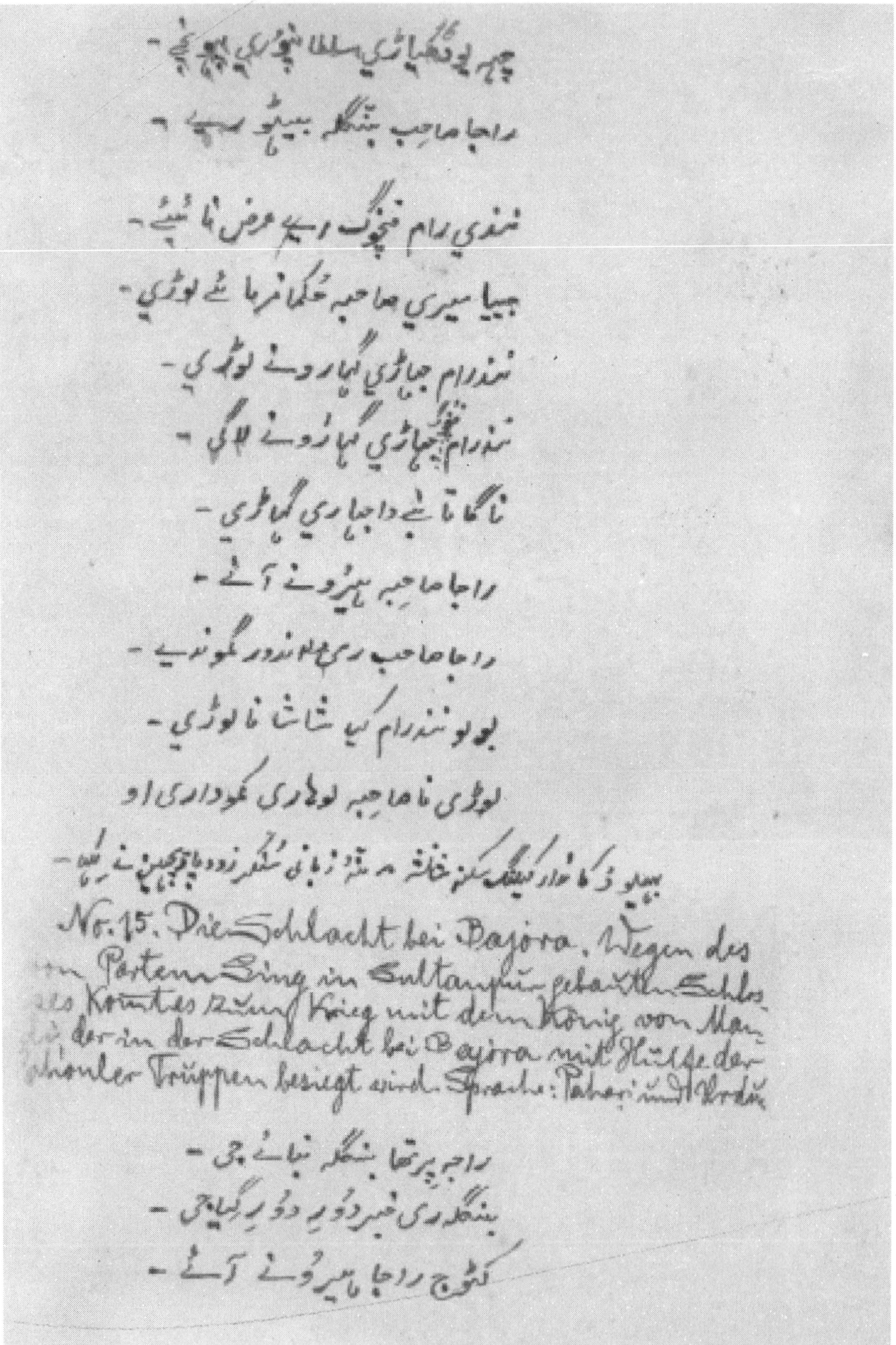

No. 15. Die Schlacht bei Bajóra. Wegen des
...m Partem Sing in Sultanpur gebauten Schlos-
...es Kommt es zum Krieg mit dem König von Man-
...di der in der Schlacht bei Bajóra mit Hülfe der
...länder Truppen besiegt wird. Sprache: Pahari und Urdu

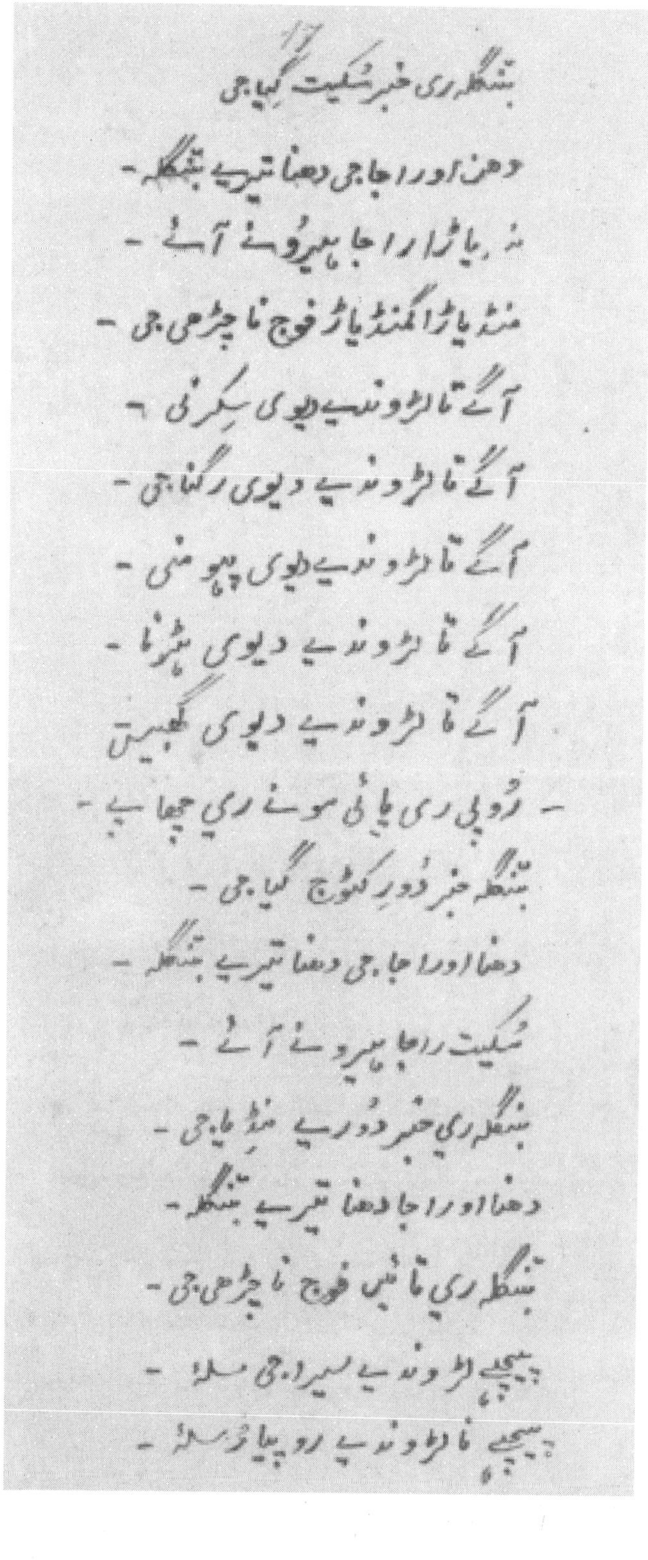
بنگلہ ری خبر شکیت گیا جی

دھن اور راجا جی دھنا تیرے بنگلہ -

بنہ بابڑا راجا ہیروں سے آئے -

منڈیا بڑا گمنڈیا بڑ فوج نا چڑھی جی -

آگے تا ڈھوند سے دیوی سکرنی -

آگے تا ڈھوند سے دیوی رگنا جی -

آگے تا ڈھوند سے دیوی پہومنی -

آگے تا ڈھوند سے دیوی ہڑنا -

آگے تا ڈھوند سے دیوی گجیسن

- ڈوبی ری بابی سونے ری چھجا ہے -

بنگلہ خبر ڈور کوچ گیا جی -

دھنا اور راجا جی دھنا تیرے بنگلہ -

شکیت راجا ہیرو سے آئے -

بنگلہ ری خبر ڈور سے منڈیا جی -

دھنا اور راجا دھنا تیرے بنگلہ -

بنگلہ ری تانب فوج نا چڑھی جی -

پیچھے ڈھوند سے سیرا جی مسلا -

پیچھے تا ڈھوند سے روپیا ترمسلا -

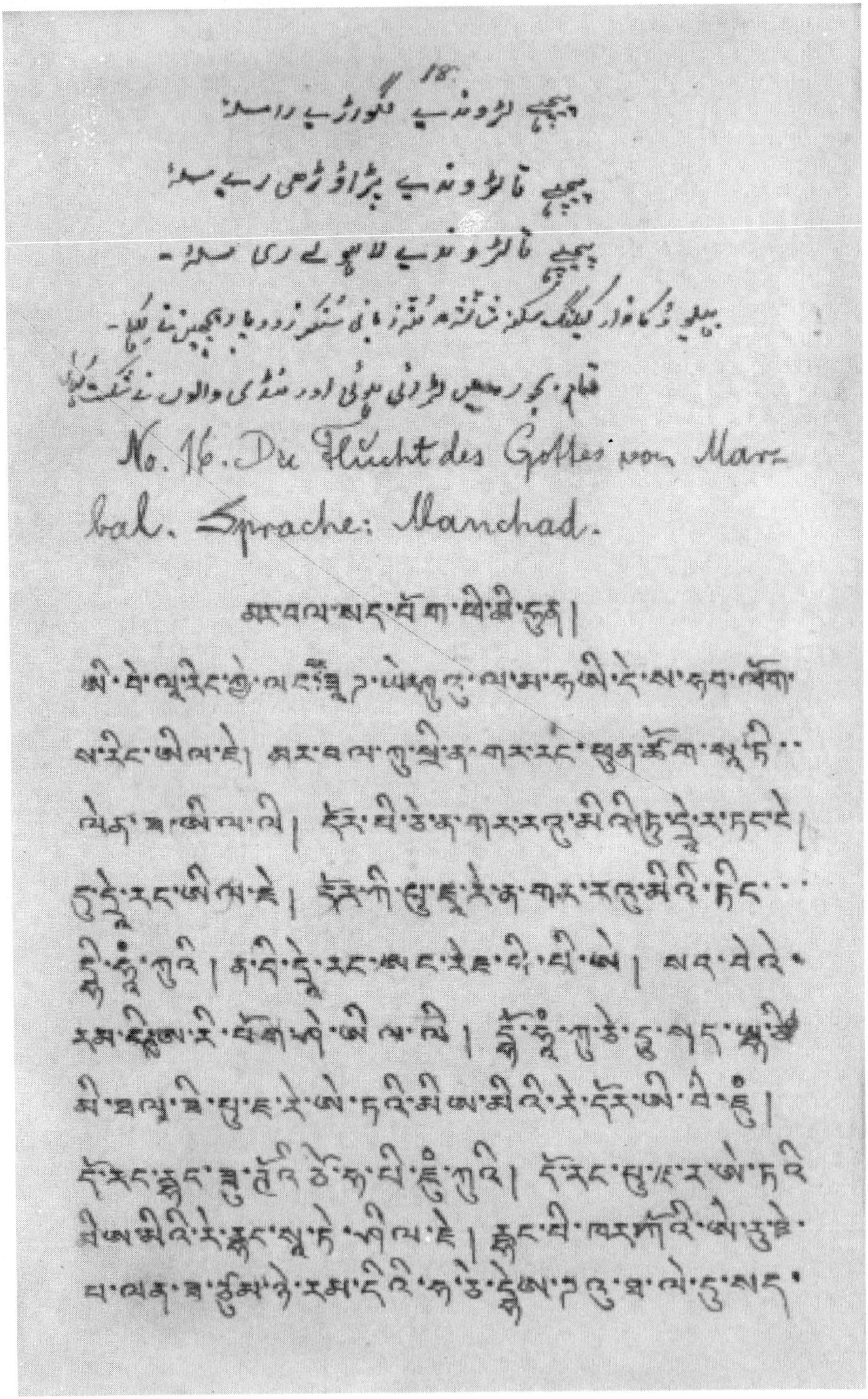

No. 16. Die Flucht des Gottes von Marbal. Sprache: Manchad.

ཉི་མ་རང་སྐྱེ་ན་ནི་ནི། ན་རི་རྒྱན་རྡོ་ཡན་ཟླ་བ་མི་འི་ཟེ་ལོག་ཏེ་ཏ།

འི་རྡོ་རྡོ་ཞེ་ཆོ་ཏོ། མཐུགས་ལ་ཏུ་ཏུ་ཡོད་ཡེ་ཤི་འི་བི་རྡོ་དེ་ཡུར་ན་བར་ཏ།

དེའི་ཡུལ་ཆེན་ཞ་རྩ་ཡེ་ག་ཙོ་ཏར་ལོ་ཏོ།

No. 17. Vertreibung der Ladakher aus Spiti.

Wahrscheinlich nach der Schlacht bei Basgo, c. 1647?42

Sprache: Westtibetisch.

དང་པོ་ལ་དྭགས་པ་རྣམས་ལ་ཀྱི་ས་སྤྱི་ཏི་པ་ལ་དགྲ་བཅོ་ཅེས་

ཀྱི་ལོ་རྒྱུས་ནི།

དེའི་དུས་ལ། ལ་དྭགས་པ་ཀུན་སྤྱི་ཏི་ཡུལ་ལ་སོང་སྟེ།

ཕྱུག་བཅོས་བཏང་སྐྱེ་ནོར་ཚོངས་བཀོ་ས། ས་མོ་ཀུན་གྱི་

སྒོ་རྒྱ་ལ་སོགས་པའི་བདག་སྐྱེ་ཚོང་ག་ཡང་བཅོམ་སྟེ་ཁྱེར་ས།

སྤྱི་ཏི་པ་ཚོང་ག་རི་ལ་ཕོར་ཏེ་སོང་། དེ་ཇུག་གི་དན་ཆེན་ལ་

དྭགས་པས་ལན་མང་པོ་བཅོས་པ་སང་། སྤྱི་ཏི་པས་འདི་

ཇུག་ཐབས་ཤིག་བཅོས། རང་གོ་ནོར་རྒྱལ་ལ་ཚོང་མ་རེ་ལ་

ཁྱེར་ཏེ་ཕྱིས། དེ་ཇུག་ཀ་སོར་སྤྱི་ཏིའི་ཚོ་དང་སྤྱི་ཏི་པ་ཕྱུག་

མོ་ཀུན་གྱི་སད་རྟུང་ཡང་རི་ལ་ཕྱིས་ཏེ་ཡོད། དེ་ནས་ཡང་ལན་

ཅིག་ལ་དྭགས་པ་ཀུན་སྤྱི་ཏི་ལ་བསྐྱི་བས་ཏེ་དགུན་ཅིག་དེ་རུ་

བསྡད་སོང་། དེ་ནས་ལོ་ག་སར་གྱི་དུས་རན་ཏེ་སྤྱི་ཏི་པ་ཀུན་

གྱིས་འདི་ཇུག་ཐབས་བཅོས། ལ་དྭགས་པ་ཚོང་མ་ཡུ་ལ་ཚོ

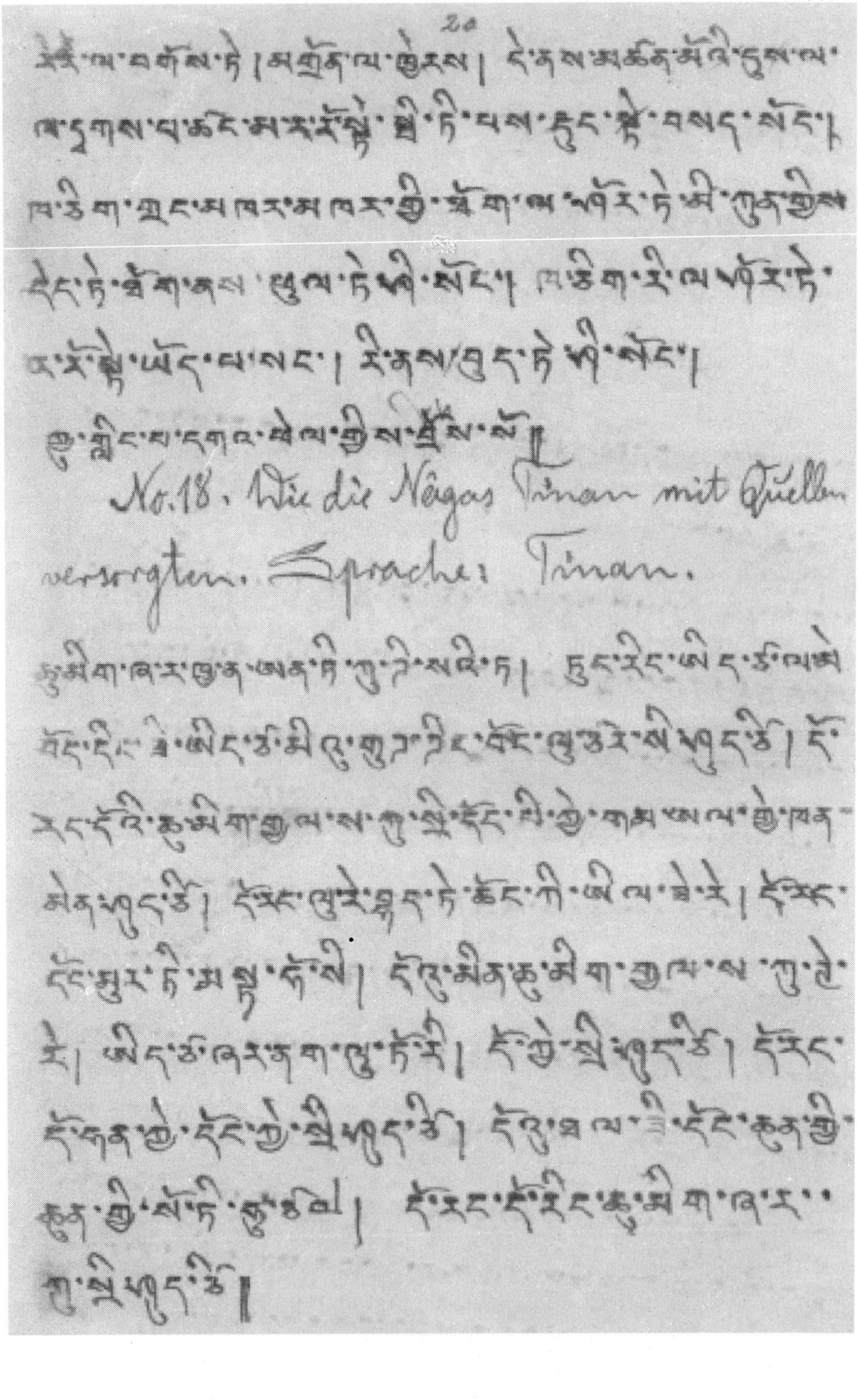

No. 18. Wie die Nâgas Tinan mit Quellen versorgten. Sprache: Tinan.

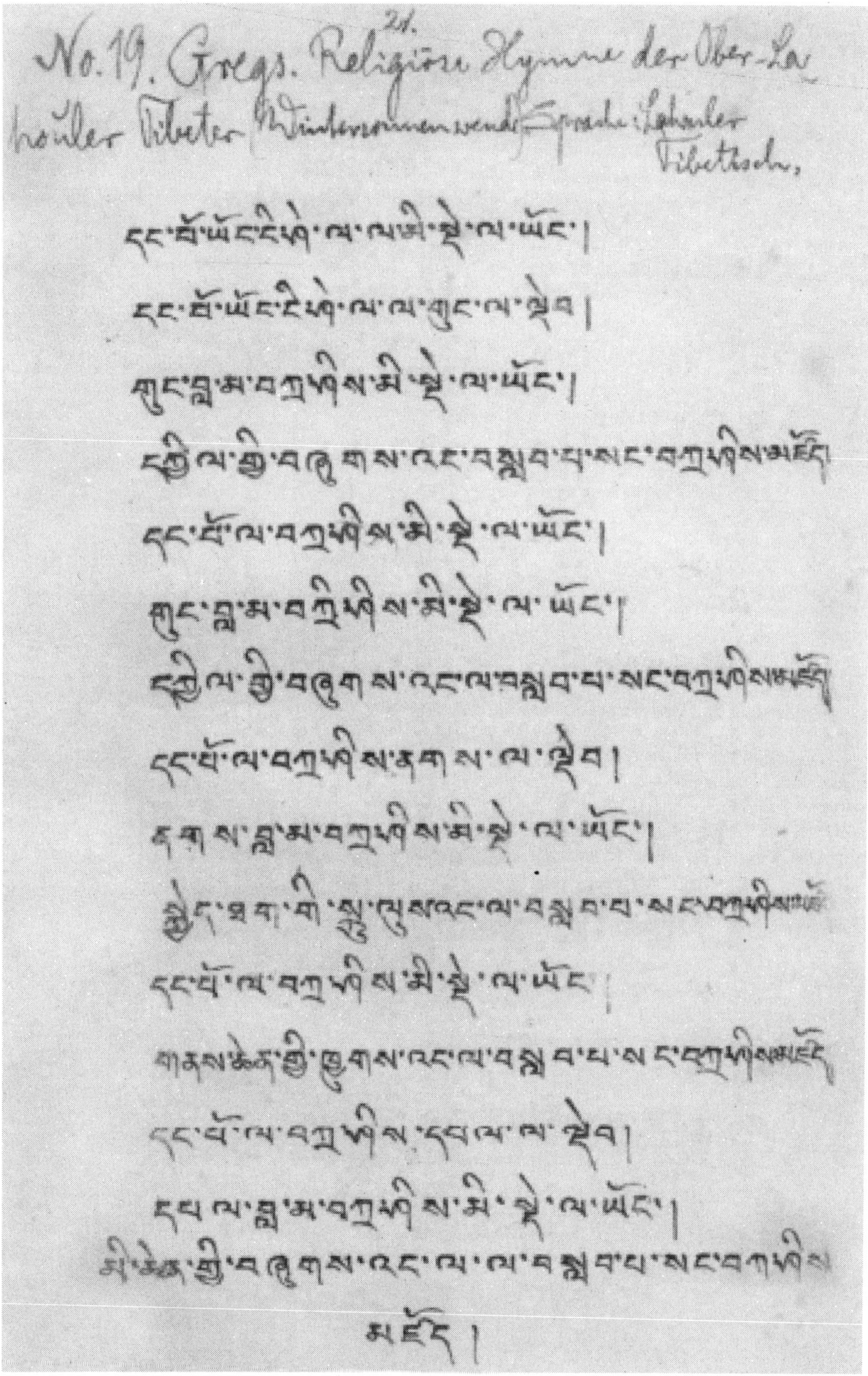

No. 19. Gregs. Religiöse Hymne der Ober-Lahouler Tibeter (Wintersonnenwende) Sprache: Lahauler Tibetisch,

དང་པོ་ཡོང་དེ་ཕྱི་ལ་ལ་མི་སྐྱེ་ལ་ཡོང་།

དང་པོ་ཡོང་དེ་ཕྱི་ལ་ལ་གུང་ལ་ལྷེབ།

གུང་བླ་མ་བཀྲ་ཤིས་མི་སྐྱེ་ལ་ཡོང་།

དཀྱིལ་ཀྱི་བཞུགས་འདང་བསླབ་པ་སང་བཀྲ་ཤིས་མཇོད།

དང་པོ་ལ་བཀྲ་ཤིས་མི་སྐྱེ་ལ་ཡོང་།

གུང་བླ་མ་བཀྲི་ཤིས་མི་སྐྱེ་ལ་ཡོང་།

དཀྱིལ་ཀྱི་བཞུགས་འདང་ལ་བསླབ་པ་སང་བཀྲ་ཤིས་མཇོད།

དང་པོ་ལ་བཀྲ་ཤིས་ནག་ས་ལ་ལྷེབ།

ནག་ས་བླ་མ་བཀྲ་ཤིས་མི་སྐྱེ་ལ་ཡོང་།

སྙིང་ཟག་གི་སྐྱུ་ལུས་འདང་ལ་བསླབ་པ་སང་བཀྲ་ཤིས་མཇོ

དང་པོ་ལ་བཀྲ་ཤིས་མི་སྐྱེ་ལ་ཡོང་།

གནས་ཆེན་ཀྱི་ཕྱུགས་འདང་ལ་བསླབ་པ་སང་བཀྲ་ཤིས་མཇོད།

དང་པོ་ལ་བཀྲ་ཤིས་དཔལ་ལ་ལྷེབ།

དཔལ་ལ་བླ་མ་བཀྲ་ཤིས་མི་སྐྱེ་ལ་ཡོང་།

མི་ཚེ་ཀྱི་བཞུགས་འདང་ལ་ལ་བསླབ་པ་སང་བཀ་ཤིས་

མཇོད།

22.

No. 20. Gregs. Religiöse Hymne der Ober-Lahouler Tibeter. (Wintersonnenwende) Sprache: Lahouler Tibetische

སྔོ་ལོ་གསེར་ཐོད་མ་སྒྲི་བའི་སྒྲུ་དང་སྒྲུའི་སྒྲི།

ཤག་ཀ་མ་མ་ཡི་སྒྲི།

ཉི་ལོ་གཡུ་ཐོད་སྒྲི་བའི་སྒྲུ་དང་སྒྲུའི་སྒྲི།

བྲག་མ་མ་ཡི་སྒྲི།

ལྷུང་མ་བལ་ཐོད་སྒྲུ་དང་སྒྲུའི་སྒྲི།

ཀྱུ་མི་ག་མ་ཡི་སྒྲི།

ཁྱམ་བྱུག་དར་ཐོད་སྒྲུ་དང་སྒྲུ་ཡི་སྒྲི།

ཤང་ཁྲང་སྔོན་མོའི་སྒྲི།

༄༅་ཡང་གོང་པ་འབྲུག་རི་ག་འཛིན་གྱི་ས་བ་ཤད་རྒྱལ་པ་མཆོད་རྟ་སྒྲི

No. 21. Tod der Prinzessin Parmoli, Tochter des Jo Bali Rām c. 1840. Sprache: Pahari.

نیگی بلی رام کیلانگے ری کوٹھی -

دیشی پرمولی گارڈے جو ڈلائی جی او

نانا بلی رام ماپیشک کا نہیں جی او -

نیگی بلی رام گھر سے جو گوگئے جی او -

آدھو بتی بیشک ہوئی جی او -

-

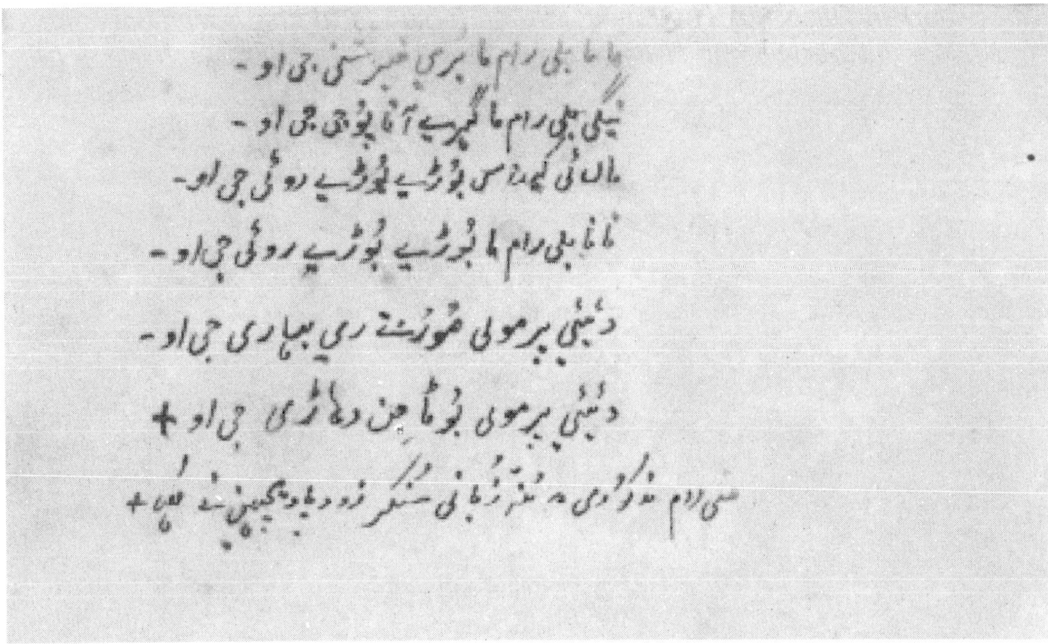

ماما بلی رام ما بری خبر سنی جی او -
نیگی بلی رام ما گھر سے آنا پوچی جی او -
مال نی کیہ داس بوڑھے بوڑھے روئی جی او -
نانا بلی رام ما بوڑھے بوڑھے روئی جی او -
ڈبنی پر موی ھونشے ری بھاری جی او -
ڈبنی پر موی بوٹا جن دہاڑی جی او +
[illegible] +

D. St. Mark in Tinan by A.H. Francke, 1908 (Marku's thrin zang aen nu tsog kan shud tsi. Markh'i 'phrin bzang Ti-nan cKad du bzhugs) by A.H. Francke, Kyelang 1908.

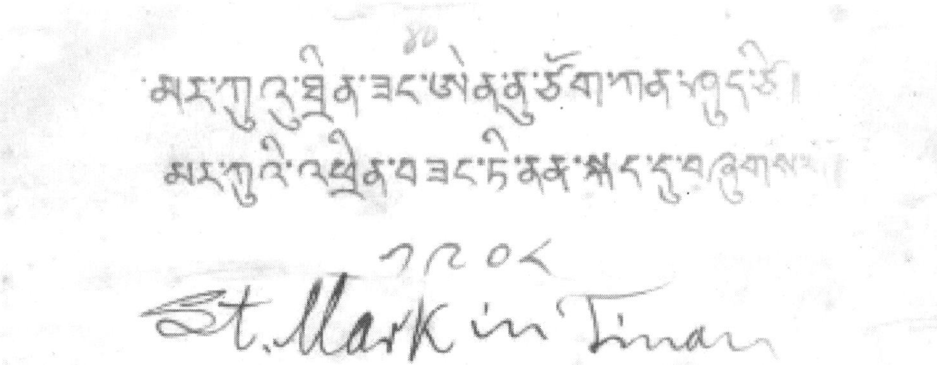

༡། རི་ང་ཡི་ཕུ་མ་ཕིག་ཀ་གོན་ཅིག་ཏུ་ཡོ་ཅི་ཕུད་ཅི་རོ་འུ་ཀེ་

ཏུང་འཕེང་གི་ཕུད་ཅི།

༢། ཏུང་རིང་གོན་ཅིག་ཏུ་ཡི་ ནུ་ལ་རན་ཞི་པེ་ཀུ་ཀེ། ང་ཁན་ཞི། ཀྱི་ཡིང་ཕུ་ཏུ་ཡི་ཡོ་ཀེ་ཀ་ཞེ་ཅི་ཏུང་རིང་ཅི་རང་ཅི་ཏོལ། ངོ་ཡོ་ཀེ་ཀ་ཞེ་ཅི་ཏུང་རིང་ཡ་སྐུ་ཆག་ཀན་ལན་ཏུ།

༣ ཞེ་མ་འུ་ཐང་རིང་ཟེ་ཡི་ཀད་ཡིང་གྱོལ་ཀུ་ཀེ། ཡོན་དག་ཏུ་ཡ་སྐུ་ཀེ་ཕི་ལད་ཏི། རོ་འུ་ཡམ་ཅིམ་ཡ་སྐུ་ཀེ་ཕི་ལད་ཏི། ཡོན་གྱོལ་ཀད་ལ་ཟེ་པ་འུ་ཅིག་ཀན་ཕུ་འི། · ༢༥

༤ ཡོ་ཏ་ཆན་ཆེ་མི་འི་བད་ཏེ་ཏིང་བེ་མ་འུ་ཐང་རིང་སྦུ་འི་རན་ཀྱི། ཞེམ་ཀུ་ར་པེ་རང་། ལྷ་པ་དག་པེམ་སྦུ་འི་འུ་ཆེ་འི་ཕག་ང་རྣ་ཏི།

༥ རོ་འུ་ཐལ་ཟེ་ཡ་ཏུ་རྣ་རེ་ཕག་ཡེ། ཡེ་རྐུ་ཕག་ལེམ་མ་འུ་མི་འི་བད་ཏེ་རོ་འུ་ཀ་ཆང་ཡེ་ཀྱི། ལྷ་པ་པ་འུ་ཐལ་ཟེ་གྱོད་པ་ལ་ཟེ་པ་བད་ཏེ་ཏེ། ཡོ་ཏ་ཆན་ཆེ་ཡོ་ར་དག་ཀུ་སྤྱི་འུ་བེ་ཐྲ་རིང་སྦུ་འི་རྣ་ཏི།

༦ ཡོ་ཏ་ཆན་ཆེ་ལ་ཁ་ཁ་འུ་ཅིམ་ཟེ་ལ་སི་ཁམ་ཡེ། ཏེ་ག་ཏུ་ཚེ་ར་ཚེ་ར་ཟ་ཏོ་རི། ཟ་འི་ཁིང་ཞི་ཁ་ཡེ་ཀྲི་འུ་ཡང་གོ་ཟ་རི།

༧ ངོ་རང་ཡོ་ཏ་ཆན་ཆེ། ཀྱི་བེ་ཅི་ཐལ་ཟེ་ཀྱི་པེ་ཅི་ཁིང་ཅན་ཡན་ཏུ།

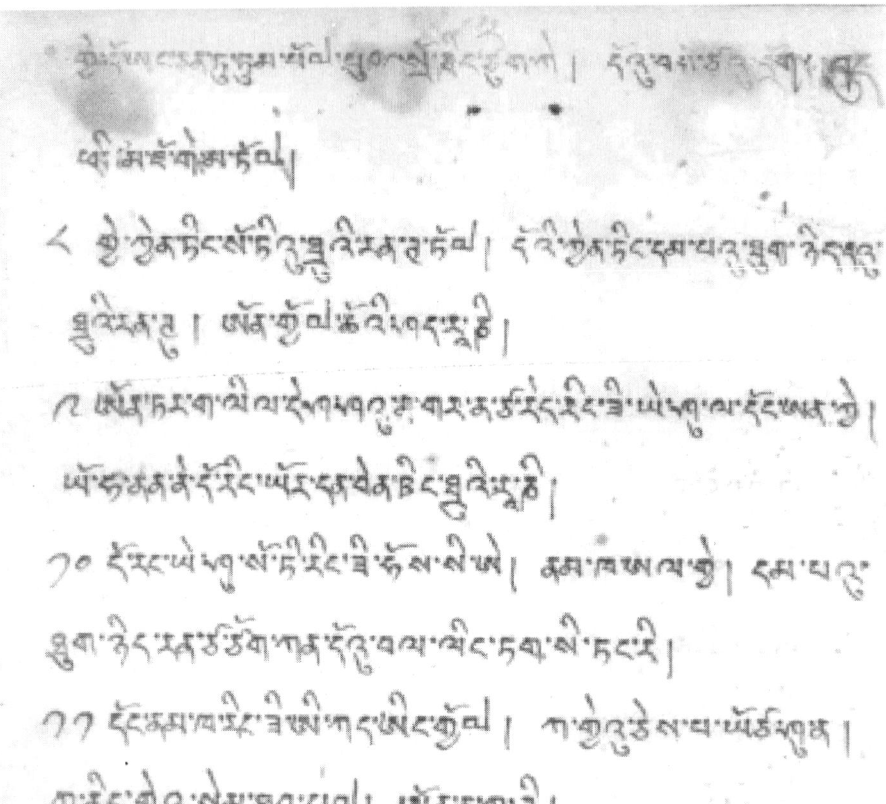

ཡན་ཅི་ཏོ་ཏོ། དོ་ནུ་ཐ་ལ་ཟེ་ལེམ་སྦུ་ར་ཐེ་ལང་ཅེ། ཐྲིན་ཐ་ལ་ཟེ

ངད་ཐ་ལད་ཏི། ཡོན་ན་ཕག་དི།

༡༥། ངོ་ཝི་ལྷ་རིང་ཡེ་ཕྱུ་ག་ལི་ལ་ཚོ་ནུ་དབ་ཟིང་ཡམ་ཅི་ཏར། ལེམ
ཡེ་ཡན་དུ་ཡྭ་ཡ་ཚོ་རྒྱུག་ཉི་མི་ལ། ཉ་ཚོམ་ཅི་པ་ཕྱུད་ཅི་ཡེ། ཉིད་སོ་
ཏི་ནུ་ནང་ཚང་ཅི་ཏང་ཅི་ཡེ།

༡༦། དོ་གྱུ་ཉི་ཨི་ས་རིང་། ང་ཉི་ར་ཅེད་ཅེ། ཤེ་ནུ་ཐ་ལང་ཟེ་ཡན་ཅི
ཏི། ཤེ་ཅེན་ཏིང་མི་ནུ་ཉིད་ཚང་ཅི་ཡུ་ཧལ།

༡༨། ཡོན་ན་གུད་ཅེ། ཉིད་ཅེད་ཅེ་ཡེ་ཕྱུ་ནུ་ཐ་ལང་ཟེ་ཡི་ལི་གུ།

༡༩། ངོ་རང་རྫོད་ཏན་ངོ་པོ་རིང་ཡི་ལ་ཏར། ཟེ་བད་ཡྭ་ནུ་ཡོ་ཅ་གུ་
ཉི་མི་ལ་ཡ་གོབ་ཡེ་ཡོ་ཀ་ནན་གུ་སྲི་ཡ་ཚོ་རྒྱུག་ག་གུ། རྫུ་ནུ་ནང་
ཉིད་པེམ་བ་རྗོབ་པི་ཏང་ཝེ། དོ་གུ་ཏིང་ཡེ་ཕྱུ་ཝི། དིང་ཡན་ཏ་ཅི། གུད་
ཅི་ཡེ།

༢༠། རྫུ་ཡེ་ཡ་ཏ་ཡེ་ཡོག་པོ་རེ་ཅེད་ཅེ། ཡེ་ཕྱུ་ནུ་ཐ་ལང་ཟེ
ཡན་ཅི་ཡི་ལ་ལི་གུ།

༢༡། དོ་རང་ཀ་པར་ན་རྒྱམ་གུ་སྲི་ཆ་གར་རང་ཡི་ལ་ཅེ། ཡ་ཝི
ཏོ་ཡར་ར་ནུ་རྗག་མེ་ཟིང་ཚོ་ཝི་ཕག་ཅིམ་རྒྱུ་ས་སྐྱུང་ཡི་ལ་གྱི།
ཚོ་ཝི་ཕག་དི།

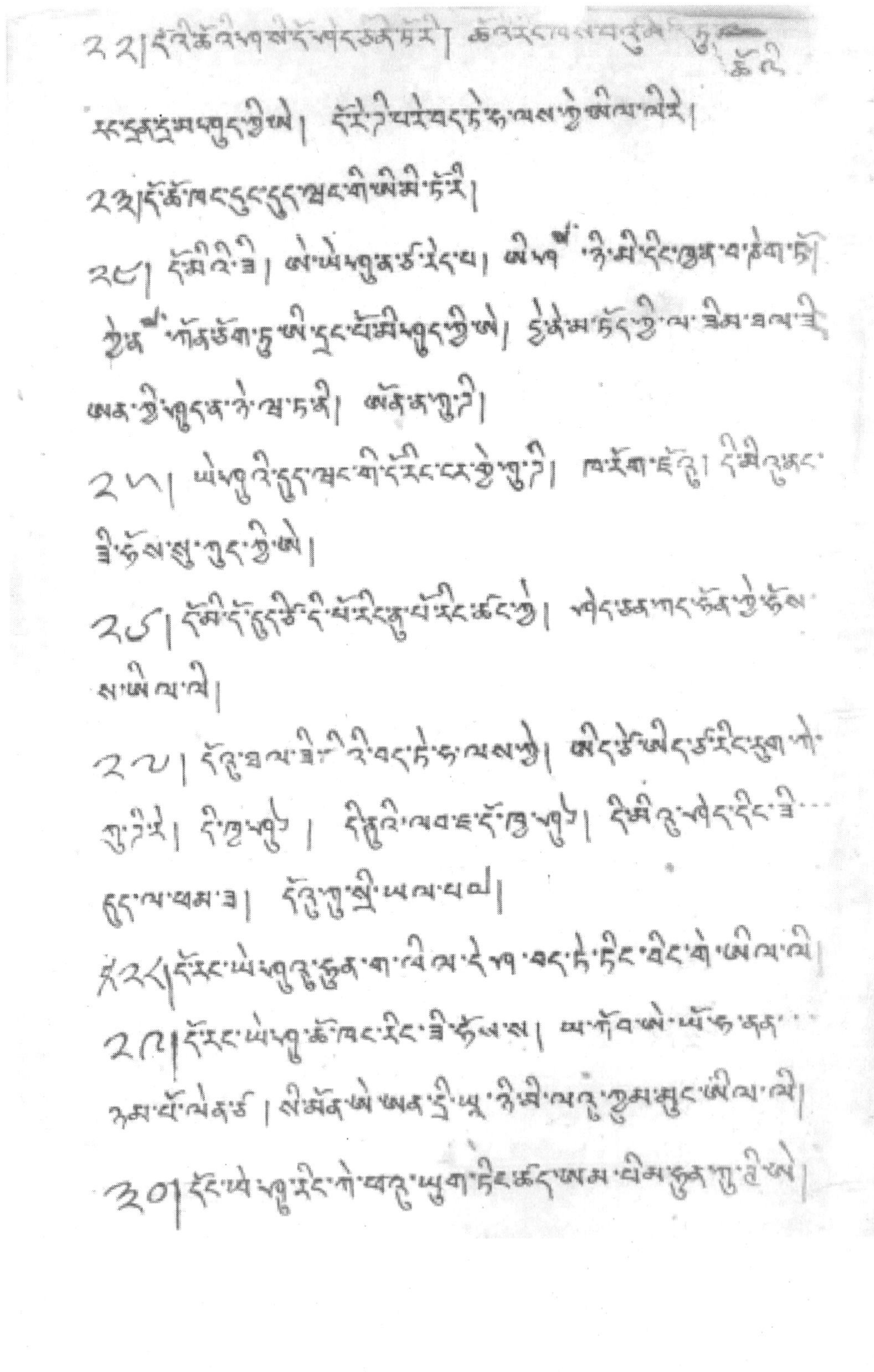

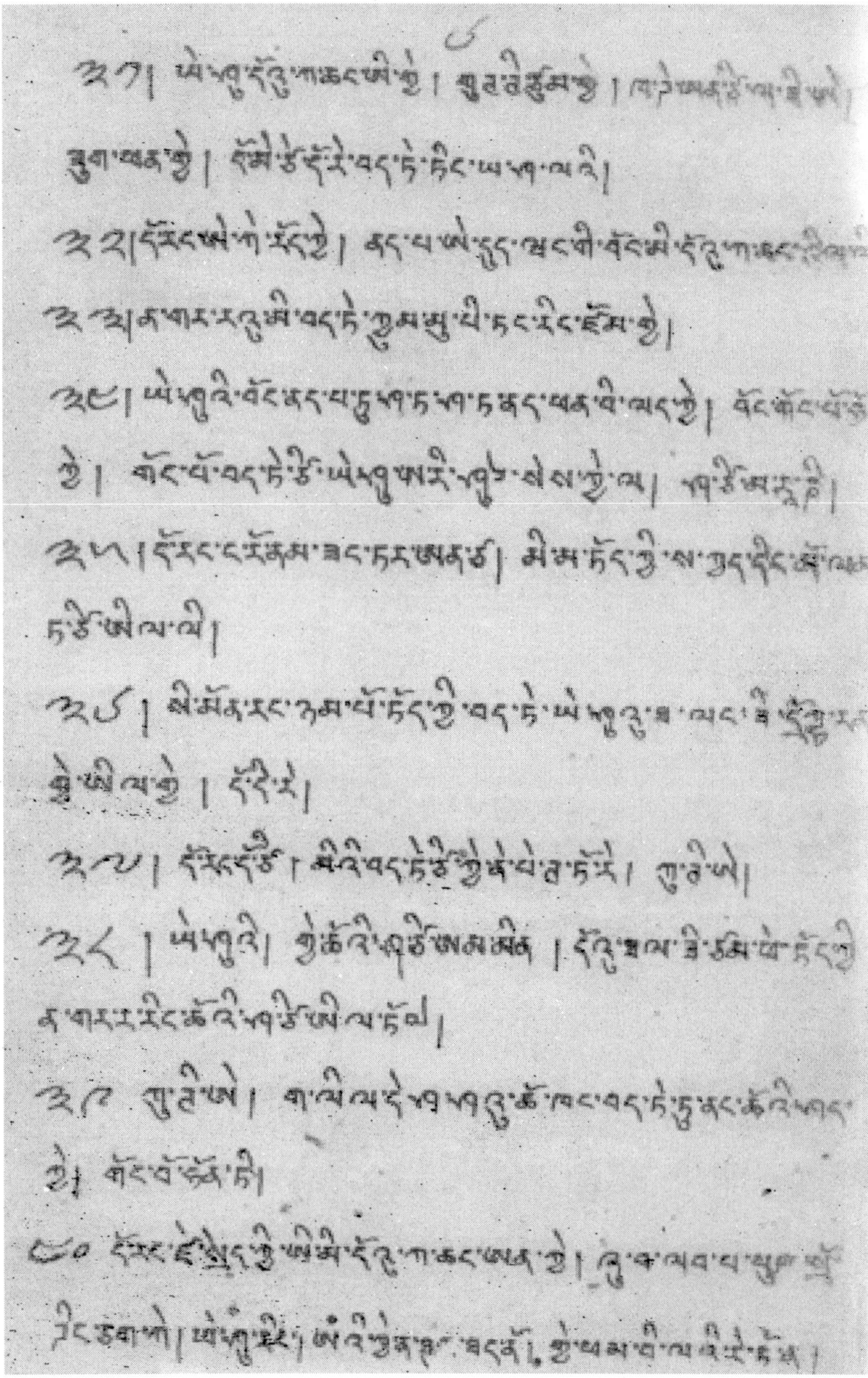

༣༡། ཡེ་ཤུ་དོ་ཏུ་ཀ་ཚང་ཡི་གི། སྒུ་ཞི་ཚུམ་གི། ཁ་ཏེ་ཡན་ཙི་ལ་ཞི་ཡེ། [illegible]
སྒུག་ཡན་གི། དོ་མེ་ཙི་དོ་རེ་བད་ཏེ་ཏིང་ཡ་ཤ་ལ་འི།
༣༢། དོ་རིང་ཡེ་ཀ་རོང་གི། ནད་པ་ཡེ་དུད་ཟང་གི་བོང་མི་དོ་ཏུ་ཀ་ཚང་[illegible]
༣༣། ནགར་རཏུ་མི་བད་ཏེ་ཀུམ་སྒུ་ཡི་ཏང་རིང་རྫོམ་གི།
༣༤། ཡེ་ཤུ་འི་བོང་ནད་པ་ཏུ་ཤག་ཏ་ཤག་ཏ་ནད་ཡན་བི་ལད་གི། བོང་གོང་པོ་[illegible]
གི། གོང་པོ་བད་ཏེ་ཙི་ཡེ་ཤུ་ཡ་རི་ཤུ་སེ་ལ་ཀྱི་ལ། ཤ་ཙི་ཡ་རྣ་ཏི།
༣༥། དོ་རང་ང་རོ་ནམ་ཟང་ཏར་ཡན་ཙ། མི་མ་ཏོད་ཀྱི་ས་ཀུད་དིང་ཚོ་[illegible]
ཏ་ཙི་ཡེ་ལ་ལི།
༣༦། སེ་མོན་རང་ཉམ་པོ་ཏོད་ཀྱི་བད་ཏེ་ཡེ་ཤུ་ཟུ་ཟ་ལང་ཞི་[illegible]
སྒེ་ཡི་ལ་གི། དོ་དི་རི།
༣༧། དོ་རིང་དོ་ཙི། མི་འི་བད་ཏེ་ཙི་ཀྱི་ཞེ་པེ་ཟ་ཏོ་རི། ཀུ་ཞི་ཡེ།
༣༨། ཡེ་ཤུ་འི། གི་ཚོ་འི་ཤུ་ཙི་ཡམ་མིན། དོ་ཏུ་ཟལ་ཟི་ཙམ་པོ་ཏོད་ཀྱི
ན་གར་ར་རིང་ཚོ་འི་ཤག་ཙི་ཡི་ལ་ཏོལ།
༣༩ ཀུ་ཞི་ཡེ། ག་ལི་ལ་དེ་ཤག་ཤག་ཏུ་ཚོ་ཁང་བད་ཏེ་ཏུ་ནང་ཚོ་འི་ཤང
གི། བོང་བོ་ཚོ་ཏི།
༤༠ དོ་རང་རྗེ་སྒུད་ཀྱི་ཡི་མི་དོ་ཏུ་ཀ་ཚང་ཡན་གི། ཏུ་ཀ་ལབ་པ་[illegible]
ཏེང་ཙག་ཀེ། ཡེ་ཤུ་རིང་། ཡོཾ་འི་ཀྱི་ན་ཟ་བད་དོ། ཀྱི་ཡམ་པི་ལ་ལི་རི་ཏི་ཡ།

༨༡། ཡེ་ཤུའི་སྒྲུག་རྗེ་ཡང་ཀྱི། ཀུན་ཀྱང་ཀྱི། དགེའི་འིང་ཐོག་ཏེ།

༨༢། ཀྱི་ཡོན་ཏན་རན་ཞ་རྟོལ། ཇེ་ཤི་ཤུ། ཀུ་ཞི་ཡེ། རྗེ་པན་ཀྱི། དགེ་
ཇེ་ཤི་ཤུའི།

༨༣། དོ་རང་ཡེ་ཤུའི་དགེ་རྒྱམ་སྐྱུང་ཟེ་ཙར་ཀྱི།

༨༤། དོ་རིང་ཀུ་ཏི། ཀྱིའི་མིའི་ཏིང་ཀྱ་ལ་ལེ་ཟ་ཀུ་ཧྲུ། ལམ་འདུ་ག་ཆང་...
ཨེ་ལ་ཀྱི། ཡེ་ཤུ་འདུ་ཟུག་གན་ཧྲུ། ནད་པམ་ཞེམ་ཚོད་པ་འདུ་ཐལ་ཟེ། སོ་ཤེའི་
ཀྱ་ཕྱུད་མེན། ཡོན་རྐྱོལ་ཡེ་ཚོད་པ་ལ་འདུ། མིའི་བད་ཏེ་ཏུ་དུམ་པོལ་གོལ་ཏེ་
ཨམ་པེམ་ཐལ་ཟེ་ཡོན་ཏན་ལ་ཟེ་ཏེ་ས་ཀུད་ཀྱི་ལ།

༨༥། དགེ་ཡེ་ལ་ཀྱི། བོང་ཕྱུད་ཕྱུ་ཟ། གསུམ་མདུ་ཏུན་ཞིང་མི་ལ་དང་ཀྱེ
དོ་འདུ་ནལ་ཟ་ཡེ་ཤུ་དོན་གར་རདུ་ཚང་ཡེ་ཞེམ་ཡལ་ཀྱི། ཤི་རིང་ཞེ་མ་འདུ་ཐང་
རིང་རྡོད་ཀྱི་ལ། པིའི་ལ་ཚོགས་སེང་ཟེ་བོང་མི་དོ་འདུ་ག་ཆང་རྫོམ་རི་རེ།

ཇེ་ཧྲི་ལེ་འདུ་འདུ་ཚང་།

༡། བོངམ་ཤུད་ཀྱི། ག་པར་ཏན་ཏུག་ཀུ་ཤྲི་ཡེ་ཙ་གར་ཙང་ཡེ་ལ་ལི། ཡེ་ཤུ་
ཨེ་ཀྱམ་སྐྱུང་ཡེ་ཞེམ་ཏུན་ཟ་ཙི་ཡེ།

༢། བོང་སི་རྫོམ་ཀྱི། ཐེམ་ཏང་མ་སོག་པ། དོ་ཏིང་ཚོའི་ཤག་ཞི།

༣། ཡོན་ཏ་རཡི་ཁོང་ཁི་མི་ཡི་མི་ཡི་འི་ཟེ་ཀུར་ཀྱི། ཡེ་ཤུ་འདུ་ཏུམ་པོལ
ཤན་ཏི་རེ།

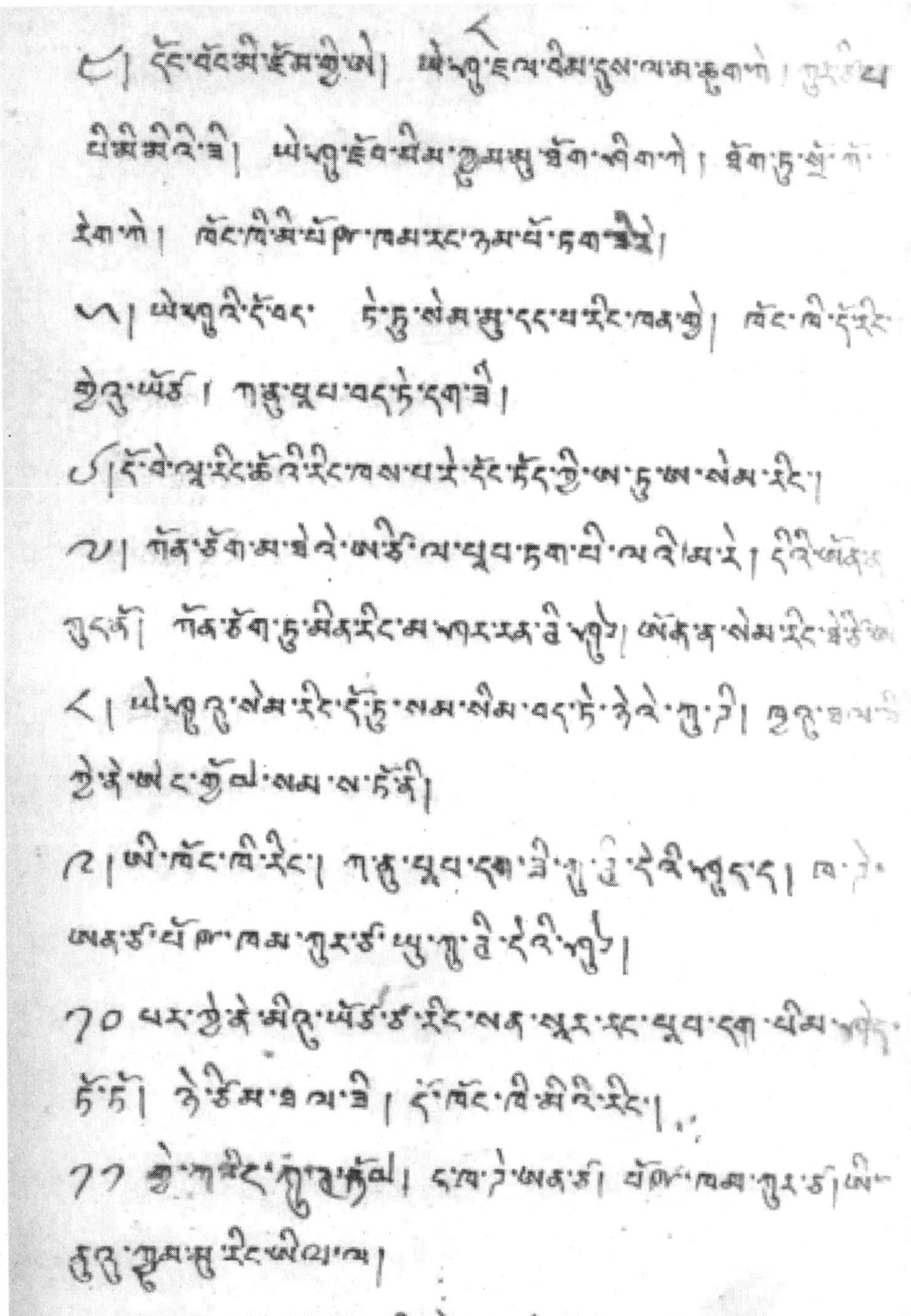

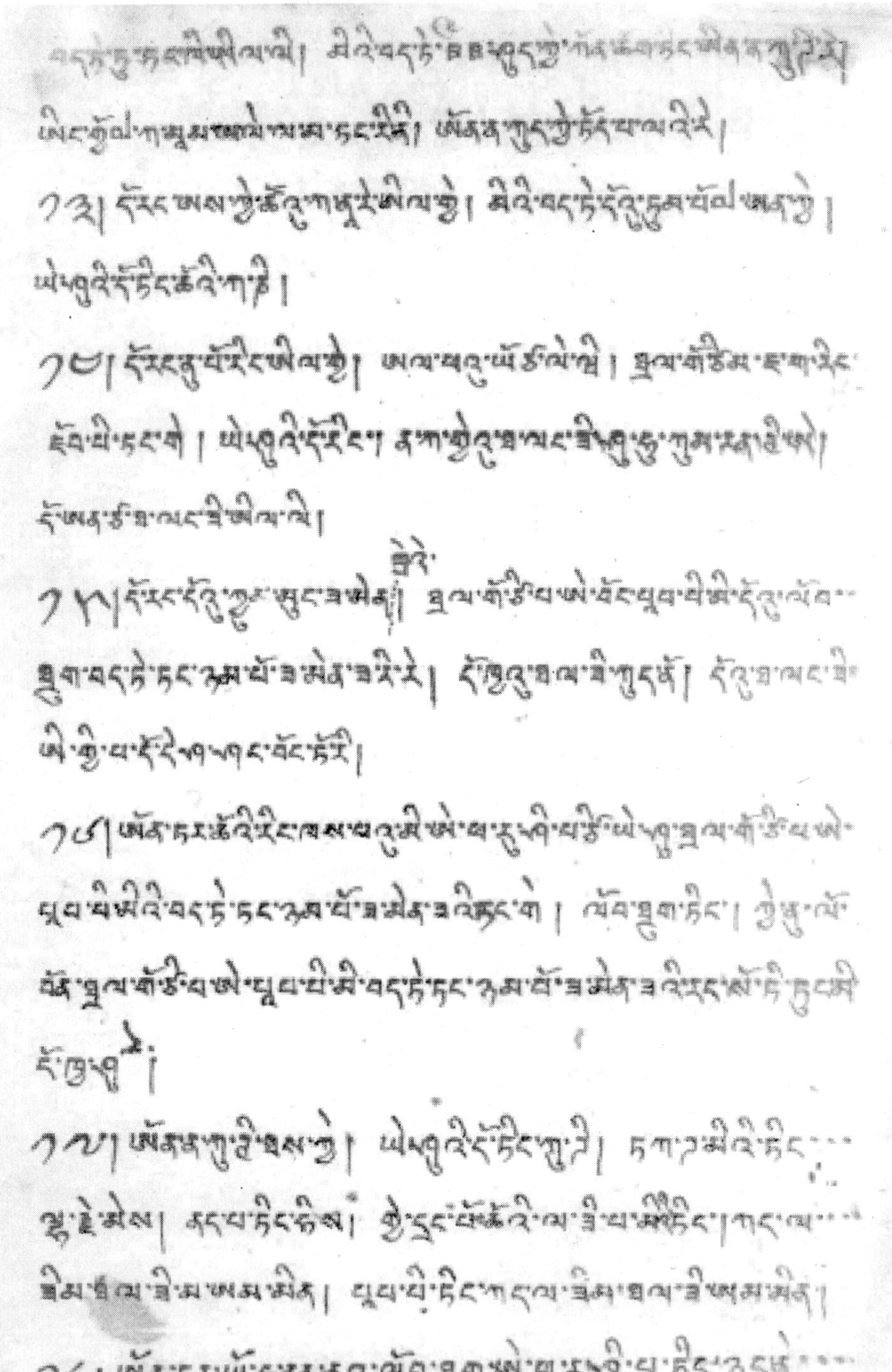

ལ་ཞིམ་སྣུམ་ཏོད་ཀྱི་ཡས། གཙན་མི་ཡང་ཀྱི་ཡི་པུ་རྡོར་ཀྱུ་ཟ་རེ། ཆིང ཁྲི་རེ། ཡོ་ཏ་ཚན

ཡེ་པ་རྡུ་ཤི་ལ་ཏུ་ཁོབ་རྒྱལ་བང་ཏེ་ཉུང་ཚེ་རིང་ཚོད་ཀྱེ་ཀ། ཡེ་རྫུ་ཉུ་ལོབ་རྒྱུག་ཏ

ཉུང་ཚེ་རིང་ཁྱུ་རིངས་ཚོབ་པ་ཏོ་རེ།

༡༩། ཡོན་ཏན་ཀྱུ་ཚིམ་ལན་ཏིང་ཡེ་ཤུ་ཟེ། མག་པ་ཉམ་པོ་ཚོད་ཏ་ར། བག་ཏོན

རྒྱ་དོན་ པོ་རེ་ཉུང་ཚེ་རིང་ཚོབ་ཡི་རྒྱུང་ཏོམ། མག་པ་རང་ཉམ་པོ་ཚོད་ཏ་ར།

ཉུང་ཚེ་རིང་ཚོབ་ཡི་མ་རྒྱུང་།

༢༠། མག་པ་རང་གི་སྨྲ་བེ་ལྷ་རིང་ཡིན་ནོ། ཡོན་ཏར་ཉུང་ཚེ་རིང་ཚོད་ཏོ་རེ།

༢༡། ཡི་ལན། ཨ་ཅོག་ཡུའི་ཁམ་རིང་ནུའི་ཏ་ལྷམ་ཏ་ཅ་ཏོ་རེ། ཏད་ནོ།

ངོ་ནུའི་ཏ་ལ་ཅོ་ཡུའི་ཁམ་ཞལ་ཀྱེ། ཏུང་རིང་བེ་ཅོ་སྨྲ་རྒྱ་ཏེ་ཞིག་ཤུད་ཏོ།

༢༢། ཀི་ཏ་ནུའི་ཀྲུན་དུམ་སུ་ཆང་ཡུའི་ཀྱལ་པ་ཉུང་ཨ་ཅོ་ལམ་ཀྱེ་ཉུ་རེ།

ཡས་ཅོ་ཡ་ཀྱེ་ནོ། ནུའི་ཀྲུན་དུམ་སུ་ཆང་ཟེ་ཀྱལ་པ་གོ་ཡས་ཡི་ལད་ཀྱེ།

ཐང་ཏོམ་ས་ཡི་ལ་ཀྱེ། ཀྱལ་པ་ཏུལ་ཀྱི་ཡི་ལ་ཏོ། ངོ་ཉུ་ཐལ་ཟི་ནུའི་ཀྲུན་

དུམ་སུ་ཆང་ནུའི་ཀྱལ་པ་ཉུང་ཡུ་ཏུ་རེ། མོ་ལ་ཏེ།

༢༣། དོ་རང་ཡེ་ཤུ་ཡའི་ཏོ་ཡར་མེ་ཞིང་ཏུ་ཉུ་ཀྲི་ཏད་ཀྱི་ཡན་ཏར། ལོབ་རྒྱུག་

ཏེ་ཅོ་ཡམ་ཅོ་ཏར་རྒྱུར་ཏོག་ཞི་རེ།

༢༤། པ་རྡུ་ཤི་པ་ཅི། ཀ་ནུ་ཅོ་ལྷོ་དི་ཀམ་ཡའི་ཏོ་ཡར་ར་ཉུ་ཐག་མེ་ཞིང་

ལ་ཞི་མེལ་ཀུ་ཏི་རེ།

༢༥། ཡེ་ཤུའི་དོ་ཏིང་། ངབེང་ཡེ་ངབེད་ཏུ་ཡོག་པོ་ཏིང་ཀྲུག་གོད་ཀྱེ།

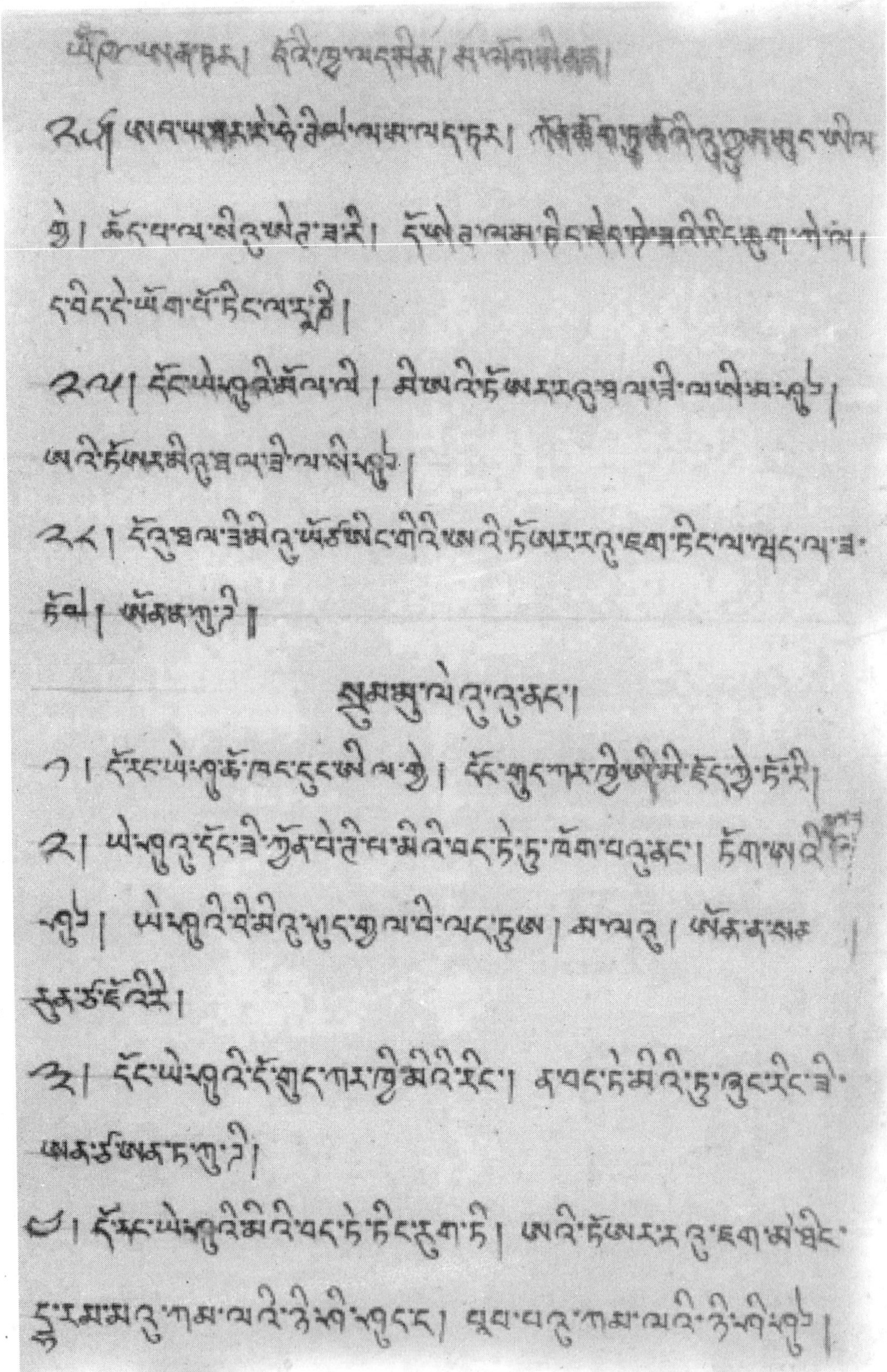

སྒུག་ཐར་པ་ལ་འཇི་ཉེ་མི་སྐྱོང་ད། སྒུག་ཞག་ཞེ་ཉེ་མི་སྐྱོ་ཀ་ཤན་རྒྱུ་ཀ།

༦། དེ་ཙི་ལན་གྱུ་ལ་ལོ་མ་སྐྱ་ཧེར། ཡེ་ཤུ་རིང་ཆེན་པ་ཡན་ཀྱི། ངོམ་བད་ཧེ་ཧུ་
སེམས་ཀུང་གི་ཧ་ངེ་ཙི་ཡེ། ཏོང་ཁོག་སྒྲུབ་ལད་ཀྱི། སྐྱིད་ཀར་གྱི་དོ་རིང། ང་་
ཡི་ཧུའུ་སྐྱིད་ཤིང་ཏུ། ཀུ་ཏེ་ཡེ། དོམ་ཞི་ཞི་ཡིན་ཐུའུ་ཀུང་ཤིང་ཙི་ཡེ། ནད་
ཕན་ཀྱི་ཡི་ལ་ལི།

༧། དོ་རང་ལ་རྟུ་ཤི་པ་རེ་ལི་རིང་ཡི་ལ་གྱི། ཉེ་རོ་དོའུ་ཡོག་པོ་ཧང་ཉམ་པོ་
རྫམ་ཀྱི། ཡེ་ཤུ་མཚེམ་ཐབ་ཡེ་ཏི་རིང་ཏབ་ལ་ཞི་ར།

༨། ཡས་ཀྱི་ཡེ་ཤུ་ཡིན་ཐུའུ་འོབ་སྒྲུག་ཧང་ཉམ་པོ་ཚོ་ཧུ་བིང་ཡི་ལ་གྱི
ཡི་པོང་རྒྱུ་ཏ་མི་ག་ལི་ལ་དེ་ཤ་ཡེ། ཡ་རྒྱུ་དྷྲེ་ཤ་ཡེ།

༩། ཡེ་རྟུ་ཤ་ལོམ་ཡེ། ཡི་ཧུམ་ཡྰ་ཡེ། ཡོར་དན་པན་ཞི་ཧུའུ་སྐྱ་ར་ང་ཏོང་ཀྱི
ཤ་ཀར་ཡེ། ཚོ་ཧྥོ་ཧེ་དོན་ཀུ་སྲིན་ཀར་རང་ཟེ་ཡན་ཀྱི་དོ་རེ་བད་ཧེ་དོ་ཧུ་ཐ་ལང་ཟི
མི་ལ་ལི་ར། དོམ་ཞི་བད་ཧེ་ཙི་ཡེ་ཤུ་ཧུ་ཆེ་ཞིག་ཀ་སྨམ་ཧུ་རྒྱན་ཐ་ཆེ་ཡེ།
དོ་ཧུ་ཀ་ཚང་ཙོམ་ཟི་རི།

༡༠། དོ་རང་ཡེ་ཤུ་ཞི་འོབ་སྒྲུག་ཧིང་ཀུ་ཏི། དེ་ཝོང་མི་ཤུད་ཀྱི་ཡེ། ཀྱེ་རིང་
ཏུབ་ས་ཡམ་པེམ་པེད་ཧོང་ཙེ། དོ་ཧུ་ཐ་ལ་ཟེ་ཀྱི་རིང་ཡེ་ཙི་ཀྱི་ཙི་ཏུ་ཆག་
ཀན་ལད་ཧི།

༡༠། དོ་ཀྱུ་ཧུ་ཐབ་ལ་ཟེ་ཀུང་ཙོ། ཝེང་མི་ཞི་ཏུ་ཚང་ཡམ་བི་ལད་ཀྱི།
ལམ་ཧེ་ང་ང་བར་དོ་ཡེ་རྒྱུག་ང་ལ་ཧོང་ཀྱི་མི་ཞི་ཙི་དོ་རིང་ཀྱུད་ཐོག་ཧི་ར།

༡༡། དོ་རང་དུད་ཁང་གི་མིའི་བད་ཏོ་ཅི་དོ་ཏ་ང་ཅི་རང་ཉམ་པོ། ཞུ་ལ་བ་མཁ་ཀྱུ
ཏ་དེ་རེ།

༡༢། ཡེ་ཤུའི་དོ་ཏིང་། སྐྱེ་ཟླ་ཕྱུད་པོང་བོང་ཡི་ཐ་ལ་ཞུ་ཀུན་ནས་ཀྱི། ཨམ་སྨན་ཀྱི།
༡༣། དོ་རང་བ་ཆ་ཆ་རིང་ཡི་ལ་ཀྱི། ཨ་ཏི་ངབ་ཀྱི་ལ། དོ་རིང་ཀ་ད་ལ་ད་ཀྱི། དོ་ཀྱུ
ཀ་ཆང་ཡི་ལ་ལི་རེ།
༡༤། དོང་ལུ་ཉི་ཟི་མི་ཨེ་ན་རིང་བི་ཆེ་ཀེ། ཆོ་འི་ཀན་ཞི་ཡེ།
༡༥། མིའི་རྒྱུ་ན་དཔལ་མ་པི་ལ་ཐེ་ཨེ། དུད་ཁོ་ན་ཚེམ་ཤེད་ལ་སྣ་ཏེ།
༡༦། ཡོན་ཏ་ར་སི་མོན་ནུ་མིན་པ་ཡ་ཀུན་ཀྱི་ཅག་ཏེ།
༡༧། ཟེ་བད་ཡ་ཞུ་ཡོང་ ཡ་གོབ་ཨེ། དོ་ཟུ་ནུ་ཀ་ཡོ་ཧན་ན། དོ་ཀྱུ་ཏུ་མེན་
བེ་ནེ་ར་ར་པེམ་ཀུན་ཀྱི་ཅག་ཏེ། ཨེན་ནུ་ཀད་དེད་དུག་ཏུ་ཡོཙ་ཀུན་ཏེ།
༡༨། ཨན་དྲི་ཡ་ཝ་ཨེ། ཝི་ལིབ། བར་ཐོ་ལོ་མ། ཐོ་མ། མཱ་ཐེ་ཡུ། ཡ་ཀོབ་ཨལ་ཕེ་
ཡ་ཞུ་ཡོཙ། ཐད་དུ། སི་མོན་ཀན་ཨན་པ།
༡༩། ཡུ་དཱ་ཀ་ར་ཡོད་པ། ཡི་ཧུ་ར་ཡེ་ཤུ་ཟུའི་རི་ཏུ་ཤུ་ར་ཉིང་རན་རི་པ་
དོ་རང་ཉམ་པོ་ལུ་ཉི་ཛི་མི་ཏ་རི།
༢༠། དོ་རང་ཡི་ཀྱུམ་མུང་ཨམ་ཀྱི། ཨ་ལ་ཀྱི་བོང་མི་ཛོམ་ཀྱི། ཡེ་ཤུ་
ཨེ་ལོབ་ཐུག་ཏེ་ང་ཟ་སྨེན་ཟ་འི་མི་ལོང་མ་ཨན་ཏེ།
༢༡། དོ་རང་ཉེ་ན་དུང་པོ་བད་ཏེ་ཅི་དོ་ཐ་ས་ཀྱི། ཡེ་ཤུ་ཤིད་བམ་ཀྱི་ཤུ་ཏི
ཀུན་ཀྱི། དོ་ཛོམ་ཅེ་ཡི་འ་ལི་རེ།

༢༢། ཆ་འདི་རིང་ཁལ་ལ་འདྲ་མི་ས་ཆུ་གཞུ་ལམ་ཆེ་ཡོད་ཀྱི་འདུག ། དེ་ཉི་ལ་བཟང་བོ་སྐྱང་
ཡུལ། ཧུད་དུ་གུ་ལ་བཙོད་སྣང་རིང་ཟེ་བོད་པོ་ཆོས་ཚིགས་ཀུ་ཞེ་པས།

༢༣། ཡེ་ཤུ་འདི་ངོ་བདག་ཏེ་རིང་ཡང་ཏ་བཀྲ་ནས་ཤེ། ལོ་གཞན་ཀྱི་ཀྱུ་ཏེ། ཧུད་ཅེ་ཧུད་
སྐུ་ཅན་ཆོས་ཀྱུ།

༢༤། ཡེ་ཧོ་ལ་ཨི་ལུ་དོང་ཛག་ཏ་ཤུད་ཅོ། དོ་ཧོ་ཛ་ཡ་ཀ་ཀམ་ཚེ་ཏ།

༢༥། ཡེ་ཀུམ་སྐུ་ཚང་ཛག་ཏ་ཤུད་ཅོ། དོ་ཀུམ་ཡ་ཀ་ཀམ་ཚེ་ཏ།

༢༦། ཡ་ས་ཀྱི་ཧུད་ཡེ་ཧུན་དུ་བ་ཚང་ཛག་ཏ་ཤུད་ཅོ། བ་ཀ་ཀམ་ཚེ་ཏ།

༢༧། ཡ་ཅི་ལ་ཡི་བ་འོ་ལུ་ཀུམ་སྐུང་ཡི་ལ་ཤེ། དོ་ལུ་མ་ཀ་ཏུ་ཁམ་པས།
ཁོར་ཀུ་ཟི་མ་རེ། ཏུང་རིང་དོ་པ་འོ་ལུ་གུད་པ་ཆུ་ཅི་ཏི་ལ། དོ་རང་དོ་རིང་ཀྱུ
ཏོད་ཀྱི་བདག་ཏེ་ཀུ་ཟི་ཆུག་ཏོ།

༢༨། ཤེ་ཤེན་ཏིང་དུང་པོ་ཀུ་ཙ་ཏོལ། མི་འདི་ཟི་ལ་སི་པུ་བ་ཡེ་གོན་ཅིག་ཏུ
མིན་རིང་མ་ཤར་སྣུ་ཤི་བདག་ཏེ་དག་ཏོ།

༢༩། ཡ་ཅི་ལ་དམ་པ་ལུ་སྐུག་ཉེད་དུ་མིན་ཏིང་མ་ཤར་རན་ཞི་པ་དོ་རིང་
ཡ་ལ་ལེ་ལ་དག་ཡི་མ་ཡན། ཏུའི་ཀུན་ཏིང་ཆད་པ་ཡོག་ཏོ།

༣༠། ཡོན་ན་ཁུ་རིང་ཀུ་ཏེ་ཀུད་ཅོ། དོ་ཅི་དེ་མི་ནོར་ཧུད་ཅེ་ཧུམ་ལེ་ཤུ་
ཀུད་ཀྱི་ཀུ་ཞིམ་པ་ལ་ཟི་ཀྱུ་ཏི།

༣༡། ཡོན་ཏར་ཡེ་ཤུ་ཡ་མ་ཡེ་ཧུག་ར་པིད་ཀྱི། པི་རིང་ཛོད་ཀྱི་
ཡི་མི་ཡེ་ཤུ་རིང་ཀད་ལ་ཟི་ཙར་ཏི་རེ།

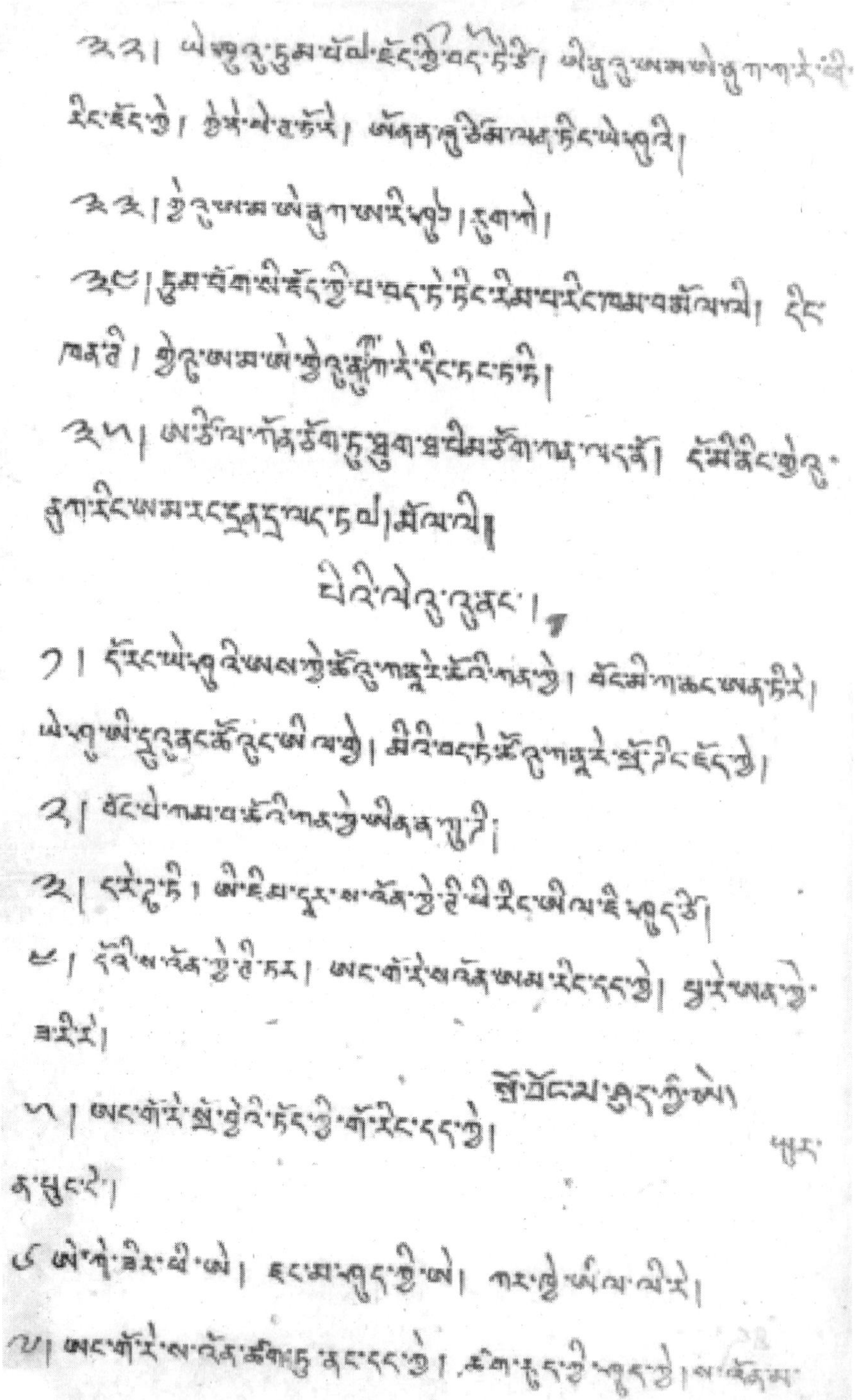

༢༢། [illegible]། [illegible]

[illegible]། [illegible]། [illegible]།

༢༣། [illegible]། [illegible]།

༢༤། [illegible]། [illegible]

[illegible]། [illegible]།

༢༥། [illegible]། [illegible]

[illegible]། [illegible]།

[illegible]།

༡། [illegible]། [illegible]།

[illegible]། [illegible]།

༢། [illegible]།

༣། [illegible]། [illegible]།

༤། [illegible]། [illegible]། [illegible]

[illegible]།

[illegible]

༥། [illegible]། [illegible]

[illegible]།

༦ [illegible]། [illegible]། [illegible]།

༧། [illegible]། [illegible]། [illegible]

ཚིག་དེ།   ༡༦

༨ ཡང་གོ་ར་ཏི་ཤི་ངར་དེ་རིང་དང་སྟེ། བྱུང་ངེ། ཕལ་པོ་ཆེ་ཀ། ཡང་
གོ་དེང་ནི་ཟ་ཏུ་ལྷ་བྱན། ཡང་གོ་དེང་བྱུམ་ནི་ཟ་བྱན། ཡང་གོ་དེང་དུ་བྱན་ཚིག་དེ
༩། དོར་ང་ཀྱུ་ཏི། ཡ་དེ་ང་ང་རེ་ཏི་མི་རེ་ཞ་ཏོད་ཏོ། རེ་ཏི་དེ།

༡༠། དོར་ང་ཡིན་ཟ་ཡིད་ཙ་ཧྲིད་ཏར། ལྷ་ནི་ཞི་མེ་ལོའི་བྱུག་ཏང་ཟེའི་དོ་ཙེ།
དི་པེ་ཏུ་ དོན་ཁང་ཀྱི་རང་ཀྱུ་ཀྱུ་ཏི་རེ།

༡༡། ཡེ་ཤུ་འི་མོ་ལ་ལི། ཀོན་ཅོག་ཏུ་རྣམ་ཟ་ཏུ་ཕྱག་ལི་བྱུད་ཀྱེན་ཏེང་ཏ་ཡོར
རྣམ་ལི་ཏོ་ཏེ། ཞི་རིང་ཏོད་ཀྱི་ད་ཏི་པེ་པེ་ཙེ། ཀྱེའི་ཀྱུལ་ལེ་རྣམ་ཤི་མང་ཙེ།

༡༢། དོ་ཙི་མི་གཙེ་ཏང་དེ་ལ། མ་ནི་ལྷ་ཏོ་རེ། རེ་ཞེ་ཟ་ལ་ཀྱེ་ལ། ཙམ་ཡོ་
ཏོ་རེ། ལེམ་མ་བྱུར་ཡིམ་ཟལ་ཟི། དོ་ཏུ་ཕུ་པ་མ་ནལ།

༡༣། དོར་ང་ཡེ་ཤུ་འི་མོ་ལ་ལི། ཀྱེན་ཙེ་དི་པེ་ཏུ་དོན་ཏག་ཏ་མ་གོ་ཏོ།
ཕྱི་ལི་པེ་རེ་ཏུ་དོན་ཏག་ཀྱུན་ཏ་གོ་ཏ་ཏི།

༡༤། ལ་འོན་པ་ཙི་པ་དོའི་ཀོན་ཆོག་ཏུ་ཚོའི་ཏ་ཙལ།

༡༥། ཡེམ་ཙང་དང་ཀྱི་ལ་འོན་རང་དུན་དུ་ཡ་རི་ཤུ་ཀྱུ་ཏུད་ཏོ། ཚོའི་ཟི
ཡེ། ལེམ་ཟང་ཀྱེ་ལ། དུང་ཕྱུར་ཙ་ཡན་ཀྱེ། སྟོ་ཏ་དུ་ཏང་ཀྱེ་ཤི་ལ་འོན་ཀོག་ཀ
ཤིལ་ཙལ།

༡༦། གོ་རིང་ལ་འོན་ཀྱེ་ཤི་དོ་ཡ་རི་ཤུ་ཀྱུ་ཏུད་ཏོ། ཚོའི་ཟ་ཙི་ཡེ། ལེམ་
ཟད་ཀྱེ་ལ།

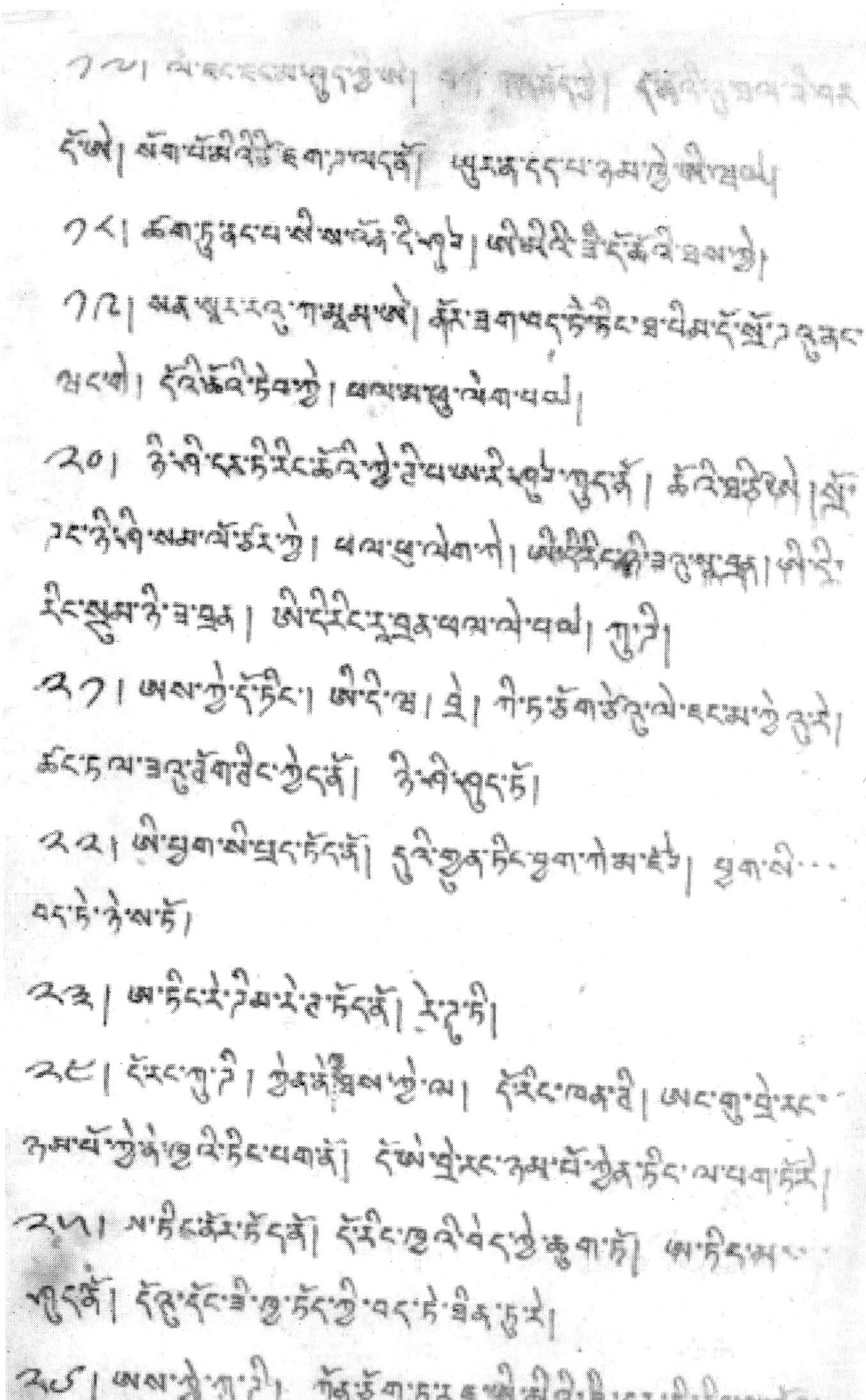

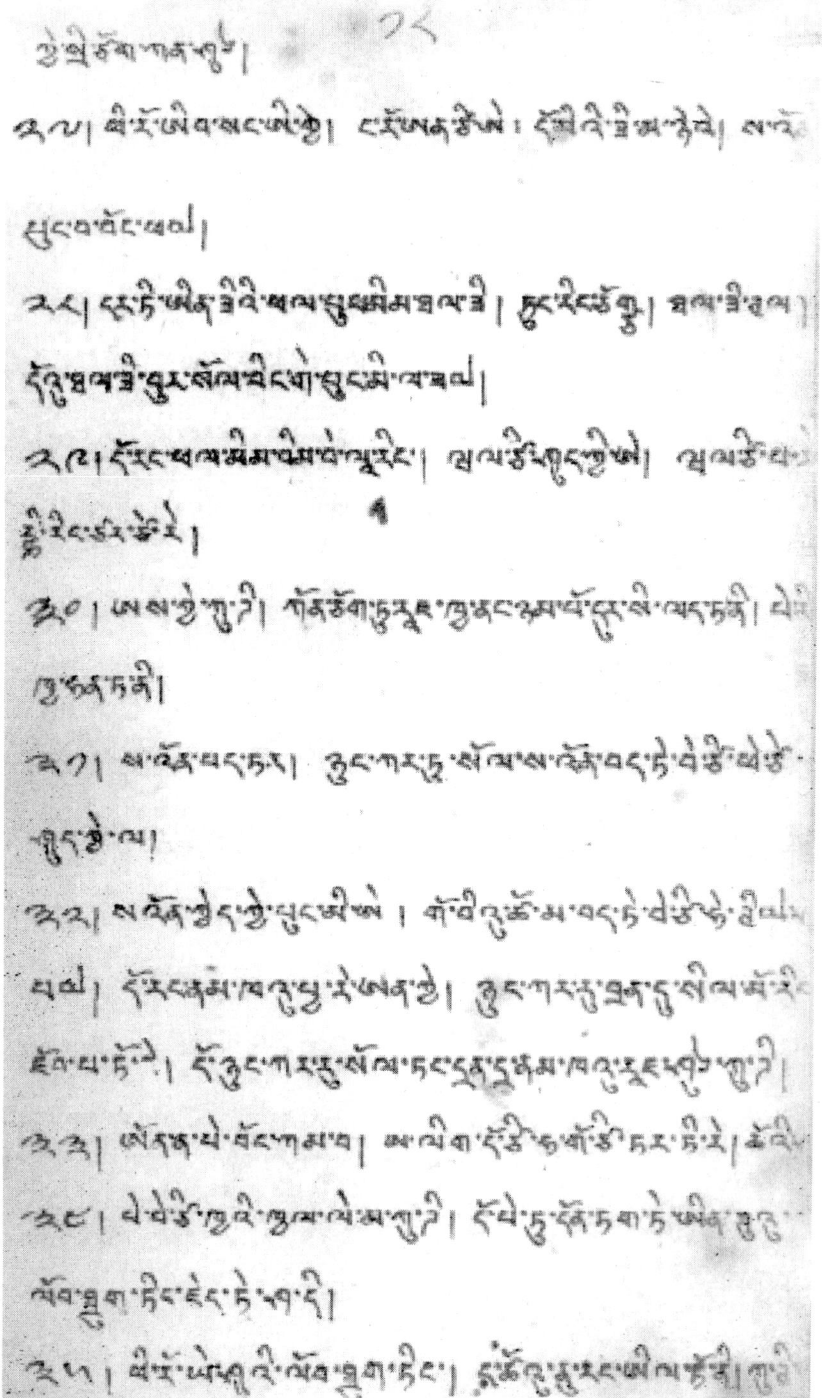

༣༦། ངེ་ཅན་རེ་བ་དང་ཧ་ཁུར་ཡོང་བར་ཞིག་རེ། ... ཐུ་མི།
རྡུ་དུ་ཆང་ཆོ་ཁྱུང་ཡི་ཤྭ། ཁྱུའི་བོད་ཧྲུ་དོ་ཧྲད་ཅུམ་པོ་པའི་ལ་ལི་རེ།

༣༧། ངོ་རང་ཡི་པོད་ཅན་འདུས་ཡས་ཀྱི། ཧྲུ་ཧྲུ་དང་ཡས་ཀྱི། ཧྲུ་ལོ་ཧི་ཕི་ལོ་
ཡི་ལ་ལི།

༣༨། ཡེ་ཤུ་ཧྲུ་དྲུ་ཧྲུབ་ཧི་ང་། ཀུན་སྐུ་ཧོག་ཞིང་བ་ལོག་ཀ་ལ་ཀྱི། ངོམ་བ་མཆོད་ཀྱི་
ཡོ། ངོ་ཅི་ཡི་བལ་ཧྲ་ཟི་ལད་ཀྱི། ཡེ་ལོ་བོན། ཧྲེན་ནེ་སྦྱི་ཞེ་ཡེ་ཀྱི་ལ། ངོ་རི་ང་མ་
ཁན་ཞ་ཧོ་ཟ་ཡས། ཞུ་ཅི་ཡེ།

༣༩། ཡེ་ཤུ་ཁང་ཀྱི། འདས་ཧི་ང་དར་ཀྱི། སོ་ཧི་རི་ངམོ་ལ་ཧི། དཀར་རོག་ཧོ། ཡོད།
ན་ཀུ་ཞི་ཡེ། འདས་ཆག་ཀེ། ཚོ་ལ་ཞི་རི།

༤༠། ངོ་རང་ལོབ་སྒྲུག་ཧེ་ཧིང་། ཁྱུའུ་ཐལ་ཟི་ཀྱིན་ནེ་ཡིང་ཀྱོ་བ་ལེམ་ཀུད་ཁ་ཐ།
ཧོ་ཧི། ཡའི་ཧ་ལ་ཀྱིན་ཧིང་དད་པ་མ་ཧ་ཧི་ཡས། ཡོན་ན་རྡུག་ཧི།

༤༡། ངོང་ངོ་ཧིང་བོང་བེད་ཡས་ཀྱི། ཡི་དི་འི་ཡེ་དི་རིང་ཀུ་རི་རེ། འདས་ཡེ་ལོ་ཧི
ལ་དི་མི་དུ་ཡ་རིང་པ་ལ་པལ། ངོ་ཡ་རི་ཤུ། ཀུ་རི་རེ།།

དྷ་ཡི་དུ་དུ་ནང་།

༡། ངོ་རང་ཚོ་དུ་སྒུ་རང་བོ་རས་བ་དུ་ཕྱུ་ལ་ཧིང་ཡམ་ཀྱི།

༢། ཡེ་ཤུ་དྲུ་དུ་ཆང་ཟི་ལོ་ས་རིང་ཧོ་ལ་ས་ཡམ་ཧར། ཧྲུ་ཁྱང་གི་ཡི་
རོམ་ཁང་བིང་ཟི་ངོ་ཀྱུ་ཅི་ཡས་ཧ།

༣། ངོ་ཡི་འི་མི་རོམ་ཁང་རིང་བྲང་ལ་ལུད་ཀྱི། ཡ་ཧིང་ང་ངོ་ཅག་ཟག

ངང་རྒྱུ་མི་སྐྱ་ཕྲལ་ལ་ཏེ།

༤། ཏུང་རིང་དོ་མི་ཏུ་ཤུད་པང་ཅག་ཐག་དང་རྒྱུད་ཀྱི་ལ།

༥། དའི་ཅག་ས་ག་ཐག་ཀེ། ཡ་ཙེ་ལ་དོ་ཏུ་ལ་ཙེ་མ་ཏར་གྱི་ཡེ། རྒྱ་ཏི་དོན་པ་ཏི།
བཀྲ་ཡེ་རྨ་ཁང་རིང་རྫོང་གྱི། ད་ཀྱུ་ཏབ་པ་ཡིན་རྒྱུ་ཏུ་རྒྱག་ཞི་རབ་དོག་ཡི་
རྣ་ཏི།

༦། དོ་མི་འི་ཞི་ཡེ་ཤུ་ལྷོ་འི་ཙེ་ཏང་གེ། གྲུལ་པ་ཡམ་ཀྱི། ཕྱུག་སྤྱོ་ཉིང་
རྫི་སྒྲ་སྒྱེ། ཀང་སེད་ཅན་དང་།

༧། ཡེ་ཡེ་ཤུ། ཀོན་ཅོག་ཐོའི་དོ་ཏུ་ཡོཙེ། ཡེ་ནེ་དིང་ཀྱུ་ན་ཉམ་པོ་རྫོང་ཀྱིས།
སྐྱེ་ཀོན་ཅོག་གོལ་ཧི་རིང་ཀྱིད་ཀྱི། ཡིནས་ཏུ་བ་ཕུལ་ཙ་ཧེལ། སྐྱེ་རིང་པར་
ཏོ་ཐ་ཀན་རྒྱུ་ཡོན་ན་ཏུ་བ་ཕུལ་ལི།

༨། ཡེ་ཤུའི་གོང་པོ་རིང་། དོ་མི་ཏུ་དོང་ཞི་ཆོས་སུ། ཀའ་གལ་རྫོད་ཀྱི་ཡེ།

༩། གོང་བོ་རིང་། ཀ་རྒྱ་མིན་ཀྱུ་ཤུར་རྒྱུག་ཀ། གོང་པོ་འེ། རྗེན་ཧེ་བོང་ཤུད་
ཟང་། མིན་ཏིང་རྒྱ་ཏ་ཀུ་ཝི་ཤུར།

༡༠། རྗེན་ཧེ་དེ་ཡུལ་ཏིང་ཞི་ཀོན་ཐ་ཀོན་ཏུ།

༡༡། ཡོན་ཏར་དོ་བཀྲ་ཀྲ་ཏུ་ཡི་དབ་ཞིང་ལག་ཏུ་ཡི་ཧེ་ཏིལ་རྒྱ་ཀ་རག་པ
ཏོ་རི་རེ།

༡༢། གོང་པོ་རེ་ཙེ་ཡེ་ཤུ་རིང་། རྗེན་ཧེ་ལག་ཏེ་ཏུ་ཀང་ཡི་བི་རང་གྲུ
ཡོནས་ཏུ་ཙེ་ཡེ། ཡེ་ཤུའི་ཡི་གི་རྒྱ་ཏི།

༡༣། ང་གོང་མ་བད་ཏེ་ཆོས་ལེ་ལེ། ལག་ཏུ་རྒྱུ་ཏ་ཏ་ཟུང་ཏང་ཡོང་ངེ། ལྗིང་ཉྫྷར་

ཏང་གྱི་ལག་ཏུ་རྒྱུ་ཏ་བད་ཏེ་གོ་རིང་ཟེ་གུར་ཏིང་ཁན་གྱི་ཚོང་པ། ལོ་ཏི་ཟུམ་ཏང་ནང་གྱི་

སེ་རི་རེ།

༡༤། ལག་ རང་གྱི་པ་རེ་པོ་རྒྱ་ཀྱེ། ན་གར་པ་ལེ་ཡུལ་བད་ཏེ་ཏུ་མི་འི་ཏིང་ཀྱི་སྐད་

ཀྱི་ངོ་པག་ཅེལ། ངོ་རེ་ཀྱི་པུད་ཅེས་ཁན་ཞི་པན་ཏི་རེ།

༡༥། ཡེ་ཤུ་ཞུ་ཏུམ་པོལ་ཡིན་གྱི་ལེ། ཏུང་རིང་དུད་ཚང་གི་ངོ་མི་ཏི་ང་རིང་ལ

ཀྱི། ངོ་ངོང་ཁམ་ཁམ་ཟ་ཏོད་ཀྱི་ཏང་ཟང་། ཞེ་རི་རེ།

༡༦། ངོ་རང་ངོ་ཀ་སྨུམ་ཏང་ལེ་ད་ཅི་ངོ་ཏིང་དུད་ཚང་གི་ངོ་རང་ལག་ཏུ་ཏུ་ཏ་ཏ

ཏིང་ཀྱི་པུད་ཀྱི་ངོ་བད་ཏེ་པག་དེ་རེ།

༡༧། ངོ་རང་ངོ་རེ་བད་ཏེ་ཅི། རྗེན་ཟུ་དེ་ཡུལ་ཏིང་ཟེ་ཆོས་ལ་ཀྱི་ནམ་

ཡི་གེ་ཅིས། ཡོན་མོ་ཞུ་ཟེ་རེ།

༡༨། ངོ་ཊ་ཡེ་ཤུ་རྣ་ཟུ་མང་ཡོང་ངེ། ཏུང་རིང་དུད་ཚང་གི་ངོ་མི་ཞི་ཟེ།

ཀྱི་ལ་ཀྱི་སྐུ་ཐ་ལང་ཟེ་ལམ་ཡི་རང་ཤུ་ཞུས་ཀྱི་ལ།

༡༩། ཡེ་ཤུའི་ལམ་ཡིམ་རང་གེ་ངོ་རིང་མོ་ལ་ལི། ང་ཀ་རྒྱུམ་སྐུ་རིང་ཡི

ཡེན་སྐུ་ཞིང་མད་བད་ཏེ་ཏིང་། ཅི་བོ་ཞི་ཀ་ཚིང་ཀྱུ་ན་ཟུག་ཟེ་ཀན་ཏེ་ཀ་ཅི་ཅི

ཡོན་ན་པོ་ལ་ལི།

༢༠། ངོ་ཡི་ཀྱེ། ལྷན་གར་ཀུ་ཤི་དེ་པག་དང་ཀྱེ། ཡེ་ཤུ་འི་ཀྱ་ཀྱ་ལ་ལི

བད་ཏེ་པཀད་ཀྱེ། མི་འི་བད་ཏེ་ལམ་ཙན་ཤུ་འི་རེ།

༢༡ །ཨ་ལ་སྐྱེ་ཡེ་སྒྲུ་དུ་བྱུང་ཐུང་བ། རྒྱ་དང་པོད་ཀྱི། འོང་མི་པོ་ལྷ་རྒྱལ་པོ།

ཇོམ་ཀྱི། ཡེ་སྒྲུ་ཆོ་ཟླ་དཔའ་ཟིང་ཟླ་སྐ་སྐྱེ།

༢༢ །ཨེ་ཕྱུ་ཞི་པ་ཡ་ཨིར་ཀྱ་གྲི་དོ་ཨན་ཀྱི། ཡེ་སྒྲུ་ཏ་ང་ཅེ་ཡེ། སྤྱུག

སྦྲ་ཀྲིང་ཚག་ཀ།

༢༣། སྐྱེ་ཟླ་སྐྱེ་མེཙ་མི་ལྡི་པོའི་སྒྲུང་གྱི་ཧོ་ཧོ། སྐྱེ་ནེ་ཨམ་ཀྱི་བ་ལ་ཏོག་ཏིང་

ཀུད་སྐྱེ་ངོ། ནད་ཕན་ཧོ། ཨོན་ན་ཚན་ཏན་ལྦུ་ཟེ།

༢༤། ཡེ་སྒྲུ་དོང་ཨམ་ཏར། འོང་མི་དོ་ཟླ་ཐ་ལང་ཟི་རྒྱབ་ས་ཨན་ཧི་རེ།

༢༥། དོ་ཞེ་ལྷ་རིང་ཁྲུའི་ཨེ་མེ་ཙི། སྣ་ཉི་ཛེ་མིང་ཐ་ལང་སེ་ཟླ་ནང་པོག་ཀ།

༢༦། འོང་ལ་རྡེ་ཙེ་ཁན་ཀྱི་ལ། འོང་བར་དོ་ཉོང་བེ། ཆོར་བད་ཧེ་ཀོད་ཀྱི་ལ

ཕན་ཐོག་པི་མ་ཡ་ལ་ཏི།

༢༧། དོ་རིང་ཡེ་སྒྲུའི་རྒྱན་ཐ་ཅེ་ཡེ། ཨིན་ན་སམ་སེ་རི།

༢༨། དོ་ཟླ་ཁམ་རིང་ཀུད་ཐོག་ནོ། ཕན་ཧོལ། སམ་ས། མིའི་ཧུ་རྒྱ་ཅེ་ཟ

ཞི་ཙང་ཟི་ཐ་ལང་ཟི་ཨན་ཀྱི། ཁམ་རིང་ཀུད་ཐོག་ཧི།

༢༩། ཨོན་ཏར་སྒྲུའི་དང་ཀྱེ། ཨིན་ཟླ་ཟླ་ཟུག་ཟུ་ཟུག་ཕམ་བི་ནེ་རི།

༣༠། ཡེ་སྒྲུའི་ཨིན་ཟླ་ཟླ་ཟུག་ཟིང་ཟི་ཨེ་སྙིད་ཧོལ་སི་ཉེ་ལེ། མིའི

བད་ཧེ་ཧུ་བི་ཙང་ཟི་ཐ་ལང་རིང་ཁན་ཀྱི་སྐྱེ་ཟླ་ཁམ་ཟིང་ཡ་ཅེ་ཀུད་ཐོག

ཧི་ཀྱུ་ཏི།

༣༡། ལྡབ་ལྷུག་ཧེ་ཅེ་ལྦུ་པ་ལའི་རེ། ཆོང་མི་ཀྱི་ནན་ཟླ་བ་སི་ཏང

ལྷ་རིང་ལ་ཚེ་ཟེ་བ་ཚལ་ཀུ་སྦྲ་དོ་ཁྲུ་མཁྱེན།

༣༢། ཡེ་ཤུ་ཡི་དོ་བདག་ནི་ཉི་ང་རེས་པ་ཁྱེན་གྱི། ཡོན་ཏན་ལ་ཟེ་པ་ཡམ་པའི་མཁྱེན།
ཡར་ཆོད་ལའི།

༣༣། དོ་རང་དོ་མེ་ཚེ་ཡིན་ཟ་རིང་གྱུ་མཁྱེན་ནི་ཉེ་ནི། བེ་ནེ། དུ་སྐྱེ་བ་པ་ཕྱུག་
ཡང་ཀྱི། ཀྱི་ལ་སྐྱིད་བད་ཀྱེ་དུང་པོ་དུང་པོ་ཁྱེ་དི།

༣༤། དོ་རང་ཡེ་ཤུ་ཡི་དོ་ལེ་ཚེ་རིང་། སྐྱེ་ཏུ་སྐྱེ་མེད། ཀའི་དང་པ་ཀྱ་ཟེ་
ཡེ། ནད་ཐན་ཀྱི་ཡི་ལ་ལི། དཀི་ཁྱི་མཁྱུད་ཀྱི་ཡི་ལ་ལ། ཐལ་ཟེ་ལ་དོ་
ནད་དིང་ཟེ་ཡོ་ཡི་མཁྱུད་ཀྱི་ཚེ་རེ་ཏོན།

༣༥། ཡོན་ཏན་ཀུ་ཏེ་ཡེ། ཡུ་ཏེ་པ་ཏུ་ཡི་ཡོ་ག་པོ་ཡན་ཀྱི་ཡིན་ན་
ཏུ་བ་ལའི། ཡི་ཏུ་ཏུ་ཀྱི་མེད་ལི་ནེ་ཡི་ལ་ལི། ཡེ་མཁྱུ་བར་དོ་རིང་ཀྱུ་ལ་ཀི
ཡམ་པི་རན་ཟ་ཏོན།

༣༦། ཡོན་ཏན་ཀུ་ཏི་ཟ་ཚེ་ཡེ། ཡེ་མཁྱུ་ལི་ཡུ་ཧི་པ་རིབ། བེམ་ལེ་ལེ
དད་པ་ལ་ཏུ། ཀུ་ཏི།

༣༧། གེ་ཐ་ཡེ། ཡ་ཀོབ་ཡེ། ཙོ་ཏུ་ཏུག་ཡོ་ཕ་ནན་སྐུ་མཐེས་བུའི།
ཀྱུ་རི་མི་ཡ་རི་ལ་ནང་ཡམ་པི་ཡམ་རྣ་ཧི།

༣༨། ཡུ་ཏི་པ་ཏུ་ཀྱུམ་སྤུང་ཡི་ལ་ཀྱི། ཀྲུབ་ཀྱི་པ་ཡེ་ཏུག་ངལ་
ལ་ཟེ་པ་བད་ཀྱེ་ཏིང་ཁྱན་ཀྱི།

༣༩། ནང་ཡན་ཀྱི་ཀུ་ཏི། ཀྱུ་རིང་ཀྲུབ་པ་ཕ་ཏུ་ཀ་རན་ཟ་ཧོ་ཏི།

ཤུ་མེ་ཙ་ལི་མ་ལི་འེ། ཡེ་བ་ལང་ཡོས་ལ་ཀྱལ་ཀུ་ཝི་ཡེ།

༩༠། ངོ་རེ་བད་ཏེ་ངོ་རིང་ཁན་ཤུ་ཀྱ་དི་རེ། ཡེ་སྐུ་ཝེ་ངོ་རོ་ཝི་རིང་ཚོན་ཤེ།
ཤུ་མེ་ཙ་ཀུ་ཡ་ཏ་ཡམ་མ་ཡེ། ཀོ་བ་ཟང་ཟེ་འེ་སྤུམ་སུ་ལོབ་སྦུག་ཏི་ངཡམ་ཏ
ཀུད་ཤེ། ཤུ་མེ་ཙ་ཏོད་ཀྱི་ཧ་ང་ཡི་ལ་ལི་རེ།

༩༡། ཤུ་མེ་ཙ་ཙ་ཀུ་གུད་ཙུམ་ཤུ་ངོ་རིང་། ཏ་ལི་ཐ་ཀུ་ཡི། ཡེན་སྐུ་ཙོག་ཀམ
ཤུ་མེ་ཙོད་ཡན་ཛུ།

༩༢། ཡོན་བ་རྒྱ་ཀུམ་རན་ཝི་ཡེ། ལྷ་ནི་ཧི་མིང་སྐུད་ཀྱི་ཤུ་མེ་ཙོ་ཁ་ཏེ་
ཡན་ཙ། ཡམ་ཅེ་ཏང་གེ། མི་འི་བད་ཏེ་ཐ་ཐ་སྐུད་ཀྱི་ཡི་ལ་ལི་རེ།

༩༣། ངོ་རང་ཀྱ་འི་ཡི་འི་ཏིང་ཀྱུ་ཞིམ་ལབ་ཛ་ཚན་ཟན་ལད་ཀྱི། ཤུ་མེ་ཙོ་
རིང་ཐ་མེན་རན་ཝིམ་རྒྱ་ཀུམ་སྣ་ཏེ༎

ཀྱུ་འི་ལེ་ཀུ་ཀུ་ཙང་།

༡། ངོ་རང་ཏོས་ས། ལོབ་སྦུག་ཏེ་ཏང་ཉམ་པོ་ཡིན་རྒྱ་ཀུ་ཡུལ་ཏིང་
ཡི་ཤུ།

༢། ཡ་འི་ཏོ་ཡར་ར་ཀུ་ཛག་མེ་སྲིང་ཚོ་ཁང་ཏུང་ཚོ་འི་སྐད་ཀྱི། བོང་
མི་འི་ཏི་ཐ་ས་ཀྱི། ཐ་ཐ་སྐུད་ཀྱི་ཀུ་འི་རེ། ངི་སྤུད་དེ་ངོ་རིང་ཀྱང་ཐི་
ཡམ་པ་ལ། ཀོན་ཙོག་ཅི་རྡོ་རིང་སྣ་སྤྲི་ངི་རིག་པ་ཀྱ་སྐུར། ཡིན་རྒྱ་ཀུ
ཀུ་ཞེ་ཏི་ལ་སྐྱིད་ཀན་ཟལ།

༣། ངི་མི་མིར་ཡམ་སུ་ཡོ་ཙ་ཤིང་ཁན་ཡ་སྐུད་ད། ཡ་ཀོབ་ཡེ།

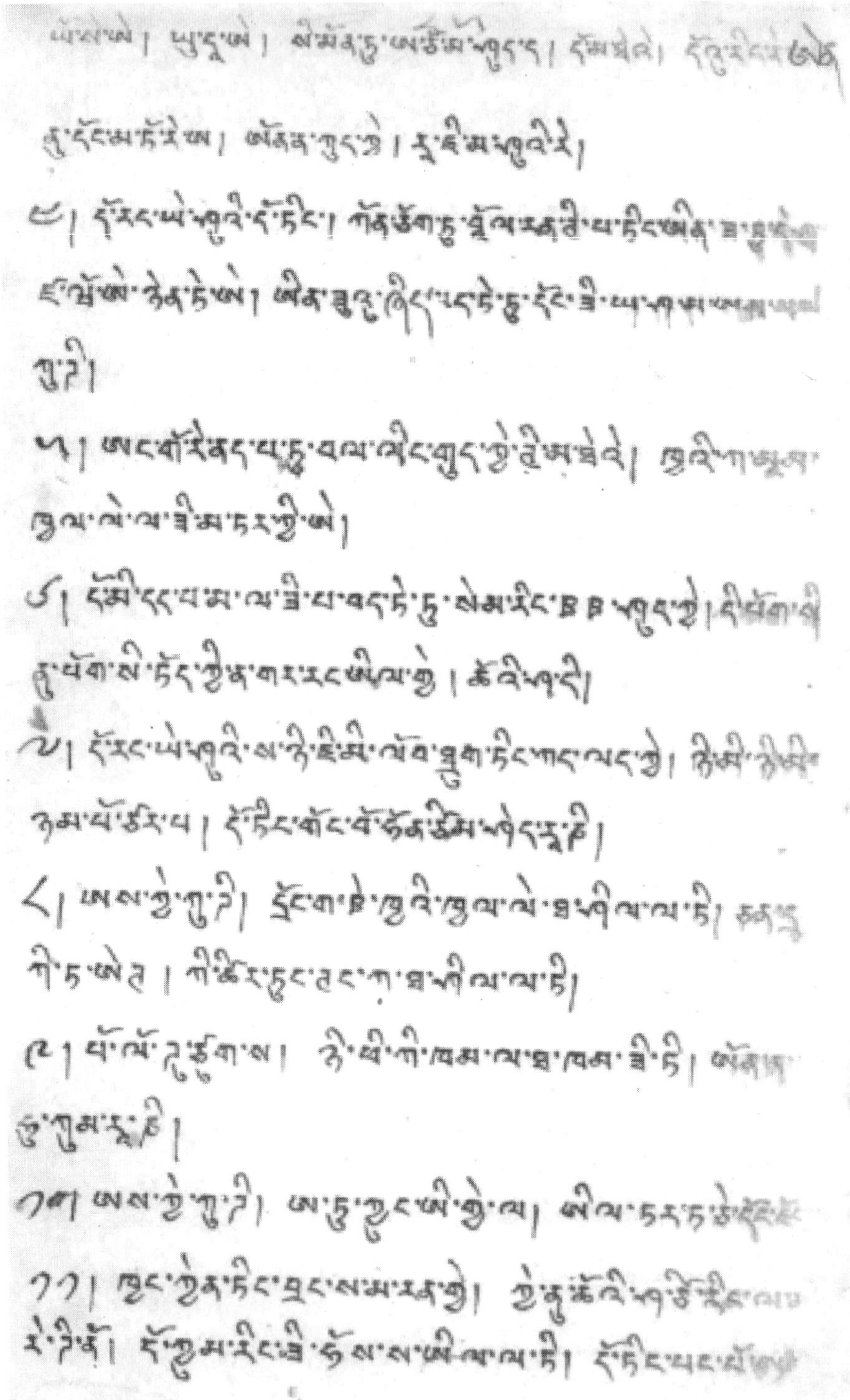

ཞིམ་ཐལ་ཟེ། པཎྜི་ཏོད་ཀྱི་རྡུ་ཀཱ་ལ་ཙུར་ཀེ། ཐེ་ཏུན་ཀེང་དྲུང་པོ་གྱུ་ཧ་

རྩེལ། དེ་ལྟར་ལ་ཟེམ་ཧག་ཀེང་དོན་གར་ཞེ་ཅི། ལོ་དམ་ཡེ་གོ་ཡོ་རར་རེང

ཆད་པ་རྒྱང་གི་ཕོག་ཏུ། ཀུ་ཏེ།

༡༢། དོ་རང་ལོབ་སྤུལ་ཏེ་ཡི་ལ་ཀྱི། ད་སེམ་གྱར་ཏི། ཡོན་ན་ཚེ་འདི་ཁ་ཟེར

༡༣། དོ་རང་དོ་ཅི་ཐང་གོང་བོ་ཚོན་གྱི། ཐོང་ནད་པ་ཀེང་ཏེ་ལ་ཆ་འི། ཁ

གི་ལ་འདི་རེ།

༡༤། ཐོ་ཞེ་ལྔ་རིང་ཡེ་ཁྲུ་ཏུ་རྒྱན་རིང་གེ། ཆེ་རོ་དེ་ཏ་རྗེ་ཐལ་གྱི་ཀུ་ཏི།

སྤུ་འི་རན་ཧི་པ་ཡོ་ཆ་ནན་ཧམ་མ་ཏ། རེ་ཁ་ཁང་ཟེ་ཡན་ཅི། དེ་འི་ཡིན

ན་ཀ་སྣ་སུ་ཀན་ཟལ།

༡༥། ཡང་གོ་རེ་མི་འདི་ཅི། དོ་ཏ་ཡེ་ལི་ཡུ་ཁྲུ། ཁྱ་འདི་ཅི། ཀེ་ཅོག

ཏུ་བློ་ལ་རན་ཧི་པ་རིང་ཟེ་ཡི་དི་རང་དྲན་དྲུ་གོན་ཅོག་ཏུ་ཡི་བློ་ལ་ནན

ཧེ་པ་ཁྲུ། ཀུ་ཏི་རེ།

༡༦། ཆེ་རོ་དེ་འི་ཡོན་ན་ཕྲད་ཐལ་གྱི། ཡིང་གི་འི་ཁོང་ཆ་བྱི་ བྱེ

ཡོ་ཏ་ནན་ཡིན་ཟ་ཁྲུ། མི་འི་ལ། ཡལ་ཀྱི་སྤྱིང་གི་ཡན་ཅི་རི།

ཀུ་ཏི།

༡༧། དོ་ཞེ་ལྔ་རིང་ཆེ་རོ་དེ་འི་ཡིན་རྒྱུ་ཁྲུ་ཀ་ཡི་ལིབ་བཏུ་མེད་

ཀོག་ཀེ། ཡིན་ཟ་རིང་མེད་ཆན་ཅི་ཡེ།

ཁང་རྒྱང་ཏོག་ཏེ།

༡༩། ཏི་རོད་ཡ་རིང་ཚོག་པ་ཡན་ཆི། ཡོ་ཏ་ཧན་ལ་ཟིན་ཆེ་ལ།
མ་ཏར་ཏི།

༢༠། ཕྱི་རིང་མ་ཏར་ཏི་ཀུན་ནོ། ཏི་ཛོ་དེ་ཝ་ཡོ་ཏ་ཧན་དང་པོ་ཡེ་ཤང་གི
མི་ལྕུ། ཚེ་ཝེ་ཝེ། ངོ་རྒྱན་ཙི་ཏར། ར་ཛ་དོ་ཝུ་དང་པོ་ཕུད་དེང་ཐད་ཆེ། ཝོ་ཏི་
ཕྱིན་དྲི་ཕྱི་ཕྱི་ལ་ཝི་ཏིས་དོ་རིང་ནག་ཀེ། ངོ་ཝུ་ཆུ་ཀུམ་ཙར་ཏི་རི།

༢༡། ངོ་རང་ཆེ་ཛོ་དེ་ཝེ་ཡིན་༎ ཟུ་བ་ཛིར། ཏ་ལྡར་ཀུ་པ་ནི་ཕྲུ་ཏུག་ཀ
མི་ལ་ཡེ། ག་ལི་ལ་དེ་ཀ་ཤ་ཁྲུ་ཀུ་ར་ལྡར་ཐད་ཏེ་ཏིང་། ཡིན་རྒྱུ་ཕྱིན
ཟིམ་ཛག་ཕྲུ་ཡི་ས་ཕྱིན་ལྡ་ཏི།

༢༢། ཡོན་ཏར་ཏེ་རོད་ཡ་ཝུ་སྤྱི་མེ་ཙོ་ནང་ཡན་ཆི། ཕྱོར་ཡི་ཡེ། ཏེ
རོ་དེ་ཡེ་དྲོན་པོ་དུ་ཝང་ཐ་དི་རེ། ངོ་ཝུ་ཟ་ལ་ཟི་ར་ཛེ་ཀྱི་མཚོ་རིང་།
ཡེ་ཤུ་མེ་ཙོ། ཀ་ཕྱུ་བ་ག་ལི་ས་རིང་ཐད་ཀྱི་ལ། ཤི་རིང་ཀུ་དུ། ཤེ་
རན་ཞལ། ངོ་མ་ཚོག་ཀེ་ལ།

༢༣། ཤུ་གནྡྲི་ལར་ཆི། ཝེད་ལྡ་ཝི་ཏ་ཙེ་ཡེད་ཀྱི་ལ། རན་ཞལ་
ཀུད་ཆི། ཆང་ཀ་ལ་ཝི།

༢༤། ཤི་མེ་ཙོ་ཡི་ཤི་ཡ་མ་རིང་། ན་ཕྱུ་ནང་ཤུ་ཀུག་ཀ་ཤི་
རིང་ཀུ་དུ་ཀུ་ཞི་ཡེ། ཡ་མེ། ཕྲུ་ཝི་རན་ཞི་པ་ཡོ་ཏ་ཧན་ཧཱུ།

ནས་ལོག་ཕར་སྒྲ་སྒྲུང་ཆེ་ཀུ་རུ། །ཕྱུག་སྐྱི།

༢༥། ཤུ་ཤེ་ཙ་ཕྱུར་ནར་རྫ་ཁྲུ་ཀ་ཆང་ཡི་གྱི། ཡོན་ན་ཡེ་ཕྱུར་ཕ་གྱི་རིང་
སྐྱུའི་རན་ཐེ་པ་ཡོ་ཧྲ་ཆན་ཆ་ཁྲུ་བ་ལ་ལོག་པེ་ཏ་ཕ་ལྟ་ཁྲུ་ཕང་རང་སྒྲུ་ཀྲུ་བ་ལའི།
༢༦། དོ་རིང་ར་ཛ་ཤོ་ཆེ་ར་ཛེ་ཕ་སྦུ་ད་གྱི་ལ། རྡོན་པོ་ཏུ་ཏྲུམ་པོལ་སྒྲུ་
ག་སྐྱུ་ཡེ་ཚད་ཀ་ལ་ཐྲི་ཡེ། ཡིན་ཐྲུ་ཁྲུ་ཕུད་རིང་ཐྲི་སྒྲུར་པི་མ་ཏར་ཏི།
༢༧། ཤི་ལ་ཅོ་བ་ཙར་གྱི། ཡོ་ཧྲ་ཆན་ཕ་ཁྲུ་བ་ལ་ལོག་ལེན་ཙོ་ཆུན་ཏ
ཡོན་ན་ཕྲུ་ཀྲུམ་རྣ་ཏི།
༢༨། དོ་ཤི་ལ་ཅོ་པ་ཙོན་ཁང་དྲུང་ཡི་གྱི། ཡོ་ཧྲ་ཆན་ཆ་ཁྲུ་བ་ལ་ལོག
ཐེག་ཀི། ཡི་པེ་ཏ་ལ་ཁྲུ་ཕང་གྱི་ད་གྱི། །གྱི་ཡེ་ཙ་ཅོ་རིང་རྣ་ཏི། གྱི་ཡེ་ཙོ
ཡིན་ཐྲུ་ཁྲུ་ཕམ་མ་རིབ་རྣ་ཏི།
༢༩། ཡོ་ཧྲ་ཆན་ཕ་ཁྲུ་ལོབ་ཐྲུག་ཏེ་ཏིང་ཡོན་ན་ཕྲུ་པིམ་ཆུན་
ཐ་ཅོ་ཕྱེ། རོ་ཕ་ཤི་ལ་ཅོ་ཡན་གྱི། །རོམ་ཁང་རིང་ཕྲུག་ཏི་རེ།
༣༠། དོ་རང་པེ་ཕྲུ་ཁྲུ་ལོབ་ཐྲུག་བད་ཏེ་ པེ་ཕྲུ་ཁྲུ་ཏྲུམ་པོལ་ཛོམ
གྱི། ཡིན་ཐ་ཅོ་ཁྲུ་ཁྲུ་ལ་ཤི་ཤོ། །ཚོའི་ཁྲུ་ཆ་པ་ཤི་དོ་དོ་རིང་པ་རི་རེ།
༣༡། པེ་ཕྲུ་ལི་རྟེ་ཏིང་། ད་གྱི་ཕ་རིང་ཡན་གྱི་ཤི་མ་ཏོད་ཀྱི་ཡི་ལ་
ཁྲུང་རིང་ཡི་ལ་ཏོ་ཤི། དོང་ཚེ་ཀེ་ཕ་ཙོ་རྡེད་ཏོ་ཤི། ཡོན་ན་ཁྲུ་ཁྲུ་ཐ་ལ་ཐྲི
ཀ་རི་ཀུང་ཤོ། བོང་ཤི་དི་པོ་རིང་ཏུ་པོ་རིང་ཡི་གྱི་པ་ཕྲུད་ཐང་། །ཐ་ཡོན་
ཐ་འི་མ་ལོང་ལ་མ་ཏོ་རི།

༣༢། དེ་རུ་ཐལ་ཞེ་རྒྱུ་ནང་ལ་འདེའོ། ཤེས་ཚད་ཀྱི་ཡི་ལ་ཟུང་
དེང་ཡི་ལ་ཏན།
༣༣། མི་འི་ཅི་པོ་ཏེ་ཡི་ཞི་ཏུ་ག་ཏེ། ཞེ་མི་འི་ཏིང་པ་ཏུ་ཙུན་ཀུང་
ཟུ། ཡིན་ཟ་ཧྲུམ་གར་རང་ཞི་ཚོ་ལ་ལ། ཡིད་པ་ཤུ་པོ་དྲེ་རྐྱ་རན་ཅེ།
ཡེ་ཤུ་ཞེ་ཅི་བྱུ་ན་ཤེད་ཞེ་ཞེ་ཡི་ཏི་སེ།
༣༤། ཡེ་ཤུ་ཡི་ཤིན་ཡི་ཅེ། ཞོ་མི་ཏི་བད་ཏེ་ལ་རྒྱུ་ལ་ཏོད་ཀྱི་ཙུ་ཏ
ཅོ་ག་ཀན་ཀྱུད་ཀྱི་ཡེ། ཟུག་ཞེ་ལད་ཀྱེ་ཞོང་ཚེ་ཏི་པ་ཏི་ཤུག་ཟི།
༣༥། ཏོ་རང་ཡེ་ཀེ་ཏོ་ཤིས་ཞེ་ལྷ་ཤིས། ལོན་རྒྱུག་ཏེ་ཡེ་ཤུ་ཏུ་ཙུམ
པོལ་ཀན་ཀྱེ་ཀུ་ཏི་རེ། ཏི་ལ་ཀྱུད་ཞེ་མ་ཏུ་ཟང་ཀྱུར། ཏོ་མ་ཞེ་ཁེ
ཡེ་ཀེ་ལ་ཏོ་པ་ལ།
༣༦། ཏི་མི་ཏི་བད་ཏེ་ཏིང་ཟ་མེན་པ་ཏོ། ཏེ་རུ་ཟ་ལ་ཟི་ཡི་ཡི་ཏྲུ་ཏུ།
ཏེ་རང་ཏོ་རེ་ཏ་གར་རང་ཡི་ལ་ཀྱེ། ཟ་ཡེན་ཀོ་ཟུ་རེ།
༣༧། ཡོན་ཙ་ཀུ་ཞིམ་ལན་ཏིང་ཡེ་ཤུ་འི། ཀྱེ་པོ་ཀྱུ་ཟ་འི་
རང་ཀྱུ་ཞི། ཀུ་ཞི་ཡེ། ཏོ་ཅི་ཀུ་ཏི་རེ། ཏོ་རང་ཅེན་པོ་ཡི་ལ་ཀྱེ།
ཏི་རྣ་ཞང་ཀ་ཏུ་ཡེན་པོད་ཀྱེ། ཏོ་ཏིང་ཟ་འི་རེད་རན་ཞི་ཅི་ལ་ལ།
༣༨། ཏོ་རང་ཡེ་ཤུ་འི། ད་ཀྱེ་ཞེ་ཡི་ལ་ཀྱེ། ཏིང་ལ་ལིག་ཡེ།
ཏིང་ཅིས། ཁན་ཞི། ཀུ་ཏི། ཏོ་ཅི་ཁན་ཀྱེ། ཙ་གོ་ཏེ། ཏིང་
ཡེ་ཏི་ཏི་ཟ་ཏོ་ཀུ་ཏི་རེ།

༣༩། ངོ་རང་ཡེ་ཤུ་འི་ད་མི་འི་བད་ཧེ་ཧིང་གི་སྐད་རིད་ཀྱུ་ཙང་ཏུ་མ་ཨེ་ཡུ་ཀྲུ་ཟླུ་ལ

རིལ་ཧོབ་ཕི་རཀ་ཐི། མོ་ལ་ལི།

༤༠། ཨིད་ཙ་ཨིད་ཙ་ཏུ་ལ་རིང་སྣ་མི་ཀི་ཧ་ཀེ་ཀེ་ཟ་ཀྲུ་ལྷུ་མི་ཆོབ་ཕི་ལ་བཞི་རེ།

༤༡། ཡེ་ཤུ་འི་དྲུ་ཨེ་ཊ་ཡེ་ཀེ་ཐི་ཊ་ཀུ་ར་ཊིང་ལད་ཀྱེ། ཨན་ཙི། ནམ་ཁ་མི་ལ་པ་ཤ

ཀྱེ། མོ་ལམ་ཧབ་པ། ཨེ་ཊ་བསྒྲུ་ཁྱེ། མི་འི་བད་ཧེ་ཧིང་ཚེ་ཙིན་ཟ་ལ་ཞི་ལོབ

སྒྲུག་ཧེ་ཧིང་སྣ་ཐི། ཀ་ལ་བད་ཧེ་ཧིང་ཚེ་ཙེ་སྣ་ཚི།

༤༢། ངོ་རང་མི་འི་ཙོ་ཟེ་ཞེ། གས་ཀྱེ།

༤༣། ལག་མ་ཀྱེ་སྒྲེ་ཨེ་ཊ་ཨེ་ཀ་དུ་ཁུ་བད་ཧེ་དུལ་ཀྱེ་ལྷུ་ཀེ་ཞེ་ཀྱེ

ཞིང་རི།

༤༤། ངོང་ཟ་འི་ཆུག་ཀི་མི་འི་ཏེ་ངྷ་ཏ་ཧྣར་ཧོ་ཞི་ཏེ།

༤༥། ངོ་བེ་ལྷུ་ཀྲིང་ཡེ་ཤུ་འི་ལོབ་སྒྲུག་ཧེ་ཧིང་། དཀྱེ་ཞེ་དྲུ་ཀྲུ་ཨར་ཞང་བེ

ཀྱེ་ཞེ་ཨུ་ཀྲུང་རིད་ཧྲུ་རང་བེད་སྣོ་ཡི་དྷུ་ཤ་གར་རང་ཨི་ལ་ལ་ཧི། ཀྱེ་དི་མི་ཀི

ཕད་ཧེ་ཡི་བི་རཀ་ཏུ་ལ། ཡོན་ཀ་ཙན་ཐན་ཀ་ལ་ལ་ཚོད་ཀི།

༤༦། ངོ་རེ་བད་ཧེ་ཡི་བི་རཀ་ཀྱེ། ཡེ་ཤུ་ཡི་མ་ཧོད་ཀྱི་ས་ཀྲུད་རི་ལ་མོ

ཧ་ཀྱི་ཡི་ཟ་ཙ་ཙ་རིང་ཡི་ལ་ལི།

༤༧། ངོ་རང་ཡེ་ཧོག་བེ་ལྷུ་རིང་། དྲུ་ཀོ་ཀྲུ་ཀྲུང་རིང་ཀོད་ཧ་ར། ཡེ་ཤུ

ཨིན་ཟ་ལ་ཀུད་དིང་ཨིད་ཙ་ཀྱི་སྒྲི་རི།

༤༨། ལོབ་སྒྲུག་ཧེ་ཧིད་མ་པ་ཙེ་ཀི་ལན་ཡམ་བི་ཨམ་ཟ་ལ་ཞི། ངར་

ཀན་ཐེ། ཡེ་ཤུ་འི་ཀྲུ་ལན་ཅི་ཏང་ཏེ། [illegible] ཡེ་དཀྲ་ལེ་ལྷ་མིད། ཆོ་ཐུ་[illegible]
ཞི་ཡམ་མ་ཙོ། དེ་རུ་ཀ་ཆང་ཞི་ཞལ་སྐྱི་ཡི་སྐྱི།

༩། བརྩོ་ཡེ་ཤུ་མཚོ་ཏུ་ཞོག་ཞིང་ཞི་ཡམ་མ་ཡི་ཏང་ལེ། རྒྱལ་ཤུར་ཞེ་ཞ། ཅེ་ཐུ
ར་ཏི་རེ།

༡༠། ཀྲུ་ཞལ་ཞི་ཀུ་དཀོ། བདང་ཏེ་ཅི་བོ་ཏང་ལེ་ལེ་རི་རེ། ཙོ་ཏང་ལེ་ཤུ་ལི་
དོ་ཏིང་ཕྲལེ། ཀྲི་ཤུ་ཀ་ཀ། སེམ་ལེ་ཙུ་ཞ་ལད་ཅི། ཏ་ཀ་ཏ་ཤུ་ཏི།

༡༡། ཡོན་ཏ་ཀུ་དཀྲི། ཡེ་ཤུ་གོ་ཏུ་རྒྱུ་ནང་ཡི་སྐྱི་ཡེ། ལན་ཆག་ཀེ། ཡོན་ཏྲུ
ཏེ་ཞཞ་ཤུ་ལི་རེ།

༡༢། ཀྲི་རིང་ཀུ་དཀོ། ལོབ་རྒྱུག་ཏེ་ཏུ་སེམ་པ་ལེ་ཡི་ལ་ཀྲི། ཡེ་ཞ་ཞཀྲུ།
ཀ་སྨམ་ཏང་ངེ་ལ། ཡེ་ཤུ་ཏུ་ཤི་དམ་ཏེ་རི་རེ།

༡༣། ཏོ་རང་ལྷུ་རང་ཡིད་ཐེ། གོ་ཞེ་སྨ་རེད་ཀྲུ་ཤྲི་ཀ་ཀར་རང་ཡི་ལ་སྐྱེ།

༡༤། རྟུ་ཏུ་ནང་ཞི་ཆོས་ལ་ཡི་ཡེ། མི་ལི་ཅི་དོ་ཡེ་ཤུ་ཤུར་ཏེ་ལེ།

༡༥། ཞེ་རི་ཏོད་ཀྲི་ཀ་ཀར་ར་ཏིང་དོན་གྲུ་རན་ཀྲི། ནང་པ་ཡན་ཇི་ཏུ་ཞོག་ཞིང་
དོས་ཀྲི་པ་བད་ཏེ་ཡེ་ཤུ་ཏོད་ཀྱི་རྒྱལ་རིང་ཤི་ལ་ལི་རེ།

༡༦། བྱུ་ཀ་ཀར་རང་ཡང་གོ་རྒྱལ་རིང་ཡེ་ཤུ་ཡི་ལ་སྐྱེ་ལ། དོང་ནད་པ
བད་ཏེ་ས་ལྷ་རིང་སྤྱོད་ཀྱི། ཡེ་ཤུ་རིང་དེང་ཡམ་མ་ཡི་ཆོས། ཡི་ཀྲུ་[illegible]
ཐུར་ཏིང་ཙེན་ཏིང་ཤུད་ཞོག་ཅི་རང་ཀྱུ། ལྷུ་ཞ་ལད་ཀྱི། ཡང་ཡོ་ [illegible] ཏ་ཞོག
ཀེ་ལ་དོ་ཀྱལ་ལི།།

ཀྱིའི་ལེ་འུ་ཀྲུ་ཚང།

༡། ངོ་རང་ལ་ཀྲུ་ཤཱི་པ་ཡེ་ཚོ་འི་རིང་ཁལ་པ་འུ་ཡང་གོ་རེ་མི་ཡན་ཀྱི།

༢། ངོ་ཚེ་ཡང་གོ་རེ་ལོབ་ཐུག་ཏེ་ཅི་ཤུད་མཚེ་འེ་ཟ་ལེན་ཟ་འི་ཏང་གེ། ངོ་རི་ངམ
ཟད་ཀྱེ། ཡེ་ཤྲུ་རྡུམ་པོལ་རྫོམ་རི་རེ།

༣། ལ་རྐུ་ཤཱི་པ་ཡེ་ཡ་ཅུ་དུ་པ་ཚེ་དང་པོ་མི་འི་ཏུ་གྲིམ་ཕུམ་ཀྱེ། ཡལ་ཀྱེ་
ཡལ་ཀྱེ་ཤུད་མཚེ་འེ། ཟ་ལེན་ཀུ་ལ་ལེ་ཡ་ཟ་རེ་རེ།

༤། ས་ཀྱ་རིང་ཟེ་ཡན་ཀྱེ། ཚེ་འེ་ག་ཏེ་མ་ཟ་འུ་རེ། ཕོ་པོ་ཡེ། ཅན་རེ
རག་ཟང། མན་ཟེ་ཚེ་ཚེམ་གྲིམ་འོང་ལ་ཟ་ཏོ་རེ།

༥། ངོ་རང་ལ་ཀྲུ་ཤཱི་པ་ཡེ་ཚོ་འི་རིང་ཁལ་པ་འུ་མི་འི་བད་ཏེ་ཚེ་ཡེ་
རེང། ཀྱེ་ཀྲུ་ལོབ་ཐུག་ཏེ་ཅི་ཏུང་རིང་དེ་མི་འི་ཏུ་གྲིམ་མ་འུ་ཚོག་གན་ཀྱུ་རི
མ་ལ་ཟ་ཏོ་རེ། ཡོན་ན་ཀུ་ཞིམ་ལན་ཏིང་ཡེ་ཤྲུ་འི།

༦། ཏའི། ཀྱེ་ཧེ་ཡ་འུ་ཚོ་འི་ལ་ཟེ་པ་རེ། ཀྱེན་ཏིང་ཡེ་ཤཱི་ཡཱུ་ཟེ་ཡོ
ཤཱི་རན་ལན་རན་ཤུ་ལ། ཡེ་ཤཱི་ཡཱུ་ཟེ་ཀུ་ཏི། དེ་མི་ཀྱུད་ཚེ་ཡ་ཤུ་ཤ
ཀྱེ་རིང་ཏོད་པ་ལད་ཀྱེ། ལེམ་ཀྱེ་རང་འོང་ལྦོ་འེ་ཏོད་ཅེ།

༧། དང་པོ་འུ་མི་འི་ཏུ་ཡུ་སྤྱི་དོ་ཀན་ཀྱེ་ལ། དོང་ཟེ་ཀྱེ་གོན་ཅོག་ཏིང
ཀྱལ་ལེ་ཏོད་པ་མ་ཡམ་པལ། ཡོན་ན་ཡེ་ཤཱི་ཡཱུ་ཟེ་གོན་ཅོག་ཏུ
ལྦོམ་རན་ཀྱེ་ཀུ་ཏི།

༨། ཏའི། ཡ་འུ་ཚོ་འི་ལ་ཟེ་པ་ཀྱེ་ཧེ། ཀྱེན་ཧེ་གོན་ཅོག་ཏུ་ཀྲུ་ཀུམ་

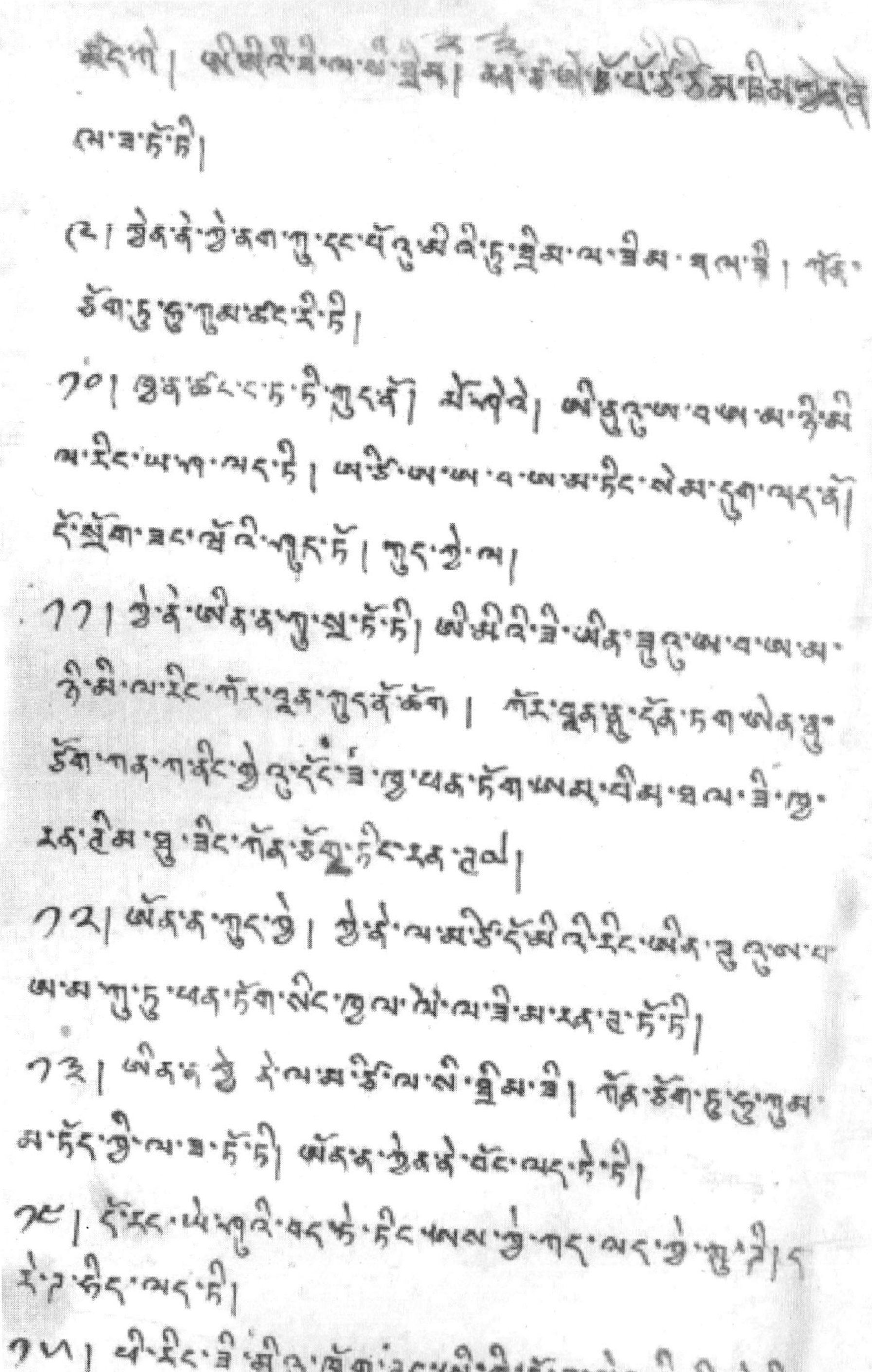

ཀླུ་ཡི་མ་རན་ནམ། མི་ཏུ་ཡང་ཟླ་རྩེས་སི་དོ་འི་མི་སེའི་ཀླུ་ཡི་རན་ནམ།

༡༥། ལས་རིང་རེ་ཏི་སྨ་རེ་ན་རོད་ནོ། རེ་ཏི་རི།

༡༦། དོ་སྡང་མི་འི་བད་ཏེ་ཏང་ཀྲི་ལྷ་ཀྲུམ་ཤུང་ཡི་ལ་ཏར། ལོབ་ཟླུག་ཏཱུ
ཡེ་ཀླུ་རིང་། དི་ཡེ་ཏུ་དོན་ཏག་ཁྲ་ཀླུད་ཀུད་ཀྱི་རུག་ཏི་རེ།

༡༧། ཡེ་ཀླུ་འི། ཀྱི་ནེ་ཡོན་ཀྱོལ་ཆ་མ་གོ་ཅི་པ་རེ་ཀླུད་ཏི་ཡམ། ཡི་རིང
ཟླི་མི་ཏུ་ལོག་པ་ཏུ་ཐང་ཡི་ལ་ཀྱི་དོའི་དོ་མི་སེའི་མ་ལ་ཟུ། དོ་ཆ་མ་གོཿ
ཏོ་ཏི་ཡམ།

༡༩། ཟ་མེ་ནམ་དོ་སྐྱོ་ཀ་ཏུ་ཐང་མེ་ཡི་ལྷལ། ཁོག་ཐུ་ཐང་ཡི་ལྷལ།
ཟ་མེན་བད་ཏེ་ཐལ་ཟི་ཡིན་ཟླུ་ཏུ་ཡམ་ཅི་དང་ཀྱི་རོས་ལ་ཡི་ལྷལ།

༢༠། ཡས་ཀྱི་ཀུ་ཏི། མི་ཏུ་ཡ ཏུ་ཡམ་ཟི་ཁྲ་རོལ་སལ། དོ་དོ་ལི་དོ
སེ་འི་ལ་ཟལ།

༢༡། ཁྲ་རིང་ཀུད་ནོ། མི་ཏུ་སྐྱོ་ཀང་ཟི་སོག་པོ་སམ་ལོ་ཡེ། རན
ཟླ་ཧི་ལ་ཟི། སོག་པོ་རྫོལ། མི་སི་ཅི།

༢༢། ཀུ་ཟི། སེར་ཏུ། ནོ་སྐྱལ་ལ་ཟི། སེམ་སོག་པོ་ཁ་ཟི།
ཆལ་རྩོལ། མིག་ལོག། སོག་པོ་ལན་རན་ཏི། རང་ཀྱལ་ལ་ཟི།

༢༣། དོ་སོག་པོ་བད་ཏེ་སྐྱོ་ཀང་ཟི་ཡི་རིང་རོལ་སི་ཡེ། མི་སེ་ལི་
ཀླུ་ཡལ།

༢༤། དོ་རང་ཡན་ཅི། ཆོར་ཡེ་ཆེ་དོན་ནུ་ལ་[illegible] རིང་ཡི་ལ་ཀྱི།

མི་ལ་ཧྲིང་ལ་མ་ཉེ་ལེ། ཡི་ཤུ་མ་སྐུ་ཚང་ཡི་ལ་གྱི། ཡོན་ཏན་ལད་ཀྱིས།

ཕྱུག་ཀེ་བང་ཟེ་མ་ཧྲི།

༢༥། ཡི་ཤུ་མེ་ཙ་རིང་གོང་པོ་དོང་གི་ཧོ་རི། ཡ་མེ་ཡོ་སྒུ་ཙུ་ཚུན་

ཟ་ཚི་རང་ཉམ་པོ། ཡན་ཏེ་ཡོ་སྒུ་རིང་ཕྱུག་ལ་འི།

༢༦། དོ་ཡ་ཧུ་དྲུ་རིག་ཁ་ཏུ་མ་ཧོ་རི། ཡ་རམ་རིག་ཁ་ཏུ་ཡོ་ཤེ་ཀ།

ཤག་ཧོ་རི། དོའི་ཡོ་སྒུ་རིང་ཀུ་ཏི། ཤི་ཏུ་ཤི་ཡེ་ཙ་ཏུ་དོང་ཟེ་གྲོང་པོ

ཚོན་ཀྱི་ཙར་ཏུ། ཡོན་ཏན་ལུ་བ་ལའི།

༢༧། ཡོ་སྒུའི་དོ་རིང་། ཏུང་རིང་ཡོ་རེ་བད་ཧེ་ཀལ་ཡི་ལ་ཟི་ཤིལ།

ཡོ་རེ་ཏུ་བརྒྱ་ཏན་ཀྱི། ཁུའི་རིང་རན་ཏི་མ་ཚོལ།

༢༨། ཡོན་ཏན་ཀུ་ཏིམ་ཤན་ཧིང་ཡ་མེ། ཟིག་སྒུ། ཡེ་ཙོ་པོ།

ཟིག་སྒུད་ཀྱི་ལ། ཙོག་ཙེ་ཏུ་ལེ་ཧང་ཧོད་ཀྱི་ཁུའི་ཙི་ལ་ཡོ་རེ་ཏུ་

པེད་ཡེ་ཊ་ཟ་ལྷ་ཧོ་རེ། ཀུ་ཏི།

༢༩། ཡོ་སྒུའི། དི་སྤྲད་ཏུ་ཐལ་ཟེ་ཡི་ལ་ལ། ཀ་རྒྱུ་གྱེ་ཡེ་ཙ་ཏུ་

དོང་ཟེ་གོང་པོ་ཚོལ་ལི་རི་ཀུ་ཏི་ཡེ།

༣༠། ཡ་མ་ཀུམ་སྐུང་ཡི་ལ་གྱི། གོང་པོ་ཚོལ་ལི་ཧོད་ཀྱི་ཡེ།

ཀྱེ་མེ་ཙི་མན་ཛི་ཏུ་ཊོག་ཏིང་དོལ་ཀྱི་ཐང་རི།

༣༡། ཧོ་རང་ཡོ་སྒུ་ཚོར་རིག་ཁ་ཏུ་ལན་ཆམ་རིང་ཟེ་ཚོལ་ལ།

ཆེ་དོན་རིག་ཡེ་ལྷ་ན་གར་རཏུ་ཡ་སྒྲ་དད་ཀྱི་ག་ལི་ལ་ཚོ་ཏུ་

དབ་སྐྱེད་ཡི་ལ་ལེ། ༢༥

༣༢། ངོ་བེ་ལྷ་རིང་ཡེ་ཀན་དུང་མི་བོང་མི་འི་ཡེ་པུ་རུ་ཏུམ་བོ་ལེ
ཤི། དེ་མི་ཏུ་བ་ལ་ལིང་གུད་སོག་ཅི་ཀེ་ལ་ཏུ་བ་ལའི།
༣༣། ཡེ་པུའི་དོ་མི་འི་ཀུ་ཡི་ཅང་བྲ་ཀོན་ཤི་པ་ཀ་པི་ལ་ཤེ།
དོ་ཏུ་རེ་ཙ་ཏུ་ནང་ཐྲེ་རྒྱ་ཤིད་ཤི། ཕོག་ཀི་ཏུ་ཀ་ལག་ལད་ཤི། ལེ་རིང་
ནོག་ཀི།

༣༤། དོ་རང་ནམ་ཁ་རིང་ཁན་ཤེ། ཀ་པུ་པ་ཤིད་ཤེ། པ་ཧུ་དུ་ཏུ་
བོལ་ལི་རིང་། ཀེ་པ་ཟ་ཀུའི། ཀེ་པ་ཟ་ཡོན་སྒུ་ཅོག་ཀན་ཡལ་
ཡོན་ན་ཀུ་ཙི་ཡེ། རེ་ཙི་ཡལ་ཟ།
༣༥། ལེ་ཏུ་དུ་ལ་པ་ས། ཀི་པི་སྦུད་ལའི་ཀར་ཀི།
༣༦། དོ་རང་ཡེ་པུའི་དོ་ཀིང་། ཡ་ཀིང་ལ་ཟ་པད་ཀི། ཡོན་ན་
ཕུ་ཀུམ་རན་ཤེ་ལ། དོ་ཅི་ཡེ་པུ་ཏུ་ཕྱུན་ཡིང་དེ་ཤེ་རི་རེ།
༣༧། མི་འི་བད་ཀུ་ཐ་ཐ་པུད་ཤེ་ཀུ་ཏི་རེ། དོའི་བད་ཀེ་ཀི་པི་
ལ་ཟབ། ཙ་ཏུ་ཧེ་རེ་ཟས་ཡི་ལ་ཟབ། ཀན་དུང་རེ་ཀིང་སྦུའི་
རན་ཙབ། ཡོན་ན་དོ་ཏུ་ཀོད་པ་ལའི་རེ།

ཤེའི་ལེ་ཏུ་དུ་ནང་།

༡། ང་བེ་ལྷ་རིང་བོང་མི་དོང་ཛོམ་ཤེ། དོ་ཀིང་ཟ་མེན་མ་པུད་ཤེ
ཡེ། ཡེ་པུའི་ལོབ་ཐུག་ཀེ་ཀིང་ཀད་ཡད་ཤེ་ཀུ་ཏི།

༢། དེ་མི་ལི་བད་ཏེ་ [illegible] ཏེ་ [illegible] ངོང་ཏེ་ [illegible] དོ་ཏིང་ཟ་འི་
མ་[illegible]། [illegible] ཁོག་རྒྱུག་ཡུམ་པ་ལ།

༣། ཡང་ཀོ་རེ་ལོ་འི་རིང་ [illegible] ཡན་ཅི་ཏོ་ཏོ་རེ། ངོ་རེ་ཡོན་གྱི་ཀྱལ་ཟུ
རིང་ཙེ་རེ་ནོ། ཡམ་རིང་ལི་འིམ་ཤད་སྐྱུད་ཏོ།

༤། ངོ་རང་ལོབ་རྒྱུག་ཏེ་ཙི་ཀྱུ་ཏི་རེ། ཡོན་ཏྲིག་མི་འི་བད་ཏེ་ཀལ་ཡི
ལ་འི་རིང་དི་ཤེ་མ་ཏུ་ཐང་རིང་རོ་ཏི་ཀྱང་ཟི་ཏན་ཏ་མི། རྒྱུག་ཏི་རེ།

༥། ཡེ་ཤུ་འི། དེང་ཡམ་ལིག་ཡེ་ཟ་ཏོ་ཏོ་ཀྱུད་ཀྱི་རྒྱུག་ཀ། ངོ་ཙི་
ཏི་ཙི་ཏོ་[illegible]་ཀྱུ་ཏི་རེ།

༦། ངོ་རང་ཡེ་ཤུ་འི་ངོ་མི་འི་ཏིང་། ད་ཀྱི་ནེ་བད་ཏེ་སྒོ་ཏིང་ཇོད་ཏི
ཀྱུད་ཀྱི་རྒྱ་ཀྱུམ་སྣ་ཏི། ཏི་ཙི་ཡེ་ཟ་ཐེན་ཀྱི། སོ་ལམ་ཏད་ཀྱི། མི་འི
ཏིང་ཚེ་ཙེམ་ཐ་ལ་ཟེ་ཡོན་རྒྱུ་ལོབ་རྒྱུག་ཏེ་ཏིང་སྣ་ཏི། ལོབ་རྒྱུག
ཏེ་ཙི་ཚད་ཀྱི་སྣ་ཏི་རེ།

༧། ཏ་རྒྱང་གི་ཤུད་ཀྱི་ཡེ། ཡེ་ཤུ་འི་ཙི་[illegible]། ཚེ་དི་ཏི།
ཀྱུ་ཏི།

༨། མི་འི་བད་ཏེ་ཙི་ཟེ་འེ། ཀལ་ཀྱེ། ལག་མ་ཀྱེ་སྒྲི་ཡེ་ཟ་ཐ་འ
དུམ་བུ་བད་ཏེ་རྒྱམ་ཏེ། ཏི་ཙི་ཀྱིར་ཏི་གིང་ཏི།

༩། དོང་ཟ་འི་རྒྱུག་ཀི་པ་མི་འི་རེ་ཏི་ཏི་[illegible]་ཏོ་ཝི་རེ།

༡༠། ངོ་རང་མི་འི་བད་ཏེ་ཙ་རེ་ཀྱི། ལོབ་རྒྱུག་ཏེ་ཕང་[illegible]

ཁང་གེ། དལ་མ་ནུ་ཐ་ཀུ་སྲུ་ཤ་གར་རང་ཙམ་ལ་ངེ།

༡༡། ངོང་པ་ཏུ་ཡེ་པུ་རི་རྟོགས་ས་ཡིན་ཀྱི། ཡེ་ཤུ་རིང་ཡིན་ན་རྒྱལ་
ཕྱིན་ཏོན་ཚོ་རྩུག་ཏི་རེ། ས་རག་འདྲ་ནང་ཡི་ཀ་སྐམ་ཀན་ཐི་ཀེ་ས་ཀུ་ཏེ་རེ།

༡༢། ཡེ་ཤུའི་ན་ཤུ་ཤ་ཕྱིབ་པ། དེ་མི་རབ་ཚོ་ཁྲུ་དྲུ་ཐལ་ཟེ་ཡི
ཀ་སྐམ་པེ་ཐ་ཏོ་རེ། ཕྱི་ཕྱིན་ཏིང་དུང་པོ་ཀུ་ཐ་ཏོལ། དེ་མི་རབ་
ཏིང་ཁྲལ་ལེ་ཀ་སྐམ་ཀན་ཐི་མ་ཡིན། ཀུ་ཏི།

༡༣། ངོ་རེ་བད་ཏེ་ཀྱིད་ཅེ། ནུ་ཏིང་ཕྱི་ནུ་རང་ཡིལ་ལི།

༡༤། ངོ་བེ་ལྷ་རོང་ལོབ་སྲུག་ཏེ་ཚོ་ཀྱུ་ག་ཟེ། མ་ཁན་ཐི་ཡེ།
ཡིད་ཙོ་ཡེ་ཐ་མ་ཞེའེ། སྐོང་དུ་དུ་ནང་མ་ཏན་ཏི་རེ།

༡༥། ངོང་ཡེ་ཡི་ལབ་ཙ་རམ་པ་ངོ་ཏིང་ཀུ་ཏེ། ཁན་ཐི།
ཏུ་ཡེ་པ་རེ་ཡེ་ཏེ་ཀོ་ཏེ་ར་ཛེ་ཏུ་ཐེ་ཀིང་ཟེ་ཐར་ཏི། ངོ་ཏང་
ཀམ་པོ་ཐ་ཀུ་རྡུ་ཏི།

༡༦། ངོ་ཙོ་ཡི་ཏིང་ཡི་ཀི་རང་ཕུད་པུ་ལྷ་ཀུ་ཏེ་རེ། ཡིན་ཏིང་ཡེ་ཐ་
ཤུད་ཟང་། ཡོན་ན་ཀུ་ཐལ།

༡༧། ཡེ་ཤུའི་དི་ཕུད་ཐལ་ཕྱི་ཀུ་ཏི། ཕྱིན་ཏིང་ཡམ་སུ་ཕྱི་
མ་ཤུད་ཕྱི་ལ། ཁྲུ་དྲུ་ཐལ་ཟེ་ཡོན་ན་ཕུད་ལ་ཟ་ཏོ་ཏི། ཡི་ལི
ཏ་ལ་ཕྱི་ནེ་ཏ་མ་གོའེ། དུང་པོ་མ་ཏེ་ལྷ་ཏ་ཏི་ཡམ། ཡེ་ལི་ཏ
ལ་ཕྱིན་ཏུ་སམ་སི་སྐུན་ངག་ཕུད་ཕྱི་ཏོ་ཏོལ།

༡༨། ཕྱིན་ཏེང་མིག་ཏོད་ཀྱི་ལ། མི་ཏིང་ཟ་ཏོ་ཏེ། རེ་ན་ཏོད་ཀྱི་ལ། ཞ་
ཟ་ཚོ་ཏོ་ཏེ། ཕྱིན་ཏིང་ཀྱལ་ལེ་ཏིང་མ་ཚོབ་པ་ལ།

༡༩། ཀྱེ་དྭ་ཡེ་ཤུ་ང་ཏ་རྣར་མི་ཏིང་ཚེ་ཙེ་ཏར། ཡ་ལེག་ཀྱིར་ཏེ་
ཀྱེ་ཙེ་དུལ་མེན། རྡུག་ཙོམ་ལན་ཏིང་གུ་ཏེ་རེ། ལྷ་ཏེ་ཚེ་ཀྱིར་ཏེ།
༢༠། ཡམ་ཀྱི་ཡེ་ཤུ་ཞི། ཏེ་ཙེ་ཡེ་ཤུ་པི་ཞི་ཁ་རྣར་མི་ཞི་ཏིང་ཚེ་ཙེ་
ཏར། ལེང་ཡེ་ཤུ་ཡ་ལེག་དུལ་མེན། རྡུག་ཙོམ་ལན་ཏིང་གུ་ཏེ་རེ།
ཏེ་ཙེ་ཀྱིར་ཏེ།

༢༡། དོ་རང་ཡེ་ཤུ་ཞི། ཀྱེ་ཏེ་ཡ་ཞི་ཏ་ལ་ཏ་མ་གོ་ཙོམ་དོ་ཀྱ་ཤུ།
༢༢། དོ་རང་ལེང་ཙོ་ཡི་དུཀ་ཀར་རང་ཡི་ལ་ཀྱེ། ཝོང་མི་ཞི་ཙོ་ཡི་ཁར
མི་ཏན་ཀྱེ། དོ་རིང་ཤུད་ཐོག་ཙོ་ཏིལ་བུད་ཏེ། ཞུ་པ་ལ་ཞི་སེ།
༢༣། ཡེ་ཤུ་ཞི་དོ་ཁ་ར་མི་ཤུ་ཞི་སྨོམ་ཀྱེ། ཚ་ཀར་རང་ཟི་ཡི་རིང་
ཡི་ལ་ཀྱེ། མིག་ཏེ་ཛེ་ལ་རིང་ཀྱོག་ཏི་ཞ་ཀ་ལག་ལོང་ཀྱེ། བལ་ལེང
ཤུད་ཀྱེབ་པ། དཀ་ཞིང་ཀྱི་ཏང་པདང། རྡུག་ཙོམ་ལན་ཏིང།
༢༤། ཞ་རི་ཁན་ཀྱི་གུ་ཏེ། སྲུབ་ཚོག་ཀཎ་མི་ཞི་ཡམ་ཙོ་ཏང་པལ།
༢༥། དོ་རང་ཡེ་ཤུ་ཞི་ཡམ་ལ་ཀྱི་མིག་ཏིང་ཤུད་ཙེ་ཀ། ཞ་ར་ཟི
ལན་ཞི་རྣ་ཏེ། དོ་ཁ་ར་མི་ཞི་ཟི་བད་ཏེ་ལ་ལན་ཏང་རི།

༢༦། དོ་རང་ཡེ་ཤུ་ཞི་དོ་མི་གུམ་ལུ་རིང་ཡི་ཝ་རན་ཀྱེ། དོ་རིང།
ཏ་ཀར་རང་ཟ་ཡི་ལ་ལ། ཚ་ཀར་རང་ཤུ་མི་ཞི་ཏིང་ཟ་ཡག་ཏུ། ཡོང་ཙན

ཀྱུ་གྲུམ་རྣ་རྟེ།

༢༧། ང་རང་ཡི་སྒྲུ་ལོབ་སྒྲུག་ཏེ་ཏང་ཉམ་པོ་དོན་གར་རང་ཟེ་་་

ཏོས་ས། ཕི་ལིབ་བུ་ཀེ་སར་ཡུ་ཀུ་སྲི་ན་གར་རང་ཡི་ལ་ལི། དངོས་དའི

ལོབ་སྒྲུག་ཏེ་ཏིང་། མི་འི་ཙོ་ཀྱི་ཡ་རི་སྒྲུ། ངོ་རིང་ཀྱུ་ཀུ་ཞ་ཏོ་རེ།

རྟུག་ཙིམ་ལན་ཏིང་ལོབ་སྒྲུག་ཏེ་ཙི་ཀུ་ཏི་རེ།

༢༨། ཡང་གོ་ཙི་སྒྲུ་ནེ་ཀོན་ཙོག་ཏུ་ནུ་ལ་རན་ཞི་པ་མཛིང་ཟེ་ཡིད་ཙོ་

སྒྲུ་ཀུ་ཞ་ཏོ་རེ།

༢༩། ཡོན་ན་ཀུད་ཀྱི་ཡི་སྒྲུའི། ཡོན་ན་ཀྱི་ནེ། ཀྱི་ཡ་རི་སྒྲུག་ཀ།

ཁུ་ཞེ་ཙ་ཏོ་ཏི། ཀུ་ཞིམ་ལན་ཏིང་། གེ་ཕེ། ཀྱི་ནེ་མ་སྒྲི་ཀ་སྒྲུད་ན།

ཀུ་ཏི།

༣༠། དོང་ཡི་སྒྲུའི་དོ་ཏིང་། ཀྱེ་འུ་རྟུན་ཡ་ཏིང་ལ་ཞ་སྒྲད་ཏི་་

ཡོན་ན་ནན་ཟན་ཀུ་ཏི།

༣༡། ཡ་ལྷ་ཀྱེ་ཀུ་ཏི། མི་འུ་པོ་ཙོ་ཡིད་གིའི་བོང་བར་དོ་ཉང་ཙེ

ཏིས། སོ་ཏོ་ཡེ། ཏེ་ཞིག་ལ་མ་ཡེ། ཚོའི་རིང་ཁལ་པ་ཙི་ཀྱི

ཚང་ངེ་སད་ཏུ་རེ། སྒྲུམ་ཀྱལ་སྒྲུད་ཀྱི་ཀྱི་སྲིང་གེ་ཡན་ཙ་ཏོལ།

ཡོན་ན་དོ་ཏིང་ཕུད་ཀྱེ།

༣༢། སྒར་ན་ཕུད་རིང་ཀུ་ཏི། དོ་ཀེ་སེ། ཡི་སྒྲུ་འུ་ཀུད་རྫོམ

ཀྱེ། ནན་ཟན་འུ་བ་ལབ་པ། ཡི་སྒྲུ་རིང་། ཡོན་ན་སྒྲུབ་ཞི་མེ

ཀུད་ཅི།

༣༣། ཡེ་ཤུ་འི་ལོབ་ཕྲུག་ཆེ་ཆིང་ཁོང་ཀྱིར་ཀྱི་ཁན་ཀྱི། ཀེ་ལ་
རིང་ངར་ཀྱི་གུ་ནི། ཀ་ཏ་དུང་ཤུ་དང་ཡ། ཀྱི་ཟུ་ཐ་ལང་ཟེ་ཡི་ལ་ལ། ཀ་ནི
ཀོན་ཆོག་ཏུ་ཡན་དོག་པ་པེ་ཞ། མི་འི་ཏུ་ཡན་དོག་པེ་ཞ་ཆོན།
༣༤། ཀུད་ཅི། ཡེ་ཤུ་འི་མི་འི་བད་ཏེ་ཡེ། ལོབ་ཕྲུག་ཏེ་ཏིང་ཀད་
ལད་ཀྱི་ནོ་ཏིང་། ཡང་གོ་མི་འི་ལ་ཀྱི་ཟུ་ཐ་ལང་ཟེ་ཡམ་པི་ཐད་
ནོ། ཡིན་ཟ་རིང་ཐ་པིམ་སེམ་ཚང་ཅོ་ཏེས། ངོ་མི་ཡིན་ཟུ་ཟུ་
ཀྱང་ཤིང་ཀུར་ཙོ་ཀྱི་ཟུ་ཐ་ལང་ཟེ་ཡམ་པི་ཏེས།
༣༥། ཡ་ཅི་ཡ་ཡིན་ཟུ་ཟུ་སྒྲོག་ཐར་པིམ་ཐབ་པེ་ད་ནོ། ངོ་མི་ཟུ
སྒྲོག་ཡཾ་ཁ་ཡི་ལ་ཏོ། ཡ་ཅི་ཡ་ཡིང་ཁེ་བྲིན་ཟང་ཏུ་ཐལ་ཟེ་
སྒྲོག་པང་ལེ་ཙར་ནོ། ངོ་མི་འི་རིང་མ་གོབ་པིམ་སྒྲོག་རྒྱུག་ཏོ།
༣༦། ཡི་མི་འི་རིང་ལན་ལྷར་ར་ཟུ་ཚོར་རྒྱུག་ཀེ་ལ། སེམ་མ་
ཟར་ནོ། ཡན་ཏོག་ཁྱུ་ཏོ་ཏོ།
༣༧། ཡིན་ཟུ་ཟུ་ལེམ་ཐར་པིམ་ཐལ་ཏི། ཡི་མི་འི་ཟེ་ཁྱུ་
པས་རན་ཏུ།
༣༨། ཡ་རི་ཡ་མི་འི་རིང་། དེ་སོག་པོ་མི་ཡེ། རན་དྲི་ཝུ་ཧི་ལ་ཟེ་པ་
་བི་ཙང་སྤྱོད་ཡན་ཀྱི། ཡིང་གོ་ཡིང་གུ་ཟུ་ཡུ་སྤྱི་ངོ་ཏིང་ཁོ་ཡི
པ་རན་ནོ། ངོ་རིང་མི་ཟུ་ཡོ་ཙོ་ཡིང་གེ་ནམ་ཁ་ཟུ་ཡོག་ཡེ།

གོན་ཅོག་ཏུ་ཟེ་ལ་ཏང་ཉམ་པོ་རིང་ཨལམ་ཕིམ་བེ་ལྷ་རིང། གོམ་ཉི

མ་རང་ན། ངོ་རིང་ཁན་སྤེ་སྤེ་རིང་ལྡེད་ཨལན་ཏོ།

ཀུ་ལེ་འུ་ཟུ་ནང།

༡། ཨལ་ཀྱེ་ཀུ་ཏི། སྤྱི་དྭང་པོ་ཀུ་ཁ་ཏོལ། རིང་རྫོད་ཀྱི་པ་ཨལངགོ

མི་འི་རེ་གོན་ཅོག་ཏུ་དྷཛ་བྱང་བིང་བེ་ཨལན་ཏར་ཚེ་ཀེ། མ་ལི་འུ་ནེ

༢། ཏུར་སྤྱུ་ལི་ཟ་ལང། པེ་སྦུའི་ཀེ་པ་ཨེ། པ་གོབེ་ཨེ། པོད

ནན་ཕྲུམ་བི་ལ་རིང་ཀད་ལད་ཀྱེ། ཨེ་སྦོའི་བཙམི་མ་ཏོར་ཀྱི

སྣ་ག་རིང་སྦི་ལ་སྤྱེ། ངོ་ཏུ་ཏང་ཁྱེ་པེ་སྦུའུ་ཟུགཕམ་ཁའུ་ཟུག

རིང་ཀྱུར་ཁྱེ་ཨི་ལ་ལི།

༣། ངོ་ཏུ་ཁམ་འོད་ཙན་ཨེ་སྤུག་ཏུ་ཚེ་ ... འི་སྦུའི། དི

... ལྦར་རང་ཨ་རི་ཨ་ཙག་ཅི་པེ་ཨོན་ཀྱོ་ལ་སྦི་འི་ལ་ཟིམ་རེ།

༤། ངོ་རང་ཨེ་ལི་པྱ་ཨེ། མོ་སྦེ་ཏི་མི་ལ་ཨན་ཀྱེ། པེ་སྦུ

རང་ཉམ་པོ་ཕྲུ་རི་རེ།

༥། ངོ་རང་ཀེ་སྦེ་པེ་སྦུ་རིང་ཀུ་ཏི། ཨེ་ཀུ་ཏུ། ཨེ་ཚེ་དིང་རྫོད་ཚོ

ཏེ་སྦི་ཏོད་ཅི། སྤྱི་སྦུ་སྤུ་ཀྱུམ་ལད་ཏལ། ཨི་ཀྱེན་ཏིང། ཨི་མོ

སྦེ་རིང། ཨི་ཨེ་ལི་པྱ་རིང་ལད་ཏལ།

༦། ཡོན་ཏན་ཁྱུ་ཕིང་ཀུ་ཏི་ཀུདཔོ། ངོ་རེ་བེ་འེ། ཨཨ་སྦུདཀྱེ།

ཁྱུ་ཕྲུ་ལི་ངོ་ཡོན་ཟ་ཅི་ལ་ཀམ་ཉེ་རི་རེ།

༧། ངོ་རང་ཡི་དྲུ་ཆོས་ས། རྗེ་བདེ་ཆེ་ཀ་བ་ཅི། ངོ་གྱི་ཤང་ནི་
ཡི་ཀད་ཡིན་ན་ཐ་ཟེ་རི། དེ་གྱི་ཟུ་སྦྱ་རི་ཡོང་སྐྱེ། ངོ་ཟུ་བྱུང་དེང་
ཡལ་ཏེ། ཡོན་ན་ཀུད་ཅི།

༨། སྤྱུམ་བི་ལོབ་སྒྲུག་ཏེ་ཅི་ཐ་ཅི་ཡེ། པི་ཏི་ཆོག་ཤིང་ཁན་ཅི།
ཡིད་ཅི་ཡེ་ཤུ་ག་ཏི། ཀྱི་ཏི་ཡ་རི་ལ་མ་ཏང་རི་རི།

༩། ངོ་རང་བཀ་ཚ་རིང་ཟི་ཏག་ཤི་ཏར། ཡེ་ཤུ་ཏི་ངོ་ཏིང་། མི་ཀྱུ་
ཡོང་ཡིང་ཝེ་ཤི་ཏི་རིང་ཟི་སྤྱིང་ཐར་ཚེ་ཀེ། སྤྱེ་ཏེ་ཀྱུ་ཏང་རི་
ཏི། ཡ་ཏིང་ལ་ཐ་ཤད་ཏི། ཡོན་ན་ཀུ་ཏི།

༡༠། ངོ་བྱུད་ཏིད་ཏེ་ཝི། ཡི་དི་ཏི་ཡི་དི་རིང་། ཤི་ཝི་རིང་ཟི་སྤྱིང་གི་
ཡན་ཅིམ་ལྷུད་ཀྱུ་ཤུ་ཏུག་ཀ།

༡༡། ཡེ་ཤུ་རིང་ཡིན་ན་ཀུ་ཏི་རེ། ཡེ་ཡེ་ཤུ། ཚེ་ཏི་རིང་ཁལ་པ་དུ་
མ་ཏི་བད་ཏེ་ཅི། ཤི་ཏི་རིང་ཟི་ཡན་ཅིམ་བེ་ཅི་ཏུང་རིང་ཡེ་ལི་ཡུ་
ཡས་ཀྱི་ཡམ་པི་རིས་ཀུད་ཅི་ཡུ་ཞ་ཏོ་རེ།

༡༢། ཀུ་ཞིམ་ལན་ཏིང་ཡེ་ཤུ་ཝི། ཡེ་ལི་ཡུ་ཏུང་རིང་ཏ་
ཡན་ཏོ། ངོ་ཝི་བད་ཏེ་དྲུང་པོ་དྲུལ་དྲིག་ལད་ཏུ། ངོ་རང་ཡི་ཀྱུ་
ཡོང་ཡིང་གི་ཝི་ཏུང་རིང་གི་ཀོན་ཅོག་ཏུ་སྦུ་ལ་རྣུ་ཤི་ཅོག་ཀན།
ཝོང་དྲུག་ངལ་ཀྱིང་ཤི་ཏིས། མི་ཝི་བད་ཏེ་ཅི་སྐྱེ་ཀྱེ་བི་ཏིལ།

༡༣། ངོས་ཟི་ཝི། ཀྱེ་སྐྱེན་ཏིང་ཀུ་ཞ་ཏོལ། ཡེ་ལི་ཡུ་

ཨམ་པོ་ཏ་ཡན་ཏེ། མི་འི་ཕོ་ཡིན་ཟླ་ཏུ་ཅིག་ཀན་དོ་རིང་ལ་བཞི་རེ། ཡོན་ན་
ལ་ཟི་ཡེ་། ཏུང་རིང་གི་ཀོན་ཅིག་ཏུ་ནོར་ལ་དབང་གྱི་ཡི་ལ་ལི། ཀུ་ཀི།

༡༤། ངང་རང་ཡེ་སྐུ་ཡིན་ཟླ་ཏུ་ལོབ་སྒྲུབ་ཏེ་ཏུ་ཀ་ཚང་ཡན་ཀྱི། བོང་མི་
དོ་ཏུ་ཏུམ་པོལ་སྐྱུད་ཀྱི་ཡེ། ཆོ་འི་རིང་ཁམ་པ་ཏུ་མི་འི་ཅོ་དོ་ཏིང་ཆོད་ཁ
ཞིམ་ཕྱུད་སྟུག་ཅོ་ཏང་རི།

༡༥། མི་འི་ཅོ་ཡེ་སྐུ་ཏང་ཅོ་ཡེ། ཐཐ་སྐྱུད་ཀྱི་བུ་ལ་སྐྱེ་ཕྱི་ལ་ཞེ་
དོ་རིང་ཕྱུག་ལ་འི་རེ།

༡༦། དོ་རང་ཡེ་སྐུ་འི་ཆོ་འི་རིང་ཁམ་པ་ཏུ་མི་འི་ཏིང་དོ་ཏུ་དོང་ཟི་ཀྱུ་ཕྱུང
ཏུག་ཅོ་ཏོ་ཏི་ཀུ་ཞི་ཡེ།

༡༧། མི་འི་ཏུ་བི་ཅང་ཟི་ཡི་དི་འི་ཡེ་སྐུ་རི་། ཡེ་ཤུ་ཏུ། ཀྱེ་ཡིང་ཤུ་ཏུ་
ཡོཅ་ཡི་ནུ་ཏུ་ཏུམ་པོལ་ཕན་མིན། དོ་ཀུ་རང་ཡི་གོང་པོ་སྤྱི་ཞེམ་ཏ་རཀྱི་པ་ལ་ཞི་ཏོ་ཏོ།

༡༨། ཡ་ལ་ལེ་གོང་པོ་འི་དོ་རྟུམ་ཏོ། ཐུག་པི་ལད་ཀྱི། ཤ་ཏུ་ནང་ཟི་
སྦུབ་ཏོས་ས་ལ། ཆ་རྟུག་ཀེ། ཟུག་ཟུ་ཁ་ཀ་ར་པ་ལ། གྱི་ཀྱི་སྤུ་ལོབ་སྦུ
ཏེ་ཏིང་དི་གོང་པོ་ཏོན་ཅིམ་ཐ་ལ་ཟི་ཀུད་ཀྱི་ལ། དོ་ཚི་མ་ཏར་ཏི་རེ།

༡༩། ཡོན་ན་ཀུ་ཞི་ཡེ་ཡེ་སྐུ་འི། ཡེ་ཀྱི་ནེ་དང་པ་མ་ཏི་རེ། གྱི་ལ
ལིག་ཐར་ཚེ་ཀེ་ཀྱིན་ཏང་ཉམ་པོ་མན་སྨ་རིག་པོལ། ཡ་ལིག་
ཐར་ཚེ་ཀེ་ཀྱིན་ཏང་ཉམ་པོ་ཛོད་ཏོལ། ང་ཡོཅ་གྱི་ལུ་ཀཚང་ཚན

༢༠། ཚུ་ཀུམ་རན་གྱི། ཡོཅ་ཡེ་སྐུ་ཏུ་ཏུམ་པོལ་དབང་ཀྱི་ཏན་ཏི་རེ།

ཡེ་ཤུ་ཏང་ཅི་ཡེ། གོང་བོ་འི་ད་ཡ་ཅོ་དེ་ཡ་རིང་ཞུ་པ་རིང་ཚེ་གི། །ཞུ་
ཏོལ་སི་ཡེ། སྦོ་ཏིང་གལ་ཀྱེ་ཡིལ་ལི།
༢༡། ངོ་རང་ཡེ་ཤུའི་ཡ་ཅོ་ཅ་ཀུ་ཡ་བ་རིང་། ཡ་ལ་ལེ་ཞེ་ཅི་ང་རིང་༔
ཡིན་ན་ཤུད་མིན་ཀུ་ཏི་ཡེ། ཡ་བེ། ཅི་སྒྲེ་ཅ་རིང་ཟི་ཤུད་མིན། ཀུ་ཏི།
༢༢། ངོ་རང་ངོ་གོང་བོ་འི་ཡ་ཅོ་ས་ཅིམ་ཐལ་ཟི་ཀི་ཏ་སེ། ཀི་ཏ་
སེ་ཏི་ཀུ་ནང་ཚང་རི། ན་ཀྱེན་ཏིང་ཐར་པི་ལ་ཞིམ་ཤེད་ཏོད་ནོ།
ཅེན་ཏིང་ཐུག་རྗེ་ལད་སྐྱེ་ཐར་པི་ལ་ཟི་ཅིས།
༢༣། ཡོན་ཆ་ཀུ་ཏིམ་ལན་ཏིང་ཡེ་ཤུའི། ཀ་ཞིང་དང་བཀུ
སེམ་ཤུད་ནོ། རེ་ཏོ། དང་པ་ལ་ཟི་པ་ཏིང་ཀྱེ་ཤུད་ཀྱི་ལ་དུབ་ལ་
ཡོང་ལ།
༢༤། ཡོན་ན་ཀུ་ཏི་ཡེ་ཡ་ཅོ་ཅ་ཀུ་ཡ་བེ་ཤེད་ཅན་བྲ་བ་ཀྱི་ཡེ་
ཤུ་རིང་། ཀྱི་དང་པ་ལ་ཟ་ཏོལ། ཡ་འི་ཏ་ལ་སྒྲེ་རིང་དང་པ་
མ་ཏི་ཀུ་སེམ་ཏོད་ནོ། ཆེལ་པི་ལཀུ། ཀུ་བ་ལའི།
༢༥། ངོ་རང་ཡེ་ཤུའི་བོད་མི་གྲལ་པ་ཡམ་པི་ཏང་གི། །གོང་
བོ་རིང་། ཡེ་གོང་བོ་བུའི་མ་ཏར་ཀྱི་པ་ཀ། ཡ་ཅོ་ཅ་ཀུ་ངོ་བོ་ཟི་
ཏོལ་སུ། ཐལ་ཟེ་ཡལ་ཀྱེ་ངོང་ཐ་ལང་ཏུ། ནན་ཐན་ཀུ་ཏི་ཡེ།
༢༦། གོང་བོ་འི་ཏ་ཀུ་ཁ་རན་ཀྱེ། ཡ་ཅོ་ཅ་ཀུ་ཟུག་བོང་
ཕུར་ཀྱེ། ཀྱོག་ཐོང་རོ་ཅོག་གན་ཤུད་ཀྱི་ཡེ། བོང་པ་འི་ཅི་

ཧ་ལི་རི་ཀླུ་ད་ཀྱི་ལ། ༤༨

༢༧། ཡེ་ཤུའི་དོ་ཤུའ་རི་རྩུམ་གྱི་ཁ་ཏེ་ལའི།

༢༨། དོ་རང་གྱུམ་སྤྲུ་རིང་ཡིན་གྱི། ཀྱིའི་མི་ཡ་རི་ལ་མ་ཏོད་ཏད།
འོབ་སྐུག་ཏེ་རི། རྗེན་ནེ་དོ་གོང་བོ་ཀྱི་རིང་ཚོན་ཚེ་མ་ཏར་ཏི་ཐི།

༢༩། རྩག་ཀེ་ཡེ་ཤུའི་ཀུ་ཏེ། རི་ཀྲུ་སྤོ་ཡོ་ལམ་ལ་ཐི་ཡེ། རེ་ནེ་རིང་
རྫོབ་ཡི་མ་ཤུ་དོ། ཀྱིའི་ཀྲུ་ལ་ཐབ་ཐིང་ཐི་མ་ཚོས་སལ།

ཀུ་ཏེ།

༣༠། དོ་རང་དོ་པོ་རིང་ཡིན་ལ་གྱི། ཡ་ཏིང་ལ་རྩུན་མ་ཏི། ག་ལིལ
རིག་ཤུང་ཡིན་ལ་གྱི།

༣༡། ཡེ་ཤུའི་ལོབ་སྐུག་ཏེ་ཏིང་ཚོའི་ཀན་གྱི་ཀུ་ཏེ། མི་ཀྱུ
ཡོ་ཙེ་ཡིང་ནེ་མིའི་ཀུ་ཀུ་ཏིང་རན་ཐི་ཡེ། ལིའི་ཡན་ཏོ། དོ་རང
ལ་ཙེ་གོད་ཀྱི། སྐུམ་གྱུག་ཏིང་སྒྲིང་ནེ་ཡན་ཙེ་ཏོལ།

༣༢། ཡོན་ན་ཀུད་ཀྱི་ལ། དོ་ཙི་ཏ་མ་གོའི། དོ་སྤུད་ཏུ་ཏོ་ཏག
ཀྱུ་ཤུ་ཀུད་ཀྱི་རྩུག་ཙི་ནེ་རི་རི།

༣༣། དོ་རང་ཀ་ལ་རན་རྩུམ་ན་གར་རང་ཡིན་ལ་གྱི། །ཀྱུམ་སྤུང
ཝིད་ཀྱི། ཡེ་ཤུའི་ལོབ་སྐུག་ཏེ་ཏིང་། ཀྱི་ནེ་ཡམ་ཙང་ཏོད་ཏར
ཀྲུ་ཐབ་ལ་ཞི་ཕུད་ལད་མེན། ཡོན་ན་རྩུག་ཀི། ༤༠
༣༤། དོ་རེ་ཁ་རག་རྫེའི་རི། དོ་ཙི་ཡམ་ཙང་ཏེ་ཞིལ་ཡ་རི།

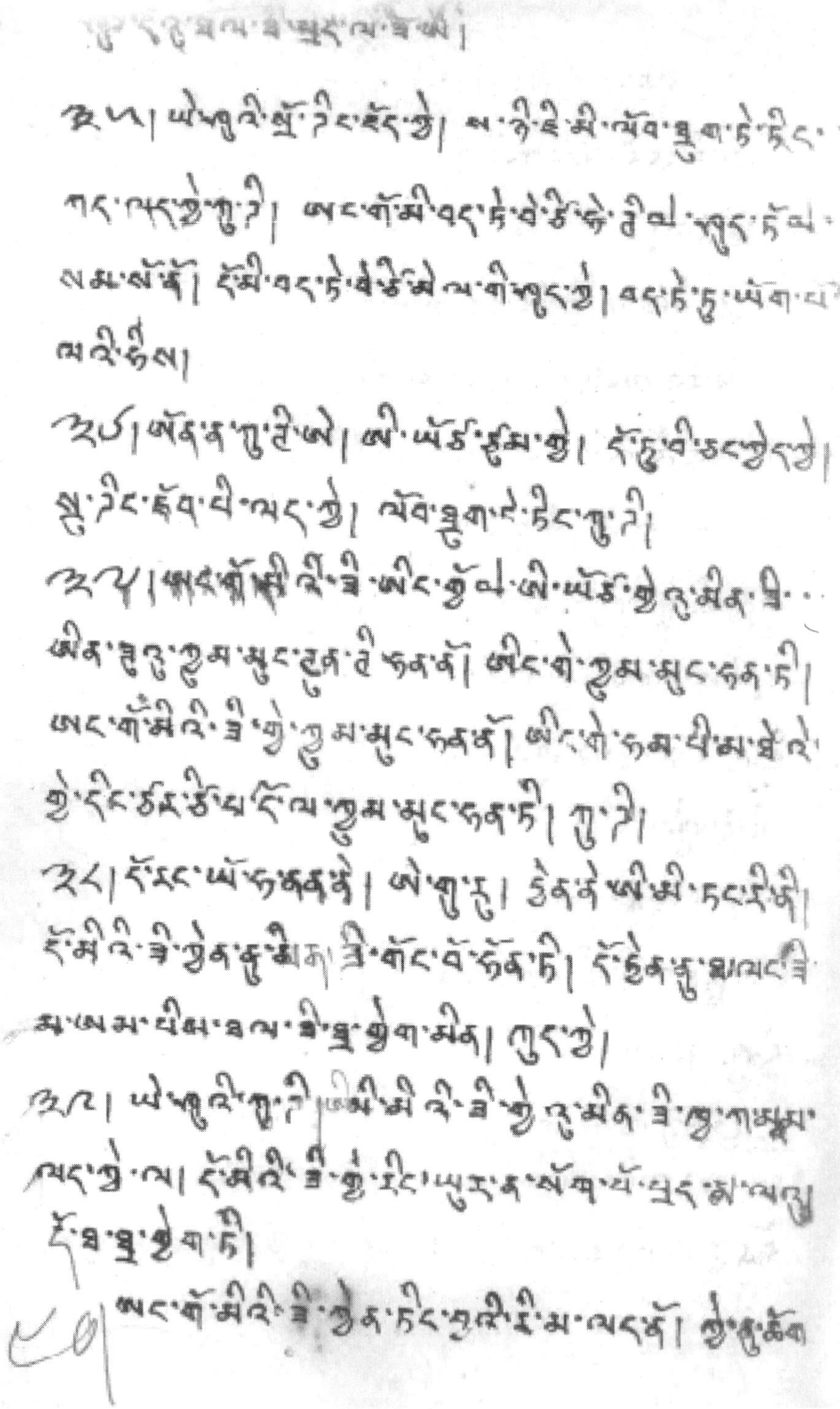

༩༡། ཡ་ཅི་ཡ་ཀྱི་ཞི་ ར་ཤི་ཀ་པ་སྐུར་ཀུད་ཆེ་ཏེ་ནེ། ཆེན་ཏི་ད་བྲི་པོ་ཕིང་
མི་ལོ་ཏི་རཚ་ཅོ། ངོ་ཝ་ཀ་ཤིག་མ་ཏི་ཡ་ཀྱི་ཏུ། ཡོན་ཙ་གྱི་ཀྱེན་ཏིང་དུང་པོ་
ཀུ་ཟ་ཏོལ།

༩༢། ཡ་ཅི་ཡ་ཀྱེ་རིང་དང་ཀ་ལ་ཟི་པ་ཉུ་བི་ཙང་ཟི་ཡི་ཤི་གྱི་ཕྱིང་
་པ་རིབ་ལད་ཅོ། ངོ་ཉུ་ཁོང་ཆང་ཡི་གར་ཚ་ཉུ་རགུ་པོ་ལ་ཀྱེ། གྱི་ཚོ
ཙང་ཚང་ཁེ་ལ། ཉི་ཤི་སྐུར།

༩༣། ཀ་ཙིང་ཡི་ཀྱུ་ཉུ་གུ་ཟ་ཏི་ཕུ་པ་ལ་ཟི་སྐུད་ཅོ། གུད་ཟེག་ཏུ
ཀ་ཉི་ཛི་གུད་ཏང་ཉམ་པོ་ཉ་ཁྱ་རིང་ཡི་བི་བེ་ཅི། གུད་མ་སྐུད་ཀྱེ། སྤོ
སྤུ་རེག་ཤང་ཡི་བི་ཉི་ཤི་སྐུར།

༩༤། ཉ་ཁྱ་ཁྱུ་སྐུར་ཀུད་ཅོ། མ་ལི་ཉི་པ་ཡོམ་ཏུ་ཡེ་མ་ལི་ཉི
མེ་ཛོ་སྐུར།

༩༥། ཀ་ཙིང་ཡི་ཀྱུ་ཉུ་པང་དུ་སྤུ་ཁེ་ཕུ་པ་ལ་ཉི་སྐུད་ཅོ། པད
ཟེག་ཏུ། ཀ་ཉི་ཛི་པང་རང་ཉ་ཁྱ་རིང་ཡི་བི་བེ་ཅི། ལ་ཟ་སྤྲོག་ཉི
རེག་ཤང་ཡི་བི་ཉི་རིག་སྐུར།

༩༦། ཉ་ཁྱ་ཁྱུ་སྐུར་ཀུད་ཅོ། མ་ལི་ཉི་པ་ཡོམ་ཏུ་ཡེ་མ་ལི་ཉི་[illegible]།
༩༧། ཀ་ཙིང་ཡི་ཀྱུ་ཉུ་མིག་ཏུ་སྤུ་ཁེ་ཕུ་པ་ལ་ཉི་སྐུད་ཅོ། མིག
ཅོན་ཏུ། ཀ་ཉི་ཛི་མིག་ཏང་ཉམ་པོ་ཉ་ཁྱ་རིང་ཡི་བི་བེ་ཅི། ཡི་མཛ

མ་ཏེ་སྨུག་ཤུ་དེ་ཁང་ཡ་ནི་ཏི་ཡག་པུ།

༢༨། ཉི་མ་ཀྱི་པུར་ཀུན་ནོ། མ་ལི་འི་ཡ་ལོམ་བུ་ལོ་མ་ལི་ལོ་པེ་པུར།

༢༩། ཡིད་ཙོ་ཡིད་ཙོ་པག་ཀྱུ་ཏུ་རེང་ཚོ་ཀྱི་ཞིམ་ཙོག་ཀན། ཡི་ཡི་ཡི་འི་
རིང་ལ་མི་འུ་ཚོ་ཀྱི་ཞི་ཉིལ།

༣༠། ཚོ་འུ་ཕན་ཏོག་བོང་པུད་ཀྱི་ལ། ཚོ་འུ་དྲི་ལག་མ་ཀྱི་ཕྱི་ནོ། ཕན
ཏོག་ཀུ་ཏོ་ཏོ། ཀྱེན་ཏང་ཉམ་པོ་ཚོ་ཡོག་ཏི། ཀྱེན་ཏེ་བད་ཏེ་དྲིག་པེ་ཙོད་ཏི༎

ལྷ་འོ་འུ་འུ་ནང་།

༡། དོ་རང་ཡེ་པུ་ཡི་ཀྱི་ཡེ། ཡོར་དན་ཞེན་ཞི་འུ་ཀུ་རང་རེག་རབ་ཁ།
ཡ་ཀུ་དུ་རེག་ཀ་འུ་ཟུར་ཏིང་ཕར་ཚེག་ཀེ་ཡི་ལ་ཀྱེ། མི་འི་ཀུ་བོང་
ཆུ་ཏ་དོ་འུ་ཀྱམ་པོལ་ཛོམ་ཀྱི། ཀུ་རིང་ཙོག་ཀན་དེ་ཏིང་ཚོ་འི་ཀན་ཞི།

༢། ངོ་བེ་ལྷ་རིང་ [illegible] ཡན་ཀྱེ། པེ་པུ་འུ་དོང་ཟི་ཀྱིན་
ཏོན་ཙིམ་ཟབ་ལ་ཟི། ཡི་མི་འི་ཟི་ཡིན་ཏུ་འུ་མེད་པོ་ཀྱིག་ཞི་
རེ་ཏོ་ཡ།

༣། ཡོན་ན་ཏུག་ཙིམ་ལན་ཏིང་ཡེ་པུ་འི་ཀུ་ཏི། མོ་པེ་འེ་ཀྱེན་
ཉིང་ཀུ་ཡུར་མིན།

༤། ཡོན་ན་ཏུག་ཙོ་ཡེ་དོ་ཙོ། མོ་པེ་འེ་ཀུ་ཕྱི་འུ་ཙོག་ཀན་
ཏ་ལྷག་ཙེ་འེ། པོ་ཀྱིག་ཞི་རེ་ཏོ།

༥། ཀུད་ཀྱི་ཡེ་པུ་འི། ཀྱེ་ཏུ་སེམ་ཀུང་གི་པུད་ཟང་། མོ་པེ་འེ

ཡོན་ཏན་རྒྱ་ཀུམ་ཙེ་ནེ། ༥༢

༦། ལན་ལྔར་བ་ཇིག་ཇི་ཏར། གོན་ཅོག་ཅི་མེ་ཙ་ཡེ་ག་ག་ལ་ཀེ་མི་ལ་
བ་ཇིག་ཏེ།

༧། དོ་ཀྲུ་ཐལ་ཟེ་མི་འི་ཙི་ཡ་བ་ཡ་མ་ཀྱིད་ཀྱི། མེད་དེང་ས་ཞིག

༨། དོ་ཀུ་ཡིད་ཙ་རྒྱག་སྐྱུད་ཀྱི། མེད་ཡེ་དག་པོ་ཇོ་ཧོག་ཏིང་ཀུད་ནོ། ཀི་
ཧི་མ་སྐུ་ཀུ། ཡིད་ཙ་རྒྱག་སྐྱུད་ཀྱི་སྐྱེ།

༩། ཀྱི་གོན་ཅོག་ཅི་ཉམ་པོ་ལད་ནོ། དོ་མི་འི་ཙི་ཕག་ཏ་ཐ་ལད་ཏི།

༡༠། དོ་རྡང་ཀྱ་མ་སྐྲང་པིད་ཀྱི། ལོབ་ཐུག་ཏེ་ཙི་ཡས་ཀྱི་དོ་ཡེ་སྤྲད་དུ་
ཐལ་ཟེ་རྟག་ཀེ།

༡༡། པེ་སྐུའི། ཡང་གོ་འི་ཡིན་རྒྱུ་མེད་ཀྱིད་ཀྱི། ཀྱའི་ནན་ནོ།
དོའི་རན་དྲི་ཝ་ཧེ་ལ་ཟལ།

༡༢། ཀི་ཏ་མི་མེ་ཙེའི་ཡིན་རྒྱུ་དག་པོ་ཀྱིད་ཀྱི། ཀྱའི་ནན་ནོ།
དོ་མེ་ཙེ་འི་རན་དྲི་ཝ་ཧེ་ལ་ཟལ།

༡༣། དོ་རང་ཙོ་ཀྱི་ཙ་པོ་རེ་དོ་ཀྲུ་ཉམ་པོལ་ནན་ཀྱི། དོ་ཏིང་ཀུད་
ཞོག་ཙི་ཏིས་ཀུད་ཀྱི་ཞུ་བ་ལ་ཟེ་ཡེ། ལོབ་ཐུག་ཏེ་ཙི་པོ་རེ་
ཀུར་ཀྱི་པ་ཀི་ཧྲང་ངར་ཀྱི།

༡༤། པེ་སྐུའི་ལོབ་ཐུག་ཏེ་ཏིང་ཁན་ཀྱི། ཐུག་མ་ཐད་ཀྱི་
མོ་ལ་ལི། པོ་རེ་མ་ཀ་ག་ཀེ། ཀྱི་ཀྲུ་རྒྱམ་པོལ་ཡམ་མ་པི་རྣ་ཀྱི

ད་ཏིང་ཀན་ཅིག་ཏུ་རྣ་ཆ་ཏོ་ཏོ། ཡོན་ན་ཀུ་ཏི།

༡༥། ཤེ་ཤེན་ཏིང་ཏྲང་པོ་ཀུ་ཟ་ཏོལ། ཡ་ཙི་ཡ་ཀོན་ཅིག་ཏུ་རྣ་
ཡོ་རེ་ཏུ་ལུག་ཟིང་མ་ཧུམ་ནོ། ནང་མ་ཁ་ཏུ།

༡༦། ཡོན་ཀུ་ཞི་ཡེ། ཡེ་ཤུའི་དོ་ཡོ་ཙ་ལྷུ་ནིང་ཐིན་གྱི། གུད་ཀྱང་ལེ།
ཙི་ལབ་ས་ལ་ཏི།

༡༧། དོ་རང་ཡི་རིང་ཚོས་ས། ཡམ་ཙང་ཁྱང་གི་ཤེ། ཡི་མི་དོ་ཏྲུ
ཏུམ་པོལ་གྲལ་ཁྱེ་ཡན་གྱི། ཕྱག་ལད་ཤེ་ཀྲུ་ཟི། ཡེ་ཤུ་ཞི་པ་
སང་གི། གོད་ཡིམ་མ་ཏི་སྤྲོག་ཆུག་ཡིམ་ཐལ་ཟེ་ཀྱི་ཀྲུ་
ལག་ཀ།

༡༨། ཁྲུ་ཙིམ་ཡན་ཏིང་ཡེ་ཤུའི། ཀའི་གྱེ་རིང་སང་ཡི་ཀུ་
ཞིམ་དོ་ཁྲ་ཤུར། ཡིད་ཙ་ཀོན་ཅིག་ག་ཞི་སང་ཡི་ཡ་རི་ལམ་ཏོ

༡༩། རན་དི་ཟླ་ཛེ་ཟ་ལབ། མི་ཟ་ས་ཏུ། ཁུད་ཟ་ཁུད་ཏུ།
ཏབ་སི་ཀྲུ་གོ་ཡ་ཏི་ཟ་ར་ཏུ། ཀྲུའི་ཏུ་ཚོར་ཀོག་ཀོ་ཟ་སྤྱིལ་ལ
ཤི་ཏུ་ཏུ་ཡ་བ་ཡ་མ་རིང་ཡ་སབ་ལབ། དོ་རིང་ཐེའི་ཏུ་ཀ
ཕད་ཏེ་ཀའི་ཉེ་ན།

༢༠། ཡོན་ན་ཀུ་ཞི་ཡེ་དོ་[illegible]ཞི། ཡེ་ཤུ་ཞི་པ། དོ་ཁང་
ཙེ་གྱི་ཙ་ཡོ་རིང་ཟེ་རྣན་མིན།

༢༡། ཡོན་ན་ཁྲུ་ཙི་ཏར། ཡེ་ཤུའི་དོ་རིང་ཁན་གྱི་ཡ་ཡ

ལབ་པ་ཀྱུ་ཏེ། ཀ་ནང་ལ་འུ་ཡོད་ཙོ་མ་ཚང་ཟེ། ཁྱེ་སྐྱིར་ཀྱུད་སོ།
ང་ཡི་ལ་ལ། ཀ་ཉིང་ཁྱེ་ཧོད་ཀྱི་བད་ཏེ་ལང་ཁྱེ། མ་ཏི་ངོ་ཏི་ང་ར་ཧྲུ།
ཡོན་ན་ལད་ནོ། ནམ་ཁ་འུ་ཞོར་ཀ་ཞིང་རྒྱུག་ཏོ། ངོ་རང་ངིང་ཡན་ཀྱེ།
ཡི་རྒྱུ་འུ་ཀྱུང་ཀྱིང་ཀྱུར་ཙོ་སྐྱེ་འུ་ཐ་ལང་ཟེ་ཡན་ཏ།

༢༢། ཡོན་ཀྱུ་ཟེ་ཡེ་ངོས་ཐད་ཀྱེ། ངོ་རྒྱུག་པོ་སྐྱབ་པིས་ཐལ་ཟེ
སེམ་མ་ཐད་ཀྱེ་རྒྱུ་པོ་རྟིང་ཡི་ལ་ལི།

༢༣། པེ་སྐྱུ་ལི་རིམ་པ་རིང་ཁན་ཀྱེ། ལོབ་སྒྲུག་ཏེ་ཏིང་ཀྱུ་ཏེ།
ཡི་རྒྱུག་པོ་མི་ཀོན་ཅོག་ཏུ་རྣམ་རྒྱུ་ཧ་འུ་ནང་ལྷང་ངི་བག་ལེ་ཀ་འི
སྐྱེ།

༢༤། ཡོན་ན་ཀྱུ་ཞིམ་ཐལ་ཟེ་ལོབ་སྒྲུག་ཏེ་ BB [illegible] སྐྱུ
ཀྱེ་ཡེ། པེ་སྐྱུ་ཨི་ཡལ་ཀྱེ་ཀྱུ་ཏེ། ཡེ་ཡོ་རེ། ཡི་མི་ཨི་ཟེ་ཡི
རྒྱུ་འུ་ཞོར་ཏིང་ཡོར་ཏད་ལད་ནོ། ཀོན་ཅོག་ཏུ་རྣམ་རིང་པི་པི་
བག་ལེ་ཀ་འི་སྐྱེ།

༢༥། རྒྱུག་པོ་མི་ཀོན་ཅོག་ཏུ་རྣམ་ཧ་འུ་ནང་ལྷང་ངི་ནི་ཙེ།
ཡི་ཨུཛ་ཀྱེ་བ་ཏུ་མིག་ཏུ་ནང་སོག་པི་སྟེབ་ཕལ་ཀྱེ་སྐྱེ།

༢༦། ལོབ་སྒྲུག་ཏེ་ཕ་མ་ཉན་སྐྱུད་ཀྱེ། ཡི་ད་འི་ཡི་དི་རིང་།
ཡོན་ན་སྐྱུད་ནོ། ལ་རི་ཐར་ཏོ། ཀྱུད་ཀྱེ།

༢༧། ཁྱུ་ཙི་ཡེ། པེ་སྐྱུ་འི་ངོ་ཏིང་ཁན་ཀྱེ། མི་འུ་མིག་ཏུ་

རྨ་པོ་ལ་དུད་པོ་ཨ་ཙར་ཀྱི་ལ། ཧོད་ཆོས་རྒྱ་རྒྱམ་ཚོལ་ཀྱི་

ལུམ་ལ་ལ། བདག་དེ་དུབ་པོ་ཡ་ལ་ཞོ།

༢༨། ཨོཾ་ན་ཀུད་ཀྱི། ཀི་ཡེ། ཨེ་ཡེ་སྐུ། རྩེན་ནེ་ཨ་མ་མ་ཁུ་

ཨ་མ་མ་ཁུ་ཀྱུ་ཏོད་ཀྱི་ངོ་བད་དེ་ཀྱེད་ཀྱི། ཨི་དུ་ཟ་ལང་ཟི་ཨལ་

མིན།

༢༩། ལྗུ་ཤི་ཨེ་ཡེ་སྐུ་ཧི། ཀྱི་ཀྱེན་ཏིད་དྲང་པོ་ཀུ་ཙ་ཏོལ། ཡི་མི་ཞི་

ཟི་ཡིང་ག་ཡེ་ཟིན་ཟད་དུ་ཟལ་ཟི་ཀི་ཏ་རྒྱམ། ཀི་ཏ་ཨ་ཚོ་ཐུག།

ཀི་ཏྲ་ལུ་བ་ཨ་མ། ཀི་ཏ་མེད། ཀི་ཏ་རི་དང་པོ་ཀྱེ་གཞོ།

༣༠། ཏོ་རིང་དི་མི་ཚོ་རིང་། རྒྱམ་ཡེ། ཨ་ཚོ་ཐུག་ཡེ། ཨ་མ་ཡེ

རི་རྣལ་ཏི་བེ་ཅི་བོང་ཆུག་ཏོ། ཟླ་ཞི་རི་ཅི་ཚོད་

པ་ཀལ་ཟིམ་ཟ་ལ་ཟི་ཨ་ལ་ཀྱེ་ཆུག་པོ་མ་ཟེ་འེ། ཟ་ལ་ཟི་ཁུ་

མི་ཚོ་རིང་ངོ་རིང་གབ་པི་མ་མ་ཏི་སྦྱོག་ཆུག་ཏོ།

༣༡། སྐུད་ཀྱི་ལ། ཏུང་རིང་ཏོད་ཀྱི་བོང་ཟ་ལ་ཟི་པིད་ཞོ་རེ།

ཟ་ལང་ཏོད་ཀྱི་བོང་ཏུང་རིང་ཡིད་ཞོ་རེ།

༣༢། ངོ་རང་ངོ་རེ་བད་ཏེ་ཨ་མ་རིང་ཚོས་ལ། ཡེ་སྐུ་ག་ཡེ

བ་རྟར་ར་རིང་ཨི་ལ་ལི་རེ། ཡེ་སྐུ་ཏུང་རིང་ཨི་བི་ཡེ།

ཆུག་རེ་ཟ་ཟ་སྐུད་ཀྱི། བེ་ལྷ་ཟ་ལང་ཟི་ཨི་ལ་ལི་རེ། ཡེ་

ཁུ་ཞི་ལོབ་ཐུག་ཏེ་ཏིང་ཀད་ལད་ཀྱི། ཨིན་ཟ་རིང་

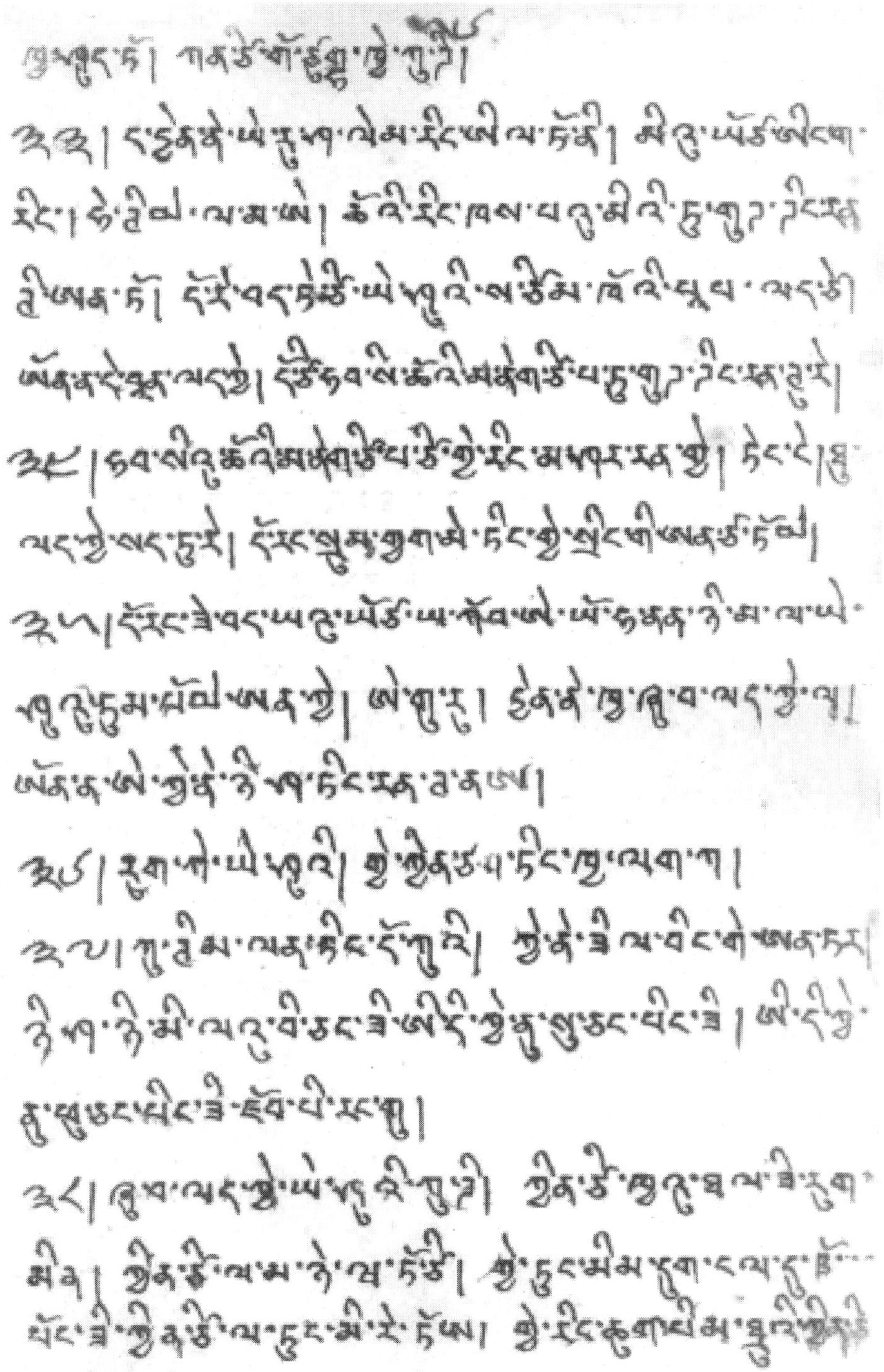

༧༩། ཡོད་ན་རྫུག་ཙེ་ཡེ་རྡོ་གུ་འི། ལྷན། རེ་རྡོ་ཡོད་མ་གུ་ཏི་གུ།

༨༠། ཡེ་ཤུ་འི་དོ་གུ་རིང་། ཀྱི་རིང་ཆུག་པེམ་བུ་འི་ཀྱིན་ཙིག་རིང་རག
སི་ར་རག་སོ་རོ། སྐྱེའུ་ཤུ་ཙང་པེང་ཟེ་ཡེ། ཤུ་ཙང་པེང་ཟེ་རྫོབ་པེ་རན་ཏེ་དོ།
ཡིང་ཤུ་ཙུ་ཤུ་ཏ་ཏིང་མ་རོ། ཡ་རྫུ་ཐ་ལ་ཟེ་དོ་ལ་ཀྱིད་ཆག་ཀན་ལ་ལི་
རོ་རོ། དོ་རིང་ཆུག་རོ། གུ་ཏི།

༨༡། ལག་མ་ལུ་མི་ལོབ་ཐུག་རེ་ཙེ་དོ་ཕྲུད་ཐ་ཙེ་ཡེ། ཡ་ཀོབ་ཡེ་ཡོད
ནན་རིང་མ་ཐ་དི་རེ།

༨༢། ཡེ་ཤུ་འི་དོ་རོ་བད་རེ་རིང་ཀད་ལད་ཀྱི་གུ་ཏི། དེ་ལན་ལུ་རུ་རང་
ཐྲིམ་པེན་སེ་དྷ་ལི་རན་ཏེ་རོ་རེ། རེ་ཏེལ་མི་འི་ཙི་རྫུ་གུམ་རན་ཏེ་རོ་རེ།

༨༣། ཀྱི་ནི་ཡོད་ན་ལ་ཟེ་མེས། ཀྱི་རུ་བེ་ཙང་ཟེ་ཡ་རི་ཡ་རེ་ཏེལ་
ཀྱུབ་པེ་ཐད་ནོ། ཀྱུ་འི་རྫུ་ཡོག་པོ་ལད་རེ།

༨༤། ཀི་ར་ཀྱི་ནི་བེ་ཙང་ཟེ་ཡི་དི་མི་ཆེན་ཀྱུད་ར་ལ་ཐེ་ཟ་ནོ། བད་རེ
རྫུ་ཡོག་པོ་ལད་རེ།

༨༥། མི་ཏུ་ཡོ་ཙེ་ཡིང་བེ་ལ་ཀྱུ་འི་མི་ལི་ཙེ་ཀྱི་རིང་ཡོག་པོ་ལ་ཟེམ་
ཡམ་མིན། ཡིང་བི་ལི་ཀྱུ་འི་རྫུ་ཡོག་པོ་ལ་ཟེ་ཡེ། བོང་མི་ཐར་
པོམ་ལ་ཟིང་ཡིང་ཤུ་ཏུ་སྐྱོབ་རན་ཏེ་ཡམ་མིན།

༨༦། རྡོ་རང་ཡེ་རི་ཀོ་ན་གར་རང་ཡི་ལ་ལི། ལོབ་ཐུག་རེ་ཡེ་
བོང་མི་རང་ཉམ་པོ་ཡེ་རི་ཀོ་ན་གར་ཙང་ཟེ་ཚོས་ལི་ཡེ། རེས་

ཀུ་ཤྲི་ཏུ་ཞ་ར་ཡོ་ཙ་བར་རྟེམ་ཀུ་ཤུ་དོ་རྟ་ཙེམ་ཐལ་ཟེ་ཨམ་ཚང་རྫ་འི།

༤༧། ཡེ་ཤུ་ན་ཙ་རིང་པ་ཨམ་ཡིམ་ཏྲུན་ཟ་ཙེ་ཨེ། བར་རྟེམ་ཟེ་ཤེད་ཙན་
ཕྱི་འདྲུ་ཀ་རན་ཕྱི། ཨེ་ཡེ་ཤུ་དབེད་ཏུ་ཡོ་ཙེ། ཕྱི་རིང་སྨུག་རྫེ་ལྡུ། ཀུད་ཕྱི་
གད་ལད་ཕྱི། ཨོན་ནའ་འདྲུ་ཀ་རན་ཧྲི་ཨེ།

༤༨། བང་མི་འི་ཙེ་དོ་རིང་། ད་ཁ་རོག་རྫེ། ཙན་ཏན་ལད་ཕྱི་ཀུད་ཕྱི་ལ་ཧྲི་
ཏྲུང་རིང་ཝེ་ཙེ་ན་འདྲུ་ཀ་རན་ཕྱི། ཨེ་དབེད་ཏུ་ཡོ་ཙེ། ཕྱི་རིང་སྨུག་རྫེ་ལྡུ།
ཀུད་ཕྱི་གད་ལད་ཕྱི།

༤༩། ཡེ་ཤུ་ཏུ་པོ་རིང་མེ་ཨེ་ལ་ཕྱི། ད་དེ་མི་ཝེ་རིང་ཨན་ཏ་ཀུ་ཤེ། ཀུ་ཤེ་
ཨེ། ཨང་གོ་ཙེ། ཞ་ར་དོ་རིང་། ད་ཡེ་ཤུ་འི་ཀ་ཚིང་ཨན་ཏ་ཀུ་ཤུ་ལ།
བད་མ་བེ་འེ། ཨན་ཙུ།

༥༠། ཨོན་ན་ཀུ་ཏི་ཨེ། དོ་མི་འི་ཟེ་ཁམ་ཚང་ཁེ། ཨན་ཙེ་ཡེ་ཤུ་
ཏྲུམ་པོ་ལ་ཨེ་ལ་ལི།

༥༡། དོ་རང་ཡེ་ཤུ་འི་ཞ་ར་རིང་། ཕྱི་ཀ་ཚིང་ཁྲུ་ལག་ཀ་ཀུ་ཏི་ཨེ་ཁར།
ཨེ་ཀུ་ཀྲུ། ཕྱི་རིང་ཏང་ཐེ་རང་ཀྲུ། ཏྲུ་བ་ལད་ཕྱི།

༥༢། ཡེ་ཤུ་འི། ད་ཨེ་ལ་ལ། ཀ་དད་པ་འདྲུ་ཕིང་ཟེ་ཕྱི་ཁ་ལི་ན།
ཨོན་ན་ཀུ་ཏི་ཨོ། དོ་མི་འདྲུ་མིག་སྲ་རི་ཤུད་ཕྱི་ཡེ་ཤུ་འདྲུ་ཐ་ཁང་ཟེ་ཤི་ལ་ལི།
སམ་ཨེ་དི་ལི་འདྲུ་འདྲུ་ཏད།

༡། དོ་རང་ཡེ་ཏྲུ་ཤག་ལམ་མ་འདྲུ་བ་རྨར་རཏྲུ་ཨམ་ཚང་ཟེ་ཏྲུན་ཀྲུ

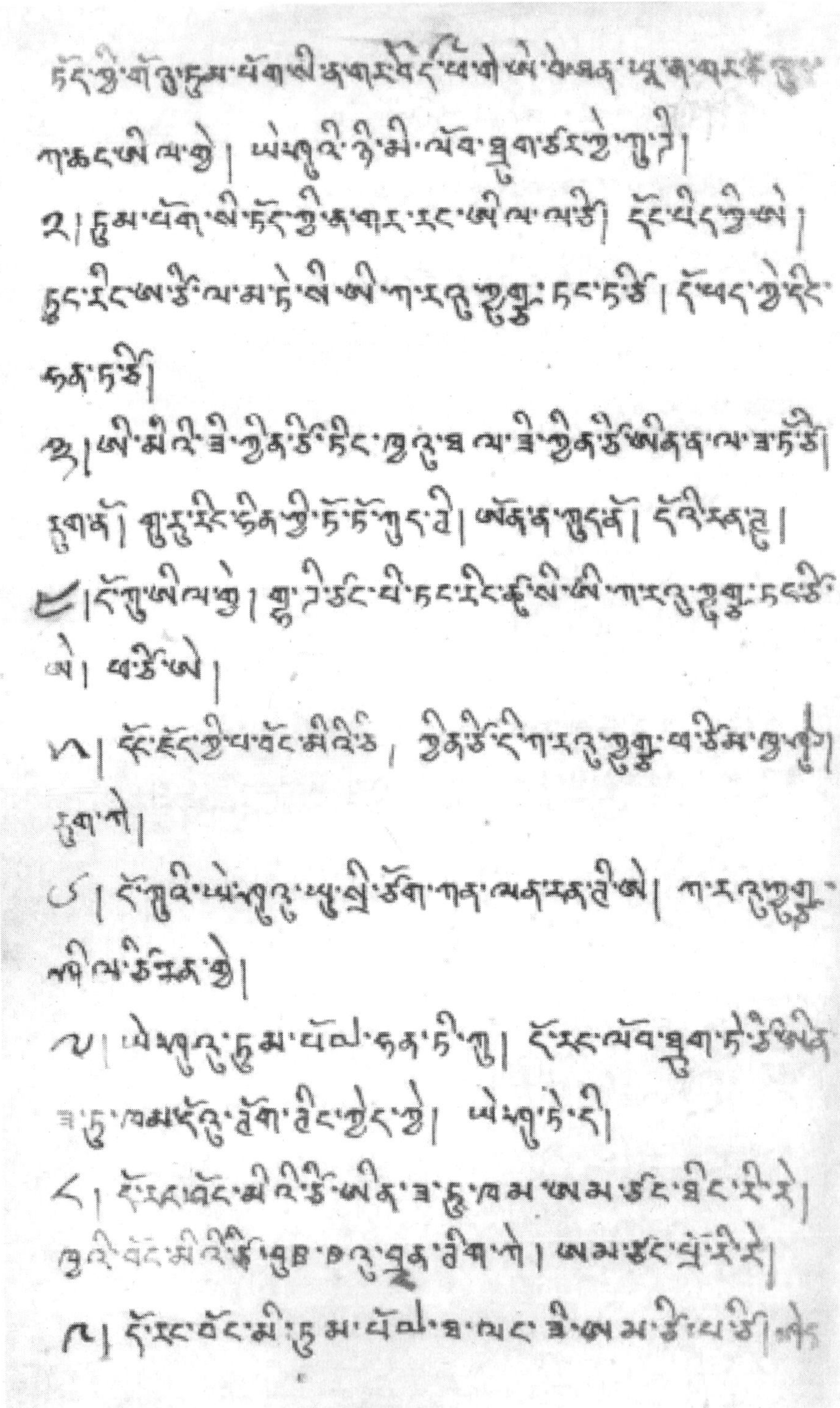

[illegible] ཡིན་ན་[illegible]། ངབ་སྐྱོ་[illegible]

གཉན་ཚོག་ཏུ་མིན་ཏིང་ཨན་གྱི་པ་དེ་ཞ་པགིལ་ཡི་ཏིལ།

༡༠། ཅིན་ཏུ་ལེ་ཊེ་ད་བིད་ར་ཛཏྲུ་སྐྲ་ལི་ཏྲུ་འི་རྟུག་ཅི་བ་དོ་ཞ་པགིལ་ཡི་ཏིལ།

༡༡། དོ་རང་ཡེ་ཕུ་ཡེ་ཏུ་ཕྱ་ལེམ་མ་ཏྲུ་ཚོ་ཁང་དུང་ཨི་ལ་གྱི། བད་ཏེ་
ཏིང་ཁ་ཊེ། གིར་དོས་ཉི་ཛི་ལོབ་བྲུག་ཏེ་ཏང་ཉམ་པོ་བེ་ཐན་ཡུ་ན་
གར་རང་ཨས་ལ་གྱི་ཡི་ལ་ལི།

༡༢། ཡོ་ར་གྱལ་བེ་ཐན་ཡུ་ན་གར་རང་ཟེ་ཏོས་ཏར། ཡོ་ཁ་ཨན་གྱི།
༡༣། ལོ་ལི་རིང་ཟེ་ལབ་ཏོད་གྱི་ལེ་ཡབ་ཀུ་སྲི་ཨིད་ཙོ་བྲུ་ཁ་ཏང་གི།
ཏོ་རིང་ཐ་ལ་ཏོ་ཏོ་ཨ་མ་ཏོ་ཁན་ཞི་ཀ་ཚང་ཡི་ལ་ལི། ལབ་ག་ཞི་ཀྲུ་ལི་
ཀྲུ་ལ་ལེ་མ་ཕུང་གྱི་ཨེ། ཡེ་ཕུ་ལི་དོ་ལེ་ཡབ་བྲུ་ཁ་རིང་།
༡༤། དིང་ཐ་ལང་ཟེ་ཨ་ཅི་ལ་ཀ་ཏུ་དོང་ཟེ་ཀྲུ་ལ་ལེ་པ་ལ་ཟ་ལི་
མེས་ཀུ་ཉི། དོ་སྤུད་ལོབ་བྲུག་ཏྲེ་ཅི་ལ་ཐ་དེ་རེ།
༡༥། དོ་རང་ཡེ་ཏུ་ཕྱ་ལེ་[illegible] བ་རྣར་རང་ཨི་ལ་གྱི། ཚོ་ཁང་དུང་ཨི་ལ་གི
དོང་ཏོད་གྱི་ལང་ཅི་པ་ཨེ་རོ་གྱི་པ་བད་ཏེ་ཏོན་ཅེ། ལ་རྣམ་ཏུ་ཙོག་
ཅོ་ཨེ། རན་ཙོ་ལང་ཙོ་པ་ཏུ་ཀུར་སི་ཚང་རི།
༡༦། ཡེ་ཕུ་ལི་ཨ་ཏིད་ལ་ཚོ་ཁང་དུ་ཨམ་ཅོ་ཀྲུ་ལྦ་ལེ་ཀུར་ཅི་
མ་རྣ་ཊེ།
༡༧། དང་ཡེ་ཕུ་ལི། ཀྲི་ཏྲུ་གར་ཕྱར་ར་རིང་མན་ཕྱར་ར་ཏྲུ་[illegible]

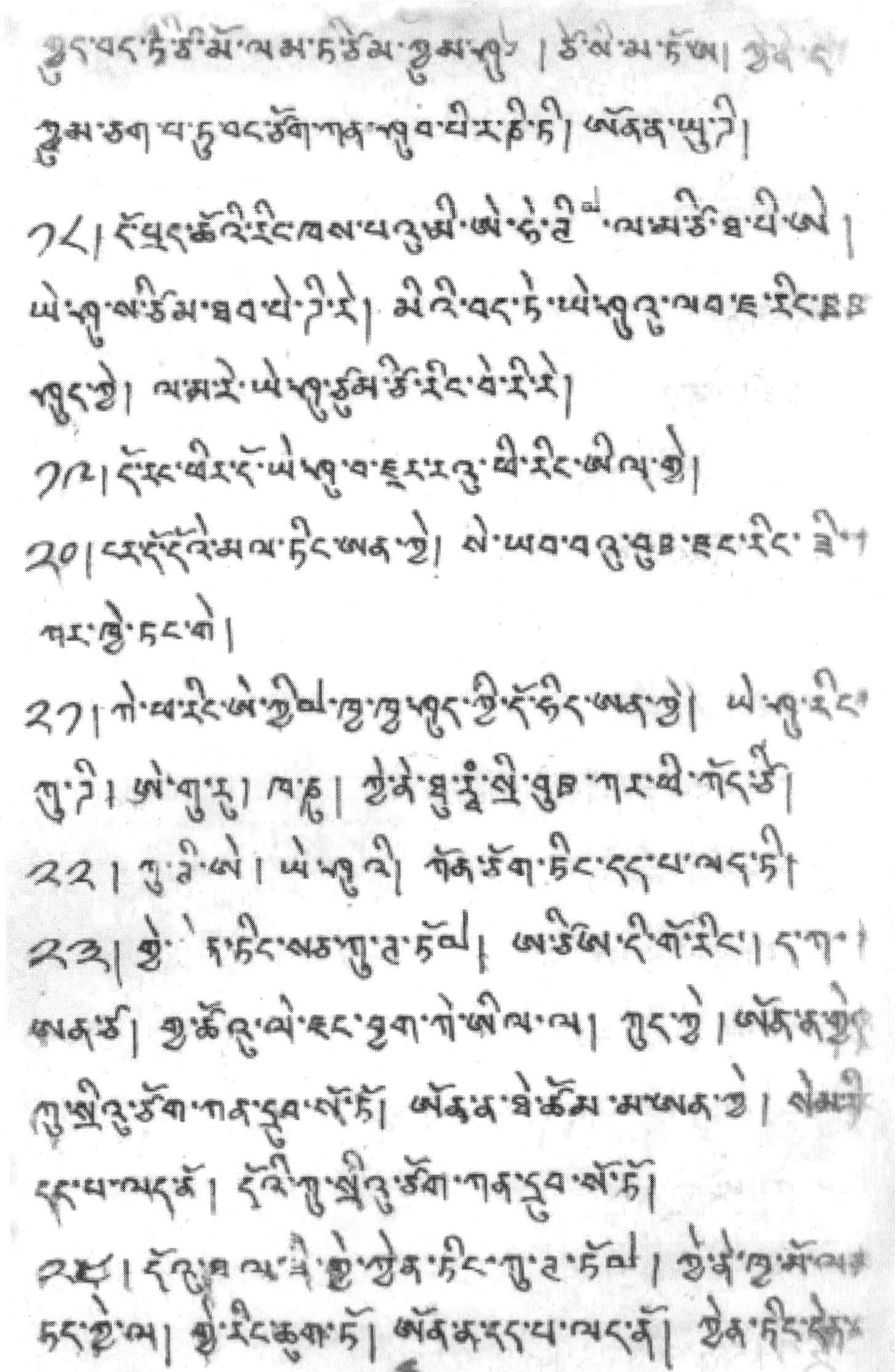

༢༥། ཀུ་འི་སྒྲོན་མོ་ལམ་དེ་ཅི་ཡིན་ཅི་ནོ། ཀུ་འི་ཡི་ཏུ་ལྟ་བ་ཅི་ཡིན་ནམ་སྐྱེ་སྐྱེ་
སྒྲེ་ཅིར་དེ། དོ་རང་སྒྲེ་ནུ་ཡ་བ་ནམ་ཁ་རིང་ཏོད་ཀྱི་དོའི་སྒྲེ་ནུ་ལྟ་བ་རིང་ལ་མན་

སྣ་རེག་ཏུ།

༢༦། སྒྲེན་ཀུ་འི་མི་འི་དེང་མཇོ་སྣ་རེག་ནོ། སྒྲེ་ནུ་ཡ་བ་ནམ་ཁ་རིང་ཏོད་ཀྱི་དོའི་
སྒྲེ་ནུ་ལྟ་བ་རིང་ལ་མཇོ་སྣ་རེག་ཏུ།

༢༧། དོ་རང་ཡ་ལ་སྐྱེ་ཡེ་ཏུ་ཤག་ལེམ་རིང་ཡི་ལ་སྐྱེ། ཡེ་ཤུ་ཆོ་ཁང་དུང་ཡི་ལ་
སྐྱེ། དེ་ཞིལ་ལ་མ་ཡེ། ཆོའི་རིང་ཁམ་པ་ནུ་མི་ཡེ། སེ་ཏྲེ་མི་འི་རེ་ཡེ་ཤུ་ཀུ་
ཏུམ་པོལ་ཡན་སྐྱེ། ཡེ་ཤུ་རིང་།

༢༨། ཡ་ཏུ་པེད་དུ་པེང་ཟེ་ཀ་འི་ཡོན་ཚ་ལ་ཟ་ཏོན། ཡ་ཅིག་ཚིང་ཡོན་ཚ་
ལ་ཞེམ་པེད་རན་མིན།

༢༩། རྟག་ཅོམ་ལན་དེང་ཡེ་ཤུ་འི་དོ་དེང་། སྒྲེ་ལ་སྒྲེ་ནུ་དོང་ཟེ་ཡེ་ལྟད་
རྟག་ཏལ། སྒྲེ་རིང་ལན་རན་ནོ། སྒྲེ་སྒྲེན་དེང་ཡ་ཏུ་པེད་དུ་པེང་ཟེ་སྐྱེ་
ཏུལ་དི་ལ་ཟ་ཏོལ་པེད་ཏལ།

༣༠། ཡོ་ཧ་ནན་ནེ་བུ་འི་རན་ཞེམ་ནམ་ཁ་རིང་ཟེ་ཡན་སྐྱེ་པུད་ང་།
མི་ཏུ་དོང་ཟེ་ཡན་སྐྱེ་པུར། དོ་ལྟད་དུ་ལན་རང་ཀུ་ཞི་ཀུ་ཞི་ཡེ།

༣༡། དོ་ཏུ་སེམ་རིང་། ནམ་ཁ་རིང་ཟེ་ཡན་སྐྱེ་པུར་ཀུད་ནོ། དོའི་ཀུ
ཏོ། དོ་རང་དོ་རིང་ཀུ་ཏུ་ཐ་ལ་ཟེ་དང་པ་མ་ལད་མིན།

༣༢། མི་ཏུ་དོང་ཟེ་ཡན་སྐྱེ་པུར་ཀུད་ནོ། དེག་པ་ཏུ་ཡི་འི་བ་དང་ཏེ

༨༢

ཞི་འི་རིམ། ཀྱཱ་ཟླ་ཐལ་ཟེ་ཤུད་ཚོ། དེ་ཀ་ཁ་ཀྲུ་མི་ཟླ་ཏུང་རིང་ཡོ་ཀྱ་ཆེན་

ཀོན་ཅོག་ཏུ་སློལ་རྩན་ཞི་པ་སྐྱོ། ཡོན་ཐ་ལམ་ལ།

༣༣། ལན་ཏིང་ཡེ་ཤུ་རིང་། ཏུན་མ་ཉེ་ཞི། ཀུ་ཞི་ཡེ། ཡེ་ཤུ་འི་དོན་

གྱི་ལ་སྤྱིན་ཏིང་ཨ་ཏུ་ཁེད་ཏུ་ཡིང་ཟེ་སྐྱེ་དི་ཐད་ཏེ་ལ་ཟ་ཏོལ། ཀུ་ཞི་རིང་

མ་ཐ་ཀ་ཀུ་ཏི།།

སླུ་ཉི་རྡི་ལེ་ཟླ་ཟླ་ནང་།

༡། དོར་ལེ་ཀན་ཏེ་རིང་གོ་སྟོན་སྒྲུ་ཀྱི། ཀྱུ་ཏི། ཨི་མི་འི་ཟེ་གུན་དུམ་སྲུ

ཟླག་བ་ཚེག་ཀེ། གྱིར་གོར་ཏིང་བེ་ཏ་རྩན་གྱི་གྱི་འི། རྒྱུ་དོང་བ་ཚེག་ཀེ།

ཨི་ཐོ་འི་ཀྲུ་སྐ་བ་ཚེག་ཏི། དོ་རང་ཟླག་རྩན་གྱི་པ་སྐྱ་ཁག་ལད་སྐྱེ།

ཀྱུ་འི་དེ་ཁ་ཁང་ཨི་ལ་ལི།

༢། དོ་རང་ལེ་ལྷ་རིང་པིད་ཀྱི། གུན་དུམ་སྲུ་པ་ལ་ཀྲུ་ཅོ་ཨི་ཡོག་པོ་

ཟླག་རྩན་གྱི་པ་སྐྱ་དོང་ཙར་ཏི།

༣། དོ་ཅི་དེ་ཡོག་པོ་སྟུམ་གྱི། ཏིང་གེ། ཀྱུ་ལ་ལེ་མ་རྩན་གྱི། ཚོན་སྟེ་

ཙར་ཏི་རེ།

༤། ཡོན་དག་ཅི་ཀྱུ་འི་ཡོག་པོ་ཙར་ཅི་ཡེ། དོ་ཅི་དོ་ཟླ་བ་ལ་ལིང་...

རག་ཀུ་ཁི་ཀྱི། མ་ཁུར་རམ་བ་ཚོན་གྱི་ཙར་ཏི་རེ།

༥། ཡས་ལས་ཀྱི་ལ། ཀྱུ་འི་ཡོག་པོ་ཙར་ཅི་ཡེ། དོ་ལ་དི་རེ། ཀྱུ་

ག་ཅན་ཡོག་པོ་ཏིང་ཏིང་གེ་ཀྱུ་འ་བོང་ལ་དི་རེ།

༦། ངོ་རང་དོ་ཡོན་དག་ཏུ་ཨིད་ཙི་ཅི་ས་པ་ཡོཙ་ཏོ་རི། འད་ཏོ་

ཐལ་ཟེ་དོཊུ་དོ་ཡོཙ་ ལ་ལྷག་རྟེན་གྱི་ཕ་ཏུ་དོང་ཙར་ཏི། དོའི

ཏི་ཡོཙ་ཙ་རིང་བེ་ཏོ་རེ། ཀུ་ཀི།

༧། ལྷག་རྟེན་གྱི་པེ་ངོ་ཏང་གེ། དིཏ་ཡོན་དག་ཏུ་ཡོཙ་ཁུད་

ཨན་ཏ་ཏི། ངོ་ལད་བོ། ཙོར་ཨེན་ཏིང་རྒྱུག་ཏོ། ཀུད་གྱི།

༨། དོཧྲུམ་ཀྱེ། ལད་ཀྱེ། ཀུན་ཏྲུམ་སྐུ་ལྷག་གཙུ་བི་སྤེར་ཚང་ཏི་རེ།

༩། ངདོ་ལྷག་གཙུ་ཡོན་དག་ཙི་ཀུ་ལད་ཏུ་ཀུད་སོ། ངོ་ཡལ

རྟེན་གྱི་པ་རེ་ལད་ཏུ། དོ་རང་དོའི་ཀུན་ཏྲུམ་སྐུ་ལྷག་ཀུའི་ཏུ་ཁ

༡༠། ཀྱེ་ནེ་ཚོའི་ཏུ་པེ་ཙ་འུ་ཙང་། པིད་ཁན་ཏེ་ཙི་ཚང་བི་རབ

ཏུ་རག་ཀུད་ཀྱི་ཨི་ལ་ལི། ཡོན་ན་པོན་ཙོག་ཙི་བ་ཏེག་གེ

༡༡། ཨེན་རྒྱུ་མི་ག་ཏུ་ཏུམ་པོལ་ཡམ་ཙན་ཏོད་ཙི། ཡོན

ལོག་མི་ཅན།

༡༢། པེ་ཀུའི་ཨོན་ན་ཀུ་ཞི་ཨེ། དོཙི། ངོ་བེ་ཏེན་ཏིང

ཏེའེ། དོཧྲུམ་ཙི་རིང་ཨད་ཀྱེ་ལ། མིའི་ཏིང་བེའེ། མ་

ཀྱེ་ཡི་ལ་ལི་ཏེ།

༡༣། ངོ་རང་དོ་ཙི། ཕ་རྒྱུམ་ཀི་པ་རེ་ཨེ། ཏེ་རོ་དེ་ཏུ་ཡོག

ཟེ་ག་ཏེ་ཏ་མི་ཡེ་ཀུའུ་པུད་དིང་ཟེ་ཀྱོན་པེ་ཞི་ཙར་ཏི་རེ།

༡༤། ངོ་རེ་ཨན་ཀྱེ་ཀུ་ཏི་རེ། ཨེ་ཀུ་ཏུ། ཀྱེ་ནེ་ཏང་བོ

ཞིབ་མོ། ཚེ་ཀྱི་ཙི་རྟེང་མ་ཁན་ཟེ་པ་མོ། ཡང་གོ་མི་འདི་རང་ལ་མ་ཐེ་
པ་སྐྱུད་ཏེ། ཕྱི་ནེ་གོན་ཅོག་ཏུ་མ་སྒྲུ་རྡུང་པོ་ཀན་ཟ་ཏན། དོ་རྗེ་ནེ་ཉེ་ཙ་ཏོ་ན།
དཔེ་ཟེའི་རང་རྗེ་རིང་བྲུ་ལ་རན་ཟེ་ཡན་ཞོག་ག་མ་ཡན་ཞོག། རན་ཟེ་ནི་ཡ་
མ་རན་ནི། ཀྱུ་ཟི་ཏེས།

༡༥། ཡོན་ན་ཀུན་ཀྱི་ལ། ཡེ་ཤུ་འི་དོ་རྟུ་བ་རེབ་ཉེའི། ཀྱུ་ཏི། ཁྱེ་རིང་
ཀྱི་ནེ་ཀྱི་འུ་དང་ཟེ་ཀྱོན་པེ་ཟ་ཏོ་ཏི། ད་ཡིད་ཙ་ཟང་ཀ་ཀྱི་རིང་ཁན་ཟི་ཏན་
ཏ་ཏི།

༡༦། དོ་ཙ་ཟང་ཀ་རན་ཀྱི། ཡེ་ཤུ་འི་ཀུ་ཏི། དི་རི་མོ་ཡེ་ཚེ་ལི་ཡ་ཏུ་སྐྱུ།
དོ་ཙི་ཏེ་ཟེའི་རང་རྗེ་འུ་སྐྱུར་ཀུ་ཟེམ་ལན་ཏིང་། ཡེ་ཤུ་འི།

༡༧། ཁྱེ་རང་རྗེ་འུ་ཏོད་ཀྱི་དོ་རང་རྗེ་རིང་རན་ཟི། ཁྱེ་གོན་ཅོག་ཏིང་ཏོ་ཏོ། གོན་
ཅོག་ཏིང་རན་ཟེ། ཀུ་ཟི་ཡེ། དོ་རེ་BB་ཀུ་འི་རེ།

༡༨། དོ་རང་ལ་དུ་གི་པ་རེ་ཡེ་ཤུ་འུ་རྒྱམ་པོལ་ཡན་ཏི་རེ། ལ་དུ་གི་པ་རྒྱ་ཚོང་
ཐོག་ཀན། ལི་འི་མི་སྤྱིད་ཀི་མ་ཡན་ཙལ་ཀུ་ཟ་ཏོ་རེ། དོ་ཙི་རྟག་ཏི་རེ།

༡༩། ཡེ་ཤུ་དུ། མོ་ཤེ་འི། ལི་མི་འུ་ཡ་ཚོ་ལི་འི་མེད་ཀྱི་ཁ། ཡོ་ཙ་ཀྱིན
ཟམ་སྐྱུད་དོ། དོ་མི་འི་ཞི་ཡ་ཚོ་འུ་མེད་ཡིན་ཟ་རིང་ཏན་ཀྱི། ཡིན་ཟུ་འུ
ཡ་ཚོ་རིང་ཡོ་ཀྱིན་ཟི་ལ་ཀྱི་ཏིས།

༢༠། དཀྱི་ཙི་མི་ཡ་ཚོ་སྒྲུག་ཏོ་རེ་རེ། ཡ་ཚོ་འི་ཡི་མེད་ཏན་ཀྱི། དོ་ལི་འི།
ཡོ་ཙ་མ་ཏོ་རི།

༤༥

༢༡། དོ་རང་དོ་འབྲུག་ཀ་ཀོ་དོ་མེད་ཀན་ཏེ། ལིའི་ཡོར་ས་བཀྲའི། དོ་བེ་
ཅེ་ཅེ་གྱི་ཙ་དོ་རིང་ལ་ཡོན་ན་ཡེ་བཀྲའི།

༢༢། ཉི་ཅི་མི་འི་ཅི་ལ་དོ་མེ་ཙ་མེད་ཀན་ཏེ། ལིའེ། ཡོ་ཙ་ས་བཀྲའི།
བད་ཏེ་བེ་ཙ་ཐལ་ཟི་དོ་མེ་ཙ་ལ་ལི་རི།

༢༣། ལི་འི་མི་འི་རེ་སྲིད་གི་ཡན་ཅེ་ཏར། དོ་མེ་ཙ་ཡ་ཏུ་མེད་བཀྲད་ཏོ།
ཁྲུ་འུ་ཐལ་ཟི་ཀུང་ནོ། དོ་མེ་ཙ་ཉི་ཅི་མི་འུ་མེད་ཏོ་རི།

༢༤། ཡོན་ན་ཏུག་ཙམ་ལན་ཏིང་པ་བཀྲའི་ཀུ་ཏི། ཤེ་ཕེ་ཚོའི་ཏུ་བེ་
ཙ་ལ་ས་ཉེ་འེ། ཀོན་ཙོག་ཏུ་ཁྱང་ལ་ས་ཉེ་འེ། པེ་ཁ་ཏོ་ཏི།

༢༥། ལི་འི་མི་འི་བད་ཏེ་སྲིད་གི་ཡན་ཅེ་ཏར། མེད་དག་པོ་བཀྲབ་
པིམ་པུད་ལ་ས་ཡན། ཀོན་ཙོ་ཀ་ཏུ་ཡོ་ཉ་ནམ་ཁ་རིང་ཏོད་ཏི་
དོ་ཏང་དུན་དུ་ཀྱུད་ཏོ།

༢༦། སོ་བཀྲ་འུ་པེ་ཙ་འུ་ཧང་། ཚོ་ལེག་ཏུ་བེ་ཙང་ཟི་པུད་ལ་
ཟི་ཏར། ཀོན་ཙོ་ཀ་ཅི། ཀྱེ་ཡབ་ར་ནམ་ཡེ། ཡིད་གད་ཡེ། ཡང་
ཀོབ་སུམ་བི་ལའུ་ཀོན་ཅོག་བཀྲུག་ཀ། ཀུ་སྲི་དོ་མ་ལོག་ཡིན་
ན། རོ་པུད་ལིའི་རིང་ཟི་ཡན་ཙམ་པུད་ས་བཀྲད་ད།

༢༧། ཀོན་ཅོག་ལིའི་མའི་ཏུ་ཀོན་ཅོག་ས་བཀྲུ། སྲིང་གི་ཏུ་ཀོན་ཅོག་
ཀྲུ། དོ་འུ་ཐལ་ཟི་ཀྱེ་ནེ་བོང་པེ་ཁ་ཏོ་ཏི། ཀུ་ཏི།

༢༨། དོ་ཟླ་ལྷ་རིང་ཚེ་འི་རིང་ཁལ་པ་འུ་ཡི་མི་འི་ཟི། དོ་ཅི་

ཡེ་ཤུ་རིང་ཆོས་ཁན་ཞི་ཡེ། ཡེ་ཤུའི་ཉི་ཡི་ལན་རན་ཞི་ཐལ་ལྟོ།

ཡེ་ཤུ་རིང་། གོན་ཅོག་ཏུ་རྒྱ་ཀྱུམ་མཉུ་ཞི་ཙང་ཟི་ཚེ་ཞིལ་ཡང་གོ་ཤུང།

ཏུག་ཀེ།

༢༩། ཡེ་ཤུའི་ཀྱུ་ཏི། གོན་ཅོག་ཏུ་རྒྱ་ཀྱུམ་མཉུ་ཞི་ཙང་ཟི་ཚེ་ཞིལ་དི་ཤུང། ཨེ་ཡིས་ར་ཨེ་ལ། ད་རེ་ཏུ་ཏི། ཨེན་ཤུ་གོན་ཅོག་ཨིད་ཙོ་ཤུང།

༣༠། སྤྲོ་ཏ་ཨེ། ཞེམ་ཨེ། ཏིད་ཨེ། བད་ཏེ་ཤེད་དང་དོ་རིང་། ཆག་ཏི། དོ་བད་ཏེ་རྒྱ་ཀྱུམ་ཞེ་ཙི་ཚེ་ཞིལ་ཤུང།

༣༡། རྒྱའི་ཨིད་ཙོ་རྒྱ་ཀྱུམ་དི་ཤུང། རྒྱན་ཨིན་ན་རིད་ཆག་པ་ཏོན། ཨོན་ན་ཨེ་ན་གར་པ་ཏིད་ཆག་ཡི་ཏིས། དི་རྒྱ་ཀྱུམ་ཏུང་རིད་གི་རྒྱ་ཀྱུམ་ངང་དུན་དུ་ཤུང། དི་ཉི་ང་རྒྱ་ཀྱུམ་ཞེ་ཙི་ཚེ་ཞིལ་རྒྱའི་ཨིད་ཙོ་ལ་མ་ཏོ།

༣༢། དོ་རང་དོ་ཆོའི་རིད་ཁས་པ་ཉུ་མིའི་ཟི། ཨེ་ཀྱུ་ཏུ། ཨིན་ན་ཉུ་ཀྱུ་སྤྲི་དོ་དུང་པོ་ཤུང། གོན་ཅོག་ཨིད་ཙོ་ཤུང། ཏོ་ག་ཞི་ཡ་སྤེལ་མ་ཏོ།

༣༣། དོ་རིད་བད་ཏེ་སྤྲོ་ཏ་ཨེ། ཞེམ་བད་ཏེ་ཨེ། བད་ཏེ་ཤེད་དང་ཆག་ཡི་ཨེ། ཨིང་ཀྱུ་ཉུ་ཅོག་ཀན་ན་གར་ར་ཉུ་མིའི་ཏིད་ལ་ཆག་ཡི་དོ། ཤི་ཀྱུ་ཨེ་ཛིན་སྤྲེཀ་ལ་ཟི་ཞེ་ཙི་ཚེ་ཞིལ་ཤུང་ཀྱུ་ཏི།

༦༧.

༣༤། ཡེ་ཤུ་འི་ཧོ་མི་འི་ཟི། རིག་པེ་ལན་རན་ཞི་ཁན་སྐྱེ། ཧོ་རིང། ཀ་ཀོན་
རྩིག་ཏུ་ནྲ་ལི་རང་ཙམ་ཡེ་ཏོ་ཏོན་ཀུ་ཏི། ཧོ་ཏྲུ་ཐ་ལ་ཟི་ཡ་ཏིང་ལ་ཡེ་ཤུ་ཏུ་
ཧོང་ཟི་པུད་རྟུག་ཙམ་ཏམ་པ་མ་ཀྱི་ཕྲི་རི།

༣༥། ཧོ་རང་ཡེ་ཤུ་འི་ཚོ་ཁང་དྲང་ཚོ་འི་ཀམ་པུ་ཡིན་པར་རྟུག་ཏི། ཚོ་
རིང་ཁལ་པ་ཏུ་མི་འི་ཙོ་མ་ཤི་ཀ་ད་བིད་ཏུ་ཡོ་ཙ་ཤུ་ཀུ་ཏེམ་ཧོ་ཀྱམ་ཤུ།

༣༦། ད་བིད་ཡིན་ཟི་འི་དམ་པ་ཏུ་ཏྲུག་ཉིད་ཙོ་བིང་བེ། ཡིན་ན་ཀུ་ཏི།
སྐྱེ་ཏུ་ཡོན་དག་ཏིང་ཀོན་ཙོག་ཙེ། ང་ཀ་སྐྱེ་ཏུ་སུ་ཙང་དུ་པིང་ཟི་ཧེ། སྐྱེ་ཀ་ཤུ་
ཀྱུ་འི་རི་བད་ཏེ་ཀ་ནུ་པང་དུ་ལེ་ཧྲང་ཀྱིད་ཐལ། ཡོན་ན་ཀུད་ཀྱེ།

༣༧། ད་བིད་དེ་མ་ཤི་ཀ་རིང་ཡོན་དག་ཀུད་ཧོ། ད་བིད་ཏུ་ཡོ་ཙ་ཀྱུད་
ཤུ་ཏེ། ཡོན་ན་རྟུག་ཏི། བང་མི་འི་ཙི་ཡེ་ཤུ་ཏུ་སྤྲད་རེ་ཏི་ཐ་དི་རི།

༣༨། ཨལ་ཀྱི་ཚོ་འི་ཀན་ཀྱི་ཀུ་ཏི། ཚོ་འི་རིང་ཁལ་པ་ཏུ་མི་འི་ཏུ་
ཧོང་ཟི་བ་ཙེག་ཏི། ཧོ་ཙོ་ཚོ་འི་ཏུ་ཁམ་ཏུད་ཀྱི་ཁམ་ཟ། ཨ་སྨུ་ཨེ་
སྐྱུ་ཏི་ཙོ་ཡམ་ཙི། མི་འི་ཙོ་ད་ཏིང་ལྟུག་ལ་ཟི་ཨེ།

༣༩། རྟུན་ཨོ་སུ་དར་སང་བད་ཏེ་བེ་ཙོ། ཡང་བེ་ཙོ་དྲལ་ཏིང་
ཧེབ་པི་ཐ་པ་ཏོ་རི།

༤༠། ཧོ་ཙི་དག་པོ་ལི་འེ་ཀྲེ་ཙ་ཏུ་ཀྱམ་ཟེ་འེ་ལ། རྟུད་ཀྱི་སོ་ལ་
ཏ་ཙ་ཏོ་ར། ཧོ་ཧྲིང་ཤེབ་ཆ་ད་པ་ཡོག་ཏོ།

༤༡། ཡོན་ཏར་ཡེ་ཤུ་ས་ཀྱམ་སུ་ཀམ་སུ་ཏུམ་པོ་ལ་རྡོང་

༥༨

མིའི་ཙི་གམ་སྨུང་ཟུང་ཀ་སྐེ་ཟི་ཧང་གེ།

༤༢། དོང་དག་པོ་མིའི་ཡིད་ཙ་མ་ཧོད་ཀྱི་མེ་ཙ་ཡན་སྐྱེ། ཀྱི་ཧི་ཧྲེ་ལལ
སྐྱེ་ཟི་ཡེ།

༤༣། ཡེ་ཤུའི་བད་ཧེ་ལོབ་བྲུག་ཧེ་ཧིང་། དེང་ཡན་ཧ་ཧེ། སྐྱེ་སྐྱེན
ཧིང་དྲུང་པོ་ཀུ་ཟ་ཧོལ། དི་ལོ་ཉམ་སྲུ་གམ་སྨུནང་ཟུང་ཀ་སྐེ་ཟི་པ་བད་
ཧེ་ཝེ་ཙི། དོ་མི་ཙི་བོང་ཀྱི་རི།

༤༤། ཁུ་ཏུ་ཐལ་ཟི་ཀུད་ཧོ། དེ་ཙི་ཡིན་ཟ་ཧྲུ་བོང་ཧོར་ཧུ་ཝི་ཀུང་ཟི་
རན་སྐྱེ། དེ་མེ་ཙི་ཡིན་ཟུ་ཏུ་ཆུང་གི་ཚོར་ཧུ་དོང་ཟི་ཞིན་སྐྱི། ཡིན་ཟུ་ཏུ་སྐྱིང་
མིམ་ཀླུལ་ཡ་ལེག་ཧོ་རི། བད་ཧེ་ཧྲུ་ཧི། ཀུ་ཏི།

ལུ་ལུམ་ལེ་ཏུ་ཏུ་ནང་།

༡། དོ་རང་ཡེ་ཤུ་ཚོ་ཁང་དུང་ཟི་ཚོས་ལི་ཡེ། ལོབ་བྲུག་ཧེ་ཧུ་ཝི་ཙང་
ཟི་ཡི་དི་འི། ཡེ་ཀུ་ཧུ། ལ་ཧུ། དི་རག་ཡེ་པང་ཟྲི་ཁྲུན་ཧོད་ཙི།

༢། ཡོན་ན་ཀུ་ཟིམ་ལན་ཧིང་ཡེ་ཤུའི་ཀུ་ཏི། དི་ཉི་གི་པང་སྐྱི་དོ
ཧང་ཧ་ཧོ་ཧི་ཡ། དེང་ཡིད་ཙ་རག་ཧུ་ཟོག་ཟིད་ཡིད་ཙ་རག་ལམ
སྐྱེ་སྲུ། བད་ཧེ་ཚིག་ཀེ་ཡི་ལ་ཧོ།

༣། དོ་རང་སྨེ་ཧུན་ཟུཁ་ཧོད་ཀྱི་བཏ་ཏང་། ཚོ་ཁང་དུ་ཧུམ་པོལ་
ཧེད་ཧར། ཁུའི་མི་མ་ཧོ་རི་རེ། ཀེ་ལ་ཡེ། ཡ་གོབ་ཡེ། ཡོ་
ན་ཡེ། ཡན་དྲི་ཡུ་པི་མི་ལེ། ཡེ་ཤུ་རིང་ཧུག་ཧི་རེ།

༤། རྡོ་བད་ཏེ་ཨལ་ལ་ལེ་སྐུད་ཏོ། རྡོ་བད་ཏེ་རྡུབ་སེམ་ཏག་ཁྲ་སྐུར། རྟེ
ཏིང་གུ་ཀི་ཏིས།

༥། ཡོན་ཉན་རྡུག་ཅེམ་ལན་ཏིང་ཡེ་སྐུའི་གུ་ཏི། ཡི་མི་འི་ཟི་སྐྱེན་ཏིང་
ལ་རྡེབ་ཨར་ལ་ཟིམ་ཐལ་ཟེ། བཅེག་ཏི།

༦། བོང་མི་འི་ཅི་སྐྱེ་ཞུ་མིན་གན་སྐྱི་ཨན་ཏོ་རེ། བོང་མི་འི་ཅི་སྐྱེ་ཨ་ཡི་
ག་སྐུག་ག་གུད་སྐྱེ། བོང་མི་འི་ཏིང་ལ་རྡེབ་རན་ཞུ་རེ།

༧། ཨས་སྐྱེ་སྐྱེ་ནེ་མག་ཡེ་ཨག་ཏུ་སྤྱུད་ཨལ་ལེ་ཐས་སྐྱེ་ལ།
བེད་ཟླ་བེ་ཏི། ཡོན་ཉན་སྐུ་བེ་ཏིན་སྐྱེ་ལ། ཐམ་ཞུ་རྡག་ཨའི་ཏ་ལ་
མ་ཡིད།

༨། མི་གུད་ཡེ་ཡོག་ཏེ་ཅི་ཡི་དི་འི་ཡེ་དི་རིང་ཏོ་ལོག་ལད་
ཏུ་རེ། སྒ་ཏ་སྒ་ཏ་དེ་ཁ་སྒང་སང་གུལ་ཡེ། ལམ་གོན་ཡེ།
ཝེད་ཨན་ཏོ། རྡོ་ཚེར་ཟི་ཨ་དང་བོ་སྐུར།

༩། རྡོ་བེ་ལྷུ་ཙིང་སྐྱེན་ཚན་ཐན་ལད་ཏི། སྐྱེ་ཞུ་ཐལ་ཟི་རྡོ་ཅི་
སྐྱེ་ནེ་ལེ་ཏེ་ཏུ་གུ་ཏ་ཏིང་རན་སྐྱེ། ཐྲིམ་ཁང་དུ་ཏུམ་བོལ་ཏིང་
ཏུ་རེ། རྡོ་ཏི་དི་པང་པོ་རྫོས་སེམ་ཐལ་ཟི། སྐྱེ་ཉེ་བ་ཛིར་ཡེ།
རར་རྫ་ཞུ་ཏུམ་བོལ་སྐྱི་ལ་ཏུ་རེ།

༡༠། གུ་འི་ཐ་མ་ཞུ་ཧག་ཏུ་ཏུམ་བོལ། དི་ལན་སྤུར་ར་ཞུ་
ཀི་གུད་པད་ཏེ་ཏིང་། ཐྲིན་ཟང་སྒ་ཅི་ཨམ་པི་ཏིས།

༡༡། དོ་ཙ་ཅི་ནི་ཀྱུའི་ཧི་ཛམ་ཀྱི། ཤིལ་ཏར། ཅིའི་ཀྱི་ཀུ་ཧི་རིས།
དོ་ཁྱུ་ཐལ་ཟེ་མིད་ཐ་ལད་ཏི། དོ་ཞེ་ལྷ་རིང་ཅིན་ཏིང་ཀྱུ་རྣ་ཡི་ཏོ་ཏ།
ཡོན་ཅ་པཀད་ཏི། ཅིན་པྲ་ཞེ་པ་ཨ་པཀུད་ཏི། ཏམ་པ་ཀུ་རྒྱུག་ཀེད་ཅེ
ཐུད་རྣ་གྱི་པཀུ།

༡༢། དོ་ཞེ་ལྷ་རིང་ཨ་ཙོ་ཞེ་ཡིན་ཧུ་ཀུ་སྐུག་ཡེ། ཡ་ཞེ་ཡིན་ཧུད
ཡོ་ཙ་མི་ལ་ཅི་པ་རེ་ཏུ་ཤུ་ཀྲིང་རན་ཧུ། ཀི་ཏ་ཡོ་ཙ་ཅི་ཡ་ཏ
ཡ་མ་རིང་ངོ་ལོག་ལད་ཀྱི། སད་ཏུ་རེ།

༡༣། ཀྱི་ཀུ་མིན་ཏུ་ཐལ་ཟི་ཀྱིན་ཏིང་ཆིག་པ་ལད་ཏུ་རེ།
ཡ་རི་ས་ཐ་མ་ཏར་ཆེ་ཀེ་ཅན་ཏན་ལད་ཀྱི་ཧོད་ཅོ། ཉན་དེལ
རྒྱུག་ཏོ།

༡༤། རི་ཀྱུན་ཡ་ཅི་ལོག་ཀ་ལ་སམ་ལོ་ཙར་ཏི། ཡལ་ཞེ
ཀྱི་ཞེ་པཀིག་ཅི་རིང་ཐད་ཀྱི། སང་གི་སེ་དོ། མ་ཁོ་ཞི་ས་ཀྱུད
དིང་ཧོབ་ཡི་ཏང་ཅོ། ཐཏཏ་རིང་པོག་ཏི།

༡༥། ཡ་རི་ཡ་ལང་ཏིང་པཀུད་པོ། ལོ་ཧང་ཐ་ཏིག་སེ་ཏི།
ཅང་ཟི་ཀྱུ་ཅོ་པཀད་ཏོན་ཅིམ་ཐལ་ཟི་ཅང་རིང་ཐ་ཡི་ལ་ལ

༡༦། ཡ་རི་ཡ་རི་རིང་ཡི་གྱི་པཀུད་ཅོ། ཁམ་ཀྱུ་ཅི་ཀྱུམ་ཀུ
སྐྱིང་ རིང་ཐ་ཡན་ཏ་ཏི།

༡༧། ཧོ་ཞེ་ལྷ་རིང་ཁོག་ཟང་སེ་ཙ་རེ་ཡ་ཀྱུ་ཀྱུ་རན་ཞི

མཆིང་དེ་ཀི་མ་བཀྱེ།

༡༨ ཀྱེ་ནི་པོག་པེམ་ཞེ་ལྷ་ཀུན་ཀི་ཞེ་ལྷ་རིང་མ་ཡམ་པེམ་ཐལ་ཀི་
མོ་ལམ་ལང་ཏི།

༡༩། དོ་གྲུ་ཐལ་ཟེ་ཀུད་ནོ། གོན་ཅོག་ཅི་སེམ་ཅན་བད་ཏེ་པ་
ཏེག་ཏེམ་ཐ་ལང་། ཡོན་ན་དུག་ངལ་མོ་ཏེ་མ་བཀུད་མིན། ཐལ་ཟེ་
ལ་མ་བཀྱེ།

༢༠། དོ་དུག་ངལ་དུ་རྟག་ཏུ་མིག་གོན་ཅོག་ཅི་ཆུང་གི་མ་ལད་
ཀྱང་། ཡིད་ཅོ་མི་ལ་མ་ཐར་ཏུ། ཡིན་ཟེ་འི་ཞི་ཏེག་སྒྲུ་མི་འི་
ཐལ་ཟེ་གོན་ཅོག་ཅི་དོ་རྟག་ཏུ་མིག་ཆུང་གི་ལའི།

༢༡། དེ་ཞེ་ལྷ་རིང་ཡི་མི་འི་ཟེ་ཀྲེན་ཏིང་། ཁན་ཏེ། མ་ཀི་ཀ་
རིང་ཏོ་ཏོ། ཀི་དོང་ཏོ་ཏོ། ཀུད་ཀྱེ་ལ། དེན་ཐ་ཆེལ་ཏི།

༢༢། ཧབ་ལི་ཙུ་མ་ཀི་ཀ་ཡི། ཧབ་ལི་ཙུ་སྦྲོལ་རན་ཞི་པ་
ཞིང་ཏོ་ས་ལ། ཡམ་ཅིན་ཀ་སྣམ་ཀན་ཏེ་ཡེ། གོན་ཅོག་ཏུ་
ཞི་ཏེག་སྒྲུ་མི་འི་ཏིང་པ་རེབ་ལ་ཟེ་ཏ་རཅོ། དོ་ཏིང་ཡ་རེབ་
ལད་ཏུ་རེ།

༢༣། དོ་ཙུ་ཐལ་ཟེ་ཀྱི་ཏེ་ཆན་ཐན་ལད་ཏི། ཁན་ཏེ། དི་བད་ཏི་
ཀྲེན་ཏིང་ཏུང་རིང་ཀུད་མིན།

༢༤། དོ་རང་དོ་དུག་ངལ་ཏུ་ཐ་ལང་ཡེ་ཀ་སྒྲུག་ཀི། ལ་ཙོ་ངལ་འི་

འདྲ་མ་ཀྱི་སྡེ། ༡༢

༢༥ ། ཞིམ་ཁ་རྡིང་ཟེ་ཀར་རྡད་ཀྱི། ལར་ག་རྡིང་ཏོད་ཀྱི་ཀར་ཏེ་ཏྲུར་ཏོ་རེ།

༢༦ ། དོ་རང་མི་འདིའབད་ཏེ་ཅི་མི་ཡྲུ་ཡོང་ཡིང་ག། ལྡེད་ཡེ་ཟི་ལ་བིང་ངོ།

ཡི་དྲུ་ཞོག་ཞིང་ལས་ཆས་ཡི་ཕྲང་ཏོ་རེ།

༢༧ ། དོ་རང་མི་ཡྲུ་ཡོ་ཅོ་ཅེ་ ... ཡོ་ན་རེ་ཅར་ཀྱི། དོ་ཡྲུ་བི་ཏེག་ལུ་མིའི་

ཐད་ཏེ་ལན་ལྷར་རཡྲུ་ཡི་འི་ཆོག་ལིང་བི་བྲུ་རེག་ཀ། ཞམ་ཁ་ཡྲུ་ཏྲུག་

ཏར་ཚེ་ག་དྲུལ་ཀྱི་ཀན་ཏྲུ་རེ།

༢༨ ། ང་ལེ་ཡབ་ཀུ་སྦྱི་ཐུབ་ཁན་ཀྱི། ཡི་པེ་ཕྱུ་སི་ཏི། དོ་ཡྲུ་ཐན་དིང་

ལྡེད་ཡན་ཀྱི། ལབ་སྤུང་ངོ། སྐྱེ་ལོ་གི་པོ་ལ་ཅིས་ཡོ་ཧོ་ཏེ། ཀུད་ཀྱི་

ཀྱི་ན་ནེ་ཐ་ཏ་ཏི།

༢༩ ། དོ་ཡྲུ་ཅོག་ཀན་ཀྱི་ན་དོ་ཏག་བད་ཏེ་དྲུབ་པི་ཏང་ཆོ། ཐ་ཆ་ཡྲུ་

ཛག་པ་ཉི་ཐེ་ཟུ་ཏི།

༣༠ ། ཀྱི་ཀྱན་ཏིང་ཐུང་པོ་ཀུ་ ... ལ། དེ་མི་རབ་གོབ་པེམ་པེ་ཀྱི་

དྲུང་རིང་དོ་བད་ཏེ་ཏྲུབ་ལོ་ཏེ།

༣༡ ། ནམ་ཁ་ ... ཏི་ཉི་ ... ལ་མ་ཏི་ལྡུད་ཀྱི་ལ། ཀྱེ་ཡྲུ་ཀུ་

སྦྱི་དོམ་ཏི་མ་ལྡུད།

༣༢ ། དོ་བད་ཏེ་དབ་ལིམ་ཏག་ལས་ཆུ་ཀྱོད་དྲུ་ཚོད་ཡས་ཏིང་ལམ་

ལྡུད།

༣༤། ད་བེ་ལྦ་པི་པིམ་རྒྱན་ཇེན་ཏེར་མཁྲུད་ཟང་། ནན་ཐན་ལང་ཏི།
དོལ་ཐ་དོས་ཏི། མོ་ལམ་ཏད་ཏི།

༣༥། ཡི་མི་ཀྱུའི་དེ་ཀ་ཁ་ཞང་ཚོང་རིང་མི་ལ་ཏར། ཡིན་ཟུ་ཊུ་རྒྱས་
ཡོག་པོ་ཏུ་ཁག་ལད་ཀྱི། ཡོག་པོ་ཏེང་ཁང་རན་ཀྱི། ཡིད་ཙོ་
ཡིད་ཙོ་མི་འི་རིང་ཡིད་ཙོ་ཡིད་ཙོ་ཏུལ་རན་ཀྱི། པི་ཏང་ཏུན་ཀྱི་པ་
རིང་། ནན་ཐན་ལ་ཏུ་ཡོན་ན་ཀྱུ་ཏི།

༣༦། དོཏུ་ཚོག་ཀན་གྱི་ཉེ་ལ་ནན་ཐན་ལང་ཏི། ཡོན་དག་
པིར་དོ་ཀི་ཏ་ཚེན་ལེད་དེང་། ཀིཧམ་ཟང་ཏར། ཀི་ངར་དོ། ཡི་
ལེ་ཡམན་ཏོ། གྱེན་ཏིང་རྒྱན་མ་ཏོ།

༣༧། དོ་རྒྱན་མ་ཏི་རིང་ཡམན་ནོ། གྱེ་ཕེ་དོས་གྱི་ཏང་ཚེམ་བེད་ཏོ་ཏོ།

༣༨། གྱེ་གྱེན་ཏིང་ཀྱེ་ཀྲུད་གྱི་ལ། ཏོ་མི་འི་བད་ཏེ་ཏིང་ལ་
ཀྲུ་ཞ་ཏོལ། གྱེ་ཀྲུ་ཞ་ཏོལ། ནན་ཐན་ལང་ཏི།

སྨུ་པི་ལེ་ཏུ་ཏུ་ནང་།

༡། དོ་རང་པེ་སག་ཏུ་ཉི་ཁི་ཛག་ཏིང་། ཡེ་ཞ་ཞ་རིང་ཞེ་མ་ཀྱེ་
ཞི མ་ཉི་ཁི་ཛག་ཡམའི་ཏ་མ་པིད་ཀྱི། ཉིར་ཀྱལ་ཏུང་
རིང་། ཚོའི་རིང་ཁས་པ་ཏུ་མི་འི་རེ་ཡེ། ཏེ་ཞིལ་ལ་མ་བད་ཁེ
ཀྱི། པེ་ཁུ་ཁས་པ་ཏུ་ཐབ་ཙོ་ཙུམ་ཙི་པེ། སཙིམ་ཐབ་པེད་ཀྱི།
ཡི་དིའི་ཡི་དི་རིང་།

༢༥༤

༢། ཉི་མའི་ཧག་ཏུ་ཝེ་ལྷ་རིང་རྩེ་མཚོ། ནགར་རཏྣ་མི་འི་རི་ཚིག་པ་ཟ་
ཏོ་རེ། ཡོནན་ཟ་ལད་ཏི། གྱུ་ཏི་རེ།

༣། དོ་རང་ཡེ་ཤུ་ཝེ་ཐན་ཡཱ་ཀུ་སྤྱེན་གར་རར། ལི་མོན་ཧེ་སྲིད་ཀྱི་རྒྱུ་
ཀྱུས་སྐུང་རྫོད་ཏར། ཟ་མེན་ཟད་ཏར། ཡི་མེ་ཚོ་ཉི་མའི་དྲི་ཟང་ཡེ། བོང་
ལ་རུ་བོ་ཏོལ་ཀན་ཀྱི། བོ་ཏོལ་ཐགྲུ་ཀྱི། དྲི་ཟང་ཡེ་ཤུ་རུ་བལ་༔
ལིང་ཐོར་ཏི།

༤། ཡང་གོ་རེ་ཤི་འི་རེ་མ་ཐད་ཀྱི། ཡི་དི་འི་ཡི་དི་རིང་ཀྱུ་ཏི། དྲི་ཟང་
ཡིན་ན་ཁྱུ་ཏེ་ཚེ་རན་མོ། ཕན་ཏོག་ཁྱུ་ཏོ་ཏོ།

༥། དོ་དྲི་ཟང་སྐྱུམ་རྟ་ཝེ་ཚོ་ལ་བོང་ཟང་ཀ་ཏིང་ལང་ཀེ། མ་ཏོད་
ཀྱི་ཏིང་རན་མོ། ཉི་མའི་ཏོད་ཚོ་ཀུད་ཀྱི། མེ་ཚོ་རིང་མ་ཐ་དི།

༦། དོ་རང་ཡེ་ཤུ་འི། དི་མེ་ཚོ་ཉི་མའི་རིང་ཧོབ་པི་རན་ཏི། ཁྱུ་རིང་
ཁོག་རྟུག་ལ་ཟི་རན་ཟ་ཏོ་ཏོ། དོའི་ཀྱེ་རིང་ཉི་མའི་ཏུས་ལད་ཀྱི།

༧། མ་ཏོད་ཀྱི་མི་འི་རེ་དྲུ་འི་ཀན་ཏིང་ཀྱེན་ཏང་ཀྱམ་པོ་ཧོད་
ཏོ་རེ། ཨལ་ལེ་ཟ་ཱ་ཙུ་ལ། དོ་ཏིང་ཡ་ཤ་ལ་ཟི་རེ་ཏོ་ཀྱེ་
རྒྱུའི་ཀྱུན་ཏིད་ཀྱེན་ཏང་ཉམ་པོ་མ་ཏོལ།

༨། དི་མེ་ཚོ་ཁྱུ་ཏར་ཀྱི་དོ་ལད་ཀྱི། དོའི་ཀྱི་རུ་རྟུག་ཟིང་དྲི་
ཟང་བོར་ཚེ་དོ། ཀྱེ་རོམ་ཁང་དུང་པི་པིམ་ཏུང་རིད་རོམ་ཁང་
དུང་ལ་ཟི་ཏིན་ཀྱི་ཟྲིམ་རྟུབ་ཀྱེ་དྲི་ཟང་བོར་ཏི།

༩། ཀྱེ་ཀྱེན་ཆེང་ལྡང་པོ་ཀུ་ཞ་ཏོལ། ཏི་ལན་ལྷུར་རང་ཁྱུང་བྱིན་ཟང་
ཀཀྲ་ཀྱེ་ལ། ཏི་མེ་ཙེ་ཡོན་ཏན་ཁྱོ་ལད་ཙེ་ཏོ་ཀྱེ་ཏ་ལ་ཞིམ་ཞལ་ཞི།ཀོང་
ཏོ། ཀུ་ཏི།

༡༠། ཏོ་རང་ལ་ཉི་ཛི་མི་ལོ་བ་ལྷུག་ཧེ་ཏུ་བི་ཚང་ཟེ་ཡིད་ཙི། ཡུ་ཏུ་ཀར
ཡོད་པ་ཀུ་ཤྲི་ཏོ། ཡེ་ཤུ་ཀྲྀ་ཤྚེའི་རི་ཏུ་ཀུ་ཀ་ཏེང་རན་ཞིམ་ཞལ་ཞི།ཏེ
ཞིལ་ལ་མ་ཏུ་ཏུམ་པོ་ཡོ་ཡིལ་ལི།

༡༡། ཏོ་ཙི་ཏོ་ཡུད་ཟ་ཙེ་ཡེ། ཐོང་ཟད་ཀྱེ། ཀཞིང་ཞང་ཀ་ཏུ་བ་ཡིག
རན་ཞ་ཞི། ཀུ་ཏི་རེ། ཏོ་ཏུ་ཞལ་ཞི་ཏོའི་ཡེ་ཤུའི་རི་ཏུ་ཀུ་ཏེང་
རན་ཞིམ་ཟབ་པེ་ཏི།

༡༢། ཏོ་རང་ཡེ་ཞ་ཞ་རིང་ཏེ་མ་ཀྱེ་ཞིམ་ཧག་མེ་ཚིང་།པེ་ལག་ཏུ
ཀུར་ཙེ་ལ་ཙོམ་བེ་ལྷ་རིང་། ལོབ་ལྷུག་པད་ཧེ་ཙེ་ཡེ་ཤུ་རིང་། ཀྱེ་ཧྲ
ཟ་ལ་ཞི་པེ་ལག་ཏུ་ཀུར་ཙེ་ཁྱུང་ལམ་ཙེ་ཏུག་ཀེ།

༡༣། ཡེ་ཤུའི་ལོབ་ལྷུག་ཧེ་ཏུ་བི་ཚང་ཞི་ཉི་མི་ཙར་ཀྱེ། ཏཞ
རེ་རང་ཡི་ལ་ལ་ཙེ། ཏོང་ཏན་ཙེ་ཀུར་ཙེ་པ་མི་ལྡང་ཏོམ་ཟོ་ཧེ་ཙེ།
ཏོའུ་ཟ་ལང་ཞི་ཡི་ལ་ལ་ཙེ།

༡༤། ཏོ་ཡང་པོ་ཀྱམ་ལྷུང་ཡི་ལ་ཧོ། ཀྱིན་ཙེ་ལ་ཡི་ལ་ཀྱེ།
ཡོན་ཏག་ཧིང་ཀུད་ཞི། ཡེ་ཤུའི་ཡིན་ཞུའུ་ལོབ་ལྷུག་ཧེ་ཧང་
ཀྱམ་པོ་པེ་ལག་ཏུ་ཀུར་ཙེ་ཟ་ཞི་མ་ཁྱུང་ཧོ་ཧོ། ཏུག་ཙེ་ཧིས།

༧༦

༡༥། ཇོ་རང་དོ་འི་སྒྲིན་ཅི་ཏིང་པོ་ཤི་ཞིང་ལི་ཟ་མེད་ཟ་འིམ་ཨེ་་
པང་མིག་ཀན་ཧུ། དོང་ཨེན་ཤུ་ཐ་ལ་ཟེ་ཆག་ཀན་ལ་དེ་ཅི།
༡༦། དོ་གུ་ཨི་ལ་སྦྱེ། བ་རྡུ་ར་རང་པིད་སྦྱེ། ཡེ་ཤུ་འི་གུ་ཀྱི་ཚོག་ཀན་
ཧུབ་ལི་རི། ཇོ་རང་དོ་གུ་འི་པེ་ལ་ག་ཏུ་གུ་ར་ཅོ་ལམ་པི་གུ།
༡༧། ཤི་ར་དོ་ཡེ་ཤུ་ལུ་ཏི་ཧི་མི་འབོབ་བྲུག་ཏེ་ཏང་ནམ་ཤོང་་
ལན་སྦྱེ།
༡༨། དོ་རེ་བང་ཏེ་ཛོད་ཀྱི་ཟ་འི་ཟ་ལ། ཡེ་ཤུ་འི་གུ་ཏི། སྦྱེ་རྒྱུ་འི་
ཙང་ཟེ་སྦྱི་རང་ནམ་པོ་ཟ་འི་པ་ཨིད་ཅེ་ཀྱི་ཤུ་འི་རི་ཏུ་གུ་ཏ་ཏེང་རན་ཧུ།
༡༩། སུ་ཐི་ཨེ་དོ་ཏིང་ཚེར་ལན་སྦྱེ། ཞི་དི་འི། སྦྱེ་ཤུག་ཀ་ལམ།
ཀྱུ་འི་ཅོ་ཀྱེ་ཤུག་ཀ་ལམ། རྟུག་ཀེ།
༢༠། ཡེ་ཤུ་འི་གུ་ཏི། ལ་ཏི་ཛི་མི་ཙུ་པི་ཙང་ཟེ་ཨིད་ཅོ་ཀྱེ་
རང་ནམ་པོ་གུད་པེ་ཏ་ལ་ཏུ་ཏང་སྦྱེ་ཐི་པ་དོ་ཤུ་ཏ།
༢༡། མི་ཏུ་ཡོ་ཅོ་ཨིང་ཀ་ཏུང་རིང་ཀོན་ཚོག་ཏུ་བློལ་རྣ་སྒྲིཨུ
ཅོན་ཀན་ལི་འི་ཏིན་སྦྱེ་ལ། མི་ཏུ་ཡོ་ཅོ་ཤུ་འི་རི་ཏུ་གུ་ཏ་ཏེང་
རག་ཐི་པ་དོ་རིང་ཏི་ཤི་མ་ཤུ་ཏ། དོ་མི་མོ་ཧེ་མ་ཀྱིན་མིན་ཅོ།
ཛོ་རིང་དོ་པི་ཅོ་ལ་ཏི་ཤི་ཀོ་རི།
༢༢ དོ་རང་ཟ་མེད་ཟད་ཏ་ར་ཡེ་ཤུ་འི་ཨེ་ཐུ་ཤིན་སྦྱེ། མོ་ལམ་
ཏབ་པ་བསྒྲུ་ཁྱེ། འབོབ་བྲུག་ཏེ་ཏིང་རན་སྦྱེ་གུ་ཏི། དི་སྦྱེ་ཨུ

རྒྱག་སྐྱེ། ཞིན་ལྷོ་ཟ་དེ། ཡོངས་ཀྱུ་ཏི།

༢༣། དོ་རྫོང་ཀར་ཡོལ་ཞིན་ལྟེ། མོ་ལམ་ཏད་ལྟེ། དོ་ཏིང་རན་ལྕི། དེ་ཕྱི་
དོ་བླ་ནང་ཟི་ཏུར་རི་རེ།

༢༤། ཨམ་ལྟེ་ཡོ་སྐྱི། དེ་ལྷེ་ཟུ་སྐྱི་སྐྱེ། དེ་རྒྱུ་ཞི་ཆད་ཀདུ་སྐྱི་ཝོང་
ཝོང་མི་ཞི་ཏུ་ཐལ་ཟི་ཝོར་ཙོ་ཨན་ཏོ།

༢༥། ཤེ་ལྟེན་ཏིང་དུང་པོ་ཀུ་ཊ་ཏོལ། དིང་ཟི་ཐ་ལང་། ཀོན་ཆོག་ཏུ་དུ་ལིཝ
ནང་རྒྱུ་ཞི་ཏུར་ཏར་ཚེ་ཀ། ཤེ་ཀུན་དུམ་ཕུ་ཚ་ཙུ་པལ་ལ་རིང་ཟི་མ་ཏུང་ག་
ཨོན་ན་ཀྱུ་ཏི།

༢༦། དོ་རང་བ་ཟུ་ལི་ཝུ་གིཏ་ཀུད་ལྟེ། དོ་རི་བད་ཏེ་ཝི་རིང་ཟེ་ཏུན་ཕུ་ཚ་ཏོད་
ལྟི་བ་ཙ་ཙ་རིང་ཡི་ལ་ལི་རེ།

༢༧། དོ་རང་ཡོ་སྐྱི་དོ་ཏིང་། དི་ཝིར་དོ་ལྟེ་ཞེ་བད་ཏེ་ཏུ་དད་པ་ཝུ་སོད
ཡ་ལ་ཤེ་ཡི་ལ་ཏོ། ཀོར་ཙོག་ཏུ་ནོ་ལ་རན་ཟི་པ་ཏུ་པེ་ཙ་ཝུ་ནང་། ཡི་ནན
ཀུ་ལྷི་ཏོ་ཏོ། ཤེ་མ་རགྱུ་ཏེང་ཏལ། ཀུར་ཙོ་རེ་བད་ཏེ་ཡན་ལྟེ་ཡི་ལ་ཏོ།
དོ་ཝོ་ལ་དུབ་ཝོ་ཏོ།

༢༨། དོ་རང་ཤེ་ལྷིང་གི་ཨན་ཙོམ་ཐ་ལང་། ཤེ་ལྟེན་ཝེ་ཕྱི་ཏུང་རིང་ག་
ལི་ལ་ཏེ་ག་སྐྱང་ཡི་ལ་ཏོལ། ཀྱུ་ཏི།

༢༩། དོ་རང་ཀ་ཝེ། དོ་རེ་བད་ཏེ་ཏུ་དད་པ་ཡ་ལ་ཤེ་ལ། ལྷེ་ཝུ་དད་པ་
མོ་ཙེ་མ་ཡ་ལ་ཀུད་ལྟེ།

༨༢

༢༠། ཡེ་ཤུ་འི། སྐྱེ་ཀ་རྒྱེང་དྲང་པོ་ཀྱུ་ཙ་ཏོལ། དི་ཡིན་རྟོ་ཀྱུ་ཀྱུ་ཀྱི་འི་ཤི་རྩེ
རྒྱུ་གཏི་རྟ་རྒྱུ་ཀ་རན་ཏ་རང་ཆེ་ཀ། ཀ་འི་སྲུ་སྲུ་རྒྱུན་ཏྲི་ཡེ་ཤུ་ལ་རི་ཤུད་དེ་ཀྱི་མ་སེམས་ཀ་
ཀྱུད་རྩེ་ཐབ་ཤི་སྐྱ་ཏོན། ཀྱུད་རྩེ་ལུ

༢༡། གེ་ཕོ་དྲུང་རིང་པོ་ཙོ་ལ་བོང་རྒྱན་ཏྲི་ཀྱུབ་པ། ཤེ་རྩེར་དང་ཉམ་ཤོ་ཤི་འི་ཤིན
རྩེ་ལ། སྐྱེ་ཡེ་ཤུ་མ་སེམས་ཀ་ཡོ་རྟེ་མ་ཀྱུབ་ཀ། ཀྱུ་རྡེ་ཡེ། ཀྱི་འི་ཙེ་ལ་ཡོན་ཏན་ཡེ་
ཀྱུ་ཏི་ར།

༢༢། དོ་རང་དོ་རྗེ་ཡོད་ཀྱི་མ་ཆེ་ཀྱུ་ཤི་ཡི་ལུག་གང་ཤིན་རྩེ། ཡེ་ཤུ་འི། སྐྱེ་མཁོ་
ལ་མ་ཏ་ཙེ་དོང་ཡིལ་ཏོལ། ཡོན་ཏང་ཆེ་ཀ་ཤིན་རིང་རྫོད་ཏི། ཀྱུད་རྩེ།

༢༣། གེ་ཕབ་ཡེ། ཕ་གཞིབ་ཡེ། ཡོ་ཏང་ཏན་ལུམ་པི་ལ་ཉམ་པོ་སྐྱིལ་ཀྱི། ཡེ་ཤུ་རིང་བོ་ཚེང
ཡེ་དང་བུད་ཡན་ཚེ།

༢༤། དོ་རྗེ་ལུམ་པི་ལ་ཏིང་། སྐྱི་ལུ་སེམས་རིང་ཤི་འིམ་ཁོ་འི་ཚིང་ཡམ་མ་པི་ཡེ། སྐྱེ་ཚེ
རིང་རྫོད་ཏི། དོས་ཐ་དོས་ཏི་ཀྱུད་རྩེ།

༢༥། རྫོད་ཏན་རྒྱུ་པོག་ཤིང་ཡིལ་ལ་སྐྱེ། དི་པེ་ལྷ་རིང་ཟེ་ཐར་པི་ལ་ཀྲུ་ཀྱུ་ཏི།

༢༦། ཡམས་ཀྱི་ཡེ་ཤུ་འི། ཡེ་སྐྱི་ལུ་ཡབ་པ། སྐྱེ་ཚེ་ལུ་རིང་ཐད་ཀྱི་ལ། ལ་ཟེ་ཏང་ཙ་ཏན། དི་རྒྱུག་
ལ་ཏུ་སྦོ་པོང་ཟེ་སྐྱི་ཐར་པི་ལ་རུ། ཤུད་སྐྱེ་ལ་སྐྱེ་ལུ་ཡམ་ཤི་མ་སྐྱེག་ཀན་མ་དུབ་ཙེ། ཡི་རྒྱུ་ཚུ་
རྒྱུག་ཐད་ཀྱི་ཙོག་ཀན་ཤུ་བི་ཚིལ།

༢༧། དོ་རང་ཡེ་ཤུ་ལུམ་མི་ལོབ་རྒྱུག་ཏེ་རྒྱུ་རྒྱུམ་པོལ་ཡན་ཚེ། དོ་རེ་དོས་པི་ཏང་
བེ། གེ་ཕ་རིང་། ཡེ་ཤི་མཚན། ཡིད་ཙོ་རྒྱ་མཚོད་ལ་ཏུ་ཟ་རྗེབ་པི་མ་རེ་ཡམ།

༢༨། སེམས་དྲང་པོ་ཤུད་རྩེ་ལ། རྒྱུག་ཟིང་ཡོད་མ་ཏོ། ཀྱི་རེ་ལྷ་པ་པ་ཀྲུ་ཏང་མ་

༨༠

ང་ཡིས་བྲལ་བ་ཟེ། མ་དོར་གྱི་མོ་ལམ་ཏ་ད་ཏི། ཡོན་ཏན་ཀུ་ཎ།

༧༩ ། ལས་ཀྱི་རྣམ་པ་རིང་ཡི་ལ་ཀྱེ། རྟུང་རིང་ཅིག་ཀན་མོ་ལམ་ཏ་དེ།

༨༠ ། རྟོང་ཟེ་ཡམ་ལས་ཀྱི་ཡན་ཀྱི། དོ་རེ་ཡལ་ལས་ཀྱི་དོལ་ཡི་ཏ་ང་ཀི། མིན་ལི་ཀི་ཡཀྲུད་ཟེ།
ལན་རན་ཀྱི་བ། ཀྱི་ཀུ་སྲི་དོ་ཡིན་ཟ་ཅེ་ལམ་ཏེ་རི་རེ།

༨༡ ། ལས་ཀྱི་ཡེ་ཤུ་ཁྱུའི་རྟུན་དུ་ཡི་ལ་ཀྱི། དོ་ཏིང་། ང་ཀྱེ་ནེ་དོལ་ཀྱི་ཀན་ཅ་ཏ་ཏི་ཡལ། ད
ཀུ་ལི། དབོ་ལ་རིང་པོད་ཀྱི་མི་ཏུ་པོ་ཅོ་ཡིང་ག ལྷ་པ་ཡི་མི་ཏི་རྟུ་ཀྲུ་ཀི་ང་རན་ཟི་ཡན་ཏོ།

༨༢ ། དོ་ལོག་ལ་ཟི་པ་ཡི་ཀི། ད་ཡན་ཅ་ཡན་ཏ་ཏི།

༨༣ ། ཡོན་ཏན་ཀུ་ཎེ་ཡེ། ལྷ་ཏི་ཧི་མི་ལོབ་རྒྱུག་ཏེ་དུ་བི་ཅང་ཟེ་ཡུ་ཀྲ་ཀུ་ཤྲི་དོ་ཡན་ཀྱི།
ཀེ་ཝུ་ལི་ལ་ས་ཡེ། ཚོ་ལི་རིང་ལམ་པ་ཏུ་མི་ཡེ། ལེ་ཏེ་ཏི་ཅོ་ད་ལི་མི་ལི་རྟུ་ཀྲ་ཀྲ་ར།
ར་ལ་དྲི་ཡེ་དྲིང་ཀུ་ར་ཅ། དོ་རང་ཉམ་པོ་དོང་ཡི་ཏི་རེ།

༨༤ ། དོ་རང་དོ་ལོག་ལ་ཟེ་ཡེ། ཡེ་ཤུ་ལེ་ཏིམ་ཐལ་ཟེ་ཡ་ཏིང་ཀྱི་ཡུ་ཀུ་རན་ཝལ། དོ
ཀྱུར། ཏི་ཝི་ལང་ཀྱི་ཝི་ལ་ཅོ་ཀི་ལ། ཡུ་ཏི།

༨༥ ། དོ་རུ་ཐལ་ཟེ་དོང་ཡི་ཡི་ཡེ། ཡེ་ཤུ་རྟུ་རྣམ་པོལ་ཡན་ཀྱི། ཡེ་ཀུ་རྟུ། ཅག་ཅལ
ཡོན་ཏན་ཀུབ་པ་ཡུ་ཀུ་རྣ་ཏི།

༨༦ ། དོ་རང་དོ་ཅི་ཡེ་ཤུ་རྣམ་རི་རེ།

༨༧ ། ཡོན་ཏ་ར་དོང་ཏོང་ཀྱི་ཡི་མི་ཝི་ཟི་ཏོལ་དུ་ཀོན་ཀྱི། ཀེ་ཝུ་ལི་ལ་མ་ཏུ་ཡོག་པོ
རིང་ཀུ་ཁ་ཀྱི་ཡི་རེ་ཝ་ཝིག་ཏི།

༨༨ ། དོ་རང་ཡེ་ཤུ་ལི་དོ་ཏིང་། ཀྱེ་ནེ་ར་ལ་དྲི་ཡེ་དྲིང་ཀུ་ར་ཅ། ཡི་ཅག་པ་རྟུམ
ཅིམ་ཅིག་ཀན་ཀྱི་རྣམ་ཅེ་ཡན་ཏོ་ཏི་ཡལ།

༤༩ ཏུ་ང་རིང་གི་དུའི་སྒྱུར་ཏིང་ཀྱིན་ཏང་ཉམ་པོ་ཚོ་ཁང་དུང་ཛོད་ཀྱི། ཚོའི་ཤད་ཀྱི་ལ། ཀྱི་ཞེ་ཀྱི་
མ་ཐུམ་མིན། གོན་ཅོག་ཏུ་སྒོ་ལ་དུབ་པི་མ་ཟ་ལ་ཟེ་ཡོན་ནར་ཀྱུ་བི་ཤིས། ཀུ་ཊི།

༥༠། ངོ་རང་ལོབ་སྒུག་ཏེ་ཙེ་ཡེ་ཤུ་ཀྱིང་ཀྱི་པོ་རྒྱ་ཁྱེ་ཡི་ལ་ལི་རེ།

༥༡། ཡེ་ཤུ་ཞུ་ཟ་ཁང་ཟེ་ཡི་ཀྱི་པ་ཡོ་མིའི་རིང་ཀུར་ཏི་ཤ་ཞེ། ཀྱིའི་ཀུ་ལ་ལོ་ཁ་མ་མ་
ཟེ། ངོང་ཏོང་ཀྱི་ཡེ། མིའི་ཙེ་ངོ་ཐུམ་ཙེ་ཡེ།

༥༢
ངའི་ཀུར་ཏི་པད་ཀྱི། ནང་ཞེ་པོ་རྒྱ་ཁྱེ་ཡི་ལ་ལི།

༥༣། ངོ་རང་ཡེ་ཤུ་ཚེ་ཞིབ་ལ་མ་ཐུ་ཏུམ་པོ་ལ་ཞིལ་ཀྱི། ངོང་ཚེ་ཞིབ་ལ་མ་ཡེ། ཚོའི་རིང་
ལས་པ་ཐུ་མིའི་རེ་ཡེ། ལེ་ཏོ་རེ་པད་ཏེ་ཛོམ་ཀྱི་ཏོ་རི་རེ།

༥༤། ཀོ་ཕ་གཙོའི་རིང་ཟེ་ཡེ་ཤུ་ཞུ་ཟ་ལང་ཟེ་ཡི་ཀྱི། ཚེ་ཞིབ་ལ་མ་ཐུ་ཀྱམ་སུང་
ཡི་ལ་ཀྱི། ཡོག་པོ་ཏུ་སྒྲོ་རིང་ཛོད་ཀྱི། མི་སྒོ་ཊི་རི།

༥༥། ཚེ་ཞིབ་ལ་མ་ཡེ་ཞུ་བ་ལ་ཟེ་པ་ཙེ་ཡེ་ཤུ་ལ་ཙེམ་ཟ་ལ་ཟེ་ཀྱོན་པེ་ཏང་ཀྱི་ལ། མ་རྒྱ་ཀི

༥༦། འོང་ཤབ་ལི་ཐུ་གོལ་ཏི་རང་ཞེ་པ་ཚོལ་ལ་ལ། སྤྲད་མ་དུག་ཟང་། ཀྱོན་མ་རྒྱག་ཏི།

༥༧། ངོ་རང་ལམ་ལི་ག་ག་ཞི་ཤབ་ལི་ཐུ་གོལ་ཏི་རང་ཞེ་མ་ཟ་ལ་ཟེ་ཚོམ་ལ། ཀུ་ཊི་རེ།

༥༨། ཙེན་ཚེ་དེ་མི་ཐུ་ངོང་ཟེ་ཟ་ལ་མིན་ཤུ་ཏི། ཀྱི་མི་ཐུ་ཀུ་ཞེ་ཞི་ལ་ལི་དེ་ཚོའི་ཁང་ཤིབ་
ཞེ། སྒྲུམ་ཀྱལ་ཏ་ར་ཚེ་ཀེ་མི་ཐུ་ཀུ་ཞེ་ཞི་མ་ལ་ལི་ཀྱ་འི་ཚོ་ཁང་པང་ཞལ། ཡོན་པ་ཀུ་ཞེ
ཟལ་ཏི།

༥༩། ཀུང་ཀྱི་ལ་ངོ་ཀུ་ཏུ་གོལ་ཏི་ལ་མ་དུག་ཏི།

༦༠། ངོ་རང་ཚེ་ཞིབ་ལ་མ་ངོ་ཏུ་བི་ཙང་ཁ་ཞེ་ཡན་ཙི། ཡེ་ཤུ་རིང་། ངོ་ཙི་ཀ་ཚིད་ཏེ་ཀྱོན་
ལ་ཁྱེ་ལ། ཀའི་ལན་རྒྱ་ལ་ལེ་མ་རང་ཞ་ཏོ་ཕྲ་ཡ། ཡོན་ན་ཏུག་ཀ་ལ།

༦༡། ཡེ་ཤུ་ལ་སྐོར་ཚོད་ཀྱི། ལས་ཨ་ཞེ་ཡེ། ངེ་ཞི་ལ་ལ་ཡེ་ཡ་ལ་ཀྱི་རྟག་ཏེ། གམ་ཡི་ག
ཚོད་པ་ལ་ཞི་ལ་ནི་གཉེན་ཅིག་ཏུ་ཡེ་ཙེ་སྤྱིར་བ་ཡ། མ་ཤུ་ཀ།

༦༢། ཡོན་ཏན་རྟག་ཅེས་ལན་ཏིང་ཡེ་ཤུ་ལ། ཀྱི་ཤུག་ག། ཀླུའི་ཀྱེ་ཅེ་མི་ཙུ་ཡོ་ཙོ་ཡིང་ག
ཀོན་ཅིག་ཏུ་ཕུ་ཙང་པིང་ཞི་རྡོབ་པི་ཡེ། ནམ་ལཙུ་ཙུ་ཙུ་རྟོག་ཞིང་ཞི་ཡམ་ངི་ཏང་ཏོ་ཏི།

༦༣། ཡོན་ཏན་ཀུ་ཞི་ཡེ། ངེ་ཞི་ལ་ལ་མེ་ཡིན་ཟུ་ཙུ་ལམ་ཞུ་ལ་ཀྱི། མི་འི་བད་ཏེ་ཏི་ཏུ་ཏི།
ཀླུའི་གོ་ཡ་ཏི་ཀླུ་ཏིས།

༦༤། དེའི་ཀོན་ཅིག་ཏུ་ཡིན་ཏེ་ཞབ་པ་ར་རྣ་ཞི་ཏོ་ཀྱིས་ཞབ་ཡིན། ངཀྱུ་ལམ་ལ་ཏོ་ཏི་ཏུག
ཅེ་ཡེ། དོ་རྩེ་མི་འི་ས་ཞི་འི་ཡུ་པ་ཤུ་ཀུ་ཏི་རེ།

༦༥། དོ་རིང་ཀླུའི་ཙེ་ཡེ་ཤུ་ཙུ་ཡོད་དེང་ཟུ་ལད་ཀྱི། མོད་རིང་ཡད་ཀབ་ཀྱི། ཟ་ལ་ཙག་ཀུལ
པ་ཡེ་ཤུ་རིང་། ཡེ་ཀོན་ཅིག་ཏུ་ཟླ་ལ་རྣ་ཞི་པ། ཡོན་ཏན་ཟ་ལ་ཙག་ཀྱི་ཞིབ་ཡ་རེ་ཤུ་ཡེ་ཟུ
ཀུང་ཀྱི། ཟ་ལ་ཙག་ཀུ་ཏི་རེ།

༦༦། དགེ་ལྷ་རིང་ཀེ་པ་བི་རིང་ཤེ་མ་ཟང་རྡོད་ཏར། ངེ་ཞི་ལ་ལམ་ཙུ་ཡི་ཡེ་ཙ་ཡོག་པོ་ཡ་ཏ་ཀྱི།

༦༧། ཀེ་ཡམ་ཡེ་ཤྲི་ཏ་ཏང་ཙེ་ཡེ། དགེ་རིང་བ་ཏ་ཀྱི་ཡ་ཀ་ལ་ཡེ་ཤུ་ཙང་ཙ་རི་ཏ་ཙུ་ཡི་ཡེ་ཤུ་ཏ་ཏན། ཀུ་ཞི་ཡེ།

༦༨། ཀེ་ཡེ་ཏབ་ཡི་ཡུ་འི། ཀྱེ་ཡ་ཇེ་ག། ཀ་ཡི་ཀུ་སྤྱི་དེ་ཙུ་དོན་ཏག་ཀུ་ཤུ་ཏད་ཀྱི་རིང་ཏ་ཡ་ཡོ
རཔ་ཀུ་ཏི། དོ་རང་དོ་ཡི་རིང་ཡེ་ལ་ཀྱི། ཡི་ཏང་ཏུ་ཏུམ་ཡོལ་ཡིད་ཀྱི་ཡེ། ཀུ་ཀུ་ཏི་འི་ངར་ཏད།

༦༩། ཡམ་ལ་ཀྱི་ཡོག་ཙོ་འི་ཀེ་ཡབ་ཏང་ཀ། དོ་ཏད་ཀྱི་བད་ཏེ་ཏིང་། དི་ལ་དོ་ཙུ་ཤྲོ་ཙུ་ཏང་ཞི
ཤུ་ཀུ་ཞི་ཡེ།

༧༠། ཀེ་ཡེ་ཡམ་ཀྱེ་ཏབ་མི་ཡུ་འི། མ་ཤུ་ཀ་ཀ་ཀུ་ཏི། བོང་མ་ཤུ་ཏ་ཙི། དོང་ཏད་ཀྱི
དོ་ཙེ་ཀེ་ཡབ་རིང་། ཀ་ཀ་ལི་ལ་དེ་ཀ་ཤུ་ཏ་ཀ། ཀ་ཏུ་ཤུ་ཏ་[illegible]། ཀ་དེན་ཏ

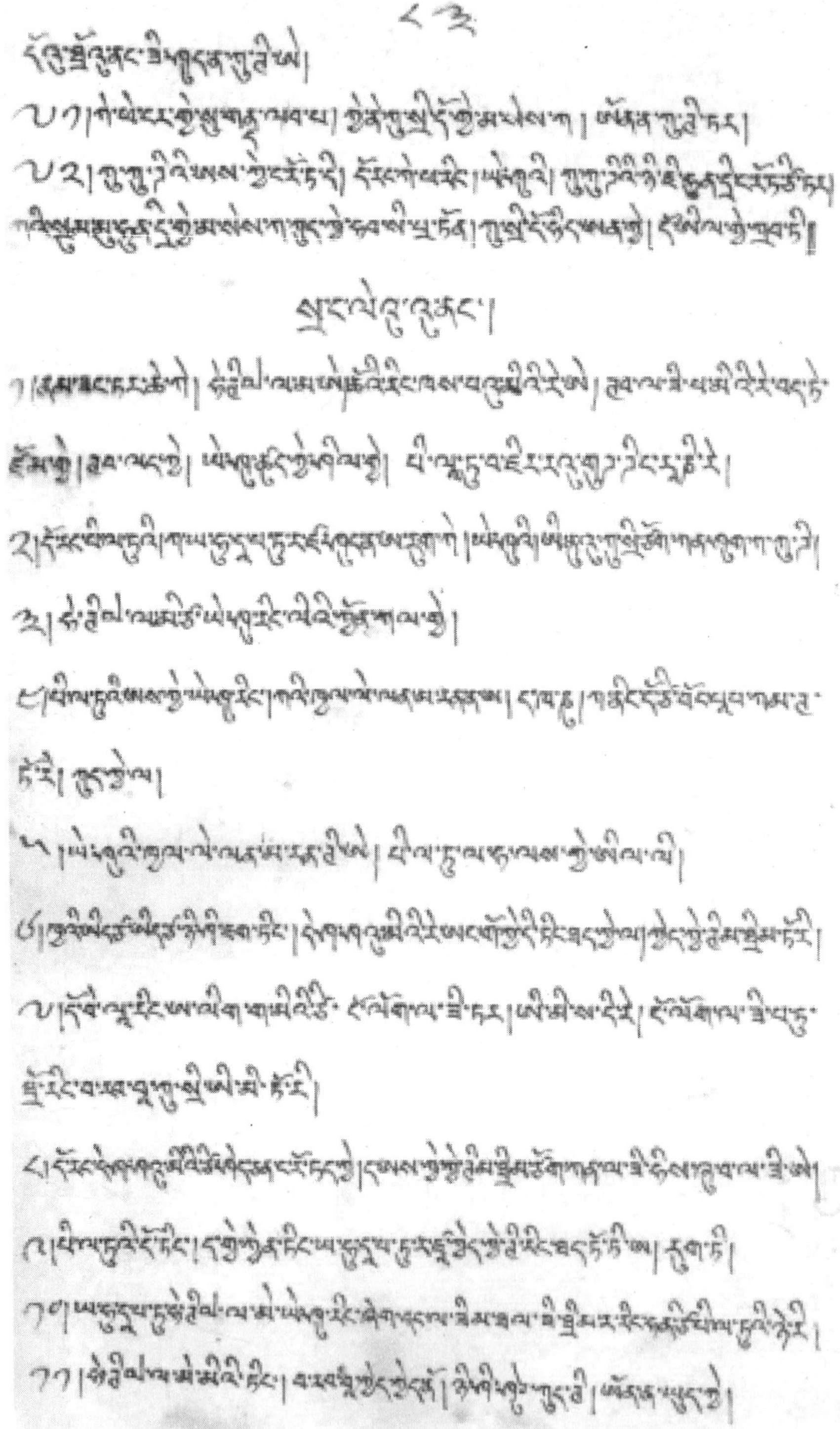

८४.

१२། ཡིག་ཕྲ་ནི་ཡམས་ཀྱེ་སྒྲ་ཏེ། ཨེ་ཨེ་ཡ་ཕྲུ་རྣ་ཡ་ཕྲ་ར་ཧ་ཀྲ་ཤྲི་ཚོམ་ནི་དྲི་རིང་གྱི་ཀྲུ་ཡན་ལག། ཕྲ་ན་ཅེ་ཡེ།

१३། ངོ་རེ་ཐབ་ཏེ་ཅེ་ཀྲུང་གི་ཕྱིད་རིང་བ་ཡེ་ཅེ་དྲིས། ཡོ་ཆེན་ད་ཀྲུག་ཏབ་པ་ཀྲུ་ཏེ་རེ།

१४། ཡིག་ཕྲ་ནི། ངོའི་ལོག་པ་ཏྲུས་ཀྲུལ་ཤེ་བྲུ་ཅེ་ཡེ། ངོ་ཅེ་ཡེ་ཅེ་ཐམ་ཏྲུ་ཀྲུག་ཏབ་པ། ཀྲུ་ཤིག་ཕྱི་རིང་བ་ཡེ་ཅེ

ཏིས་ཀྲུ་ཏེ་རེ།

१५། ངོ་རང་ཡིག་ཕྲ་ནི། ཉེ་ཀ་ཁ་ཀྲུ་མི་རེ་ཕྲ་ཐམ་ཀྱི་ཅོག་ཀ་ན་ལ་ཞི་དྲིས། ལམ་ལ། བ་སྐམ་དྲ་ཀྲེད་ཀྱེ

ཡེ་ཤུ་རིང་ཏ་ལ་ཅན་གཅིག་ཀྲུག་ཀྱི། ཀྲུང་ཤིག་ཕྱིད་རིང་བ་ཡེ་ཅེས་ཏུ་ཀྲུས་དྲི།

१६། ངོ་རང་སྤུ་ཕྲ་ལེ་བད་ཏེ་ཅི། ཡེ་ཤུ་ཀྲུས་སྐྱུ་ཞེས་ཟ་ངན་གི་ལ་ཀྱི། མི་ལེ་བད་ཏེ་ཇོམ་ལི་ལད་ཀྱི།

१७། ཡེ་ཤུ་རིང་མཐན་གྱི་ཁམས་ཁམས་རི་རེ། རང་ཏྲུ་ཀ་ལང་གི་ཅོག་ཀ་ན་སོལ་ཤག་ཕྲ་ཅ་ཀྲུར་ལ

ཀྱི། ཞལ་ལི་ཙག་ཏེ་རེ།

१८། ངོ་རང་ངོ་རིང་ཤུག་ལ་བབ། ཨེ་ཡ་ཕྲུ་རྣ་ཡ་ཕྲ་ར་ཧ་ཆམ་ཚལ་ཀྲུང་ཀྱི།

१९། ཏྲུ་ངེ་ཏྲུ་ཤབ་ལ་ལིང་ག་ཀྲུལ་ཀྱི། སྤུ་ཡད་ཀྱི། ཀྲུལ་སྤྲ་ཏེ་ཚག་ཀ། ཡེ་ཤུ་རེ་མོ་ཁམ་ཏ་ཅེས

ཅོག་ཀ་ན་ལ་ལེ་རེ།

20། ཡོ་ཆ་ཆམ་ཡམ་པ་ར་སྐམ་ཀྱི། མཆན་ཀྱི་ཁ་མ་ལ་ཅེ་ཡེ། ངོ་ཏྲུ་ཡེན་ཀྲུ་ཏུ་ཁམ་ཁམ་ཀྱི། ཀྲུང་ཤིག་ངོ་རིང

ཙ་ཡེ་ཅེ་རིང་པི་རི་ཤིག་ལ་ལེ་རེ།

१། ངོ་ཤོ་སྤྲ་རིང་། གི་ཙ་ཆེ་པ་མ་ལེག་ལམ་ངེར་ཀྲུ་ཤྲི་ཡེ། ཏ་སྒྲ་ཀྲུ་ཤྲི་ཡ་ཅེ་སྐྱ་ཀ་ཀྲུ་ཏུ་སྒྲ། ཤི་མོན

ཀྲུ ཤྲི་ངོ། རི་རིང་ཞི་ཡམ་པ་ངོང་ཡི་ཏེ། ངོ་རིང་ཀྲུང་ལད་ཀྱི་ཡེ་ཤུ་ཏུ་ཐ་ལ་ཞི་ཀྲུང་ཤིག་ཀྲུས་ཅི་སྐྱི

२། ངོ་རང་ཡེ་ཤུ་བོ་ལ་བོ་ཐ་ཀྲུ་ཤྲི་ལ་ཀྱང་ངེ་ངན་གི་ལ་ཀྱི། བོལ་བོ་ཐ་ཏུ་ཆོན་ཏག་ཡེན་ཀྲུ

ཀན་ཐོད་པ་ཏུ་ལ་ཀྱང་ཀྱི།

༢༣། དོན་རང་སྐུམ་ཞིམ་ཟས་ཆང་དང་ཀྱུར། ཏུང་མི་ཟན་སྐྱེ་ལ། ཡེ་ཤུ་ཞིམ་ཏུང་ངོ།

༢༤། ཀྱུང་ཞིག་ཟས་ནི་ཀོད་ཀྱི། ཡེ་ཤུ་ཉུ་ལམ་ཟེ་ཞིམ་ཟལ་ཞི་པོ་ཀ་ཀྱི་རེ།

༢༥། ཁམ་ཞིག་རྒྱ་ཚོད་དེ་ཀྱུང་ཞིང་རིང་ལ་ལེ་ཧྲི་ཀུ་དཀོ། སྐུམ་སྐུ་རྒྱ་ཙོད་དེ་རྒྱ་ཧྲེ་རེ།

༢༦། ཡེ་ཤུ་ཀུ་ཀོ་ཡོ་ཡར་ཏུ་ཞག་ཞེ། ཡ་ཏུ་དུ་པ་ཏུ་རང་ཤོག ཡོད་པ་རོ་ལ་བལ་ཞིག་ཞིང་ཙེ་ལི་ཧ་རི།

༢༧། ཡེ་ཤུ་རང་ཉམ་པོ། ཉི་དེ་ཙམ་པ་ཀུ་ཡོད་ཙ་ལུ་ཙང་དུ་ཡིང་ནི། ཡོད་ཙ་ལུ་ཙང་དུ་ ཡིང་ཞེ་ཀྱུ་ཞིག་ཞིང་

རྒྱ་ཧི་རེ།

༢༨། ཅོ་ཏུང་མི་ཀོ་ཙོག་ཏུ་སྒོལ་རྣ་ཤྲི་ཙོག་ཀན། དོན་ཡོལ་པ་ཏུ་སྒྲི་རིང་ཀུ་ཞེ་རེ། ཡོད་ན་དུན་ཧེ།

༢༩། མི་དེ་ཡོག་རྒྱུ་ཡོག་ལམ་ཙེ་པ་ཙེ། ཞལ་ཤུ་རང་ཀྱི། ཡེ་ཀོན་ཙོག་ཏུ་ཚོ་ལང་ཞིག་ཀེ། སྐུམ་

སྐག་ཧིང་རྒྱུ་ཞིབ་ཆེག་ཏལ་ཀུ་ཞེ་པ་ཀ།

༣༠། དཔེ་ཞེ་བ་ཙེག་ཀེ། ཀྱུང་ཞིང་རིང་ཟེ་ཧག་སུ་ཡོད་ན་མ་ཀ་རང་རྒྱ་ཧི་རེ།

༣༡། ཡོད་ན་ཡེ་ཚེ་ཞི་རིང་ཁམ་པ་ཡེ། ཏེ་ཞིལ་ལ་མ་ཙེ་ཡི་དེ་ཞི་ཡི་དེ་རིང་ཀུ་ཞེ་རེ།

ཀྱུ་རི་ཏུ་སྒོག་ཟང་པོ་ལང་སྐྱེ་ལ། ཡིན་རྒྱུ་སྒོག་ཟང་པོ་ལ་ཟེ་མ་རེ།

༣༢། དོམ་པ་ཞིག་ཡ་ཀྱུ་ལ་ཏུ་རང་ཀུ་དཀོ། དཀྱུང་ཞིང་རིང་ཟེ་ཧག་སུ། དོན་རང་ཙེ་ཞེ་ཧང་ཀེ།

དལ་ལང་ཧ་མི། ཡོད་ན་ཀུ་ཞི་རེ། ཡེ་ཤུ་རང་ཉམ་པོ་ཀྱུང་ཞིང་རིང་སྒྲུབ་ཀུ་ཞེ་ལ་མ་ཀ་རྒྱ་ཧི་ཀུ།

༣༣། དོན་རང་ཏུ་ཞིང་རྒྱ་ཙོད་རིང་ཟེ་ཀུ་རྒྱ་ཙོད་ཧ་རང་ཙེ་ཀེ། བང་ཧ་དེ་ཀ་པ་བསྟན་ཀ་ཀྱུང་ཀྱི།

༣༤། ཀུ་རྒྱ་ཙོད་དེ་ཡེ་ཤུ་ཞི་ཧ་ཉུ་ཀ་ཟན་ཀྱི་ཀུ་ཞི། ཡེ་ལི་ཡེ་ལི། ལ་མ་ཀ་

ཞག་ཐ་ཞེ། ཡོད་རྒྱུ་ཙོག་ཀན། ཡེ་ཀྱི་ཉུ་ཀོན་ཙོག ཡེ་ཀྱི་ཉུ་ཀོན་ཙོག ཀ་ཞི་

ཀྱུ་རིང་ཚང་ཙ་ཧན། ཀུ་ཞི་ཡེ།

༣༥། དོ་ཧད་ཀྱི་ཡང་ཀོ་ཙེ་དེ་སྤྱད་ཞལ་ཀྱི། དེ་ལི་ཡེ་ལི་ཡ་རིང་ཀད་ལ་ཟལ་ཀུ་ཞི

༨༥

༣༦། ངོ་མཚར་ཡེ་ཤེས་སྒྲོལ་བ་ཡི་ལ་སྐྱེ། ཆུ་སྲུལ་སྤྱན་སྐྱེ་རྣམ་ལོག་སྐྱེ། རྡོ་རྗེ་ཀུན་ནས་དྲང་སྲོང་སྐྱེ།
ཙུ་གཏམ་ཐལ་ཞེ་རྣམ། ངོ་མཚར་མི་འདི་ཞེ། ཨེ་ཁེ་པདྨ་ལྷ་ཡི་ཞིང་ཁམས་བཀོད། མཐའ་ནི་ལས་བྱུང་སྐྱེ།
༣༧། ངོ་མཚར་ཡེ་ཤེས་ཞལ་ཆེ་ཟུམ་བརྒྱུད་རྣམ་པ་ལ་ནི།
༣༨། ངོ་ཚོ་ཁང་དུ་ཡར་དཀོན་མཆོག་ཞིང་ཟླ་ཟེར་དང་ནང་ཆེ་ཀེ་དྲུལ་སྐྱེ་ཡིལ་ཀྱི།
༣༩། སྐུ་མི་མགོ་ཉི་དུ་སྐུ་ལ་སེ་པ་ཡེ་ཤེས་རྒྱ་རྒྱུ་མཚོ་ཡེ་ཚོང་སྤྱི་དོན། ཡེ་ཤེས་ཡོན་ཏན་ཀུན་རྒྱུ་རྣམ་པ་ལེའི་ཚེ་ཅི
ཡེ། དེ་མི་འཇི་ཏ་ཚན་ཐན་ཀོན་ཆོག་དུ་ལོ་ཙ་སྐྱེ། ཀྱི་ཧི།
༤༠། ཀྱིའི་ཡར་གྲིག་གཅེ་ཅི་ཅི་དོ་རི་ང་སྐྱེའི་ཤིང་ཞི་ལ་རྗེ་རེ། དོ་ཏུ་ཡི་ཅང་མི་དཔལ་ལམ་བཀྲ་དཔལ་ལམ་ཀུ
ཡེ། ཡ་ཀེ་ཝ་ཡེ་ཡོ་ལེ་ཀུ་སྤྲི་དོ་ཀུ་ཏུ་ཡམ་མ་མི་ར་ཡམ་ཀུ་སྤྲི་ཡེ།
༤༡། མ་ལོ་མེ་ཀུ་སྤྲི་ཏོ། ག་ལི་ལ་དེ་ཀ་ར་ཀང་ཞེ་ཡེ་ཤེས་རྒྱ་ཐ་ལང་ཞེ་ཡམ་པ། ཡ་བག་ལ་ཞེ་པ་ཡེ།
མེ་ཅ་རེ་ཡེ་ཤེས་རྣམ་པ་པོ་ཡེ་རྒྱལ་ལམ་བཟང་དབང་ཀྱི་པ་ཙོང་རྡོ་རྗེ་བརྟེ།
༤༢། དོ་ཧག་ཀེ་ཤི་ཧག་ཏུ་སྟུ་པ་སྒྲོ་མ་ཞིམ་ཧག། གེ་ཏ་ཨ་བ་ད་ཧག་ཏུ་ཡེ་ཙ་ཧག་ཏུ་དམར་ཤིང་དུ་ཀྱི་ཡེ།
༤༣། ཨ་ཐིམ་ཐ་པ་ཡོ་ལེ་བ། ཡི་ཏྲུ་པོ་ཏྲ་ཡ་ཞེ་པ་དེ་ནི། གི་ཏྲ་རང་རྣམ་སྐྱེ། ཞི་ར་ཡིས་ཏུ་ཏ་རུ་མ་པོ་ལ
ཡེ་སྐྱེ། ཡེ་ཤེས་ཧུ་ཏོ་སྐྱེ་སྤྲི་ཀ་ཤུ་ཀུ་ད་ཤེ་ཏུ་བ་ཡ་ནི།
༤༤། དོ་མི་ཞེ་ཀུ་ད་སྤྱི་ཐལ་ཀྱི། པེ་ལྷ་ཏུ་ཐ་ཐ་ཞ་སྦྱང་སྐྱེ། སྐུ་མི་མགོ་མི་ཏྲུ་སྟག་ལེ་པ་སྡེ། ཡེ་ཤེས་ལེའི་ཚེ་ཀ་པོ
ཏི་ཡ་ཧུ་ཀ་ཀ།
༤༥། སྐུ་མི་མགོ་མི་ཏུ་སྐུ་ལེ་པ་འཇུ་ཏོ་ཞེ་ཡོན་ཏན་རྒྱལ་པོ་ཐལ་སྐྱེ། ཡོ་ལེ་བ་པདྨ་ཚོ་རྣམ་ཅི།
༤༦། དེའི་ཡི་ཡ་རྫོགས་སྐྱེ། ཙོ་ཀུ་ཤེ་ཡི་པ་རྡེ་ཞེ་ཙོད་སྤྱི། ཡ་དུ་ཤར་ཏུན་སྐྱེ། ཀོ་ཧུང་ཀོ་ཤེག
རྟ་ཆེ་སྤྱོད་སྤྱི། ཙོ་ཏེ་ཏུ་པི་ཏ་ང་ཆེ་ཞེ་བྱུང་རྒྱལ་ཁ་བ་ཏི།

[illegible]

[illegible]

༡ [illegible]

༢ [illegible]

༣ [illegible]

༤ [illegible]

༥ [illegible]

༦ [illegible]

༧ [illegible]

༨ [illegible]

༩ [illegible]

༡༠ [illegible]

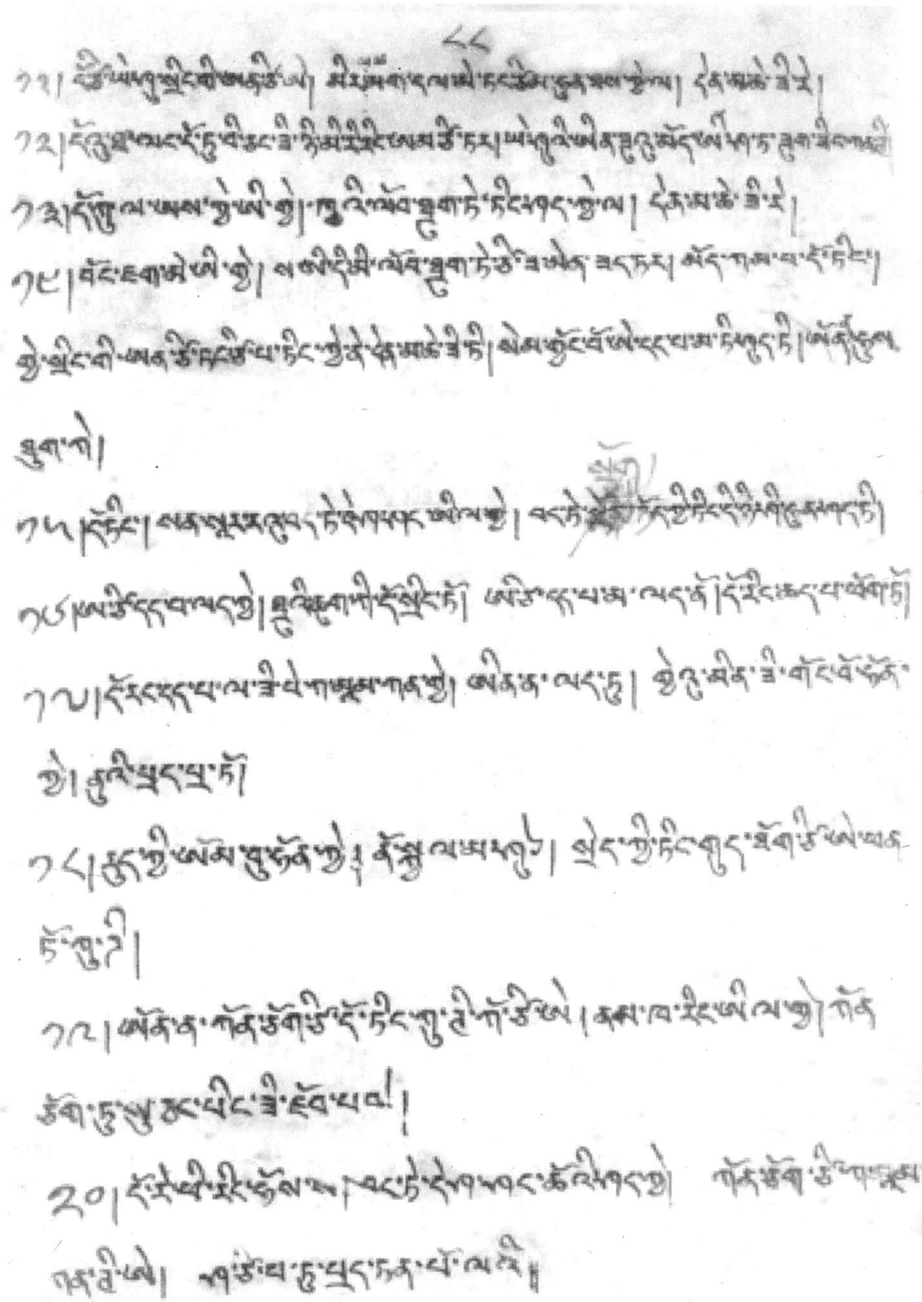

Appendix II
Rock Inscriptions of Moravians from Lahul

Two inscriptions engraved on rocks assignable to nineteenth century have been located at Kyelang and Zingzinbar which are probably the works of the Moravians of Kyelang.

***Inscription 1* :** This inscription was found inscribed on a rock in the compound at the residence of the Moravians at Lower Kyelang which reads: + *skyabs mgaon ye shus gsungs pa ji ltar mi gzhan la byed dga' ba ltar khyed rnams kyis kyang mi dzhan rnams la byos shig* (meaning *do unto others as you wish others should do unto you).* The rock on which this inscription was engraved has now been used in construction of a house in the same complex.

***Inscription 2* :** This inscription was engraved on a rock at Zingzingbar near the source of Bhaga river and it was located by Elizabeth Anne Stutchbury. The inscription reads : + *Yi-shus gsungs khong ni shi nas lang pa nyid dang dson pa nyid yin te. Su yang nga la dad pa nga shi yang gson por 'gyur ro* (meaning *Jesus said, I am the resurrection and the life. He that believeth in me though he was dead, yet he shall live).*

Appendix III
'Moravians' in India – Paparika
(published in The Hindustan Times, October 18, 1987)

"If ever I had heard the name Moravia, I probably thought of it as an imaginary country in eastern Europe - another Ruritania. In actual fact, Moravia was a country in central Europe in the early middle ages, but was conquered and became a part of the Holy Roman empire, later the Austrian empire, and is now a part of Czechoslovakia. When the Reformation came to Europe, the sturdy peasants of Moravia opted to follow the teachings of Martin Luther and became Protestants with only the Bible as their guide.

The Holy Roman empire was, as its name implied, Roman Catholic, so the Moravians were persecuted, but carried on their religion in secluded places, deep in the forests. Many left their own homeland to settle in other Protestant countries - mainly Germany, but also England. Much later, a large number from both Germany and England emigrated to America, their sect of Christianity came to be known as the Moravian Church.

In 1732, foreign missions were begun from Germany - the first to the West Indies to work among the Negro slaves. In course of time, they-also came to India. Why they left the great plains, the known world, and "British India", behind them, and went to the lonely inaccessible valleys of the Himalayas, we do not know, but it may have been that the English were hostile to them. However, they were welcomed and treated with kindness by the local rulers, and by the middle of the 19th century, had set up their missions at Leh, Keylong, Kalpa and Pooh, all but the first named being in Himachal Pradesh.

They came with their Bibles and their worldly possessions, presumably to convert the "heathen", in which they do not seem to have been very successful. Perhaps they did not really try hard or the converts soon reverted to the religions of their ancestors. However, there is still a tiny community of Christians in Leh.

What the Moravian missionaries are best remembered for are the many amenities and comforts they brought to the isolated people among whom they lived. They are credited with bringing such innovations as glass windows, and the "bukhari" - a closed stove with an outlet for smoke. What a boon it must have been in such a severe climate to be able to keep your house warm, without being smoked out!

To Lahaul they brought potatoes. Nothing but barley was grown there. Potatoes thus added variety and nutrition to the diet, saved the people from famine when crops failed, and have since become one of the greatest money earners for the cultivators. The Moravian women also taught knitting to the people of the valleys.

The Raja of Bushahr, a large but sparsely populated kingdom, seems to have been particulárly liberal and far-sighted, for he allowed the missionaries to teach his son, who grew up fluent and literate in both English and German, and very much aware of the benefits of modern education.

Few people in our country have ever heard of the Moravian missionaries. Through their bones lie in neglected and forgotten cemeteries, they themselves are not forgotten. They are still remembered in the upland valleys, with affection and gratitude, for all that they did to improve the quality of life for some of the loneliest people of the world."

Appendix IV
Snowshoes in 1897
(Translated & introduced by Gabriele Reifenberg)

"In his article, August Hermann Francke was writing to the Moravian Brotherhood's centre at Herrnhut in Germany to describe a journey full of dangers which he made in March 1897 to meet his fiancee in Amritsar. He set off from Leh with one servant and a pony on 1 March, taking a minimum of equipment.

Everywhere, including the 250-mile long track they had to complete, was covered in snow. It took the two men six days to reach Kargil. At Kargil Francke's servant insisted that they could not take the pony any further. Two porters were hired to help the travellers on the next stage of their journey to Kharbu, a small village on the eastern bank of the Dras river, about four miles from Tashgarn. They reached there after ten hours, covering just 1.5 miles an hour, and were totally exhausted. The next day, although it was still snowing heavily, they continued to Tashgarn (15 miles north-east of Dras), which they reached in the evening.

They were both depressed and felt quite hopeless, but Francke decided that he would rather die in a snowstorm than be buried alive in the - dismal shelter they had found. So he asked the headman of the village to find two more porters to help them on their way the next day. The story continues:

We were on the point of setting off again when the porters fell on their knees, lifted their hands as in prayer and pleaded stridently: "Have mercy on us, dear Sahib, and do not force us to proceed today. Even if we defy the storm we will surely be buried in a snowdrift."

I looked sternly at the poor men, ordered them to obey, and thus our day's work began. There was not a sign of the track, just a huge expanse of snow and a shower of snowflakes falling on us.

To set a good example I went first and jumped into the snow. Because of its softness, it came up to my knees I stumbled forward, fell down, disappeared completely, stood up again, fell down once more and in this way succeeded in taking five steps in five minutes.

My servant did not move from the spot, so I had to complete the struggle by myself. Totally beaten, I returned to my faithless followers. I felt like Napoleon at Waterloo!

Don't think, however, that I retreated to the inn in defeat. On the contrary I felt as though there was something of victory in my bearing and that I held my head high. How was that possible?

Two great new thoughts had flashed into my brain and I was sure we could triumph splendidly over difficulties. The first thought was to make a pair of Norwegian snowshoes and the second, a sledge. It was obvious that main obstacle to progress was the very soft snow. If we could stop ourselves sinking in and with the help of snowshoes glide over the surface, then we could get on as fast as in summer. Our baggage could then be packed into two sledges that my servant and I would pull, thus saving the money for the porters. It looked like it would be at least a week before the condition of the snow changed, so we had plenty of time.

We began our task that afternoon with the help of a blunt axe, the only tool that we could get hold of. It was not at all easy to find the necessary wood, as the severe winter had already forced the unfortunate villagers to sacrifice some of their doors. However, when my trusty servant told them I would pay the highest prices, one of them brought me a large wooden door.

The first pair of snowshoes was soon finished and ready to be tried out. I now faced an embarrassing situation. The news that I was making European winter shoes had spread throughout the village and the whole population came out to see the sahib who created such wonders. As I had never used snowshoes before, I was loath to take my first steps in front of all these people. But it had to be.

After a few difficulties I reached the slightly downward sloping expanse of snow and saw that the shoes did indeed prevent my sinking in. But how was I to move in them? As soon as I lifted one foot, the threads with which I had fastened the shoe threatened to tear. To glide downwards was equally tricky, since the forward edge of the rough shoe was not curved upwards.

I do not need to give detailed account of the opinion of the onlookers; that of my servant will suffice. He steadfastly refused to subject his feet to the same trials and nothing could persuade him to make another pair of snowshoes. So that idea had to be abandoned.

However, I felt sure that my reputation would be restored when the second idea was put into practice. The snowshoes had to be converted into sledge runners. So we began work again with enthusiasm. Time passed pleasantly, and the work was warming us up. I did not consider it necessary to try our efforts on the same day. We intended to surprise people with an early departure and to show the porters how superflus they were.

Just as we had finished our work we heard that the mail couriers from Kargil had arrived with letters (no-one had seen anything of those from Srinagar for three days), and that they were to try to continue on their way, through the snow, the next day. This news was music to our ears and we decided to attach ourselves to these officials.

The sledge was just big enough to take our belongings. We placed it on the snow – and, oh dear – it sank completely. The runners were too short. Many attempts were made to get it to move, but to no avail. It stuck fast in the snow just as firmly as the man trying to pull it. After I had lost the last remnants of belief in my own wisdom and skill, I fortunately managed to find two of the porters I had previously scorned, and we were able to join the postmen.

Despite further terrible weather, especially over the Zoji-la Pass, Francke and his companions survived the journey and he arrived safely in Amritsar, met his fiancee and was married.

(Extracted from Ladags Melong, winter 2003).

Bibliography

Asboe,Walter, 'Disposal of the Dead in Tibet', *Man,* 32: 66-67, 1932.

– –, 'Scapegoat in Western Tibet', *Man* 36: 74-75, 1936.

– –, 'Sacrifices in Western Tibet', *Man* 36: 75-76. 1936.

– –, 'The Lahoulies of Western Tibet', *Man* 36: 78, 1936.

– –, 'Agricultural Methods in Lahoul, Western Tibet', *Man* 37, 74-77, 1937.

– –, 'Pottery in Ladakh, Western Tibet', *Man* 46 (4), 1946.

Bruce, C.G., *Kulu and Lahoul,* Edward Arnold, London, 1914.

Biscoe, C.E. Tyndale, *Kashmir in Sunlight and Shade,* London, 1922.

Fillipo De Fillipi (Ed.), *An Account of Tibet, The Travels of Ippolito Desideri of Pistoia, S.J., 1712-1727,* London, 1932.

Francke, A.H., 'The Ladakhi Pre-Buddhist Marriage Ritual' (Translation and Notes), *Indian Antiquary,* April 1901, pp. 131 ff.

– –, 'The Spring Myth of the Kesar Saga', *Indian Antiquary,* August, 1901 pp. 329 ff.; January, 1902, vol. XXXI, pp. 32 ff.; March 1902, pp. 147 ff.

– –, *Dritte sammlung von Felszeichnungen aus Unter-Ladakh,* Leh, 1902 (lithgr.).

– –, 'Ladakhi Songs', *Indian Antiquary;* February, pp. 87 ff.; July 1902 pp. 304 ff.

– –, 'Notes on Rock-Carvings from Lower Ladakh', *Indian Antiquary,* vol. xxxi, 1902.

– –, Some More Rock-Carvings from Lower Ladakh, *Indian Antiquary,* vol. xxxii, 1903.

– –, *rtags-ma gchig gi nyo-glu,* Kyelang, 1904 (Translations appeared in *Indian Antiquary,* Vol. XXX, 1901, pp. 131. ff.)

– –, 'Ladakhi Stone-Implements', *Indian Antiquary,* xxxiii, 1904.

– –, 'The Rock Inscriptions at Mulbe', *Indian Antiquary,* March 1905, pp. 72 ff.

– –, The Eighteen Songs of the Bono-na Festival (Bono-nayi lu athrungsh) (Dard texts, with translation, Notes and Vocabulary), *Indian Antiquary,* May 1905, pp. 93 ff.

– –, 'Archaeological Notes on Balu-mkhar in Western Tibet', *Indian Antiquary,* vol. xxxiv, 1905.

Francke, A.H., *Erste and Zweite Sammlung tibetischer historischer Inschriften,* Leipzig, 1906.

– –, The Rock Inscriptions at Mul-bhe, *Indian Antiquary,* vol. xxxv. 1906.

– –, *First Collection of Tibetan Historical Inscriptions on Rock and Stone from Western Tibet,* Kyelang, 1906.

– –, *Second Collection of Tibetan Historical Inscriptions on Rock and Stone from Western Tibet,* Kyelang, 1907.

– –, *Saint Mark in Tinan,* Kyelang, 1907.

– –, *Die historischen und mythologischen Erinnerungen der Louler,* Kyelang, 1907.

– –, *A History of Western Tibet, One of the Unknown Empires,* 1907, reprinted, New Delhi 1977.

– –, 'Archaeology in Western Tibet', *Indian Antiquary,* vol. xxxv, 1906; vol. xxxvi, 1907

– –, 'Historische Dokumente von Khalaste in West Tibet (Ladakh)', *ZDMG,* Lxi, 1907.

– –, 'Kleine archaeologische Ertrage einer Missionsreise nach Zangskar in West-Tibet, *ZDMG,* Lx, Bd lxi. 1907.

– –, 'Remarks on a Photograph near Ating taken by the Hon. Eric Upton, during a Tour in Zanskar in 1907', *Indian Antiquary,* Nov. 1908, pp. 332-333.

– –, 'Note on Moloso', *Journal of the Royal Asiatic Society of Great Britain and Ireland,* 1908, pp. 188-189.

– –, 'References to the Bhotas in Rajatarangini', *Indian Antiquary,* vol. xxxvii. 1908

– –, 'Vorbuddistische religion Tibets', *ZDMG,* xxxviii, 1874.

– –, 'Ten Ancient Historical Songs from Western Tibet', *Indian Antiquary,* vol. xxxviii. 1909.

– –, 'Tibetan Inscription on the Stone Monument in Front of the Ta-chao-ssu Temple in Lhasa, 822 A.D.' *Epigraphia India,* vol. x, pt. iv,1909-10.

– –, 'Die Geschichte des Dogra-Krieges Nach dem Manuscript C des Ladvags rgyalrabs,' *ZDMG,* Bd. Lxiv, 1910.

– –, 'The Kingdom of gNya khri bstanpo, the First King of Tibet,' *JASB,* vol. vi., 1910.

– –, List of Minister's Names Found in the Tibetan Inscription in Front of the Ta-chao-ssu temple (Jokhang) in Lhasa, 822 AD', *Epigraphia Indica,* vol. xi, pt. vi. 1912

– –, 'Historical Documents from the Borders of Tibet', *Archaeological Survey of India, Annual Report 1909/10,* Calcutta, 1914.

– –, 'Notes on Sir Aurel Stein's Collection of Tibetan Documents from Chinese Turkestan', *JRAS,* 1914.

– –, *Antiquities of Indian Tibet,* 2 parts, reprinted, New Delhi, 1972.

– –, 'Tibetan Inscription on the Darkot Pass', A. Stein's, *Innermost Asia,* vol. ii, 1925.

Ganpat (Gompertz, M.L.A), *The Road to Lamaland (Impressions of a journey to Western Tibet)*, 1916.

Gergan, Yoseb and Walter Asboe, 'A Thousand Tibetan Proverbs & Wise Sayings from Ladakh, Spiti, Lahaul & Naris sKor-gsum', *Indian Antiquary*, New Delhi, 1976.

Harcourt, A.F.P., *The Himalayan District of Kooloo, Lahoul and Spiti*, 1872 reprinted, Delhi, 1972.

Hooper, J.S.M. *Bible Translation in India, Pakistan and Ceylon*, Bombay, 1938.

Hedin, Sven, *Trans-Himalaya*, Vol. I and II, New York, 1909.

Hutchison, J. and J.Ph. Vogel, *History of the Punjab Hill States*, Vol. I and II, Lahore. 1933.

Jaeschke, H.A., *A Tibetan-English Dictionary, London*, 1881, *reprinted* 1958.

– –, *A Short Practical Grammar of the Tibetan Language with Reference to the Spoken Dialects*, Kyelang, 1865.

– –, 'Translation of a manuscript obtained in Ladak regarding the Dancing on the Tenth Day of the Fifth Month, a Great Holiday', *JASB*, Calcutta, Vol. 34, Part I, 1865,pp. 77-80.

– –, 'Probenaus den tibetschen Legendenbuche, die hunderttausend Gesange des Milaraspa', *ZDMG*, 1869.

Khosla, G.D., *Himalayan Circuit*, London, 1956.

Marx, K. "Three Documents Relating to the History of Ladakh', *JASB*, Vol. LX, Part I, Nos. 1 -3, 1891; vol. LXIII, 1894, part. 1, No.1- 2; vol. LXXI, 1902, part 1, No. 1

Markham, C.R., *Narrative of the Mission of George Bogel to Tibet and of the Journey of Thomas Manning to Lhasa*, 1876, reprinted, New Delhi, 1971.

Moorcroft and Trebeck, *Travels in the Himalayan Provinces of Hindoostan and the Panjab; in Ladakh and Kashmir; in Peshawar, Kabul, Kunduz and Bokhara*, London, 1841 reprinted, New Delhi, 1971.

Pallis, Marco, *Peaks and Lamas*, London, 1939.

Phuntsog, Sonam, *Ladakh*, Ladakh, 2000.

Ribbach, S.H., *Culture and Society in Ladakh*, Muchen-Planegg, 1940. Translated from German by John Bray, New Delhi, 1986.

Roerich, Nicholas, *Altai-Himalaya - A Travel Diary*, 1929, reprinted by International Roerich Memorial Trust, Naggar, Kullu, 2004.

Schlagintweit E, *Buddhism in Tibet*, Leipzig -London, 1863.

Stutchbury, Elizabeth Anne, *Rediscovering Western Tibet: Gonpa, Chortens and the Continuity of Practice with a Tibetan Buddhist Community in the Indian Himalaya* (Thesis submitted for the degree of Doctor of Philosophy of the Australian National University, July 1991).

Tobdan, *History and Religions of Lahul*, New Delhi, 1984.

Tobdan & C. Dorje, *Historical Documents from Western Trans-Himalaya, Lahul, Zanskar and Ladakh*, Delhi, 1996.

Wessels, C. *Early Jesuit Travellers in Central Asia, 1603-1721,* reprinted, New Delhi, 1992.

Whistler, Hugh, *In the High Himalayas,* London, 1924.

Bhoti Works

Gergan, Yoseb, *Ladags rGyalrabs Chimed gTer,* New Delhi, 1976.

Hindi Works

Negi, Vidyasagar, 'Kinnaur ka Sanskritic Parichaya' in *Vipasha,* March-April, Shimla, 1999.

Rahul Sankritayan, *Kinner Desh,* Allahabad, 1956.

– –, *Asia ke durgam khandon me,* 1956.

Gazetteers

Punjab District Gazetteers, Kangra District, Part III, Lahul, 1897.

Punjab District Gazetteers, Kangra District, Vol. XA, 1904.

Punjab District Gazetteers, Kangra District, Vol. XXX A, Part III, Lahul, 1917.

Index